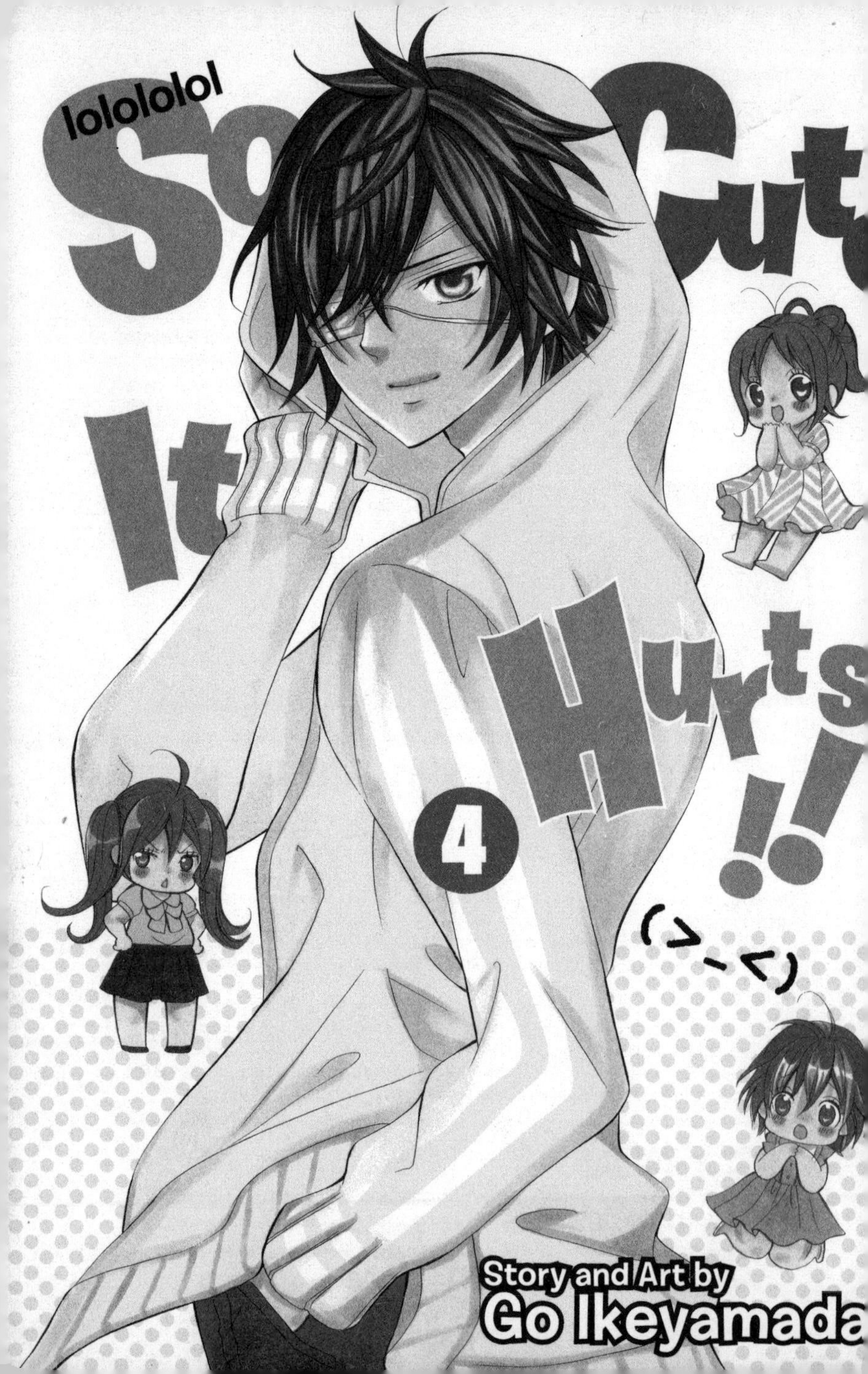
lolololol
So Cut
It
Hurts
!!
4
(>_<)
Story and Art by
Go Ikeyamada

CHARACTERS

Cross-dressing as her brother!

Nickname: Mego

Switched places at school!

Mitsuru wears bows! ☆

Cross-dressing as his sister!

Megumu Kobayashi (younger sister)
History nerd who loves video games. She likes Aoi.

Twins

Mitsuru Kobayashi (older brother)
Girls love him. Good in any sport. He falls in love with Shino.

They run into each other on the school roof

Enemies

Rescues her

Aoi Sanada
Strongest guy at school. Megumu accidentally kissed him, but he doesn't know it was her.

Azusa Tokugawa
School chairman's daughter, bully and fashion model.

Shino Takenaka
She's deaf. And she is Aoi's younger sister.

STORY

★ Mitsuru and Megumu are twins. One day they switch places and go to each other's school for a week!

★ At Akechi Boys' High, Megumu falls in love with Aoi. When she discovers that Aoi gets so uncomfortable around women that he can't even touch them, she decides to keep cross-dressing so she can be with him. Meanwhile, Mitsuru falls in love with Shino when he stops Azusa from bullying her. And Aoi and Shino turn out to be siblings!

★ Azusa and Aoi finally find out that Mitsuru and Megumu are switching places. Now that the week is over, Megumu confesses her love to Aoi as a girl. The two start going out and make a promise to go on a date on Sunday. Meanwhile, Azusa orders Mitsuru to be with her for a whole day in exchange for her keeping quiet about the twins switching places. And now a stormy Sunday closes in on our twin protagonists...!

CONTENTS

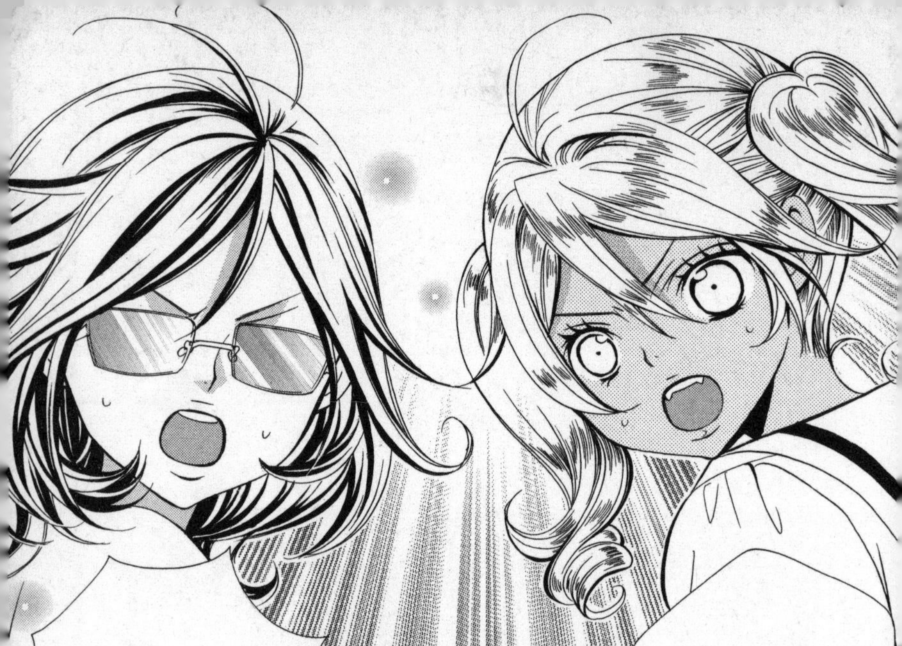
Y...
YOU HAVE A BOOOY-FRIEND?!
So Cute It Hurts!!
Chapter 16

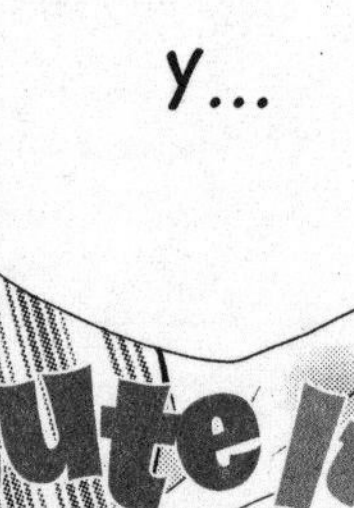

HELLO. I'M GO IKEYAMADA.
THANK YOU FOR PICKING UP VOLUME 4
OF *SO CUTE IT HURTS!!*,
MY 47TH TANKOBON!!

HAVE YOU WATCHED THE ANIME DVD THAT CAME WITH VOLUME 3 IN JAPAN? I HOPE EVERYONE ENJOYS IT. THE ANIME IS CUTE AND MERRY, AND THE PICTURES ARE BEAUTIFUL. ♡♡

VOLUME 4 IS THE FIRST-DATE ARC! I HOPE YOU ENJOY THE ROLLER COASTER LOVE SEPARATED BY TWO FEET. ♡♡

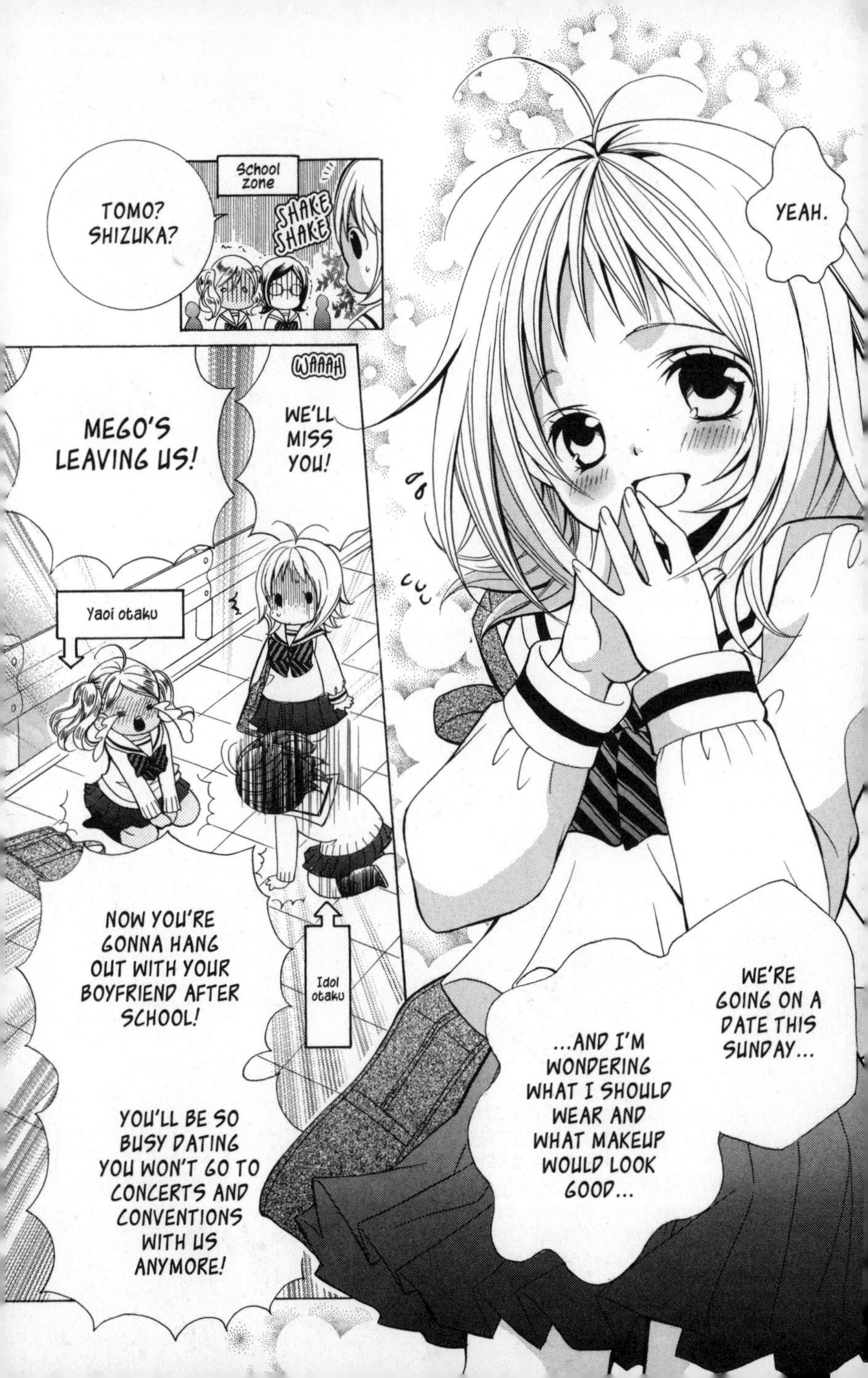

School Zone
SHAKE SHAKE
TOMO? SHIZUKA?
WAAAH
WE'LL MISS YOU!
MEGO'S LEAVING US!
Yaoi otaku
Idol otaku
NOW YOU'RE GONNA HANG OUT WITH YOUR BOYFRIEND AFTER SCHOOL!
YOU'LL BE SO BUSY DATING YOU WON'T GO TO CONCERTS AND CONVENTIONS WITH US ANYMORE!
YEAH.
WE'RE GOING ON A DATE THIS SUNDAY...
...AND I'M WONDERING WHAT I SHOULD WEAR AND WHAT MAKEUP WOULD LOOK GOOD...

SPECIAL THANKS

Yuka Ito-sama, Rieko Hirai-sama, Kayoko Takahashi-sama, Kawasaki-sama, Nagisa Sato Sensei.

Rei Nanase Sensei, Arisu Fujishiro Sensei, Mumi Mimura Sensei, Masayo Nagata-sama, Naochan-sama, Asuka Sakura Sensei, and many others.

Bookstore Dan Kinshicho Branch, Kinokuniya Shinjuku Branch, LIBRO Ikebukuro Branch, Kinokuniya Hankyu 32-Bangai Branch.

Sendai Hachimonjiya Bookstore, BOOKS HOSHINO Kintetsu Pass'e Branch, Asahiya Tennnoji MiO Branch, Kurashiki Kikuya Bookstore.

Salesperson: Hata-sama

First salesperson: Honma-sama

Previous editor: Nakata-sama

Current editor: Shoji-sama

I also sincerely express my gratitude to everyone who picked up this volume!

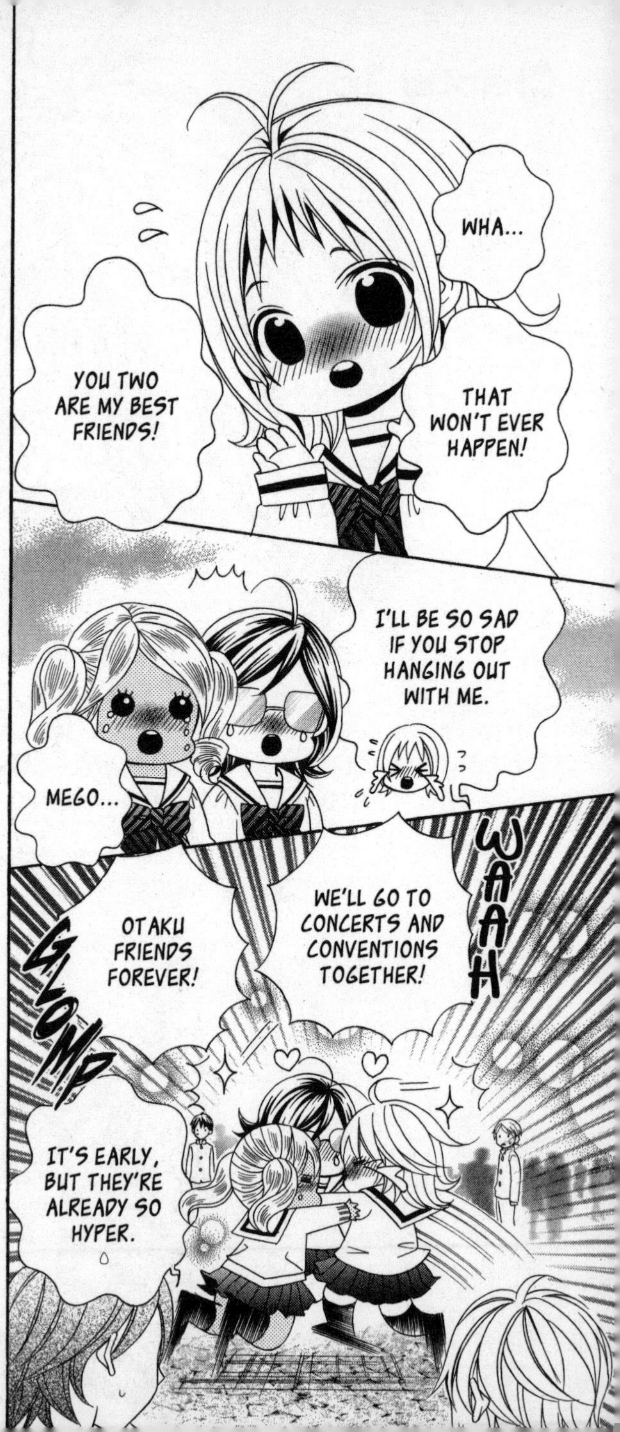
WHA...
THAT WON'T EVER HAPPEN!
YOU TWO ARE MY BEST FRIENDS!
I'LL BE SO SAD IF YOU STOP HANGING OUT WITH ME.
MEGO...
WAAH
WE'LL GO TO CONCERTS AND CONVENTIONS TOGETHER!
OTAKU FRIENDS FOREVER!
GLOMP
IT'S EARLY, BUT THEY'RE ALREADY SO HYPER.

Chapter 16

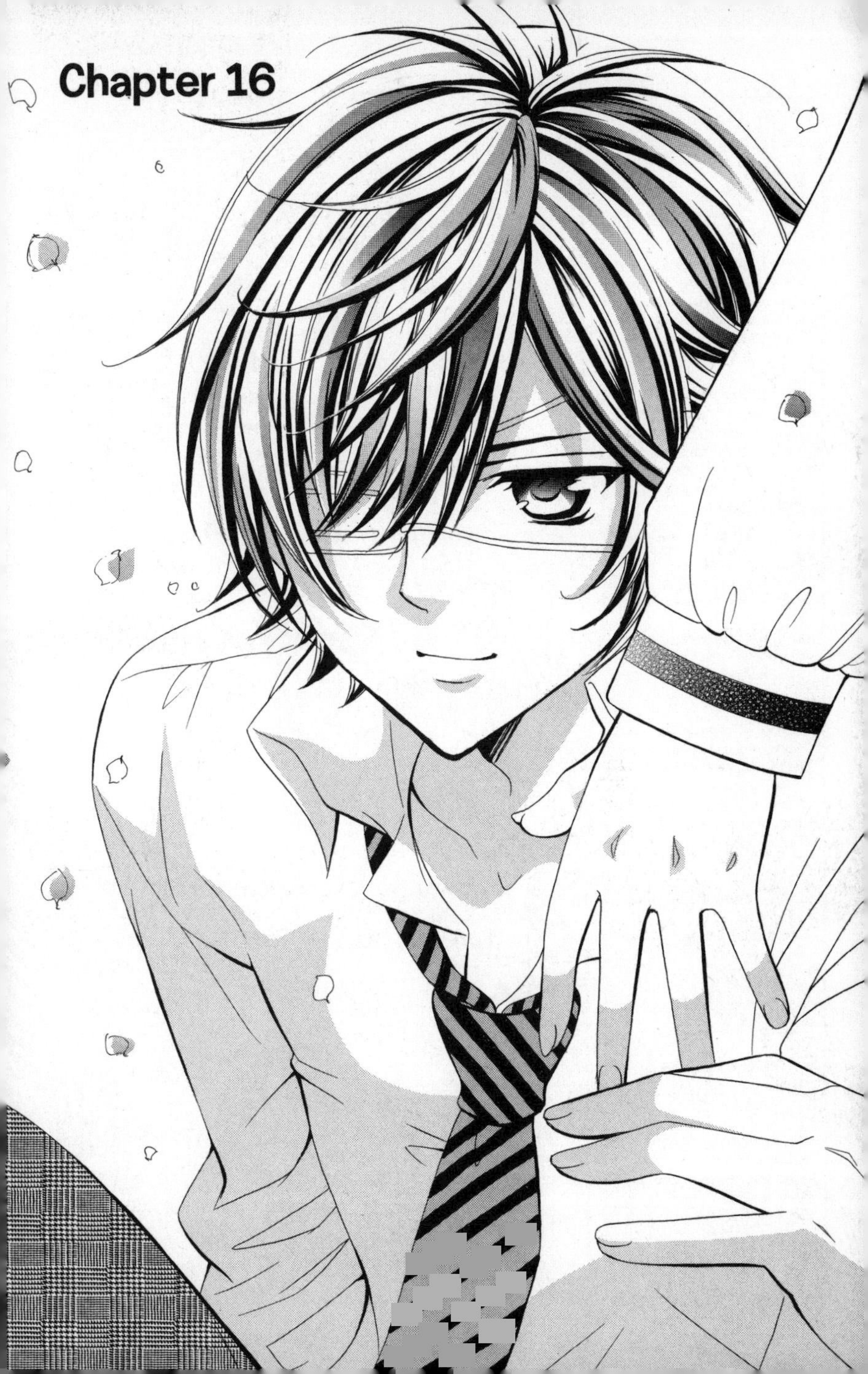

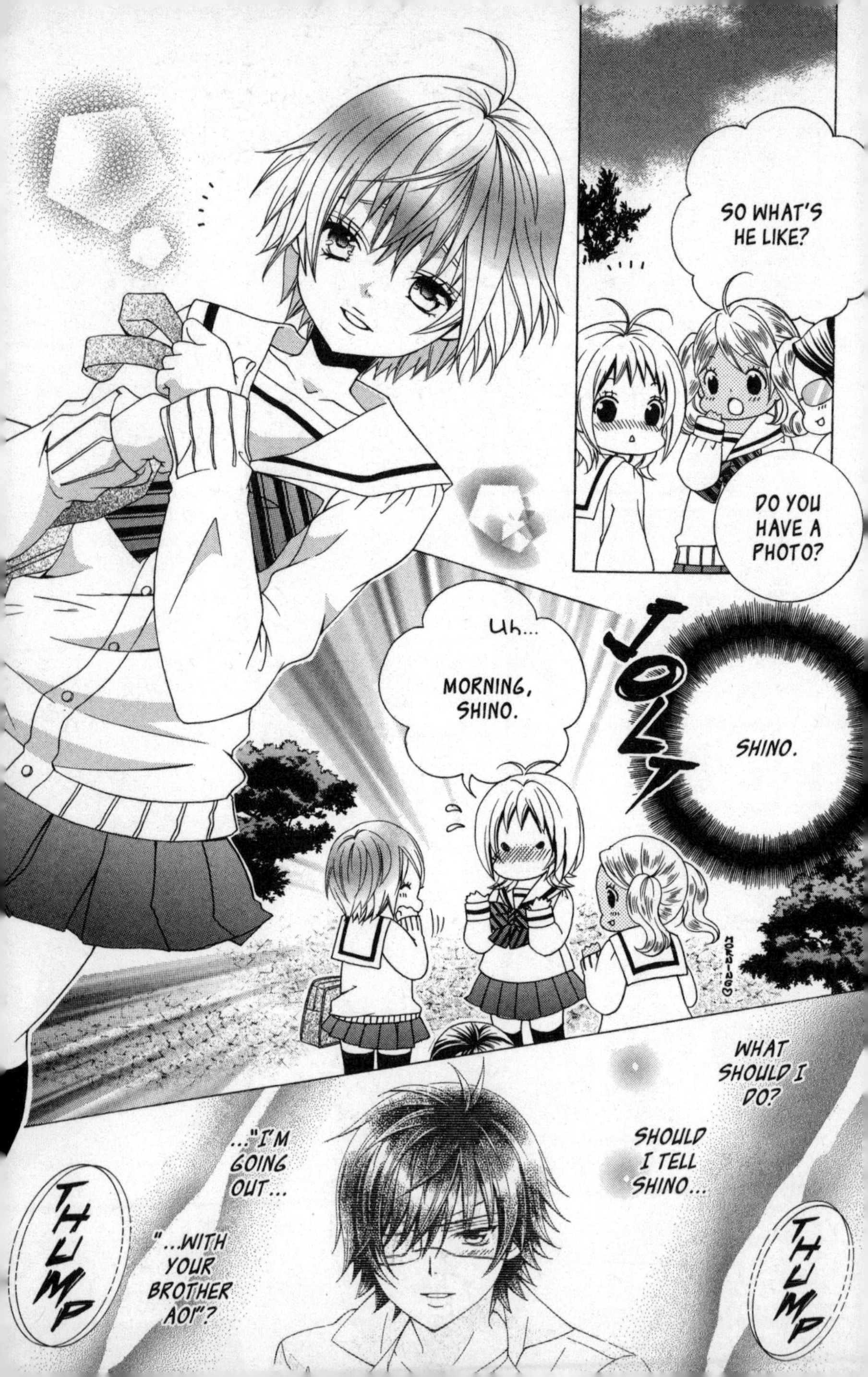
SO WHAT'S HE LIKE?
DO YOU HAVE A PHOTO?
SHINO.
JOLT
Uh... MORNING, SHINO.
MORNING♡
WHAT SHOULD I DO?
SHOULD I TELL SHINO...
THUMP
..."I'M GOING OUT...
"...WITH YOUR BROTHER AOI"?
THUMP

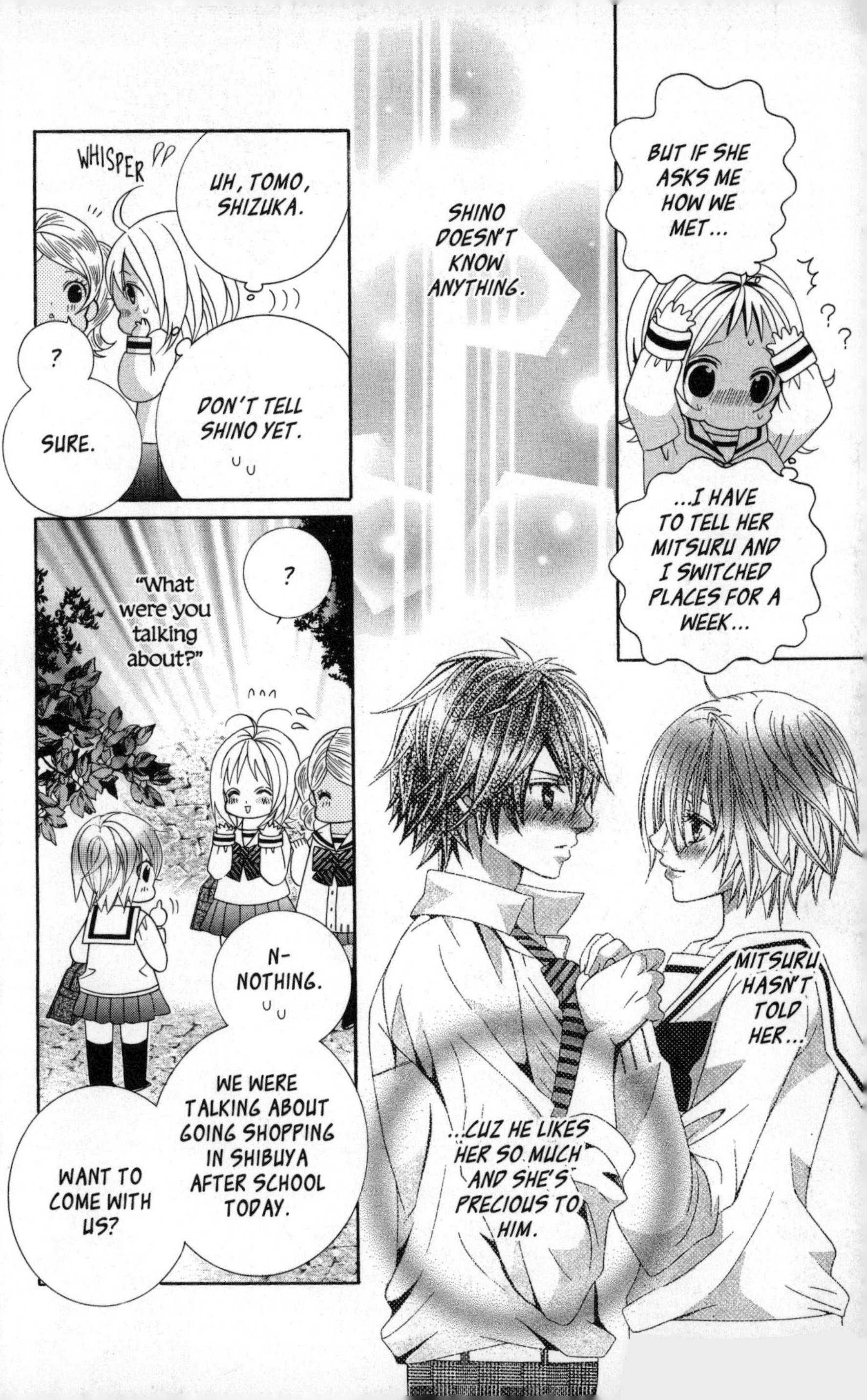
BUT IF SHE ASKS ME HOW WE MET...
...I HAVE TO TELL HER MITSURU AND I SWITCHED PLACES FOR A WEEK...
SHINO DOESN'T KNOW ANYTHING.
MITSURU HASN'T TOLD HER...
...CUZ HE LIKES HER SO MUCH AND SHE'S PRECIOUS TO HIM.
WHISPER
UH, TOMO, SHIZUKA.
DON'T TELL SHINO YET.
?
SURE.
?
"What were you talking about?"
N-NOTHING.
WE WERE TALKING ABOUT GOING SHOPPING IN SHIBUYA AFTER SCHOOL TODAY.
WANT TO COME WITH US?

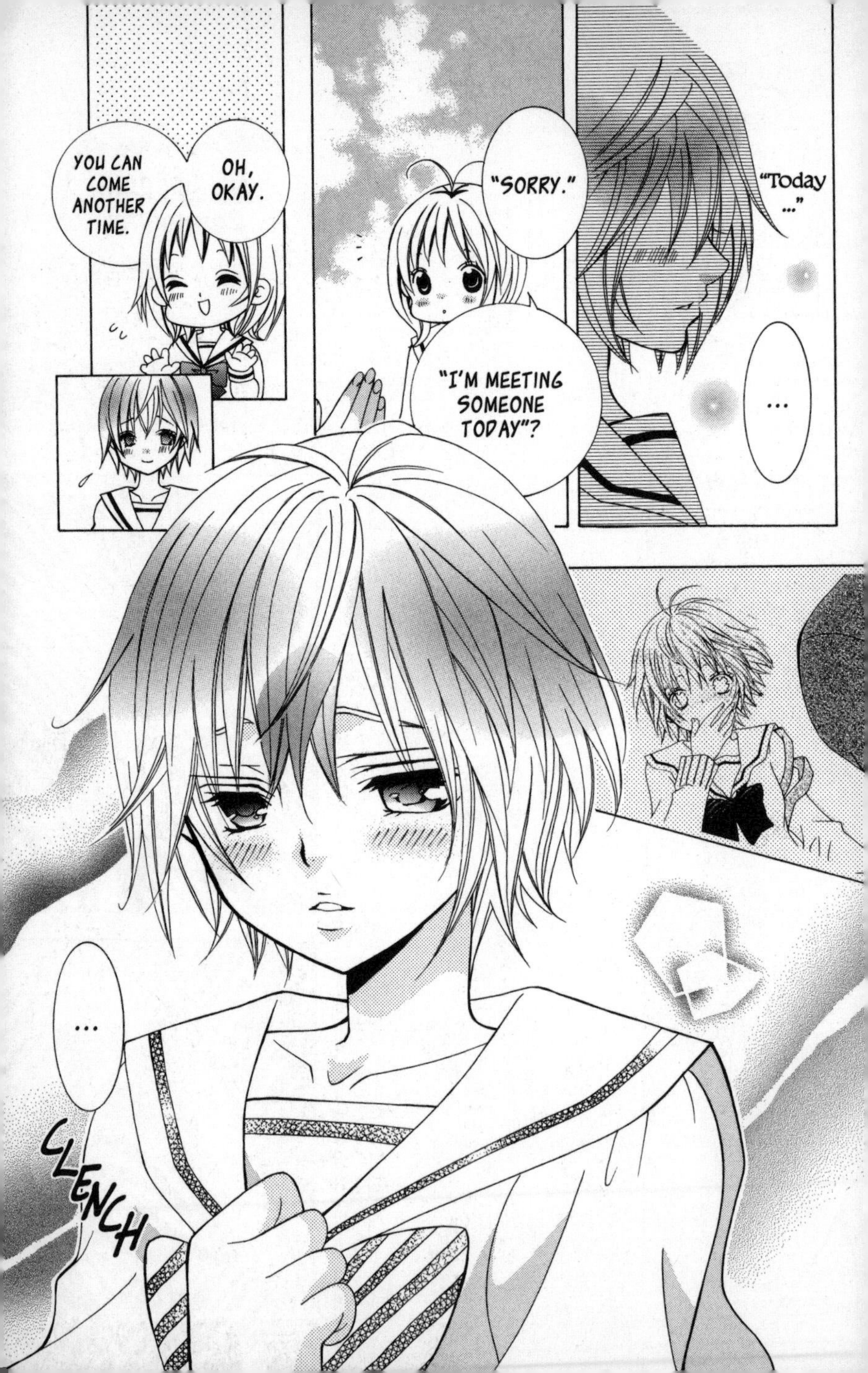
"Today ..."
...
"SORRY."
"I'M MEETING SOMEONE TODAY"?
OH, OKAY.
YOU CAN COME ANOTHER TIME.
...
CLENCH

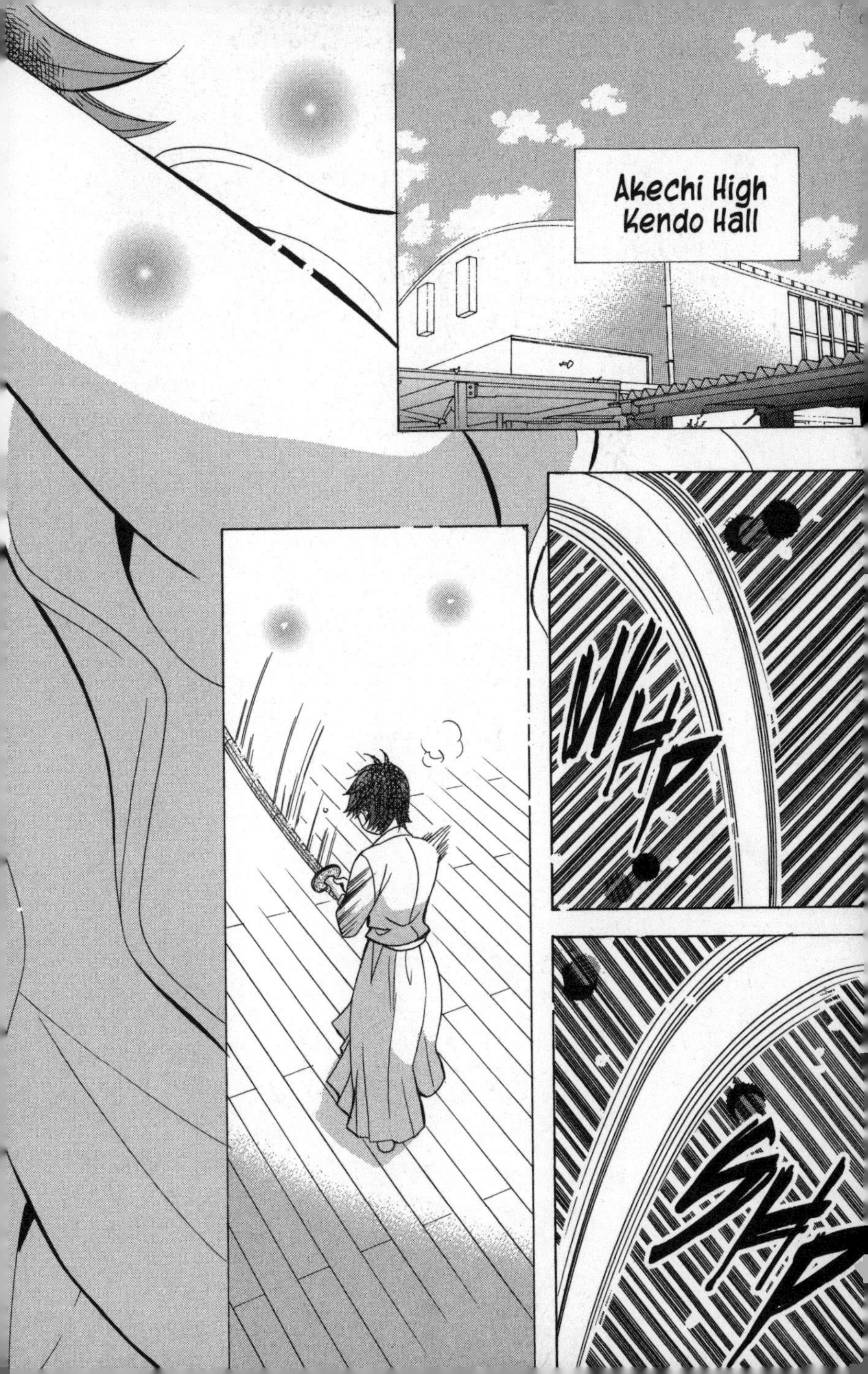
Akechi High
Kendo Hall
WHP!
SHK

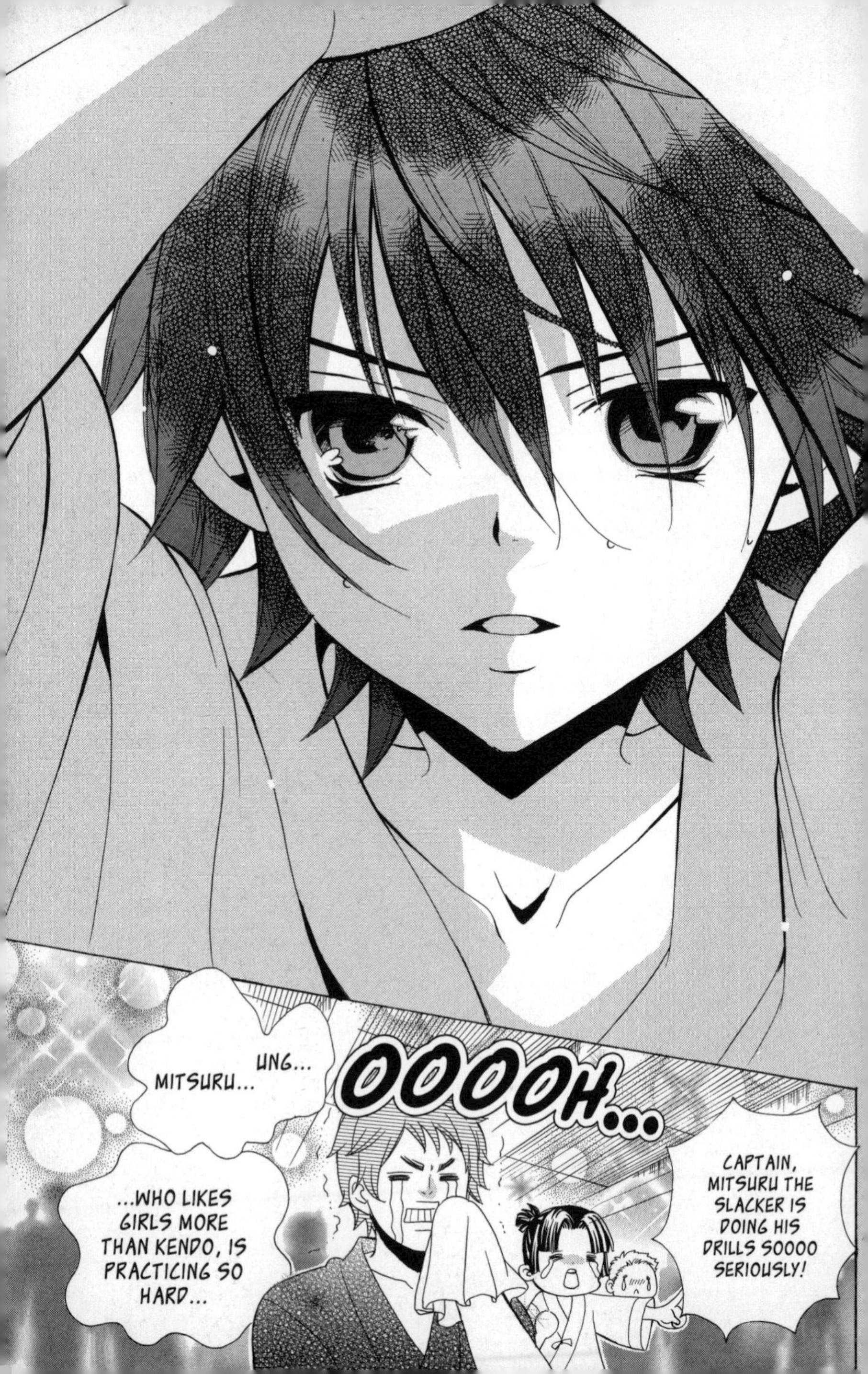
CAPTAIN, MITSURU THE SLACKER IS DOING HIS DRILLS SOOOO SERIOUSLY!
OOOOH...
UNG... MITSURU...
...WHO LIKES GIRLS MORE THAN KENDO, IS PRACTICING SO HARD...

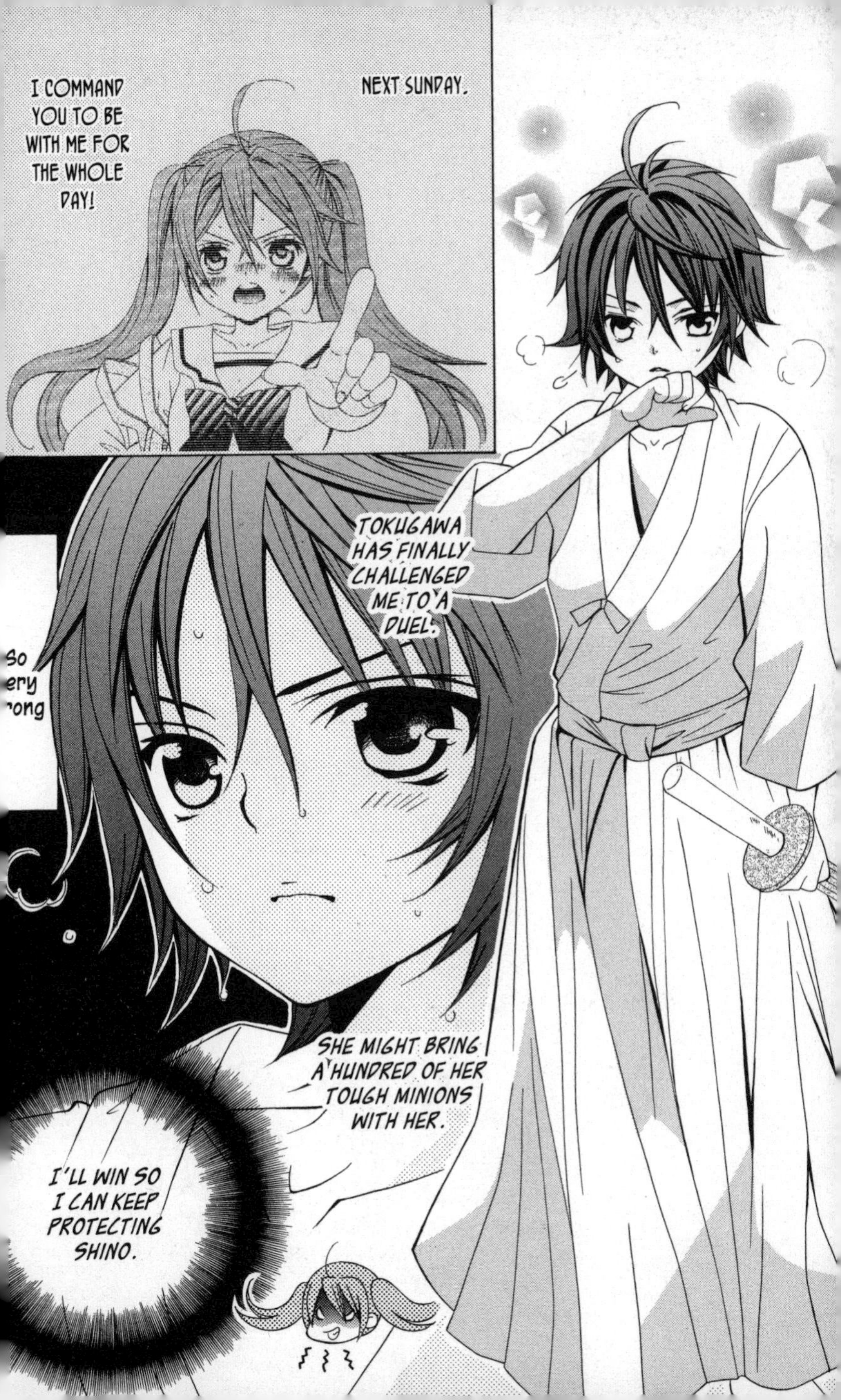
NEXT SUNDAY.
I COMMAND YOU TO BE WITH ME FOR THE WHOLE DAY!
TOKUGAWA HAS FINALLY CHALLENGED ME TO A DUEL.
SHE MIGHT BRING A HUNDRED OF HER TOUGH MINIONS WITH HER.
I'LL WIN SO I CAN KEEP PROTECTING SHINO.

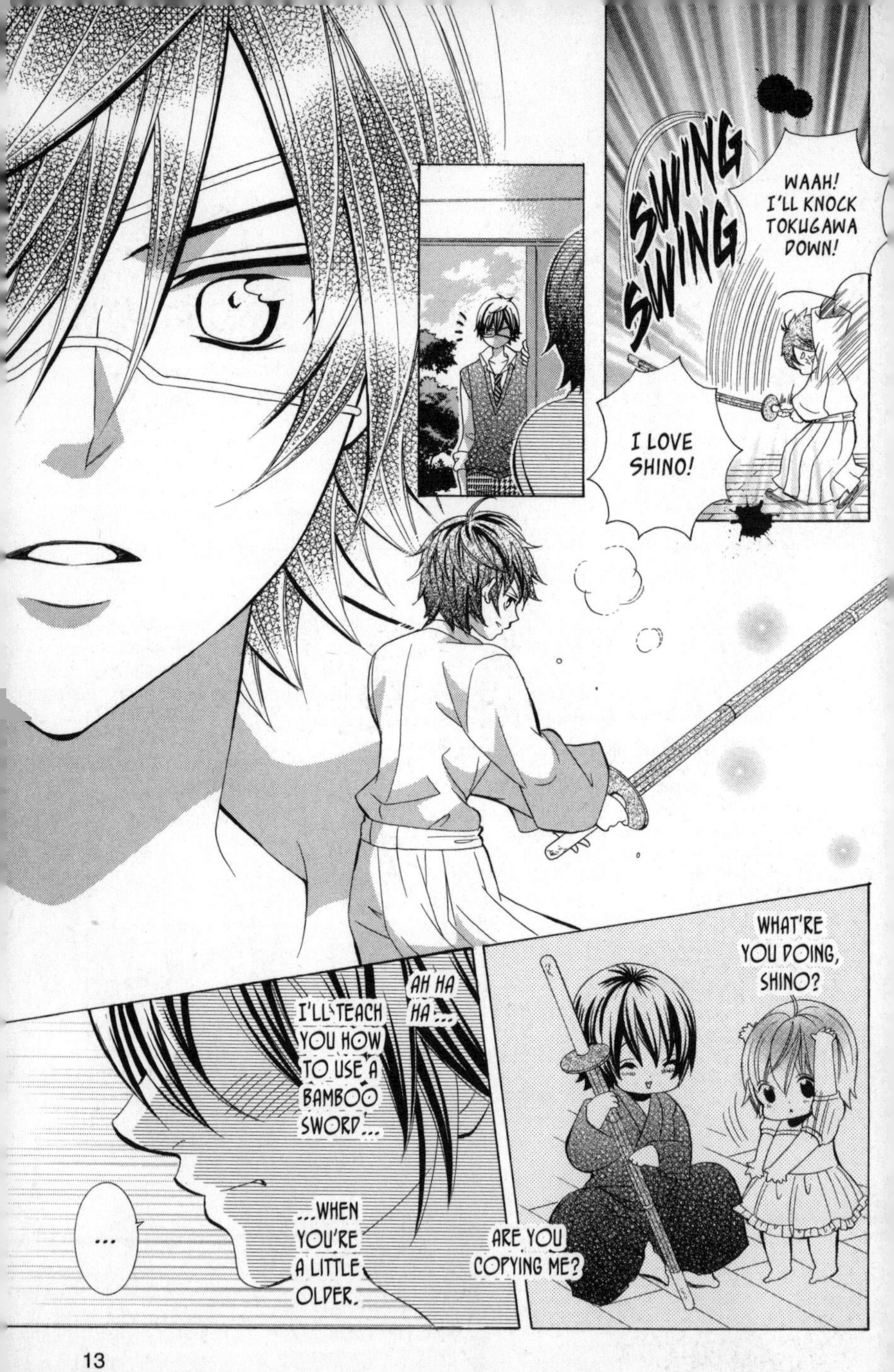
SWING SWING
WAAH! I'LL KNOCK TOKUGAWA DOWN!
I LOVE SHINO!
WHAT'RE YOU DOING, SHINO?
ARE YOU COPYING ME?
AH HA HA...
I'LL TEACH YOU HOW TO USE A BAMBOO SWORD...
...WHEN YOU'RE A LITTLE OLDER.
...

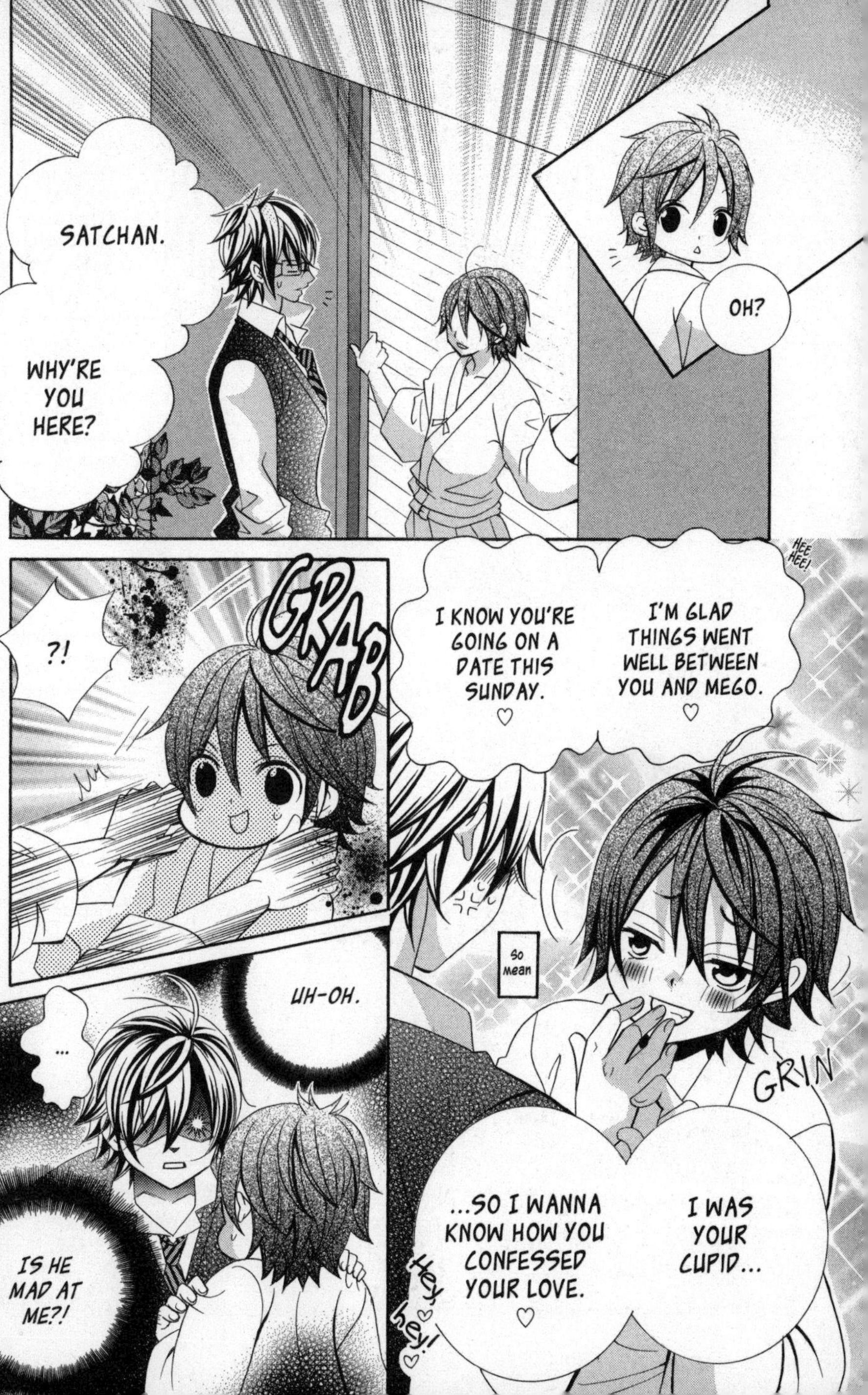
OH?
SATCHAN.
WHY'RE YOU HERE?
HEE HEE!
I'M GLAD THINGS WENT WELL BETWEEN YOU AND MEGO. ♡
I KNOW YOU'RE GOING ON A DATE THIS SUNDAY. ♡
So mean
GRIN
I WAS YOUR CUPID...
...SO I WANNA KNOW HOW YOU CONFESSED YOUR LOVE. ♡
Hey, hey! ♡
GRAB
?!
UH-OH.
...
IS HE MAD AT ME?!

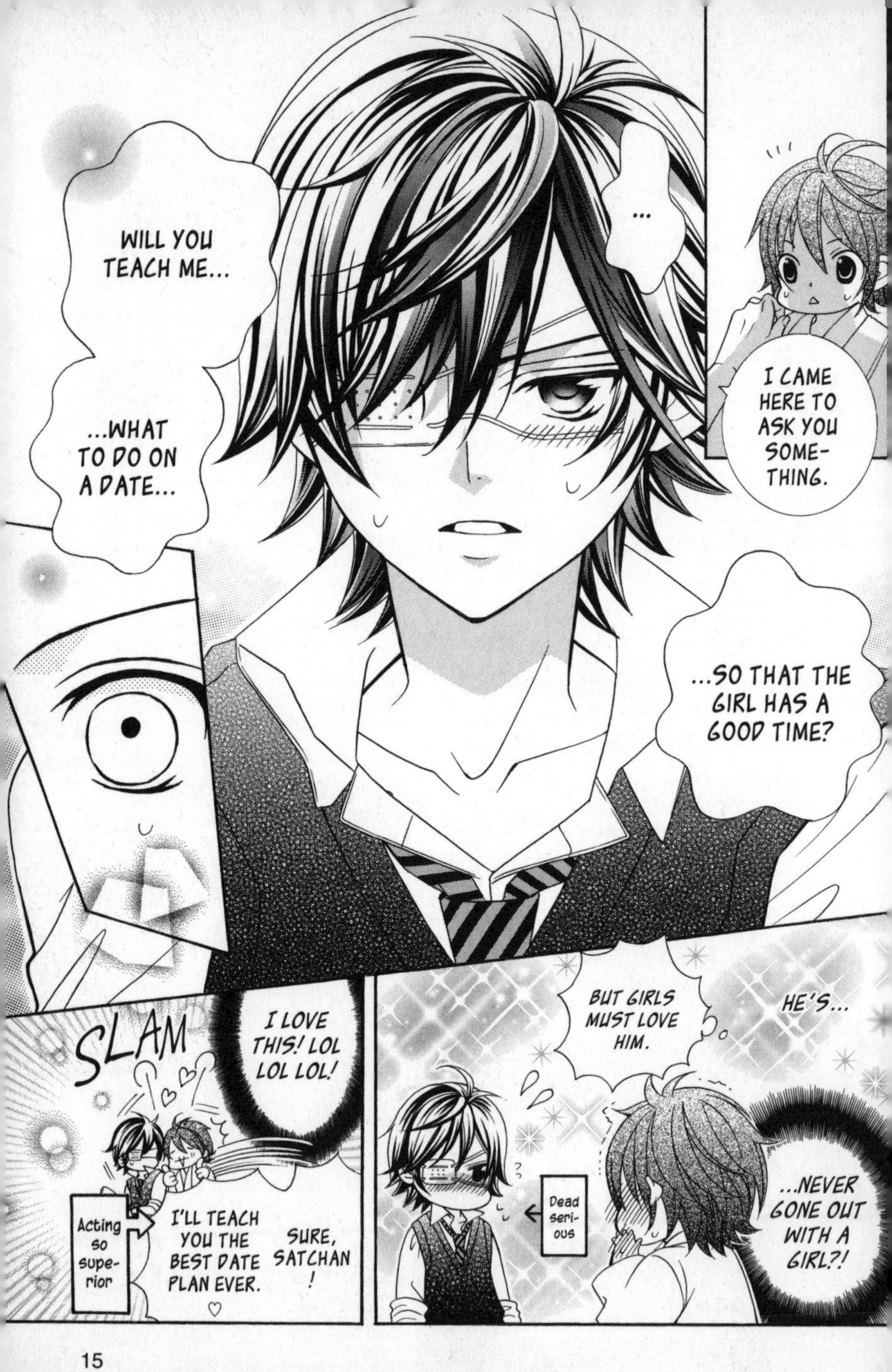
I CAME HERE TO ASK YOU SOMETHING.
...
WILL YOU TEACH ME...
...WHAT TO DO ON A DATE...
...SO THAT THE GIRL HAS A GOOD TIME?
HE'S...
...NEVER GONE OUT WITH A GIRL?!
BUT GIRLS MUST LOVE HIM.
Dead serious
I LOVE THIS! LOL LOL LOL!
SLAM
SURE, SATCHAN!
I'LL TEACH YOU THE BEST DATE PLAN EVER.
Acting so superior

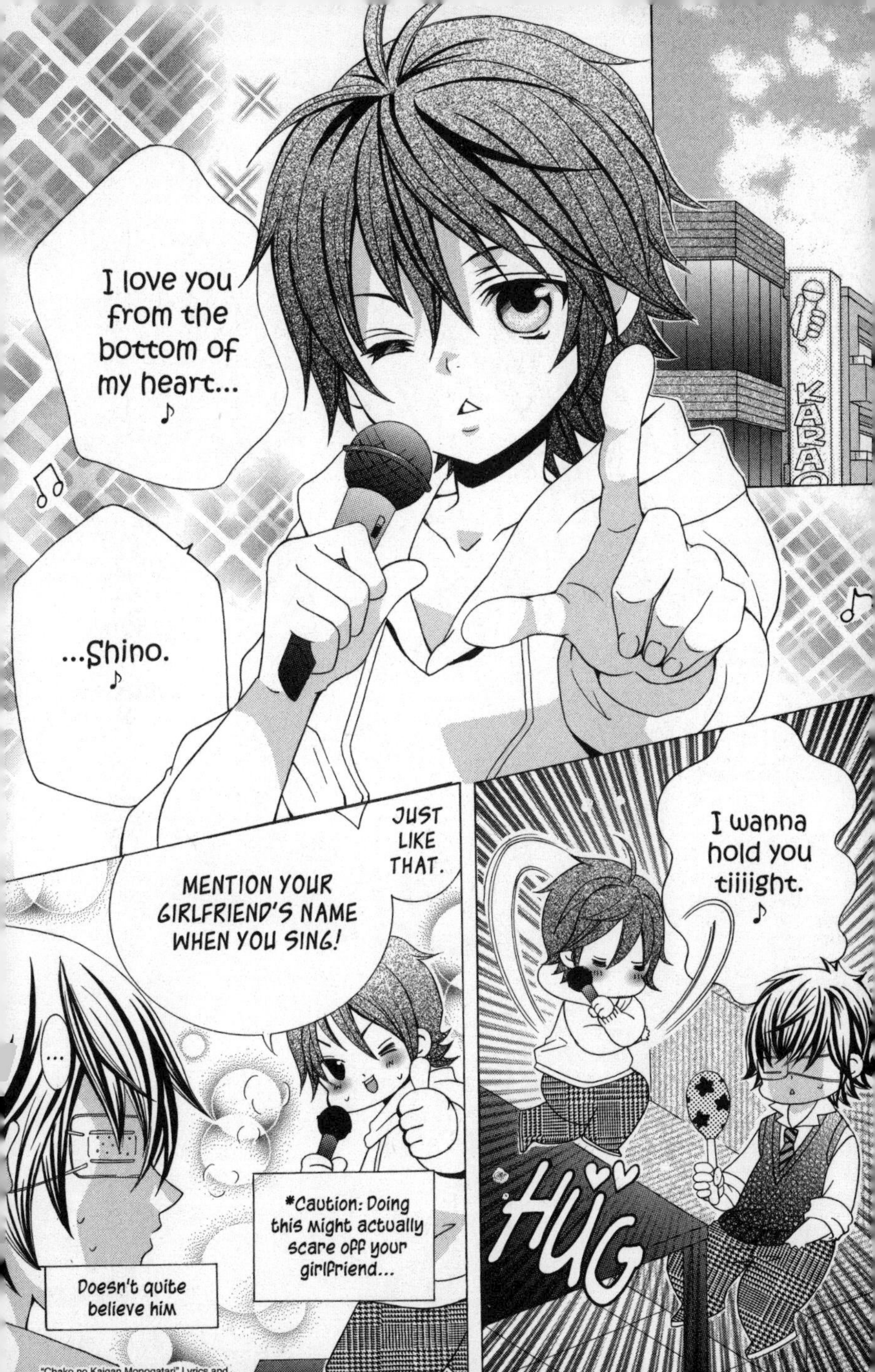
I love you from the bottom of my heart... ♪
...Shino. ♪
I wanna hold you tiiiight. ♪
HUG
JUST LIKE THAT.
MENTION YOUR GIRLFRIEND'S NAME WHEN YOU SING!
*Caution: Doing this might actually scare off your girlfriend...
...
Doesn't quite believe him

"Chako no Kaigan Monogatari" Lyrics and Music by Keisuke Kuwata

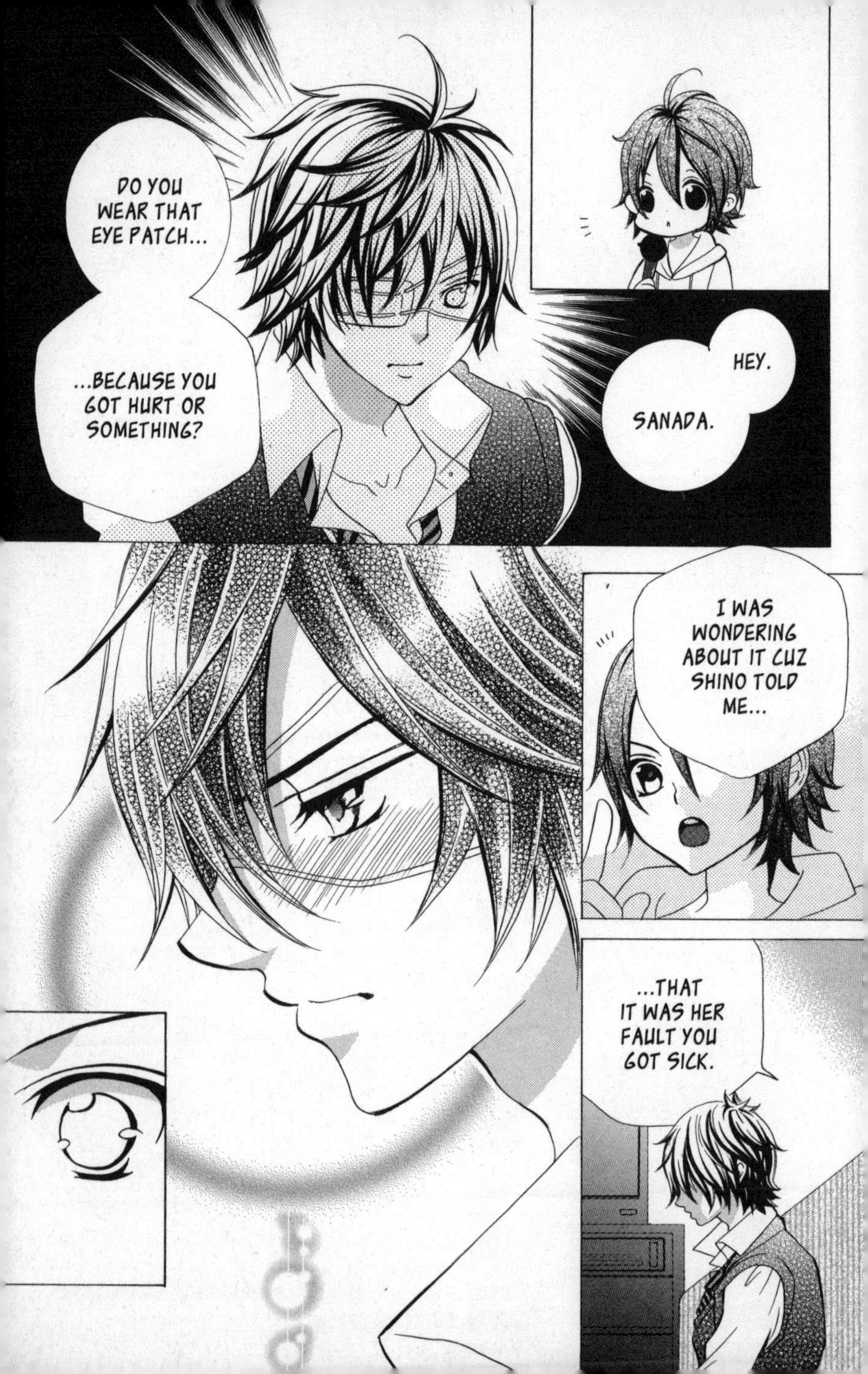
HEY.
SANADA.
DO YOU WEAR THAT EYE PATCH...
...BECAUSE YOU GOT HURT OR SOMETHING?
I WAS WONDERING ABOUT IT CUZ SHINO TOLD ME...
...THAT IT WAS HER FAULT YOU GOT SICK.

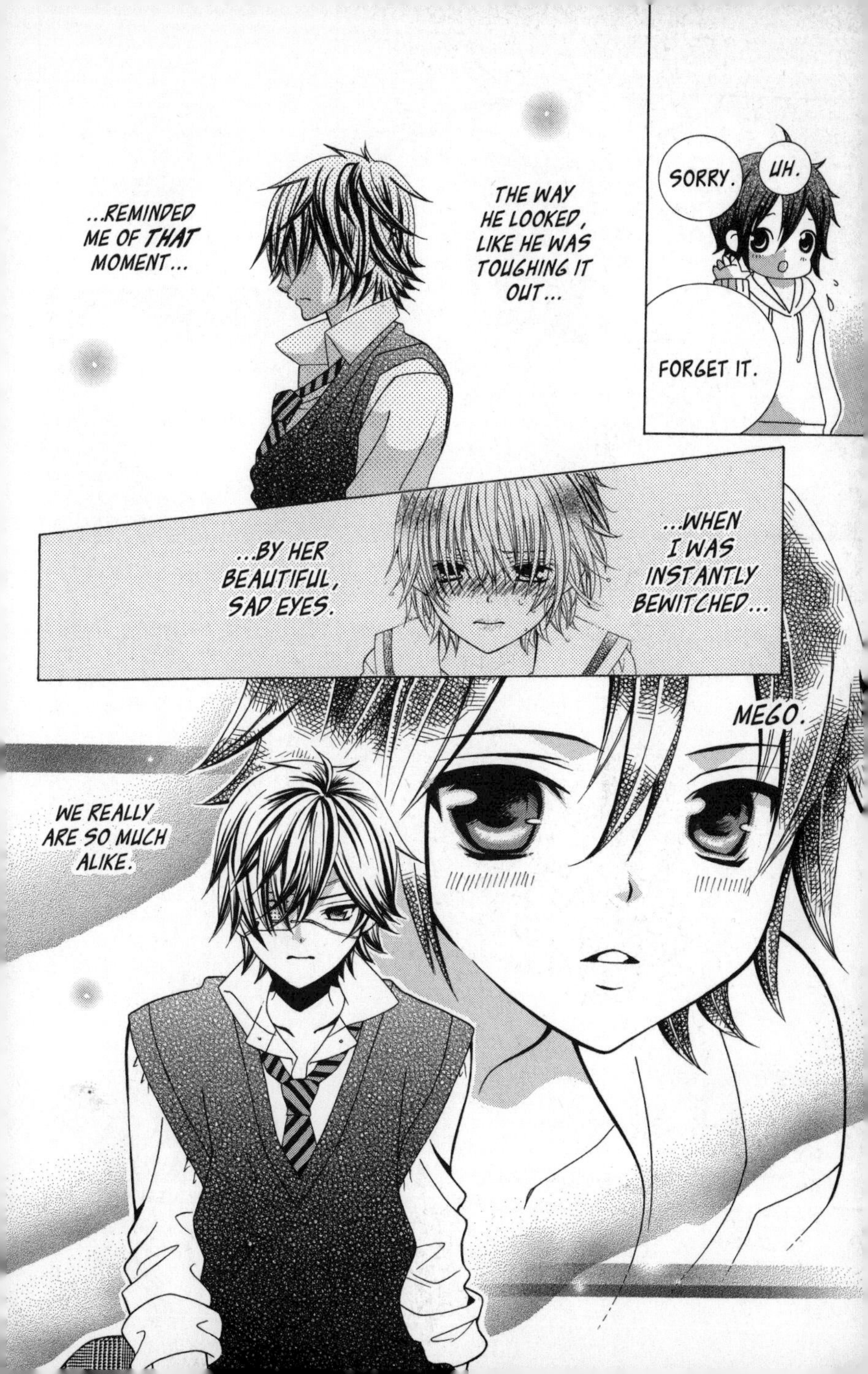
UH.
SORRY.
FORGET IT.
THE WAY HE LOOKED, LIKE HE WAS TOUGHING IT OUT...
...REMINDED ME OF THAT MOMENT...
...WHEN I WAS INSTANTLY BEWITCHED...
...BY HER BEAUTIFUL, SAD EYES.
MEGO.
WE REALLY ARE SO MUCH ALIKE.

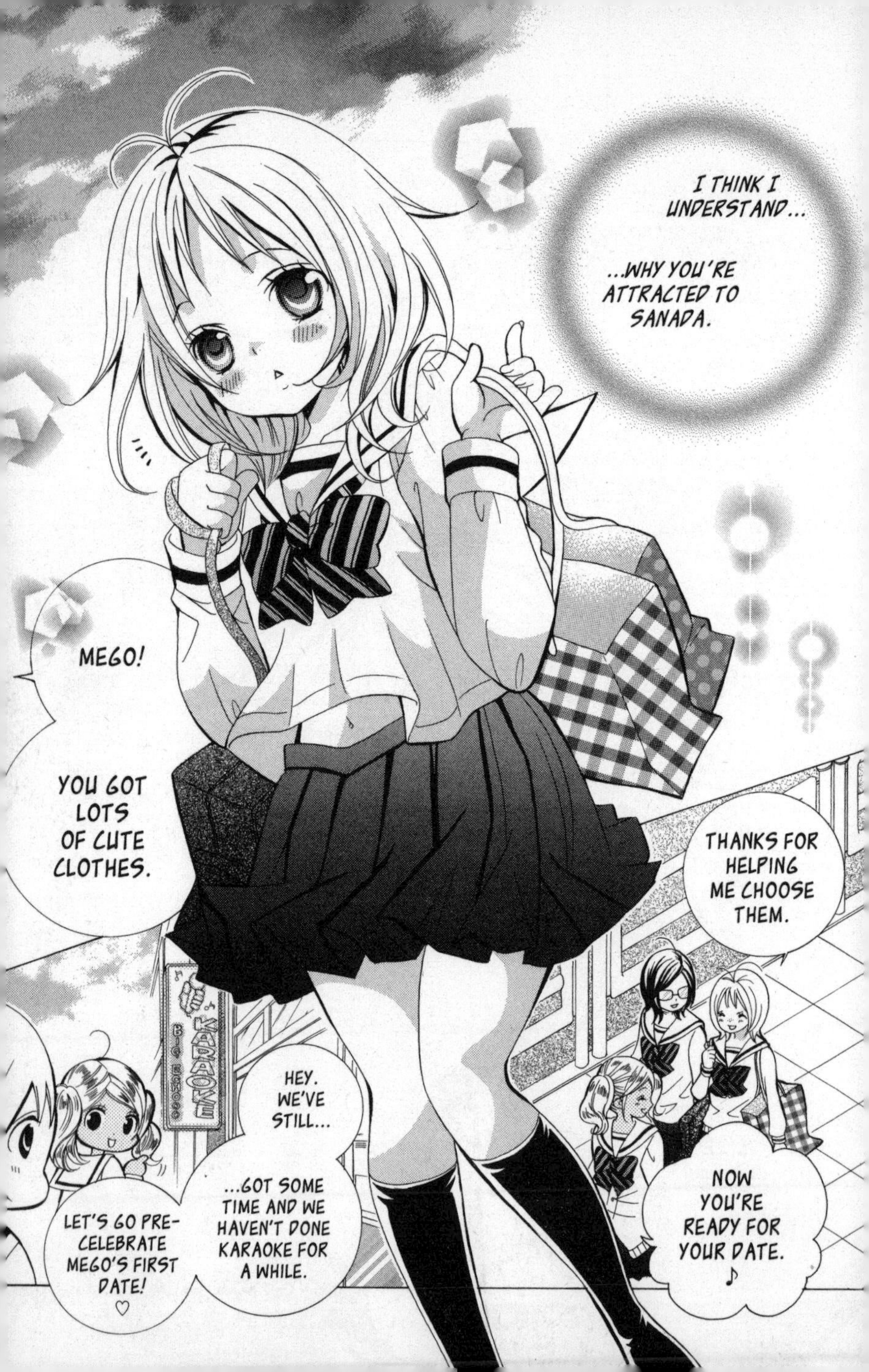
I THINK I UNDERSTAND...
...WHY YOU'RE ATTRACTED TO SANADA.
MEGO!
YOU GOT LOTS OF CUTE CLOTHES.
THANKS FOR HELPING ME CHOOSE THEM.
NOW YOU'RE READY FOR YOUR DATE. ♪
HEY. WE'VE STILL...
...GOT SOME TIME AND WE HAVEN'T DONE KARAOKE FOR A WHILE.
KARAOKE
BIG ECHO
LET'S GO PRE-CELEBRATE MEGO'S FIRST DATE! ♡

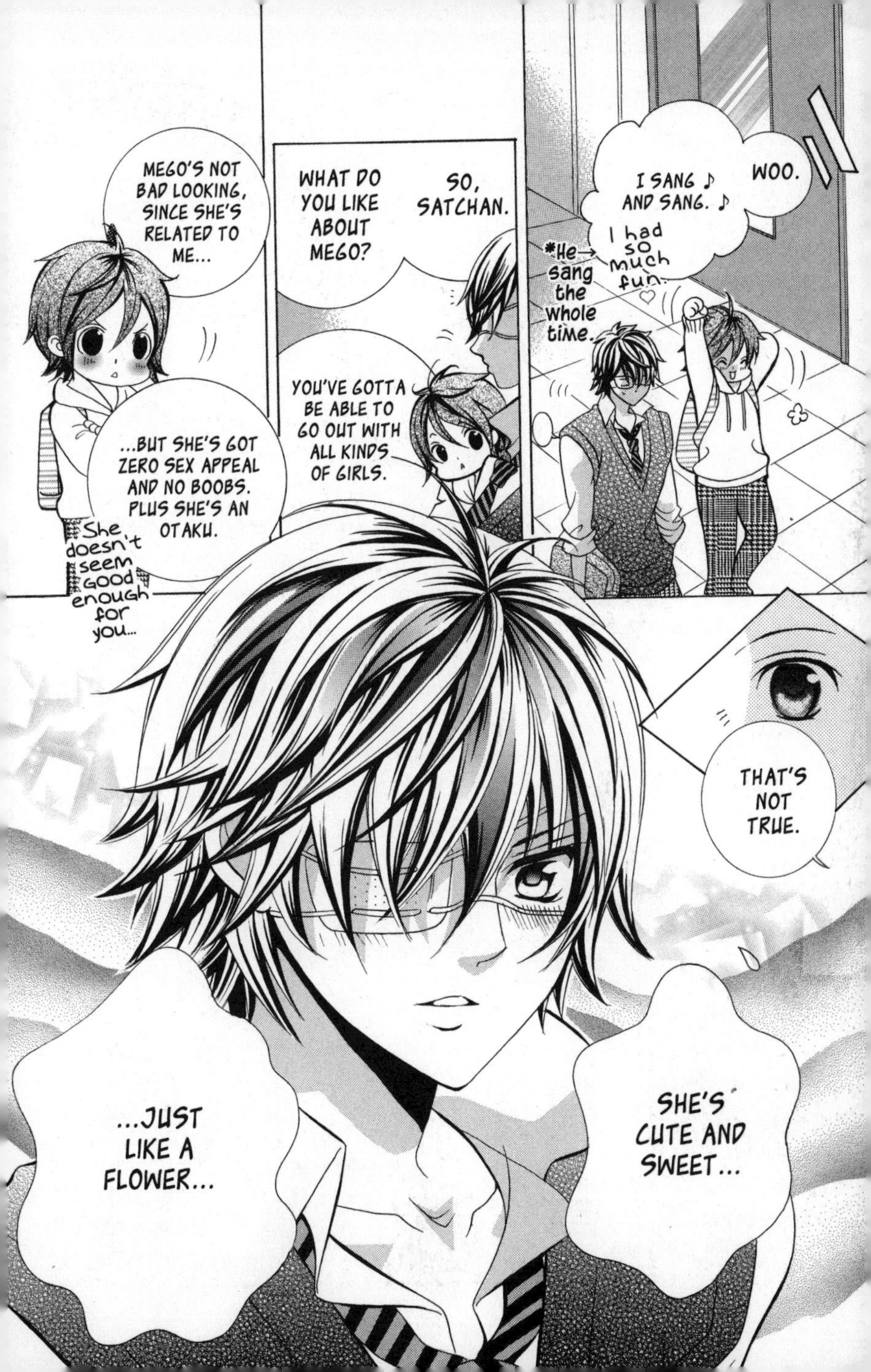
WOO.
I SANG ♪ AND SANG. ♪
I had so much fun.
*He→ sang the whole time.
SO, SATCHAN.
WHAT DO YOU LIKE ABOUT MEGO?
YOU'VE GOTTA BE ABLE TO GO OUT WITH ALL KINDS OF GIRLS.
MEGO'S NOT BAD LOOKING, SINCE SHE'S RELATED TO ME...
...BUT SHE'S GOT ZERO SEX APPEAL AND NO BOOBS. PLUS SHE'S AN OTAKU.
She doesn't seem good enough for you...
THAT'S NOT TRUE.
SHE'S CUTE AND SWEET...
...JUST LIKE A FLOWER...

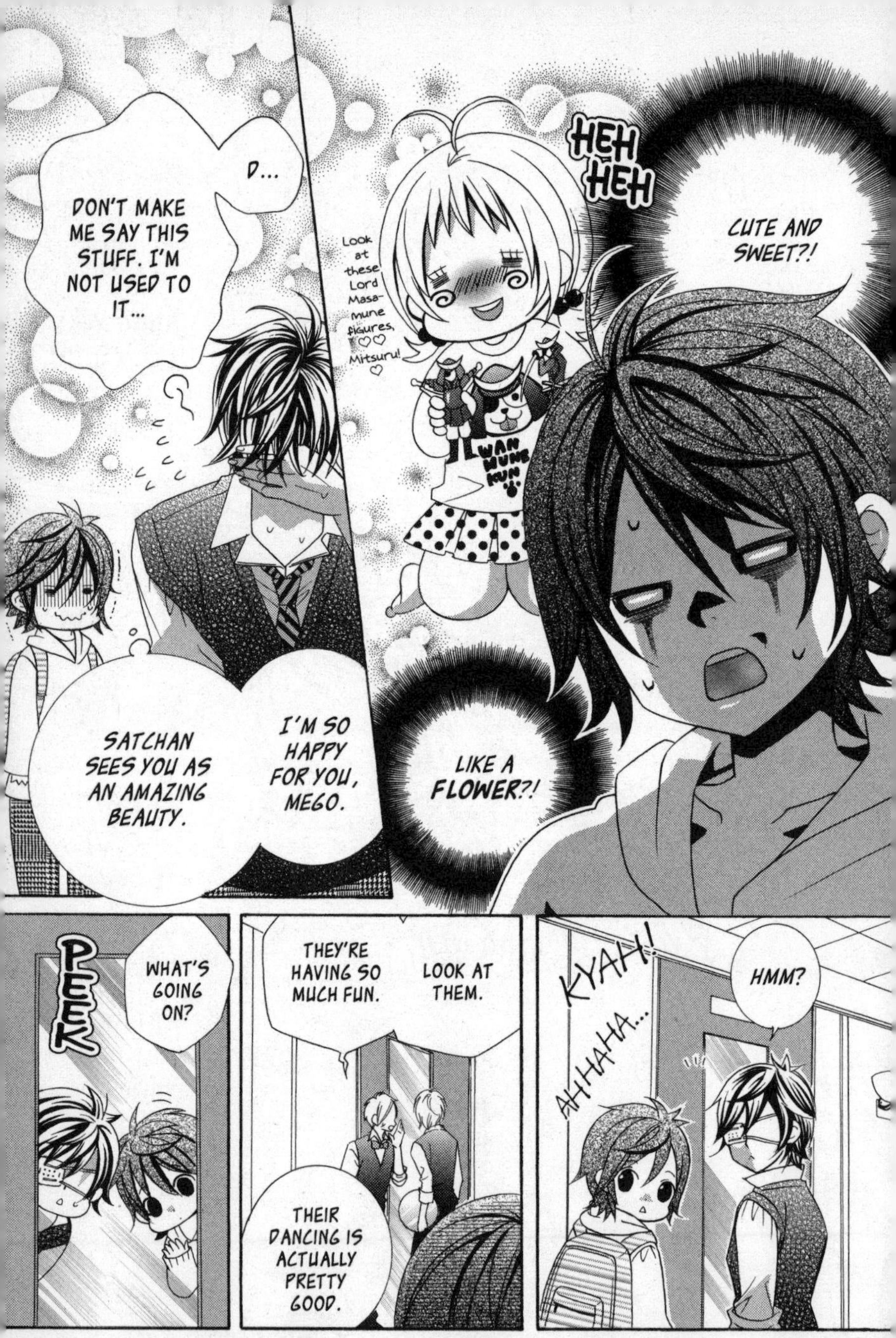
HEH HEH
CUTE AND SWEET?!
Look at these Lord Masamune figures, ♡♡ Mitsuru! ♡
WAN MUNE KUN
LIKE A FLOWER?!
D...
DON'T MAKE ME SAY THIS STUFF. I'M NOT USED TO IT...
I'M SO HAPPY FOR YOU, MEGO.
SATCHAN SEES YOU AS AN AMAZING BEAUTY.
KYAH!
HMM?
AHHAHA...
LOOK AT THEM.
THEY'RE HAVING SO MUCH FUN.
THEIR DANCING IS ACTUALLY PRETTY GOOD.
WHAT'S GOING ON?
PEEK

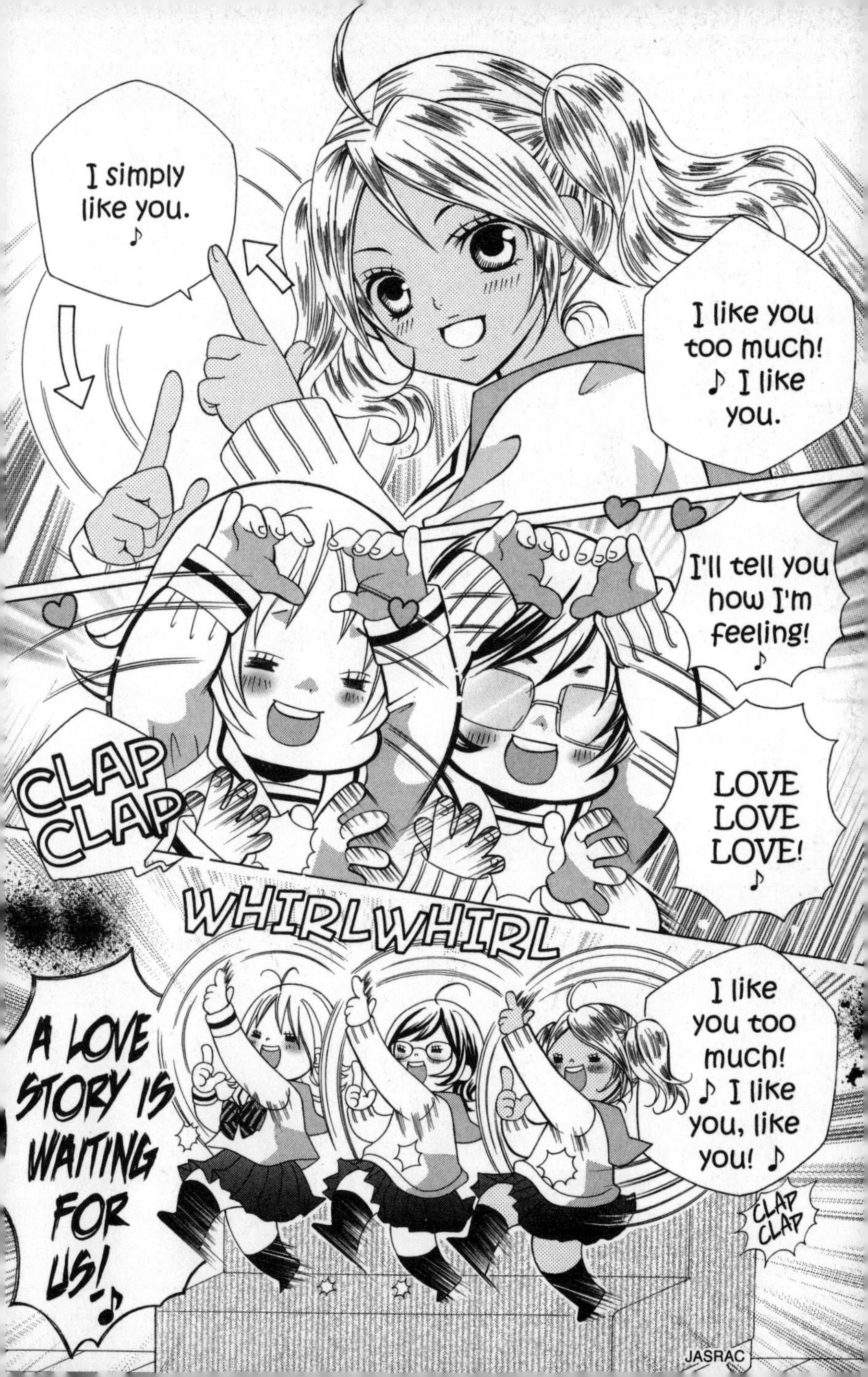
I like you too much! ♪ I like you.
I simply like you. ♪
I'll tell you how I'm feeling! ♪
LOVE LOVE LOVE! ♪
CLAP CLAP
WHIRLWHIRL
I like you too much! ♪ I like you, like you! ♪
CLAP CLAP
A LOVE STORY IS WAITING FOR US! ♪
JASRAC

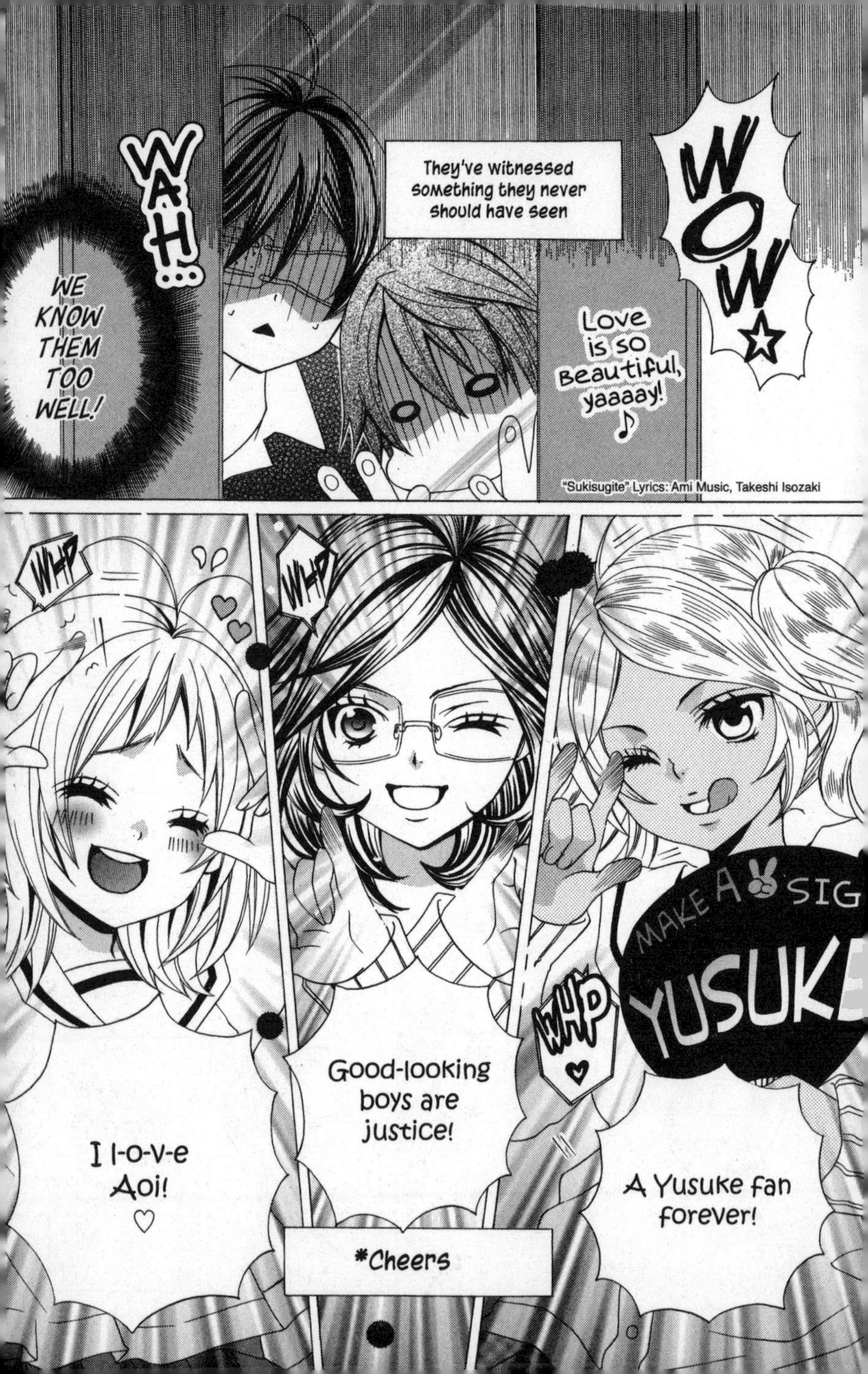
WOW☆
Love is so beautiful, yaaaay! ♪
They've witnessed something they never should have seen
WAH!!
WE KNOW THEM TOO WELL!
"Sukisugite" Lyrics: Ami Music, Takeshi Isozaki
WHP ♡
MAKE A ✌ SIG
YUSUK
A Yusuke fan forever!
WHP
Good-looking boys are justice!
*Cheers
WHP
I l-o-v-e Aoi! ♡

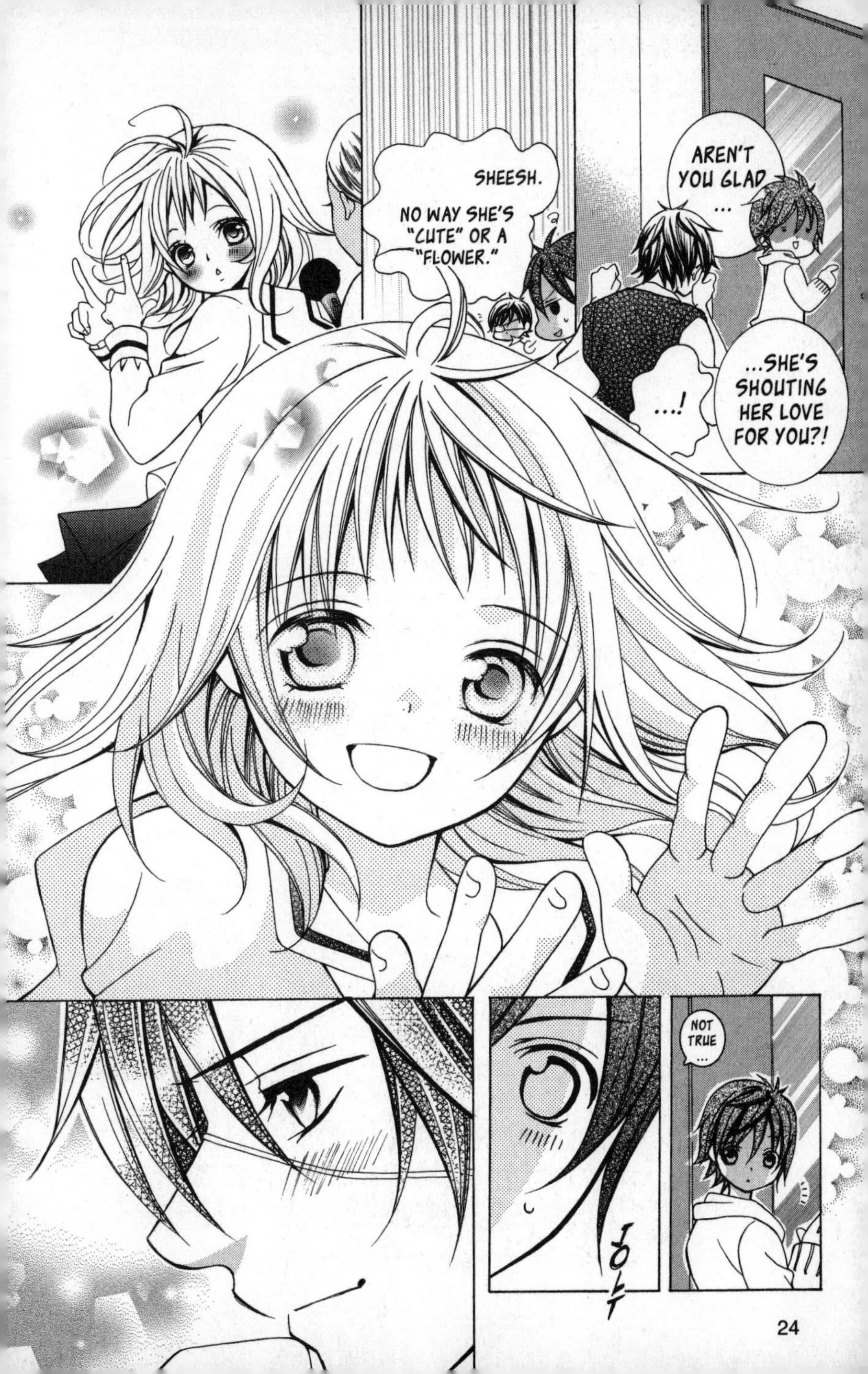
AREN'T YOU GLAD ...
...SHE'S SHOUTING HER LOVE FOR YOU?!
...!
SHEESH.
NO WAY SHE'S "CUTE" OR A "FLOWER."
NOT TRUE ...
JOLT

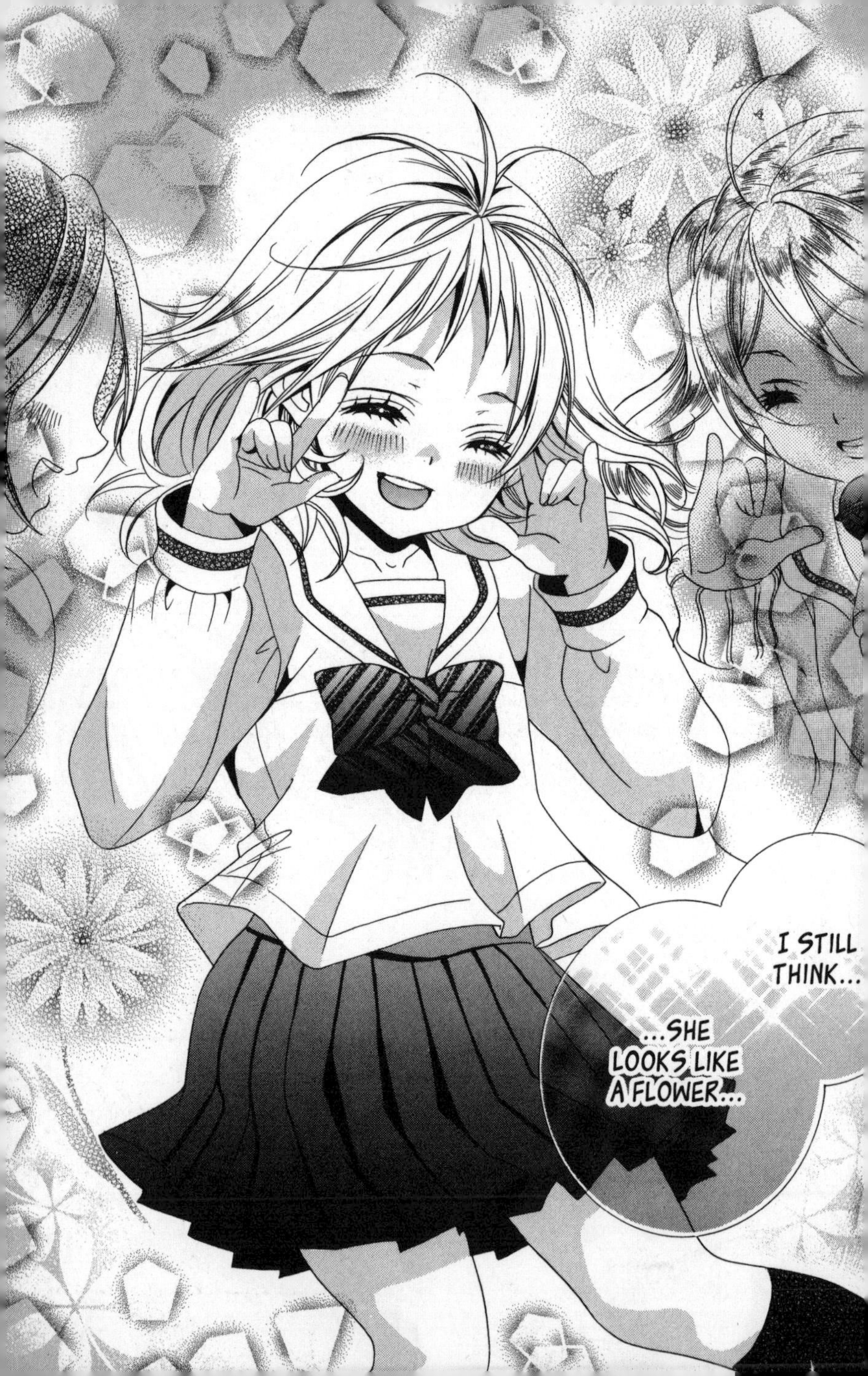
I STILL THINK...
...SHE LOOKS LIKE A FLOWER...

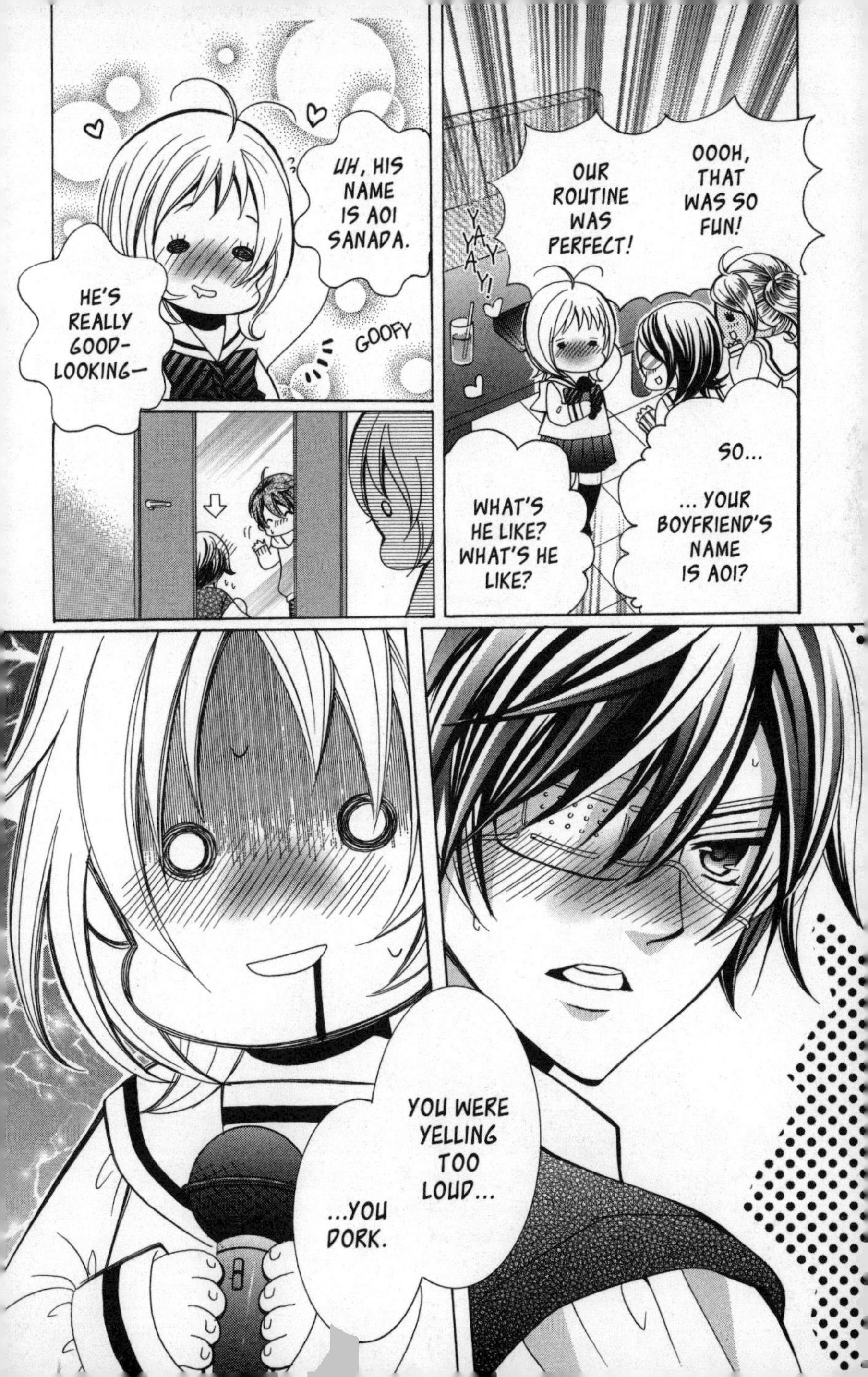
OOOH, THAT WAS SO FUN!
OUR ROUTINE WAS PERFECT!
YAY YAY!
SO...
... YOUR BOYFRIEND'S NAME IS AOI?
WHAT'S HE LIKE? WHAT'S HE LIKE?
UH, HIS NAME IS AOI SANADA.
HE'S REALLY GOOD-LOOKING—
GOOFY
YOU WERE YELLING TOO LOUD...
...YOU DORK.

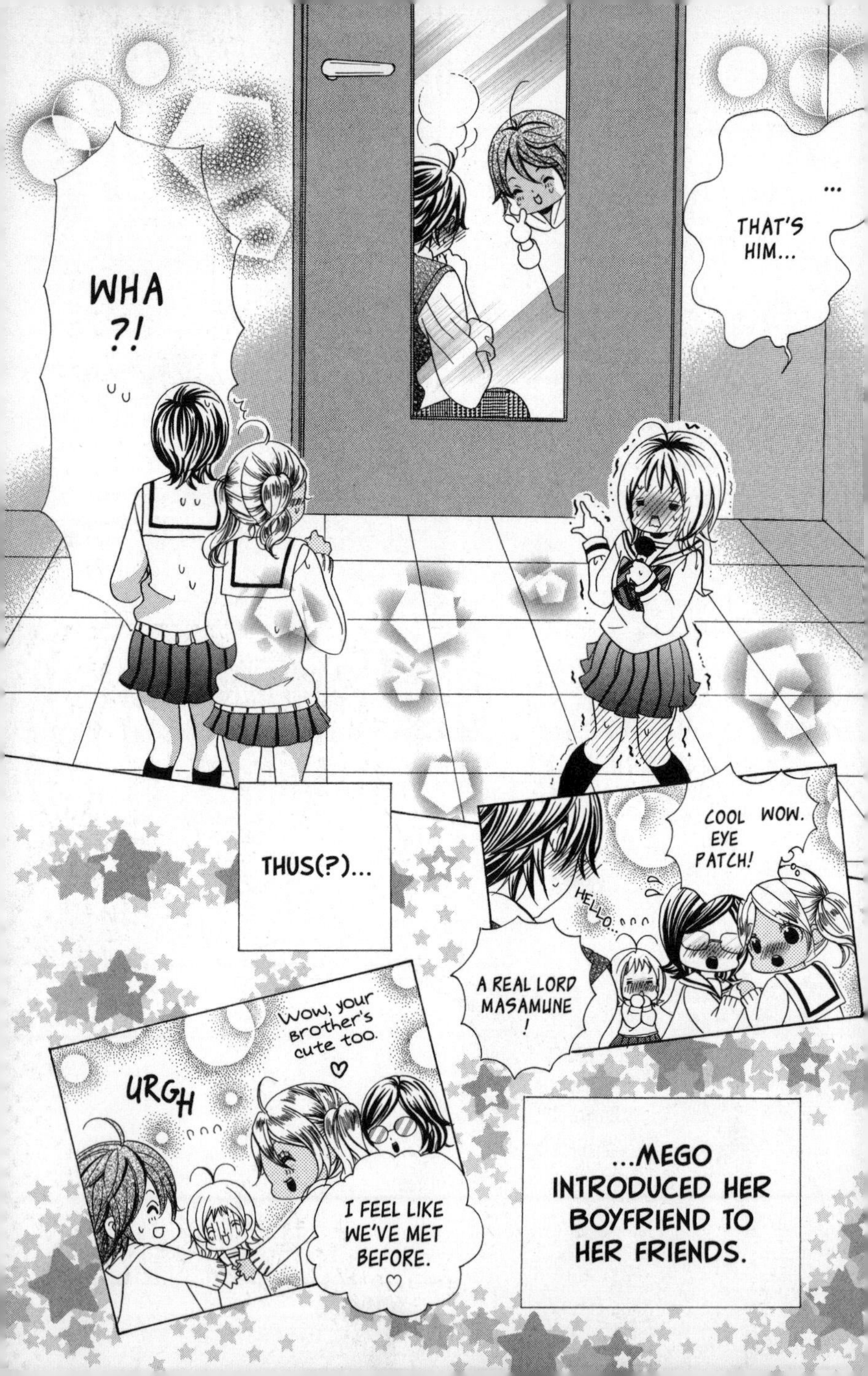
...
THAT'S HIM...
WHA ?!
WOW. COOL EYE PATCH!
HELLO...
A REAL LORD MASAMUNE!
THUS(?)...
...MEGO INTRODUCED HER BOYFRIEND TO HER FRIENDS.
Wow, your brother's cute too.
I FEEL LIKE WE'VE MET BEFORE.
URGH

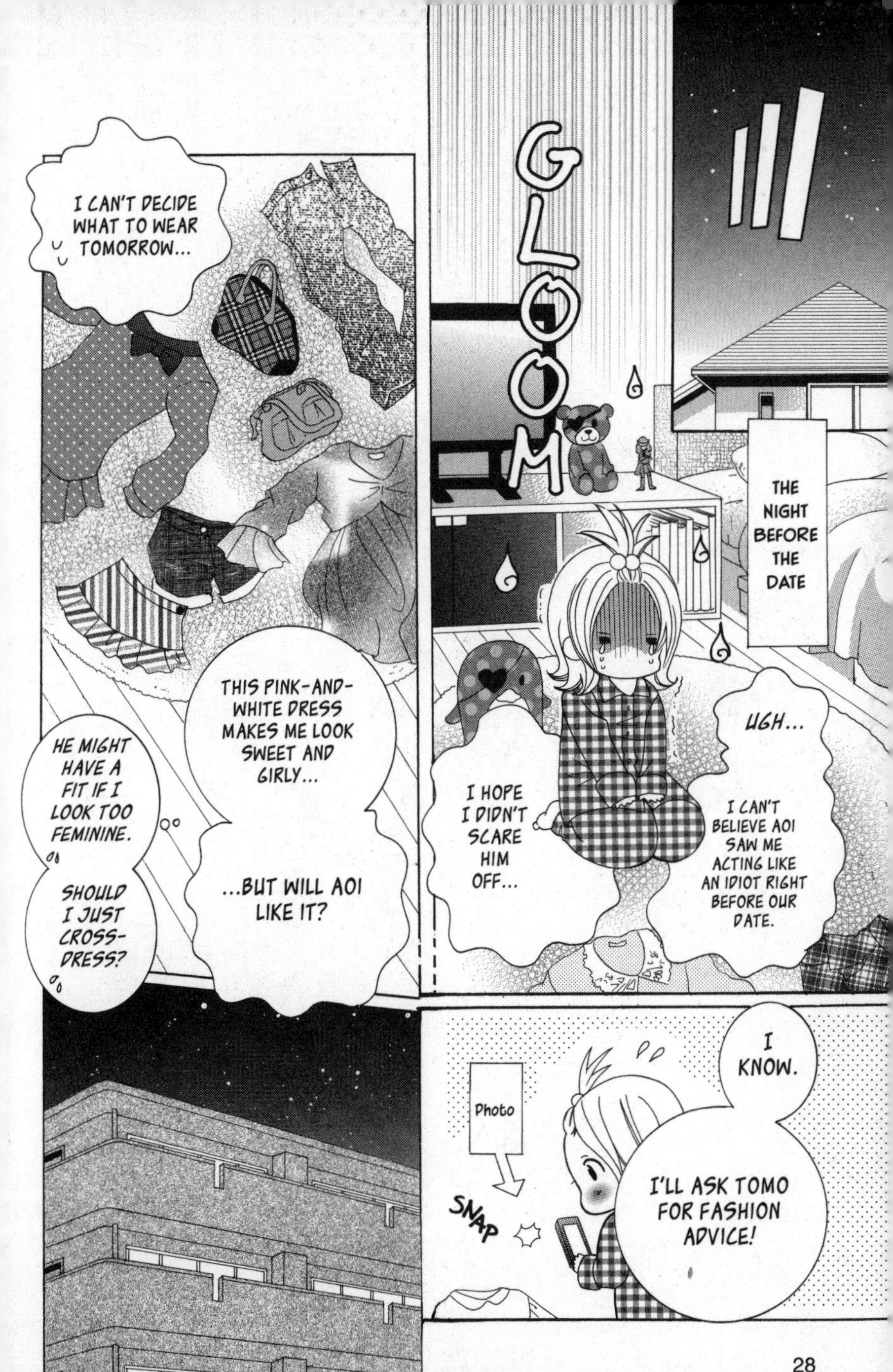
THE NIGHT BEFORE THE DATE
GLOOM
UGH...
I CAN'T BELIEVE AOI SAW ME ACTING LIKE AN IDIOT RIGHT BEFORE OUR DATE.
I HOPE I DIDN'T SCARE HIM OFF...
I CAN'T DECIDE WHAT TO WEAR TOMORROW...
THIS PINK-AND-WHITE DRESS MAKES ME LOOK SWEET AND GIRLY...
...BUT WILL AOI LIKE IT?
HE MIGHT HAVE A FIT IF I LOOK TOO FEMININE.
SHOULD I JUST CROSS-DRESS?
I KNOW.
I'LL ASK TOMO FOR FASHION ADVICE!
Photo
SNAP

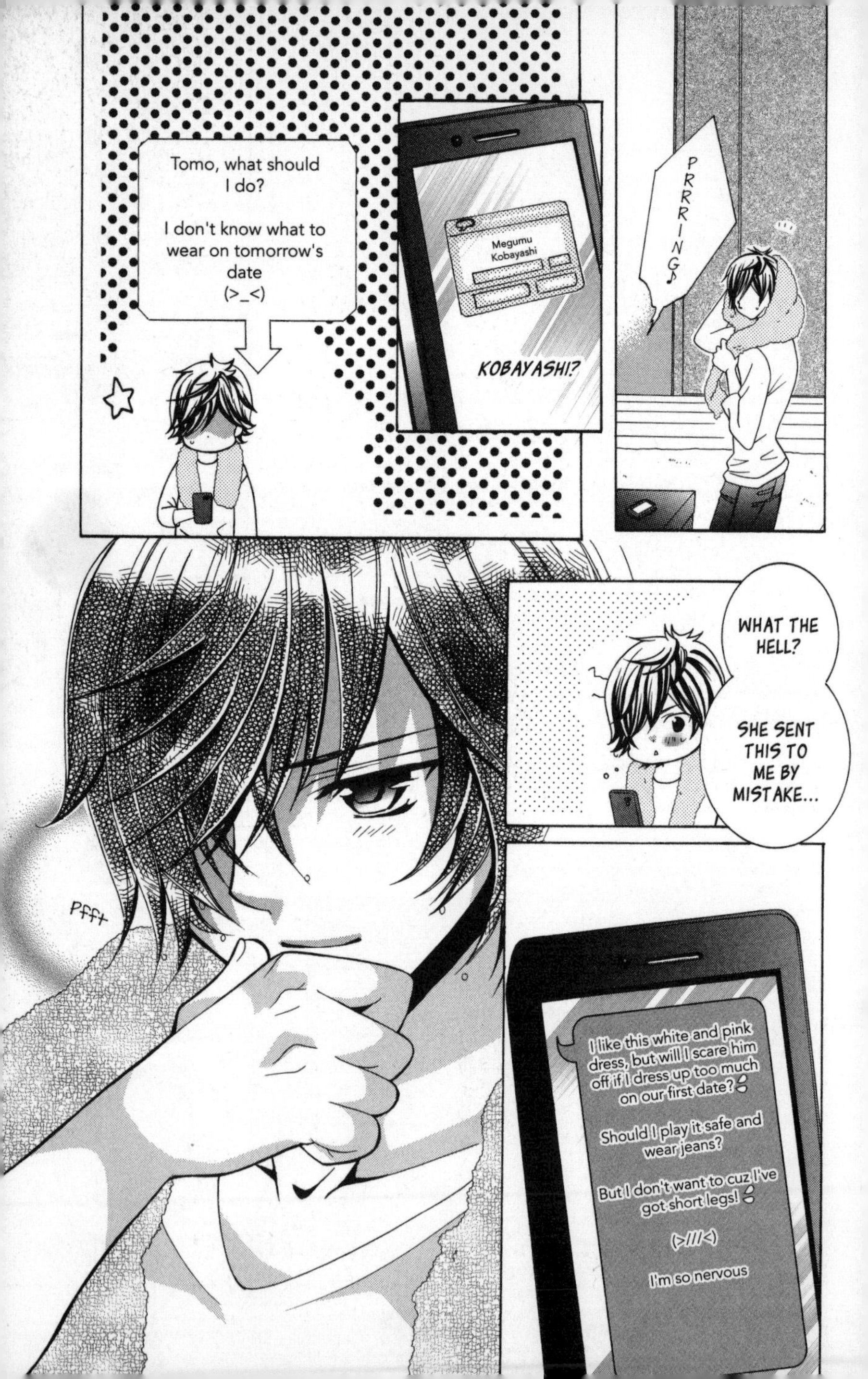
PRRRING♪
Megumu Kobayashi
KOBAYASHI!?
Tomo, what should I do?
I don't know what to wear on tomorrow's date
(>_<)
WHAT THE HELL?
SHE SENT THIS TO ME BY MISTAKE...
I like this white and pink dress, but will I scare him off if I dress up too much on our first date?
Should I play it safe and wear jeans?
But I don't want to cuz I've got short legs!
(>///<)
I'm so nervous
Pfft

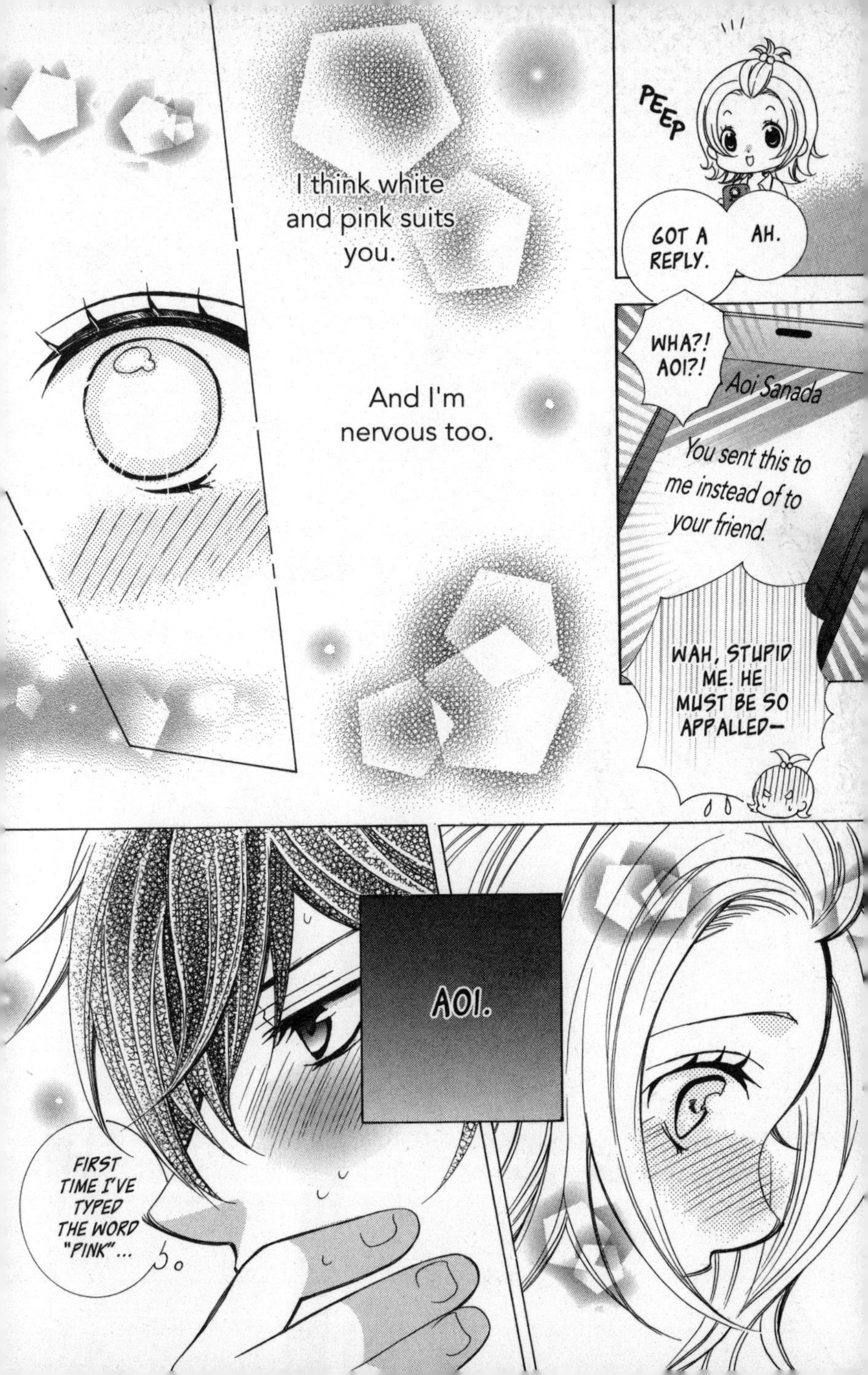
PEEP
AH.
GOT A REPLY.
WHA?! AOI?!
Aoi Sanada
You sent this to me instead of to your friend.
WAH, STUPID ME. HE MUST BE SO APPALLED—
I think white and pink suits you.
And I'm nervous too.
AOI.
FIRST TIME I'VE TYPED THE WORD "PINK"...

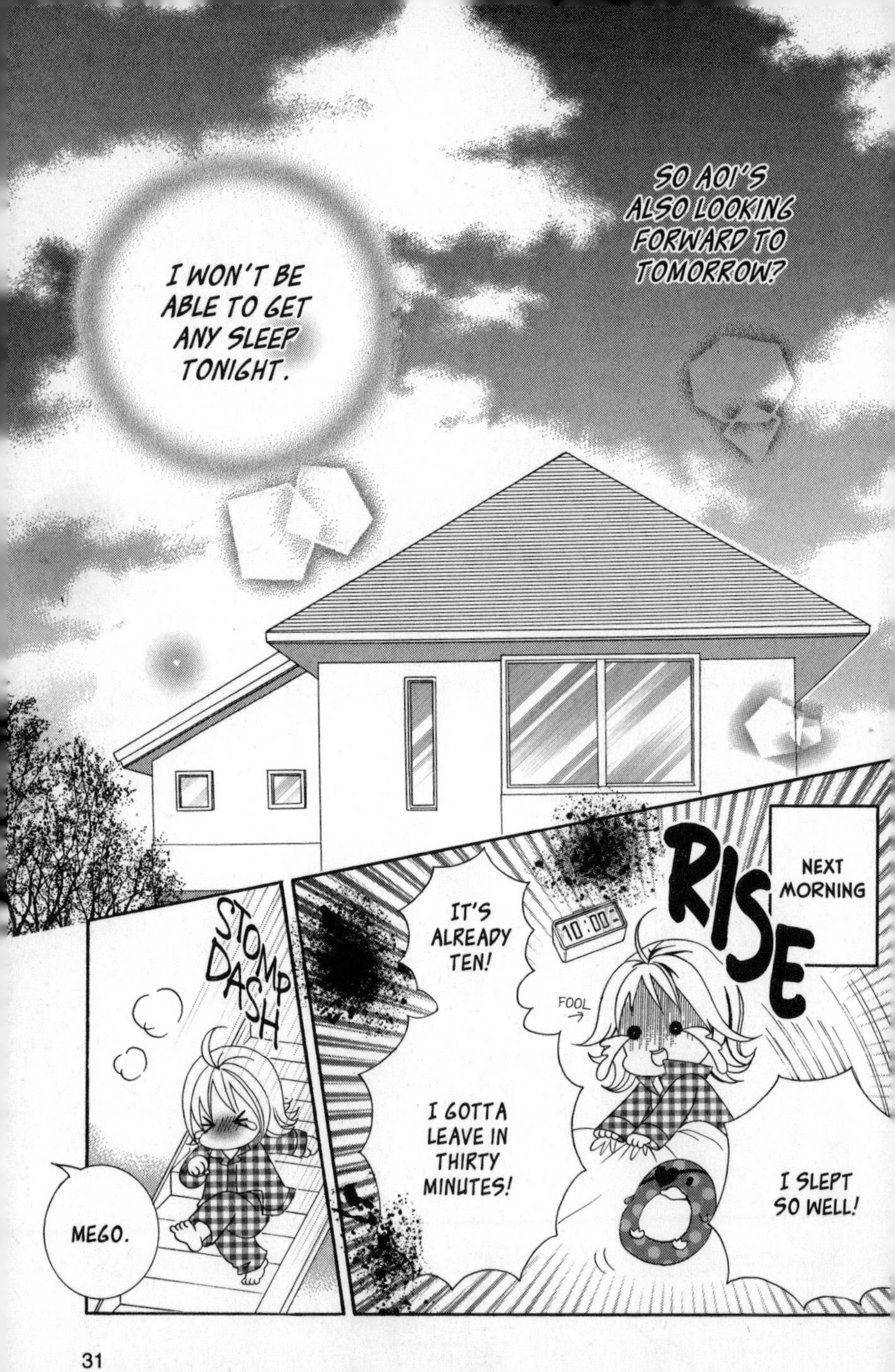
SO AOI'S ALSO LOOKING FORWARD TO TOMORROW?
I WON'T BE ABLE TO GET ANY SLEEP TONIGHT.
NEXT MORNING
RISE
I SLEPT SO WELL!
10:00
FOOL
IT'S ALREADY TEN!
I GOTTA LEAVE IN THIRTY MINUTES!
STOMP DASH
MEGO.

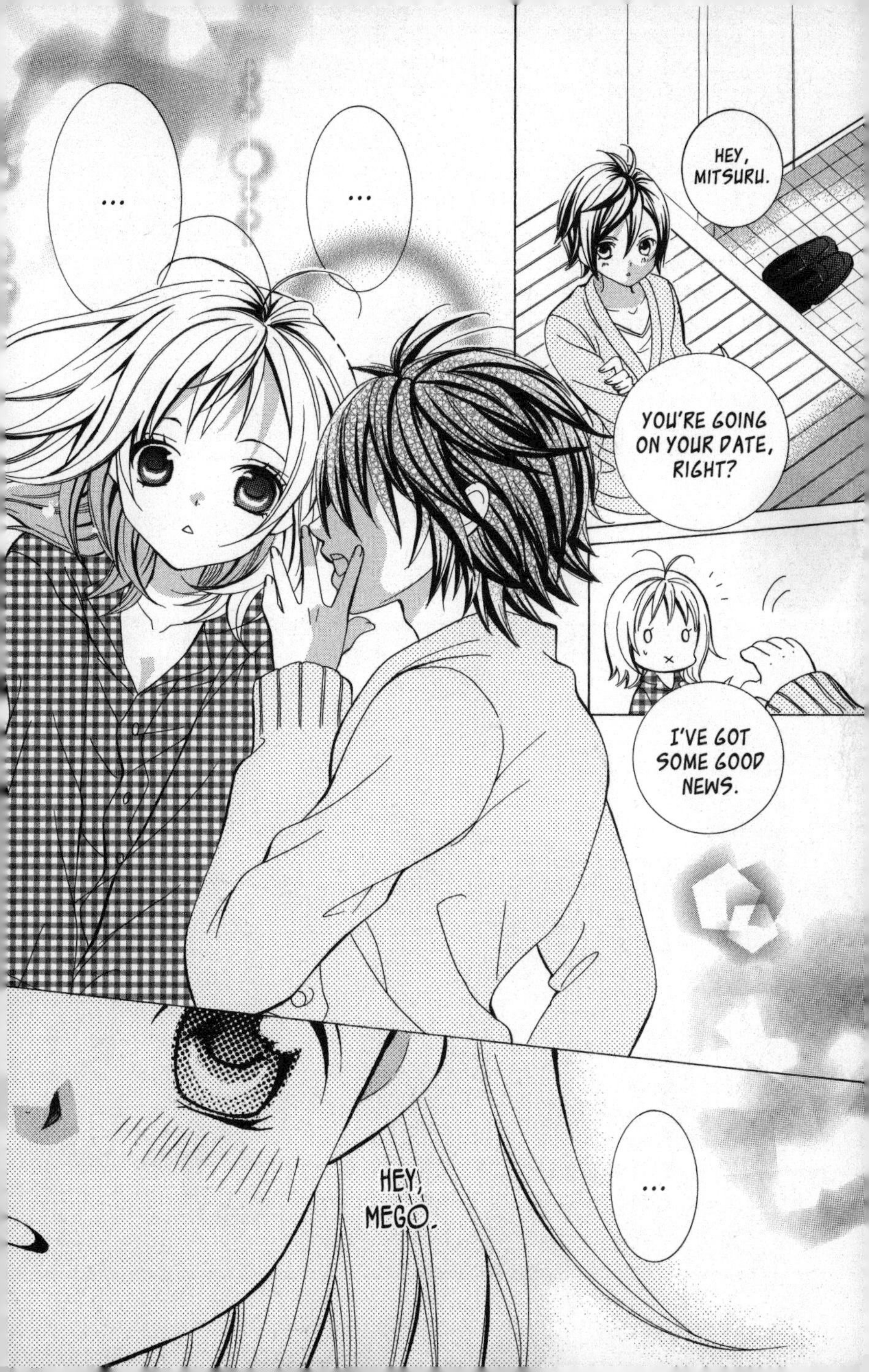
HEY, MITSURU.
YOU'RE GOING ON YOUR DATE, RIGHT?
I'VE GOT SOME GOOD NEWS.
...
...
...
HEY, MEGO.

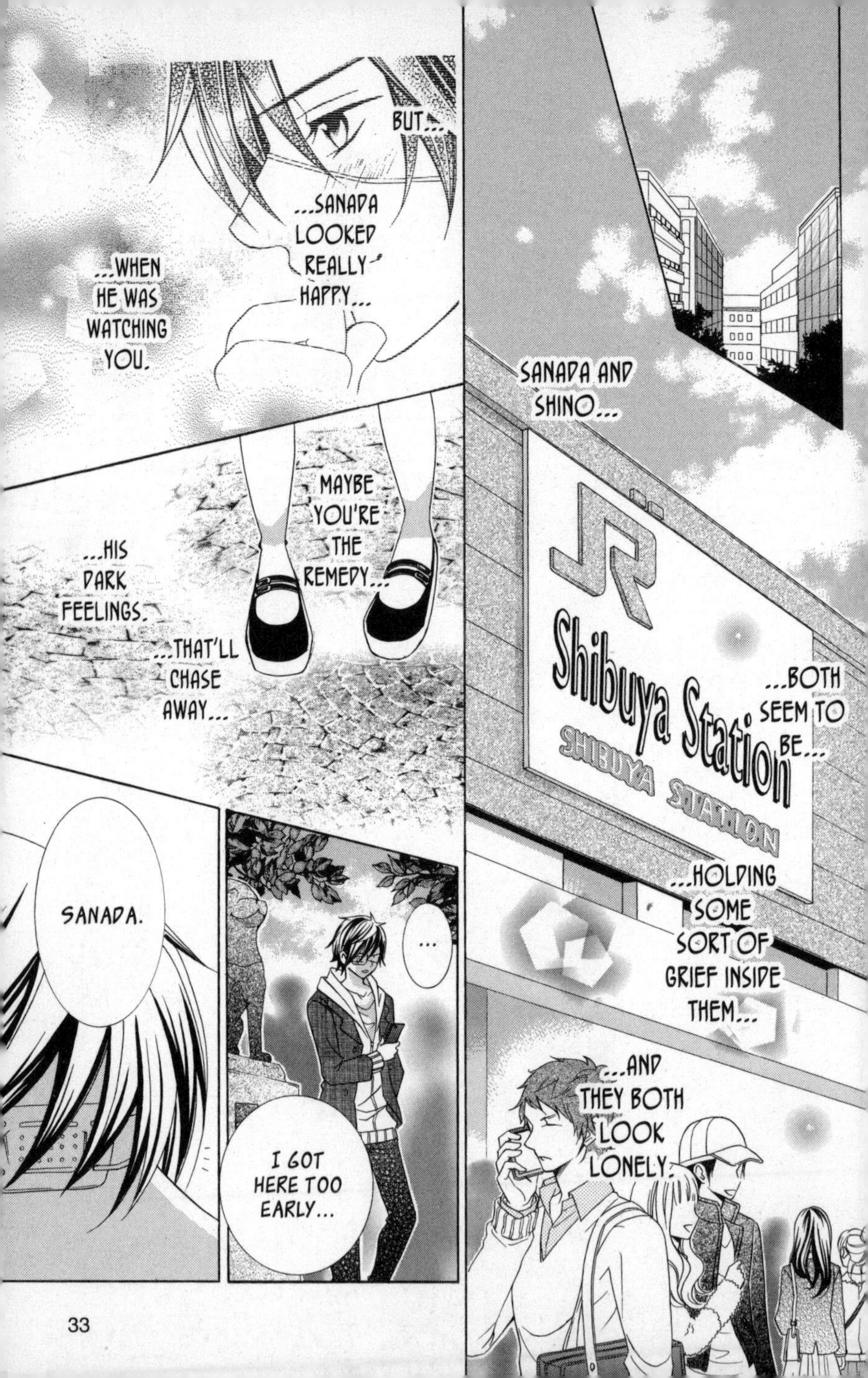
SANADA AND SHINO...
Shibuya Station
SHIBUYA STATION
...BOTH SEEM TO BE...
...HOLDING SOME SORT OF GRIEF INSIDE THEM...
...AND THEY BOTH LOOK LONELY.
BUT...
...SANADA LOOKED REALLY HAPPY...
...WHEN HE WAS WATCHING YOU.
MAYBE YOU'RE THE REMEDY...
...THAT'LL CHASE AWAY...
...HIS DARK FEELINGS.
...
I GOT HERE TOO EARLY...
SANADA.

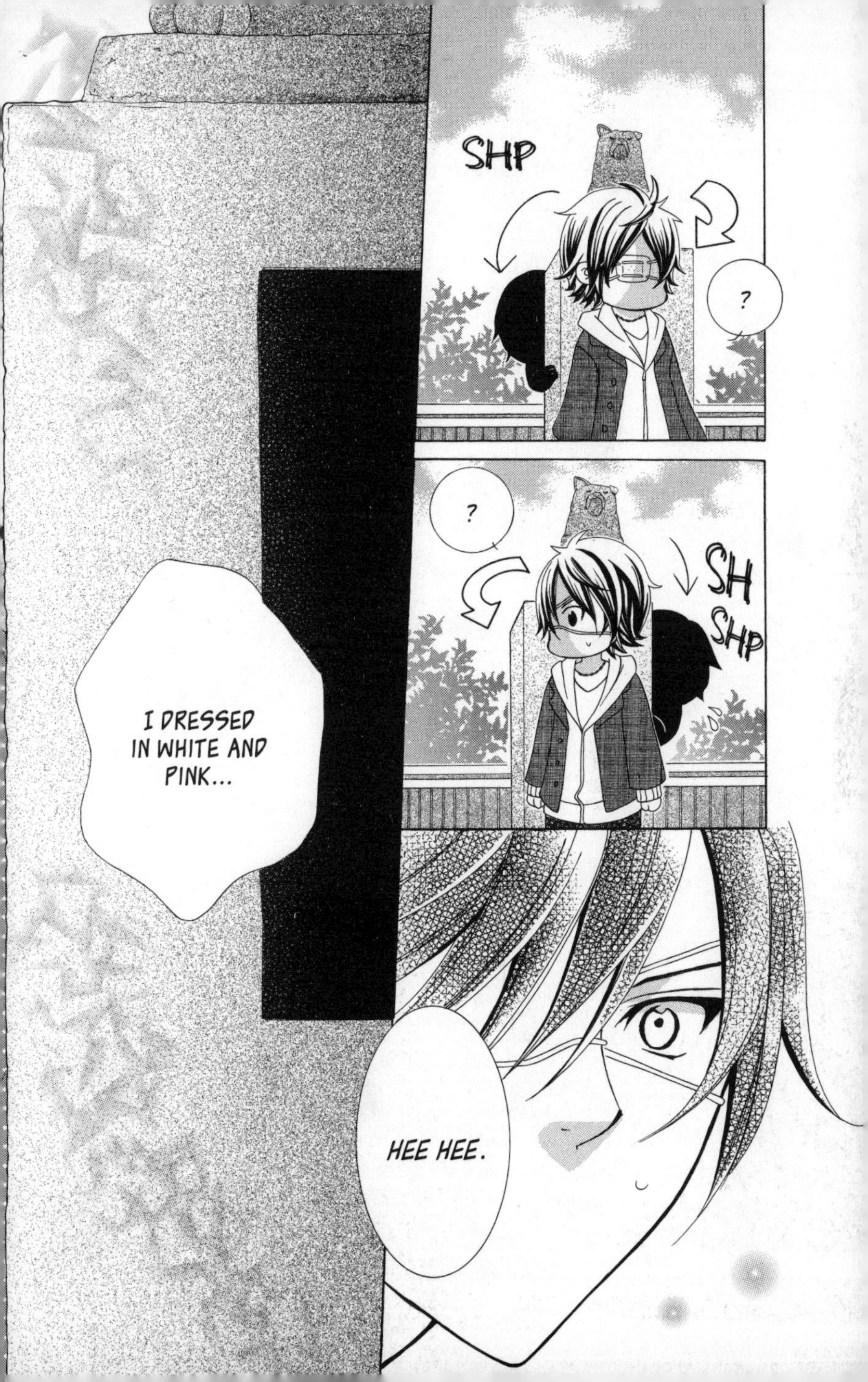
SHP
?
?
SH SHP
HEE HEE.
I DRESSED IN WHITE AND PINK...

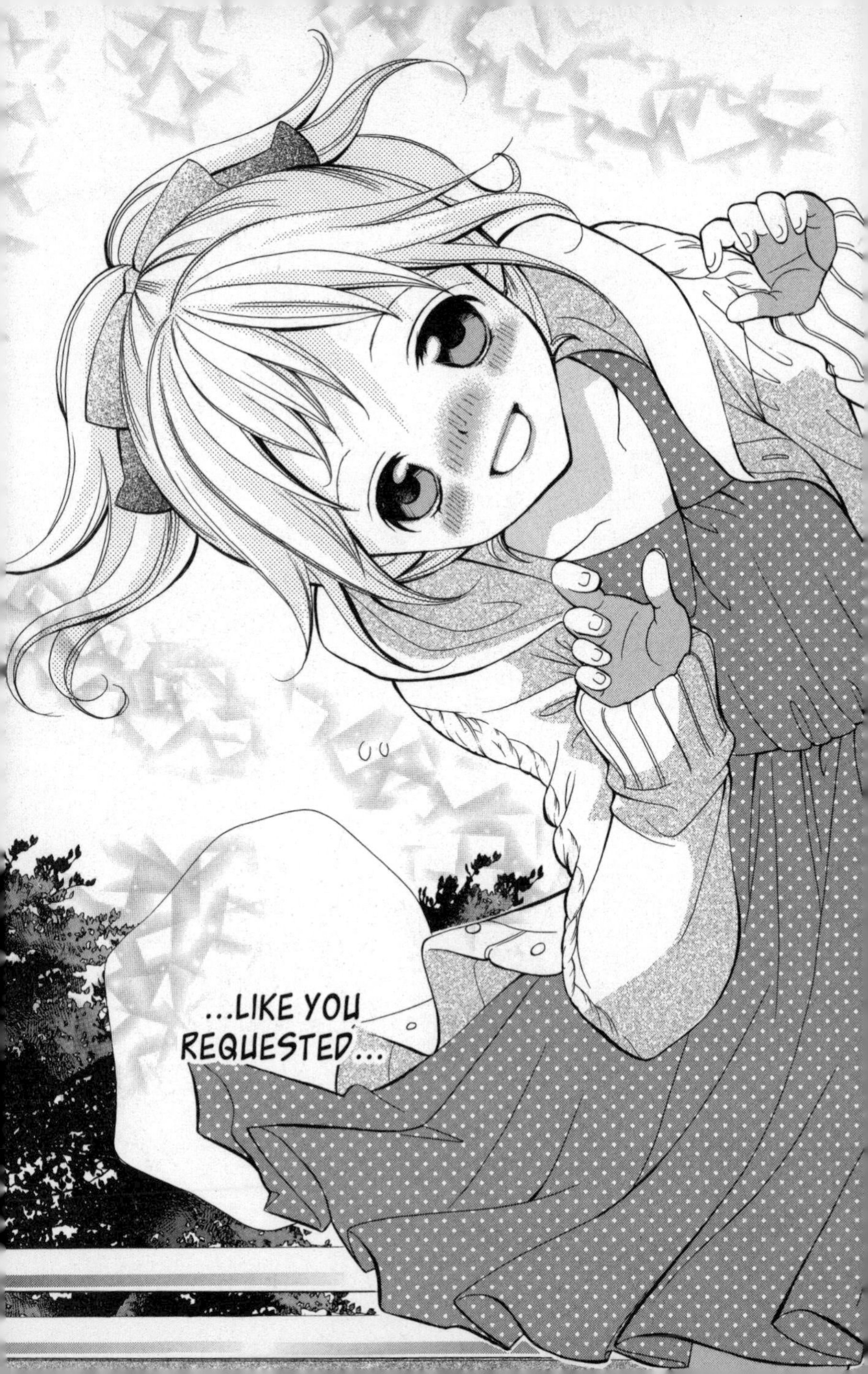
...LIKE YOU REQUESTED...

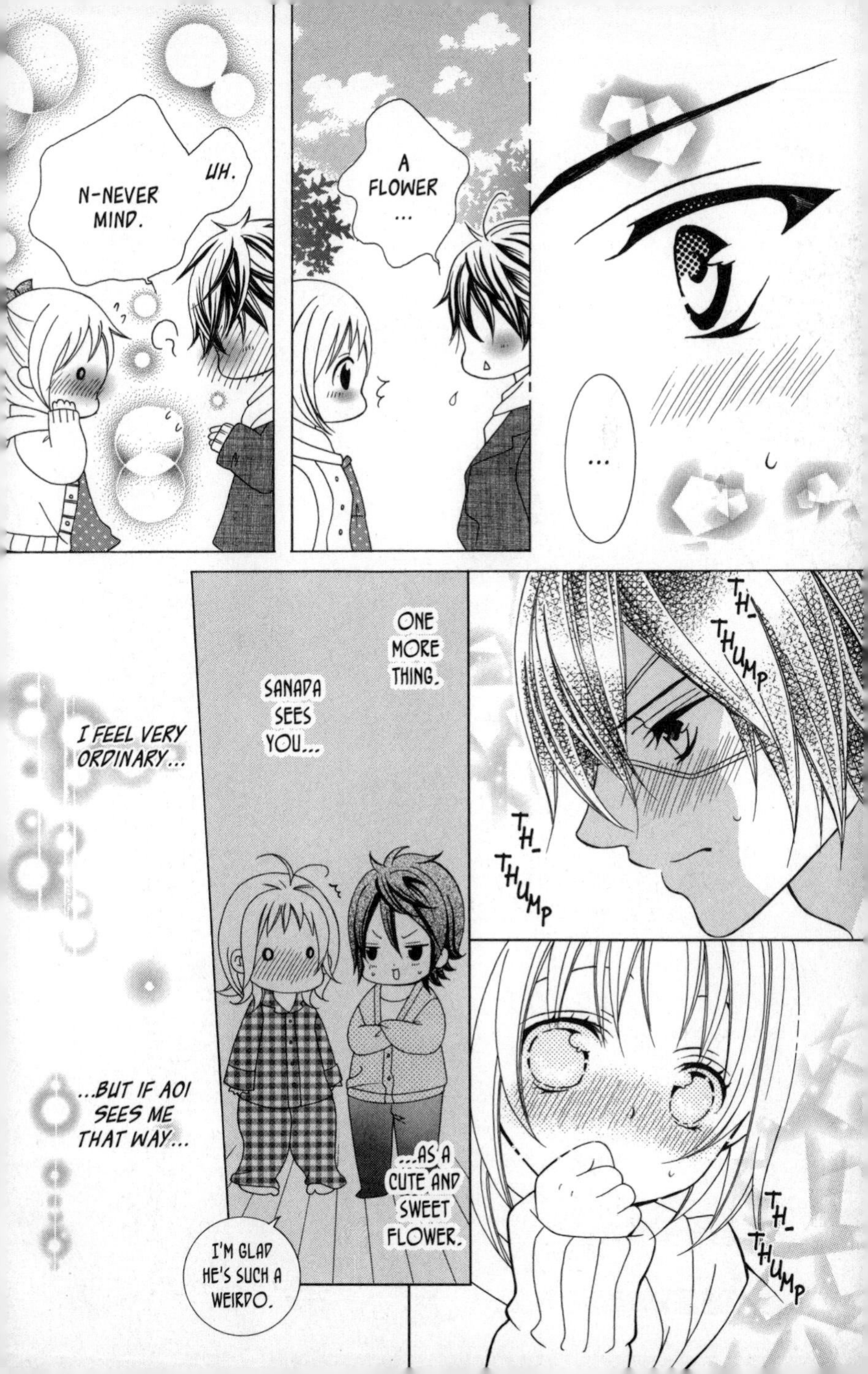
...
A FLOWER ...
UH.
N-NEVER MIND.
TH-THUMP
TH-THUMP
TH-THUMP
ONE MORE THING.
SANADA SEES YOU...
...AS A CUTE AND SWEET FLOWER.
I'M GLAD HE'S SUCH A WEIRDO.
I FEEL VERY ORDINARY...
...BUT IF AOI SEES ME THAT WAY...

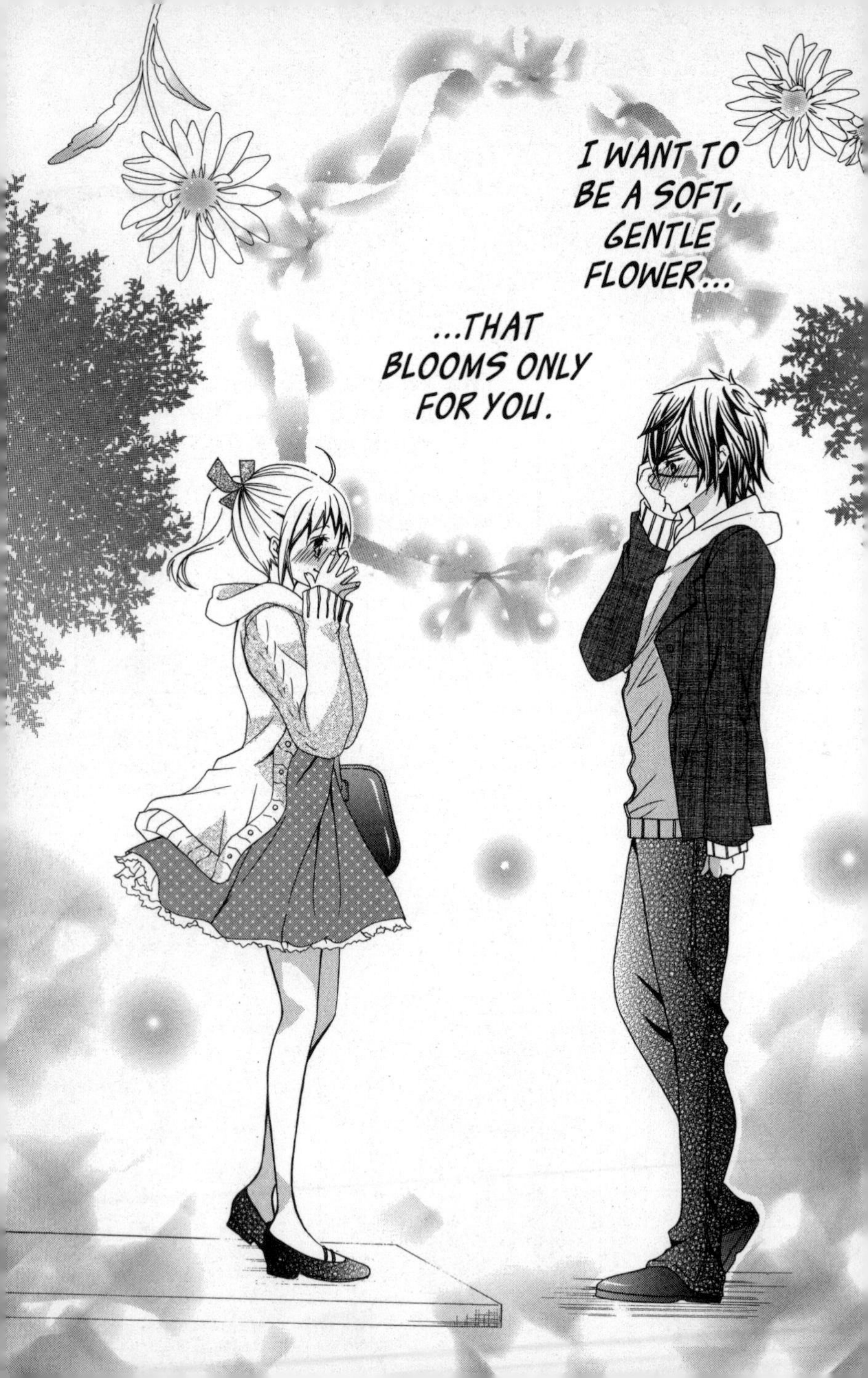
I WANT TO BE A SOFT, GENTLE FLOWER...
...THAT BLOOMS ONLY FOR YOU.

EVERYONE'S DRAWINGS

So Cute! Fan Art Feature ♥

ARE SO CUTE, THEY HURT!!

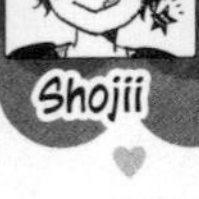

Shojii

Editor Shojii has commented on each one this time too!!

We've got lots of drawings to share this time. The feature continues on Page 110!

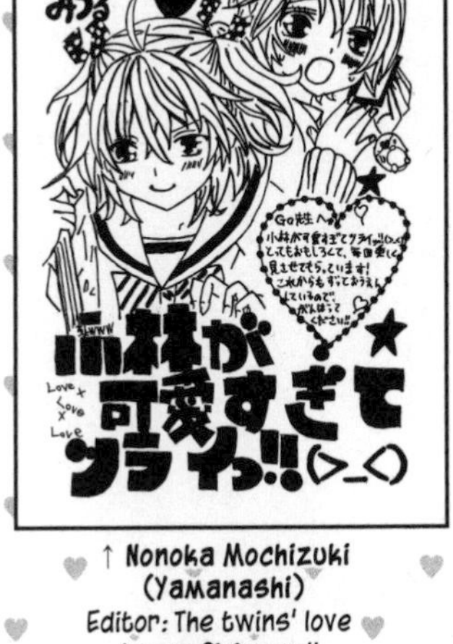
みつる
めご
小林が可愛すぎてツライっ!!(>_<)
Love x Love x Love

↑ Nonoka Mochizuki (Yamanashi)

Editor: The twins' love keeps firing up!!

Ryoka Yamamura (Yamaguchi) →

The Aoi doll is cute. ♥♥

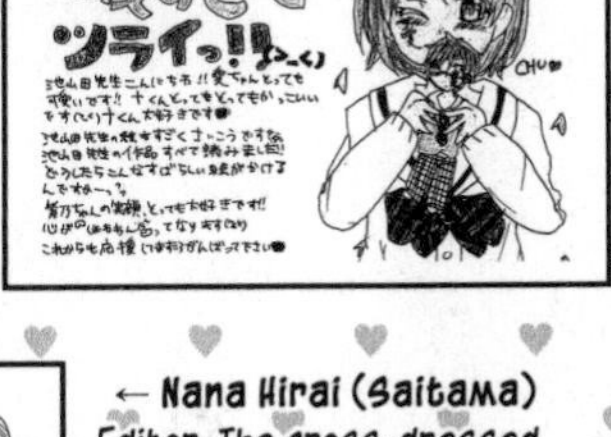
小林が可愛すぎてツライっ!!
CHU♥

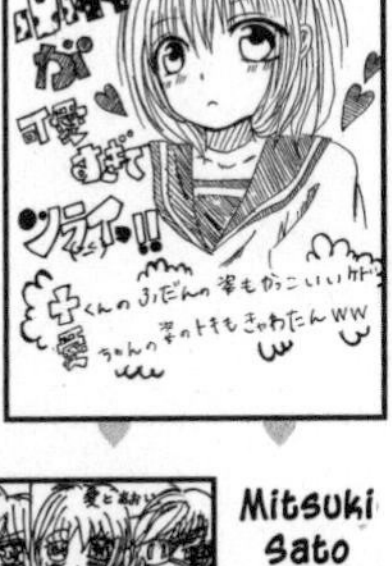
小林が可愛すぎてツライ!!

← Nana Hirai (Saitama)

Editor: The cross-dressed Mitsuru is always cute!!

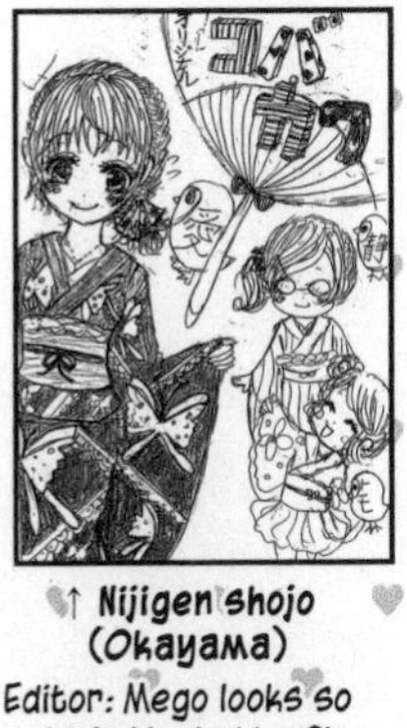

↑ Nijigen shojo (Okayama)

Editor: Mego looks so cute in the butterfly pattern kimono!!

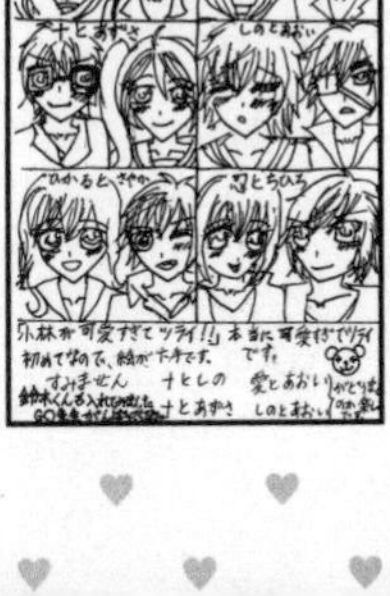
小林が可愛すぎてツライ!!

Mitsuki Sato (Saga) ←

Editor: A lot of effort went into drawing these six couples!! BTW, who's in the bottom row?!

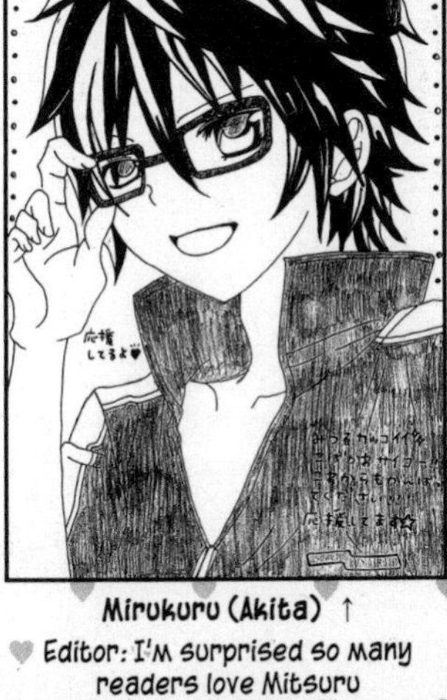
応援してるよ♥

Mirukuru (Akita) ↑

Editor: I'm surprised so many readers love Mitsuru in glasses!!

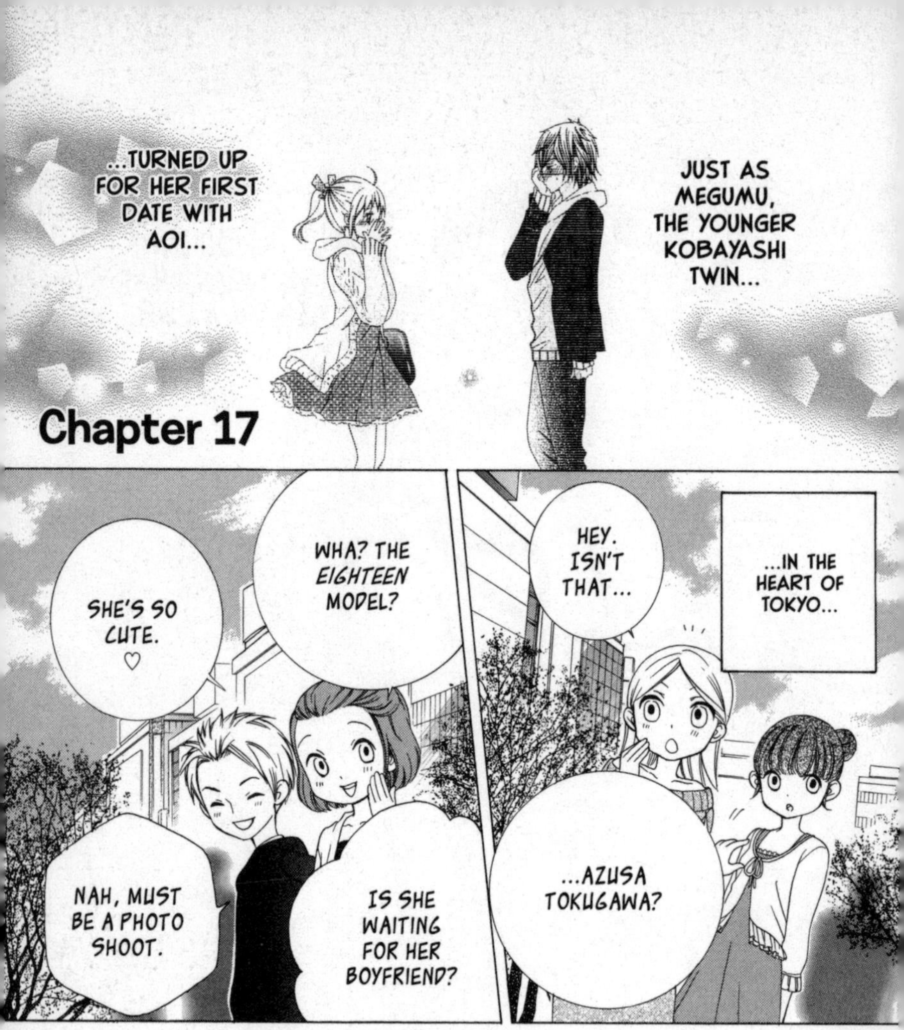
JUST AS MEGUMU, THE YOUNGER KOBAYASHI TWIN...
...TURNED UP FOR HER FIRST DATE WITH AOI...
Chapter 17
...IN THE HEART OF TOKYO...
HEY. ISN'T THAT...
...AZUSA TOKUGAWA?
WHA? THE EIGHTEEN MODEL?
SHE'S SO CUTE. ♡
IS SHE WAITING FOR HER BOYFRIEND?
NAH, MUST BE A PHOTO SHOOT.

THE MANGA NOW HAS AN OFFICIAL TWITTER ACCOUNT! ↓ @KOBAKAWA_INFO ♡ SO PLEASE TAKE A LOOK. ♡

THANK YOU FOR ALWAYS SENDING ME LOVELY LETTERS AND DRAWINGS.♡♡ IT'LL MAKE ME HAPPY IF YOU SEND YOUR THOUGHTS AND DRAWINGS AFTER READING VOLUME 4.♡

GO IKEYAMADA
C/O SHOJO BEAT
VIZ MEDIA, LLC
P.O. BOX 77010
SAN FRANCISCO, CA
94107

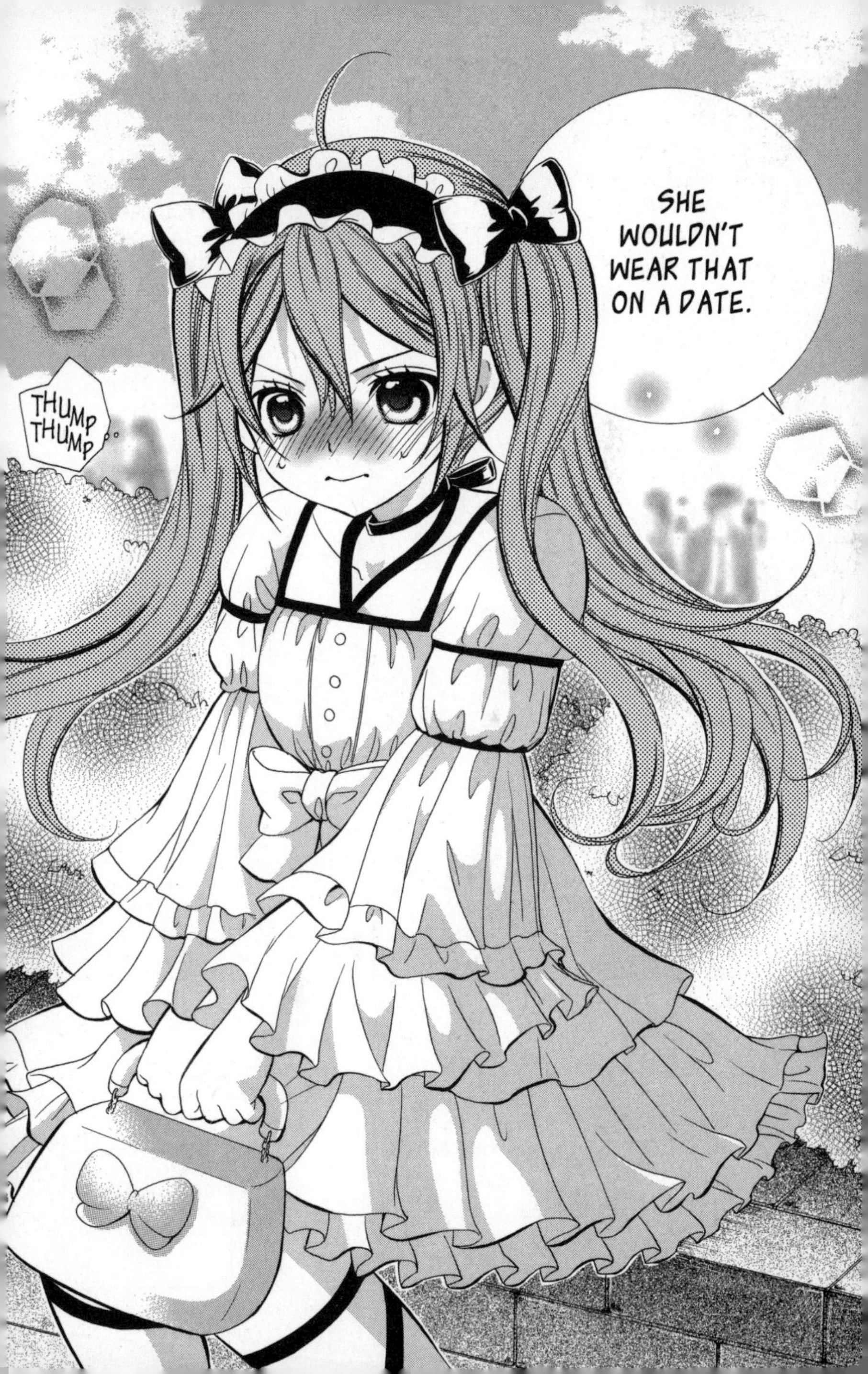
SHE WOULDN'T WEAR THAT ON A DATE.
THUMP THUMP

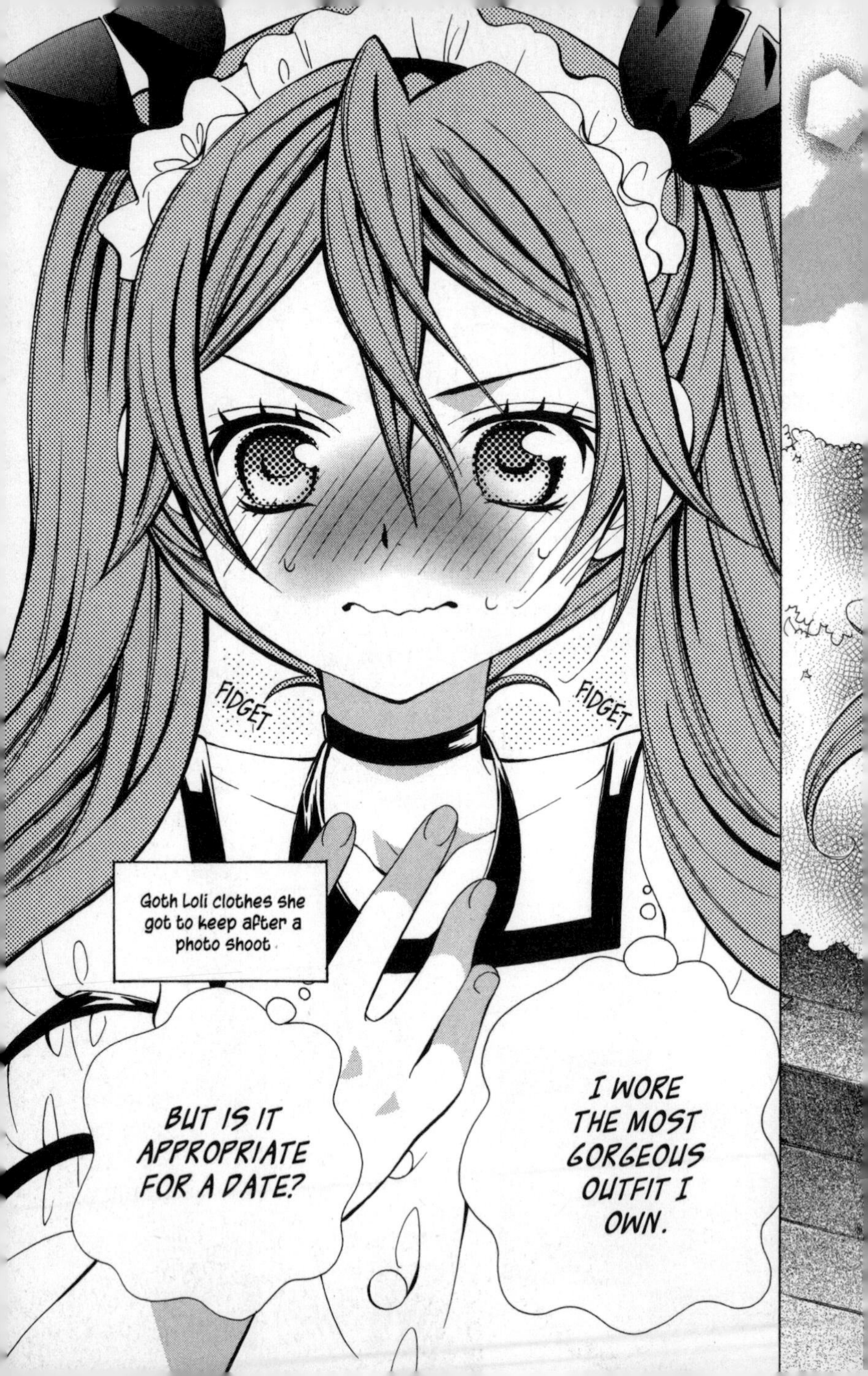
FIDGET
FIDGET
Goth Loli clothes she got to keep after a photo shoot
I WORE THE MOST GORGEOUS OUTFIT I OWN.
BUT IS IT APPROPRIATE FOR A DATE?

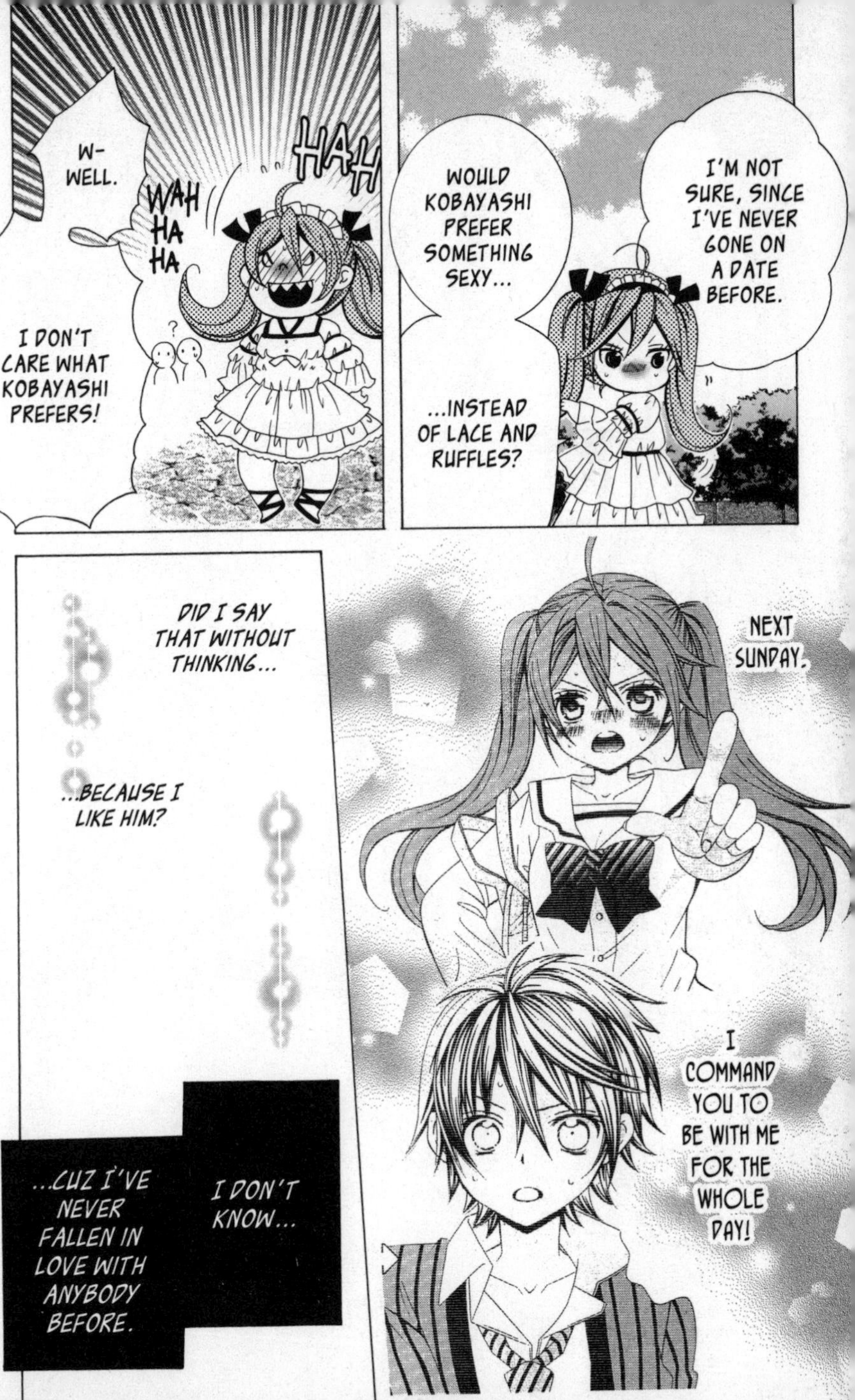
I'M NOT SURE, SINCE I'VE NEVER GONE ON A DATE BEFORE.
WOULD KOBAYASHI PREFER SOMETHING SEXY...
...INSTEAD OF LACE AND RUFFLES?
HAH
WAH HA HA
W-WELL.
I DON'T CARE WHAT KOBAYASHI PREFERS!
NEXT SUNDAY.
I COMMAND YOU TO BE WITH ME FOR THE WHOLE DAY!
DID I SAY THAT WITHOUT THINKING...
...BECAUSE I LIKE HIM?
I DON'T KNOW...
...CUZ I'VE NEVER FALLEN IN LOVE WITH ANYBODY BEFORE.

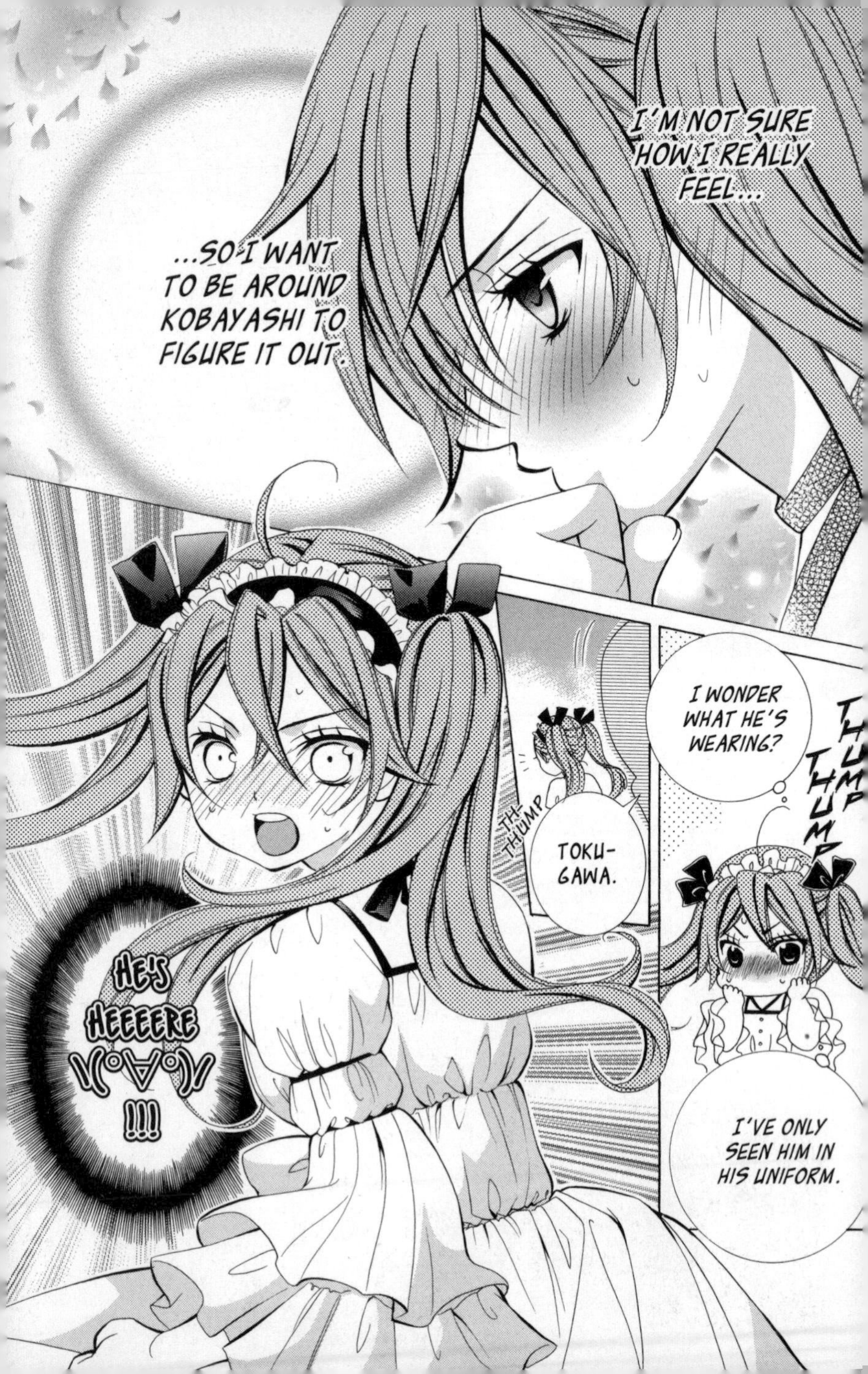
I'M NOT SURE HOW I REALLY FEEL...
...SO I WANT TO BE AROUND KOBAYASHI TO FIGURE IT OUT.
I WONDER WHAT HE'S WEARING?
THUMP THUMP
I'VE ONLY SEEN HIM IN HIS UNIFORM.
TH-THUMP
TOKU-GAWA.
HE'S HEEEEERE \(°A°)/ !!!

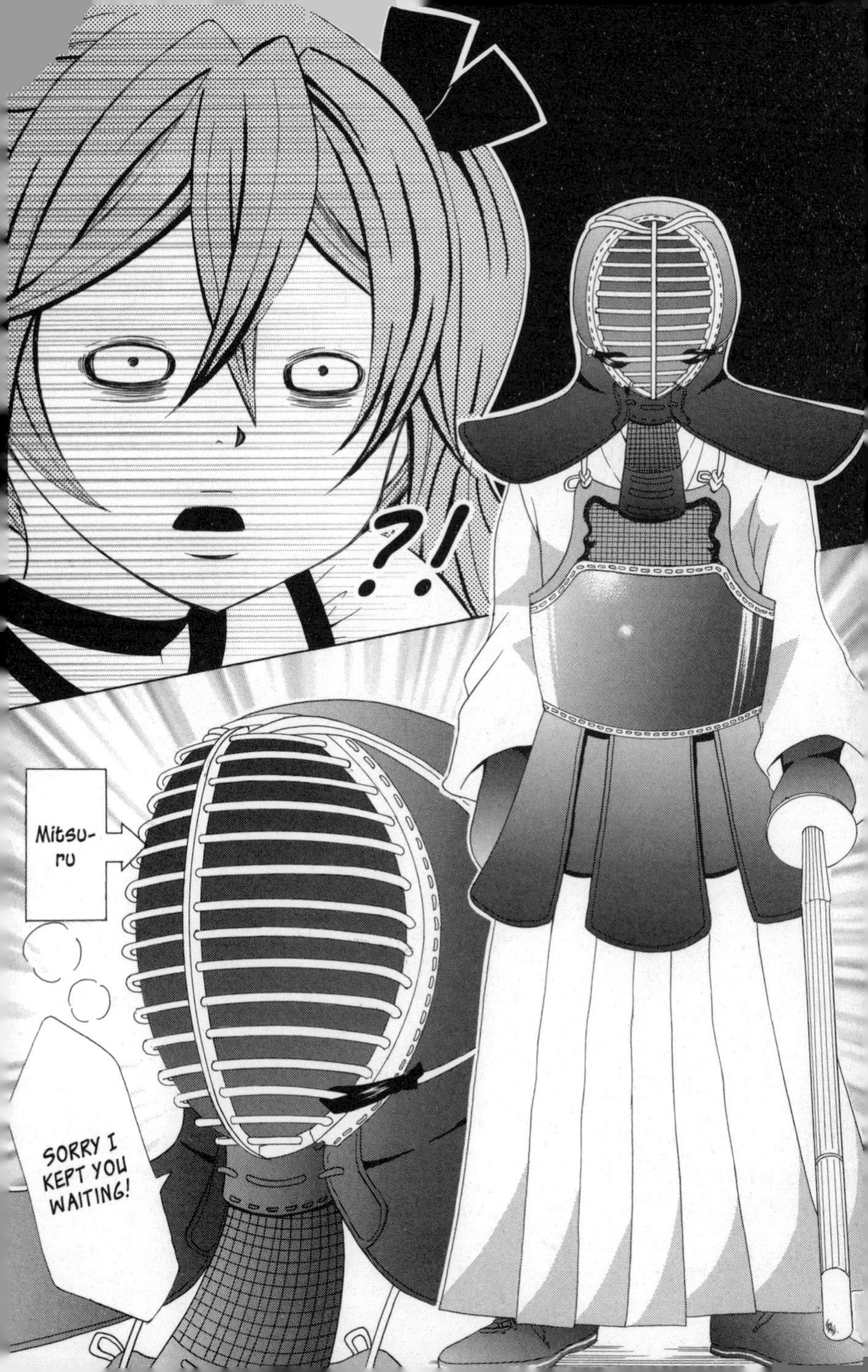

?!
Mitsu-ru
SORRY I KEPT YOU WAITING!

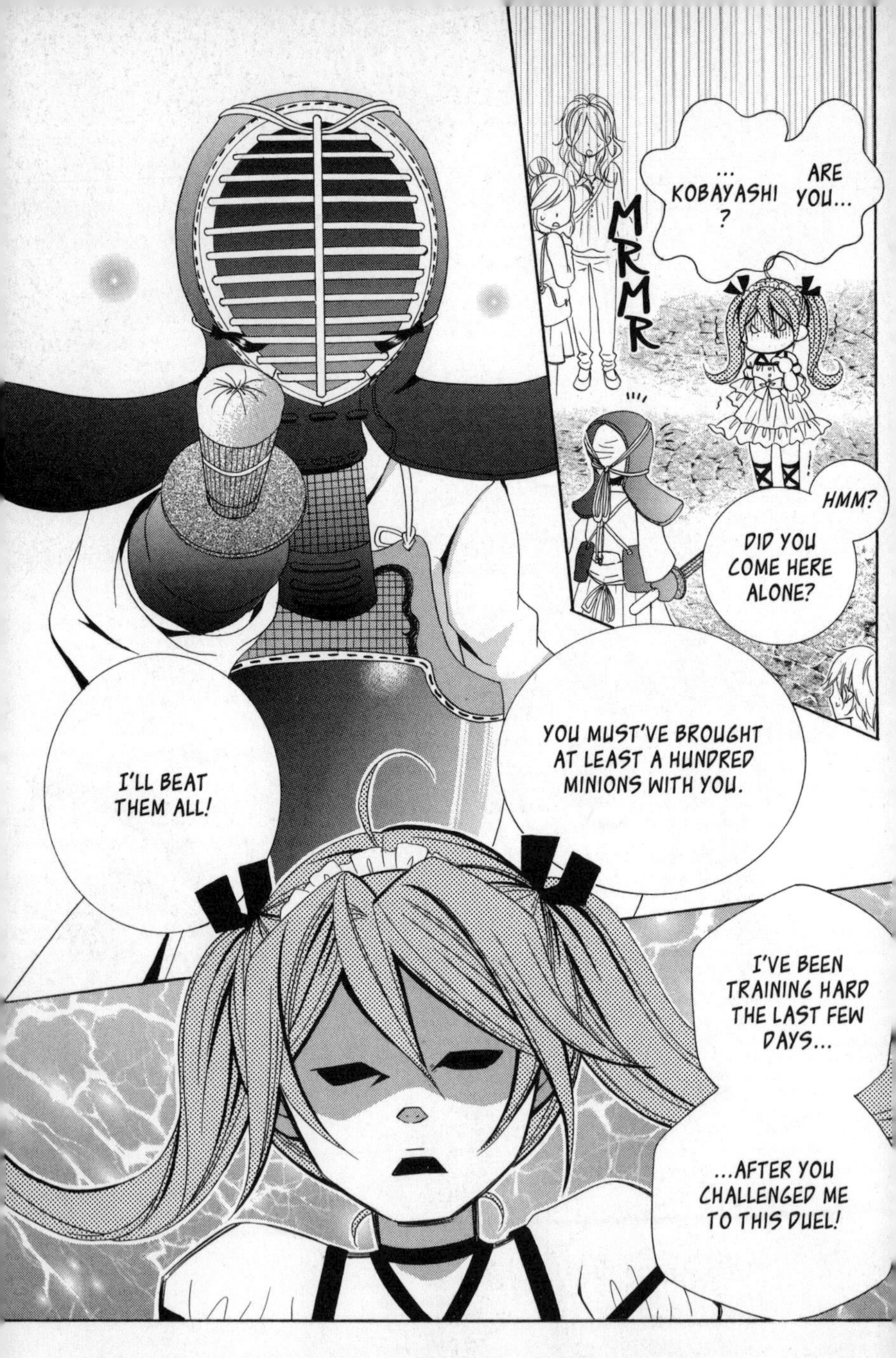
ARE YOU... ...KOBAYASHI?
MRMR
HMM?
DID YOU COME HERE ALONE?
YOU MUST'VE BROUGHT AT LEAST A HUNDRED MINIONS WITH YOU.
I'LL BEAT THEM ALL!
I'VE BEEN TRAINING HARD THE LAST FEW DAYS...
...AFTER YOU CHALLENGED ME TO THIS DUEL!

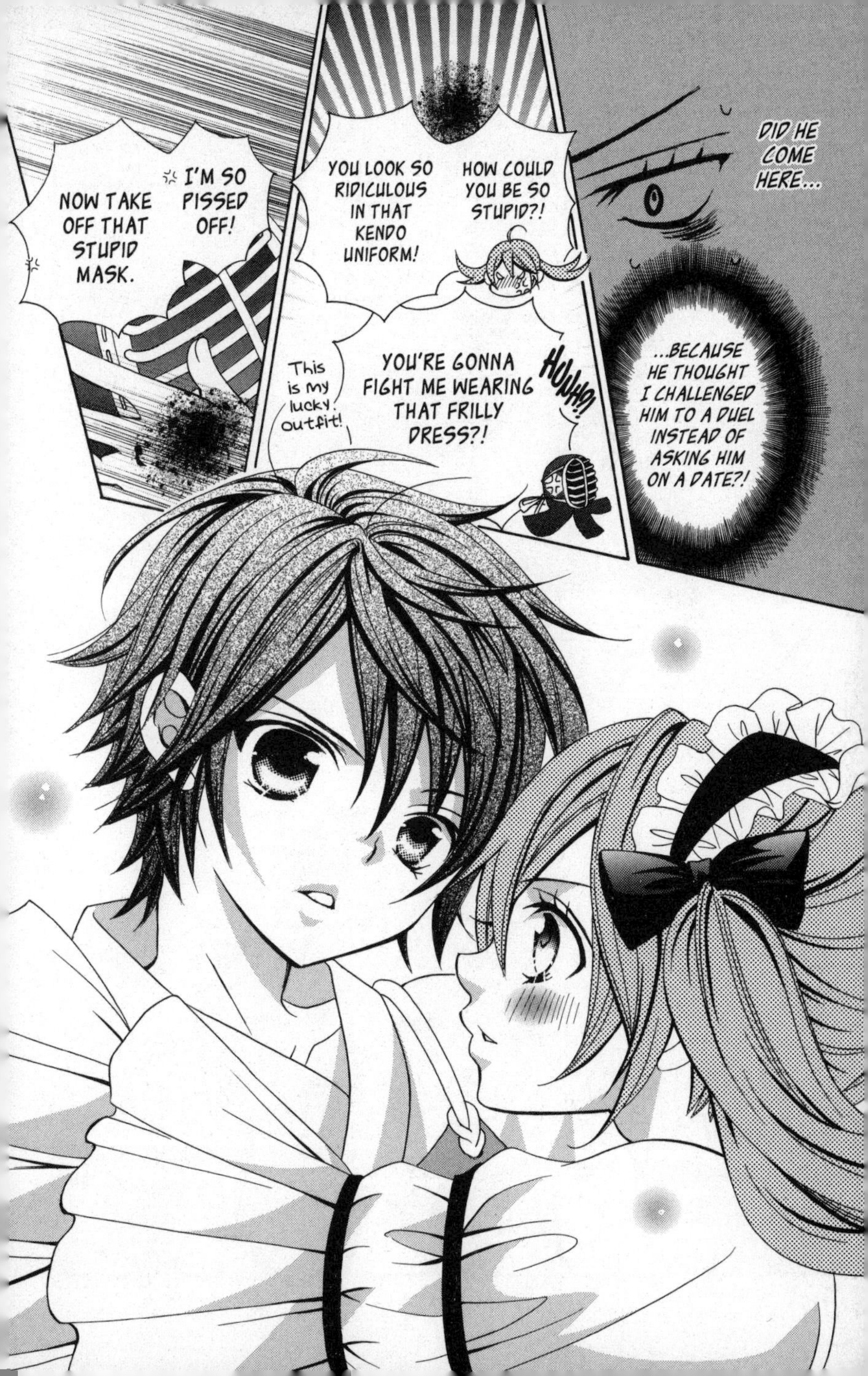
DID HE COME HERE...
...BECAUSE HE THOUGHT I CHALLENGED HIM TO A DUEL INSTEAD OF ASKING HIM ON A DATE?!
HOW COULD YOU BE SO STUPID?!
YOU LOOK SO RIDICULOUS IN THAT KENDO UNIFORM!
YOU'RE GONNA FIGHT ME WEARING THAT FRILLY DRESS?!
This is my lucky outfit!
I'M SO PISSED OFF!
NOW TAKE OFF THAT STUPID MASK.

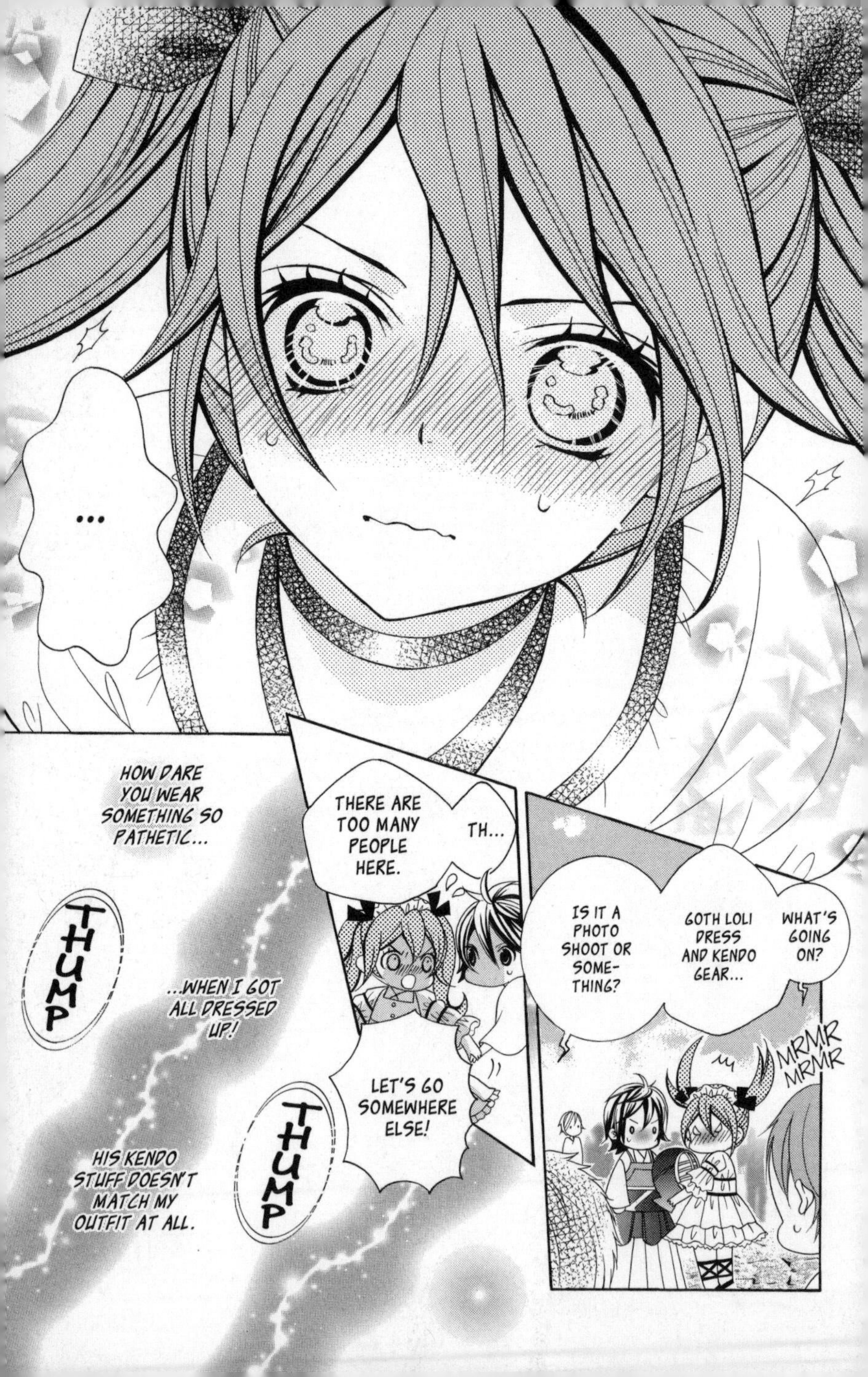
...
WHAT'S GOING ON?
GOTH LOLI DRESS AND KENDO GEAR...
IS IT A PHOTO SHOOT OR SOME-THING?
MRMR MRMR
TH...
THERE ARE TOO MANY PEOPLE HERE.
LET'S GO SOMEWHERE ELSE!
HOW DARE YOU WEAR SOMETHING SO PATHETIC...
THUMP
...WHEN I GOT ALL DRESSED UP!
HIS KENDO STUFF DOESN'T MATCH MY OUTFIT AT ALL.
THUMP

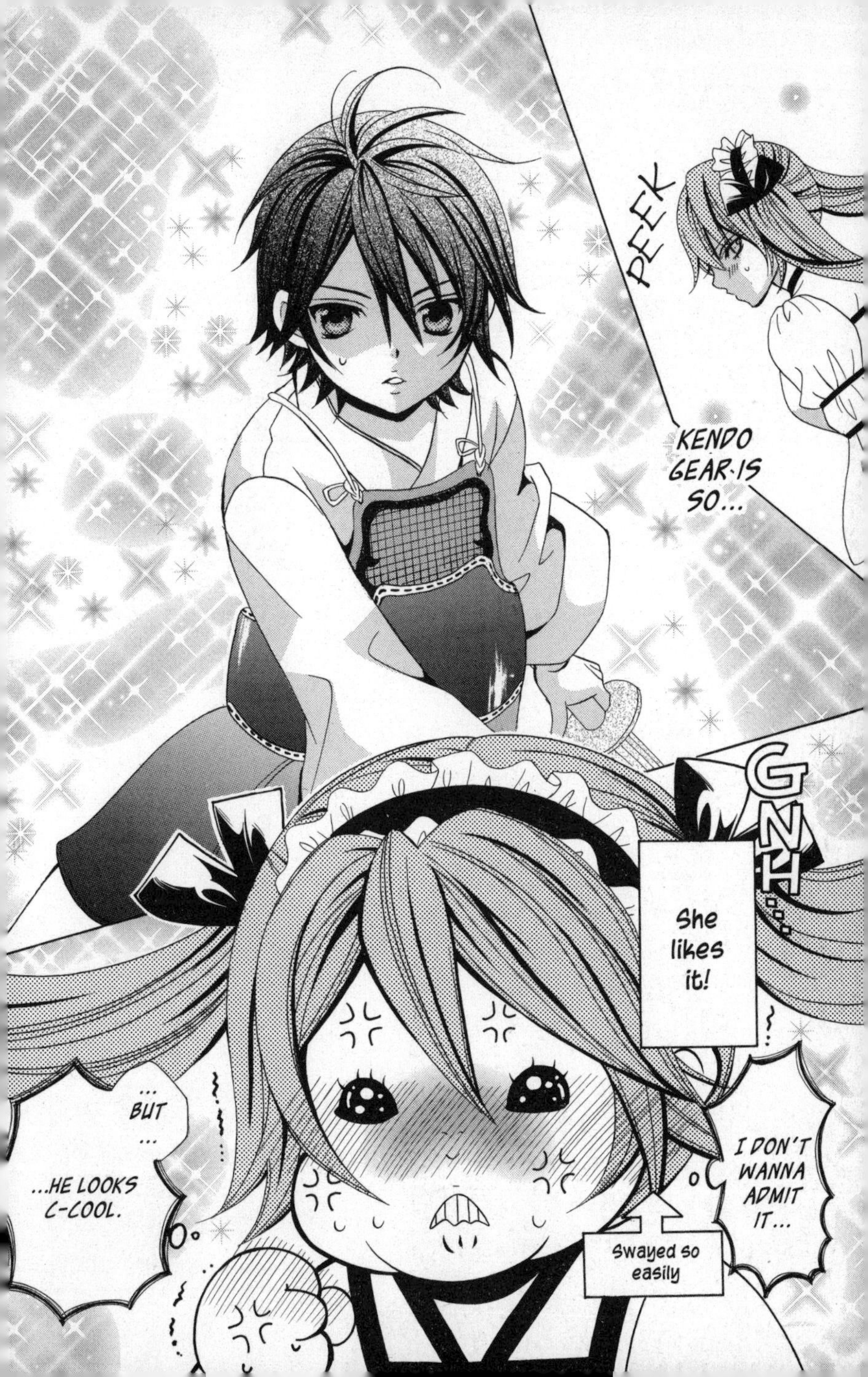
PEEK
KENDO GEAR IS SO...
GNH...
She likes it!
I DON'T WANNA ADMIT IT...
Swayed so easily
... BUT ...
...HE LOOKS C-COOL.

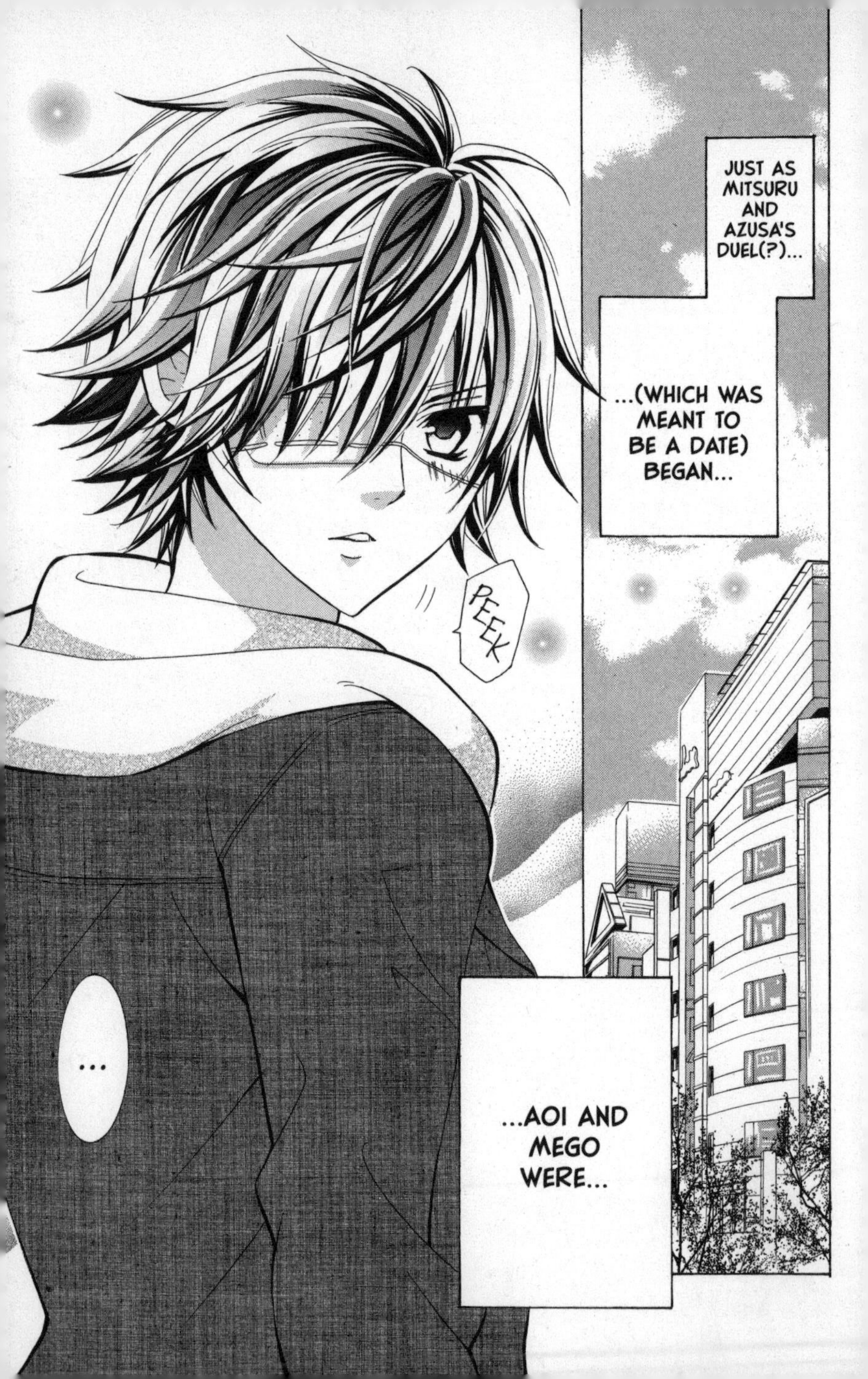

JUST AS MITSURU AND AZUSA'S DUEL(?)...
...(WHICH WAS MEANT TO BE A DATE) BEGAN...
...AOI AND MEGO WERE...
PEEK
...

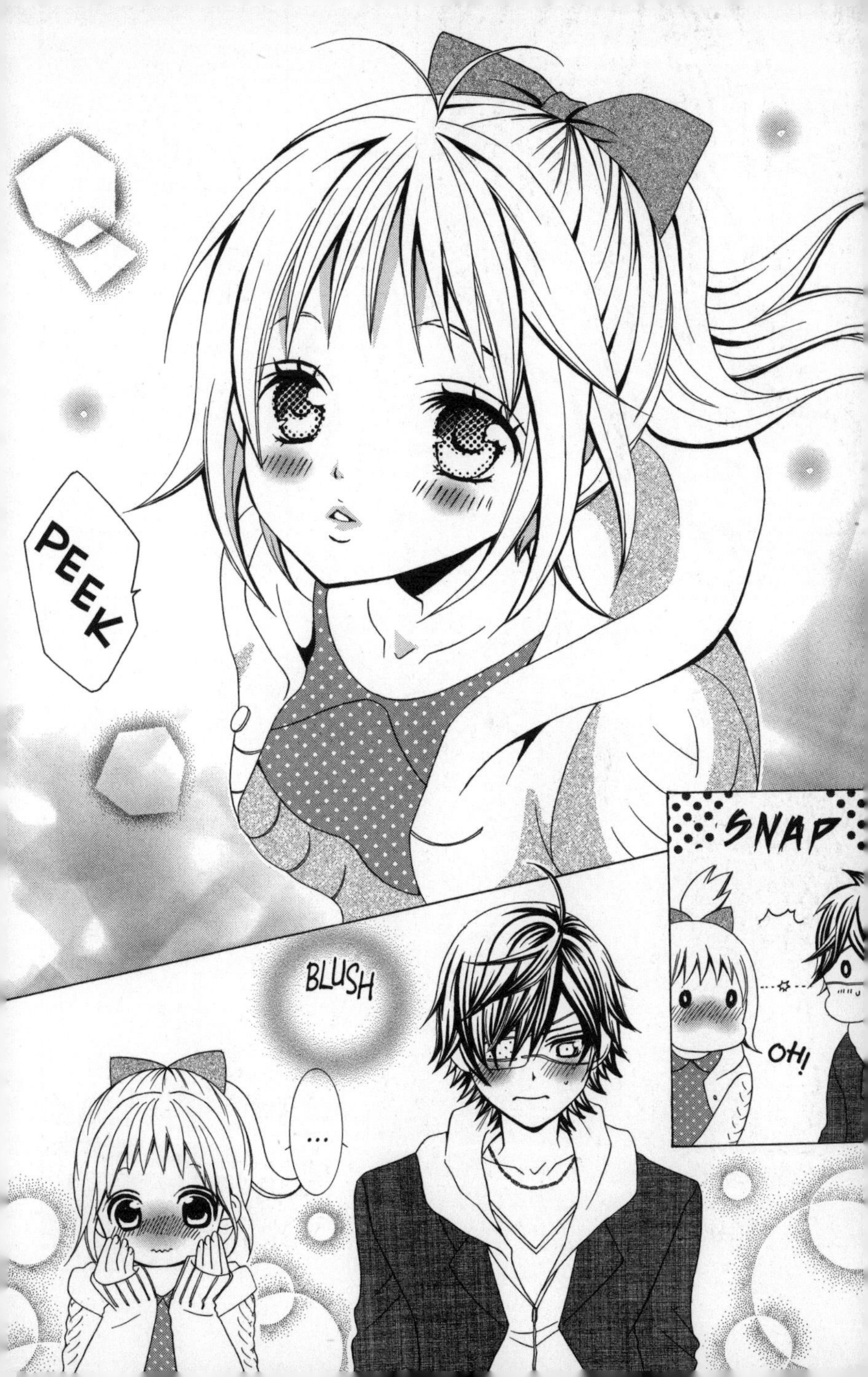
PEEK
SNAP
OH!
BLUSH
...

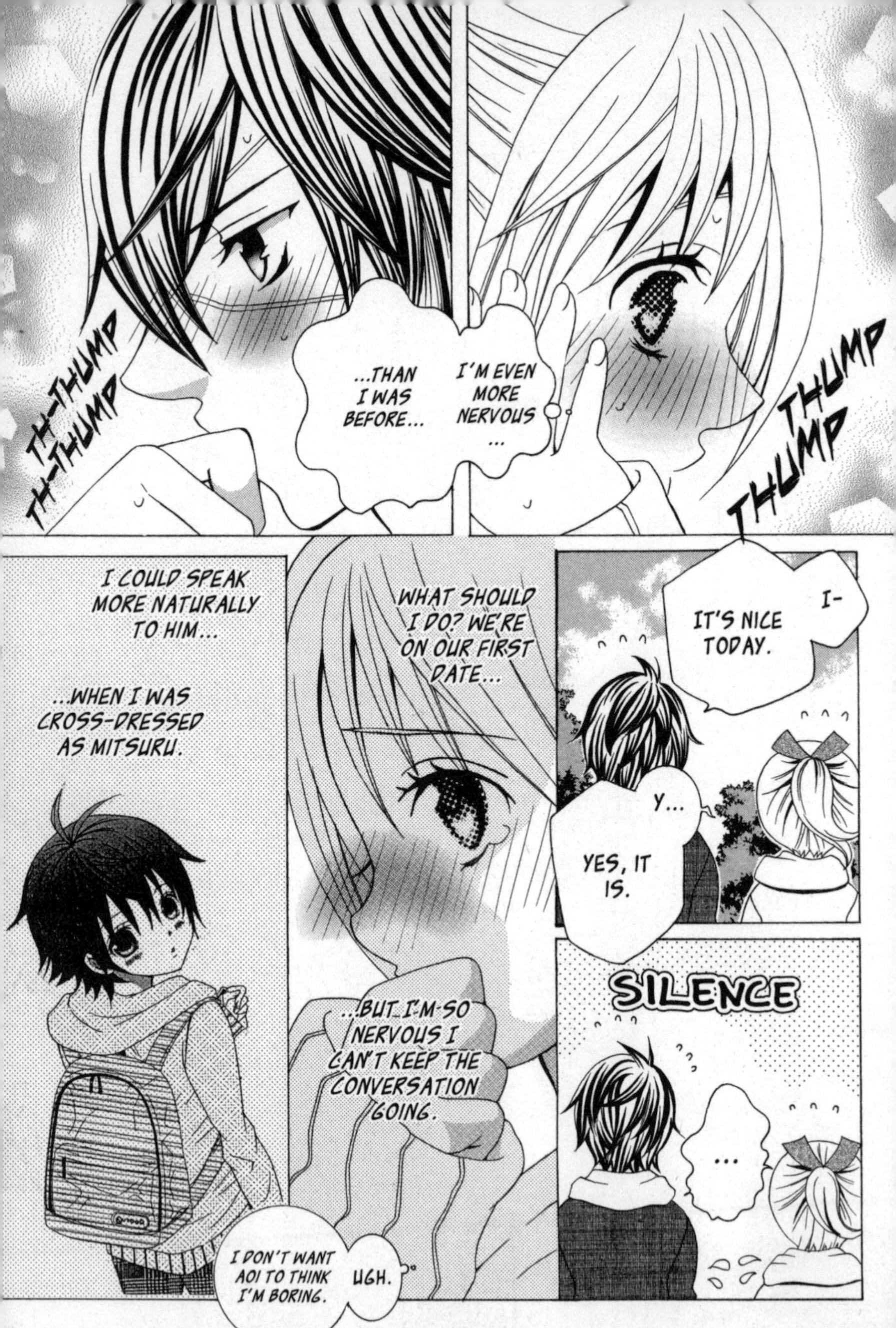
THUMP THUMP
I'M EVEN MORE NERVOUS ...
...THAN I WAS BEFORE...
TH-THUMP TH-THUMP
I-
IT'S NICE TODAY.
Y...
YES, IT IS.
SILENCE
...
WHAT SHOULD I DO? WE'RE ON OUR FIRST DATE...
...BUT I'M SO NERVOUS I CAN'T KEEP THE CONVERSATION GOING.
I COULD SPEAK MORE NATURALLY TO HIM...
...WHEN I WAS CROSS-DRESSED AS MITSURU.
UGH.
I DON'T WANT AOI TO THINK I'M BORING.

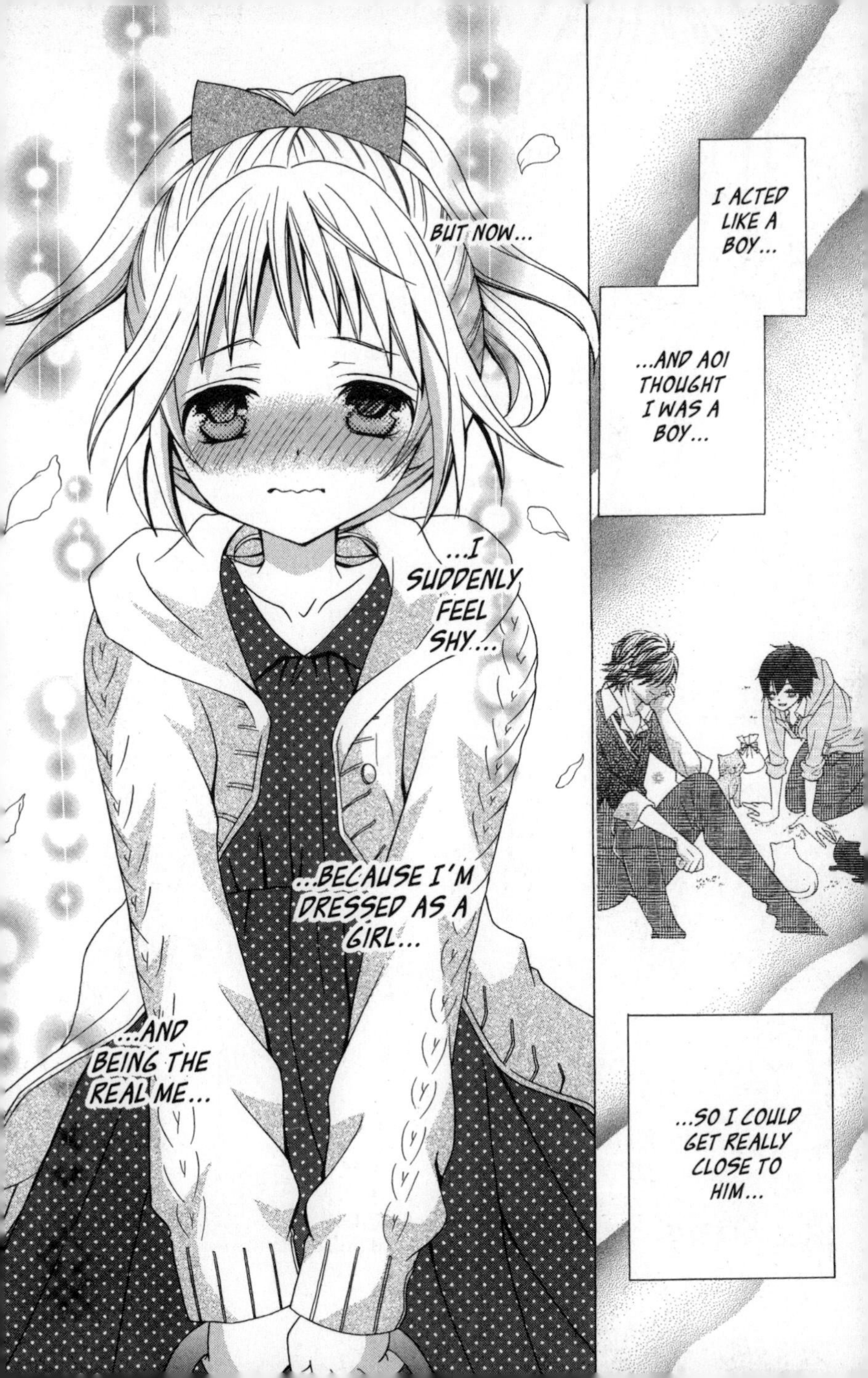
I ACTED LIKE A BOY...
...AND AOI THOUGHT I WAS A BOY...
...SO I COULD GET REALLY CLOSE TO HIM...
BUT NOW...
...I SUDDENLY FEEL SHY...
...BECAUSE I'M DRESSED AS A GIRL...
...AND BEING THE REAL ME...

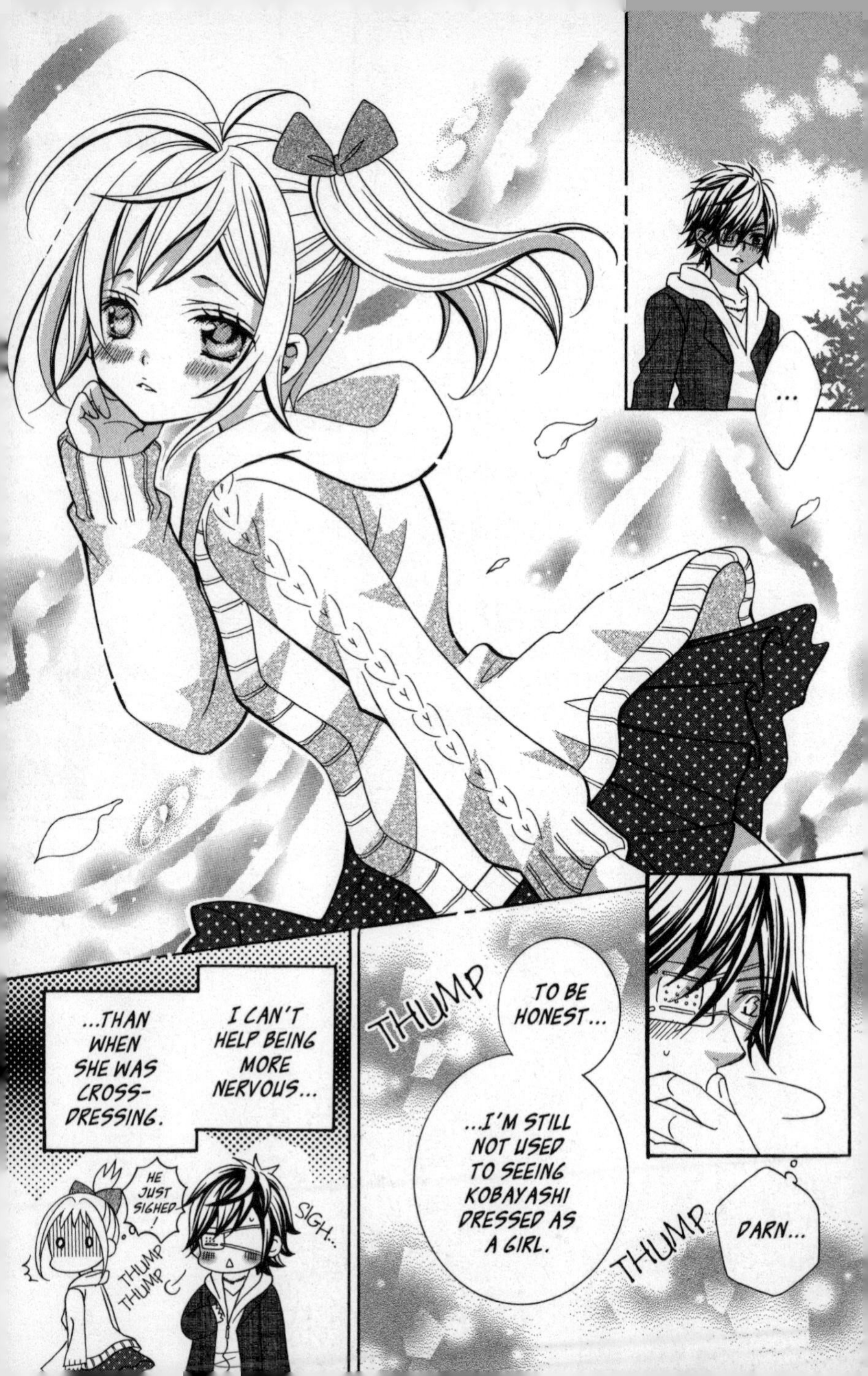
...
THUMP
TO BE HONEST...
...I'M STILL NOT USED TO SEEING KOBAYASHI DRESSED AS A GIRL.
THUMP
DARN...
I CAN'T HELP BEING MORE NERVOUS...
...THAN WHEN SHE WAS CROSS-DRESSING.
SIGH...
HE JUST SIGHED!
THUMP THUMP

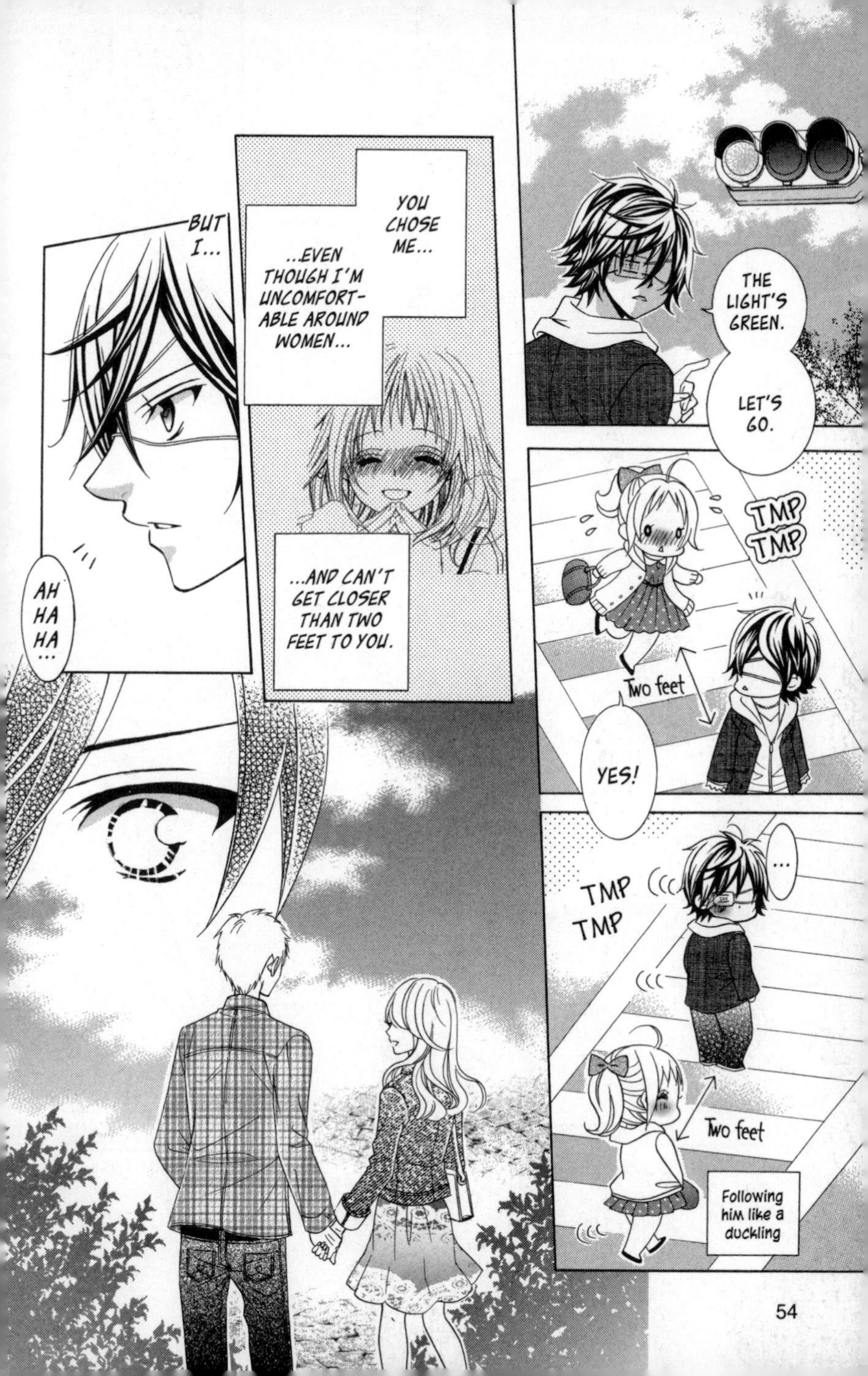
THE LIGHT'S GREEN.
LET'S GO.
TMP TMP
YES!
Two feet
...
TMP TMP
Two feet
Following him like a duckling
YOU CHOSE ME...
...EVEN THOUGH I'M UNCOMFORT-ABLE AROUND WOMEN...
...AND CAN'T GET CLOSER THAN TWO FEET TO YOU.
BUT I...
AH HA HA...

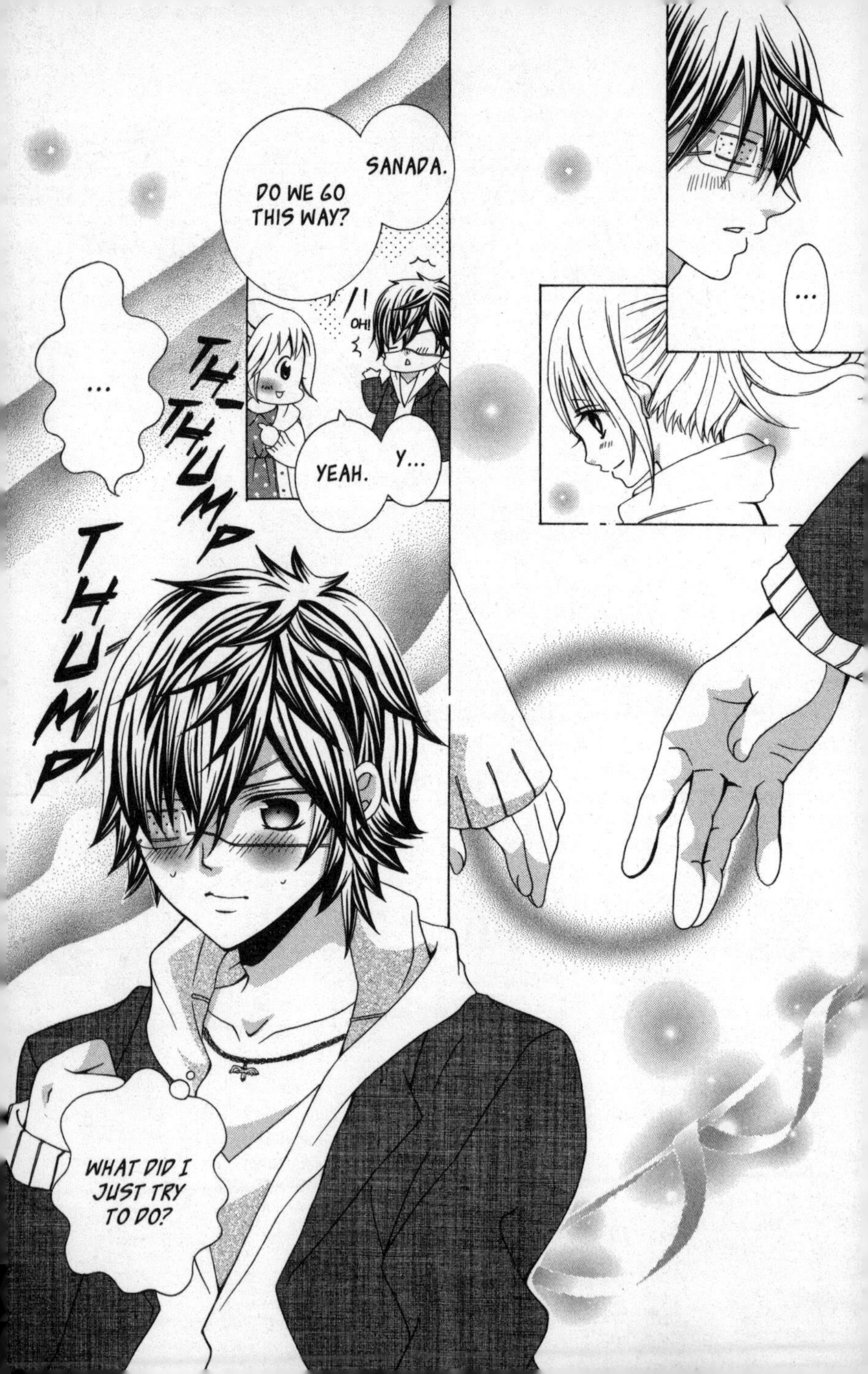
...
SANADA.
DO WE GO THIS WAY?
OH!
Y... YEAH.
...
TH-THUMP
THUMP-THUMP
WHAT DID I JUST TRY TO DO?

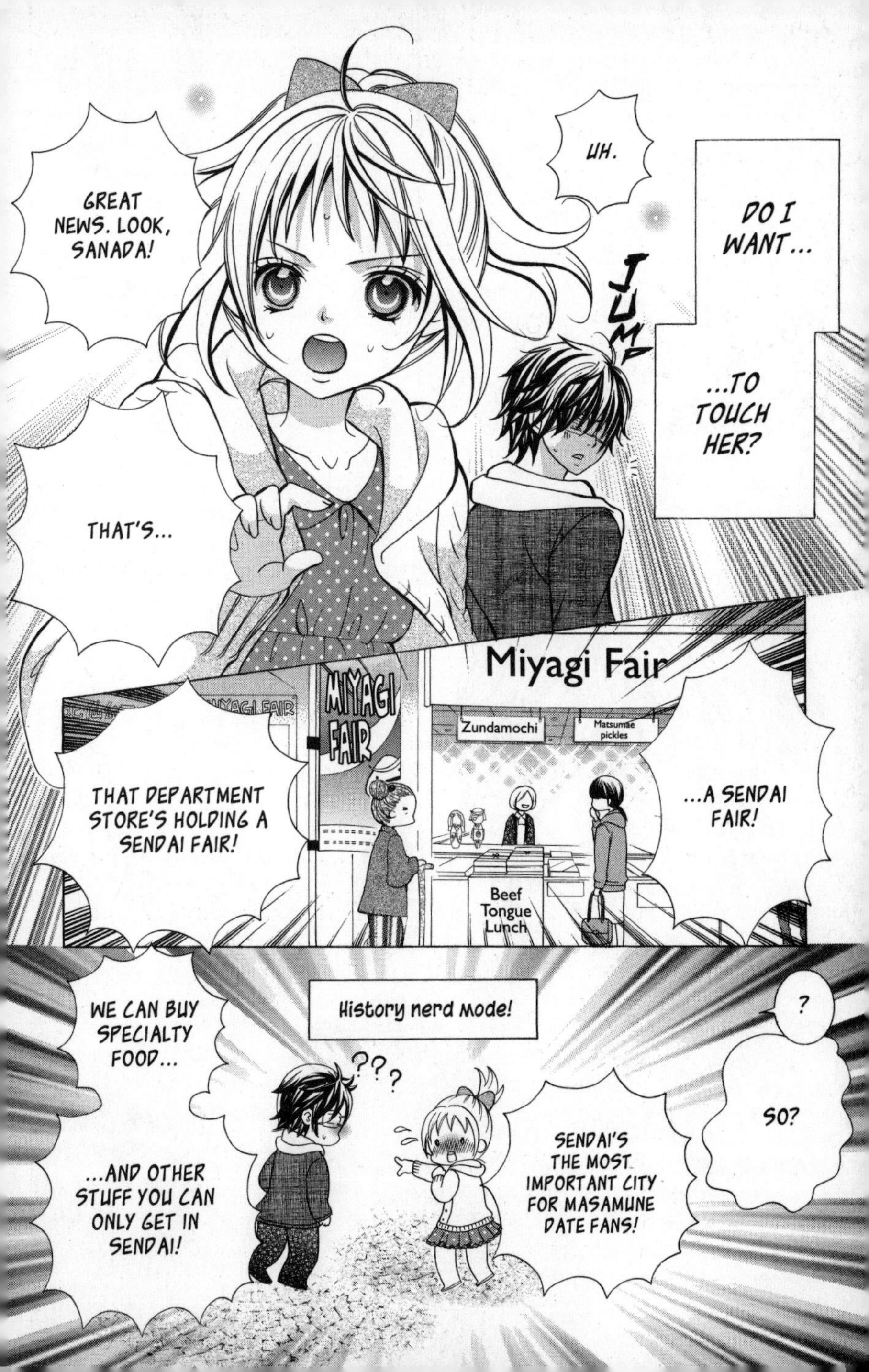
DO I WANT...
...TO TOUCH HER?
UH.
JUMP
GREAT NEWS. LOOK, SANADA!
THAT'S...
...A SENDAI FAIR!
Miyagi Fair
Zundamochi
Matsumae pickles
Beef Tongue Lunch
MIYAGI FAIR
MIYAGI FAIR
THAT DEPARTMENT STORE'S HOLDING A SENDAI FAIR!
?
SO?
History nerd mode!
SENDAI'S THE MOST IMPORTANT CITY FOR MASAMUNE DATE FANS!
???
WE CAN BUY SPECIALTY FOOD...
...AND OTHER STUFF YOU CAN ONLY GET IN SENDAI!

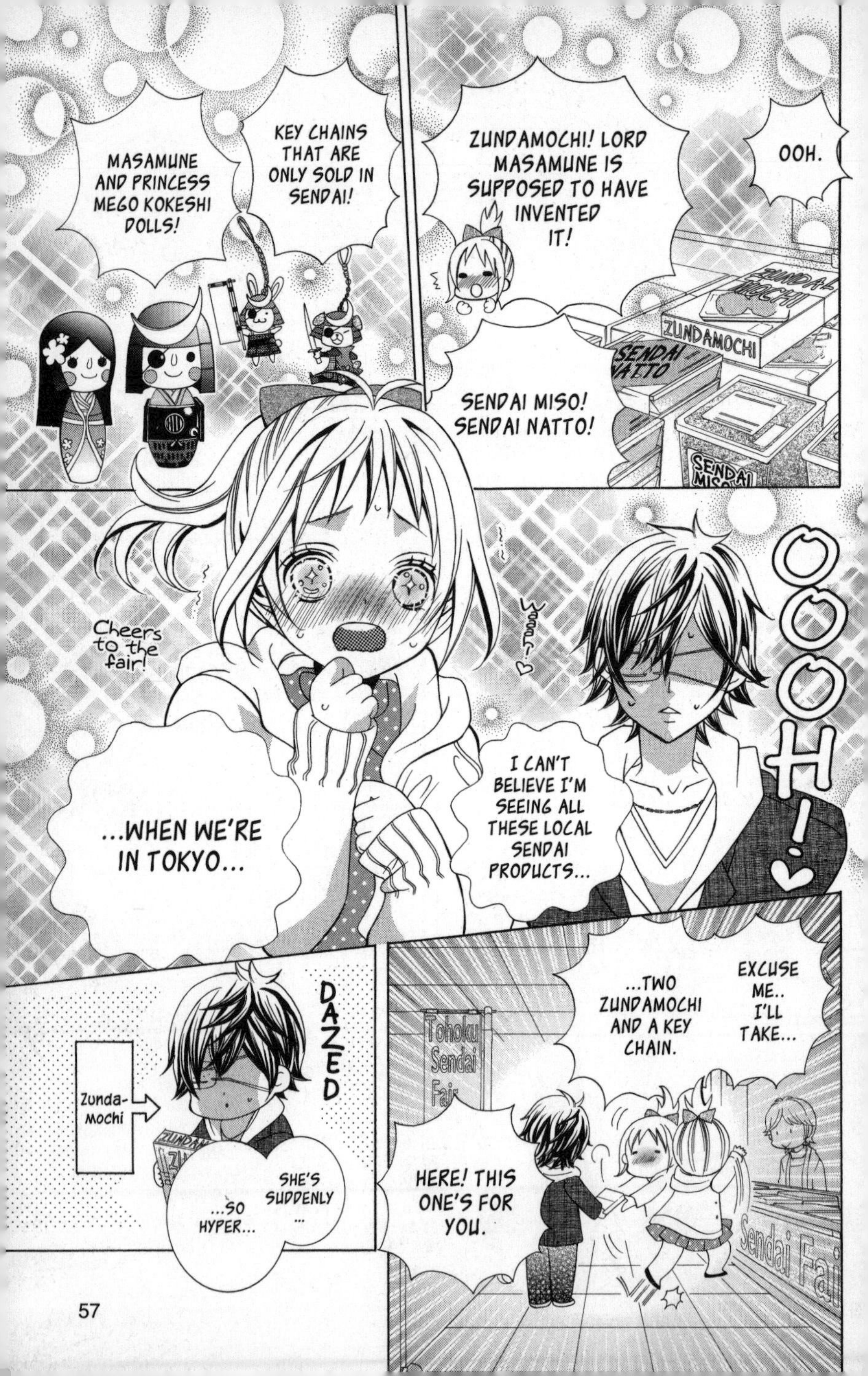
OOH.
ZUNDAMOCHI! LORD MASAMUNE IS SUPPOSED TO HAVE INVENTED IT!
ZUNDAMOCHI
SENDAI MISO! SENDAI NATTO!
KEY CHAINS THAT ARE ONLY SOLD IN SENDAI!
MASAMUNE AND PRINCESS MEGO KOKESHI DOLLS!
OOOOH!
I CAN'T BELIEVE I'M SEEING ALL THESE LOCAL SENDAI PRODUCTS...
...WHEN WE'RE IN TOKYO...
Cheers to the fair!
EXCUSE ME.. I'LL TAKE...
...TWO ZUNDAMOCHI AND A KEY CHAIN.
HERE! THIS ONE'S FOR YOU.
DAZED
Zunda-mochi
SHE'S SUDDENLY ...
...SO HYPER...

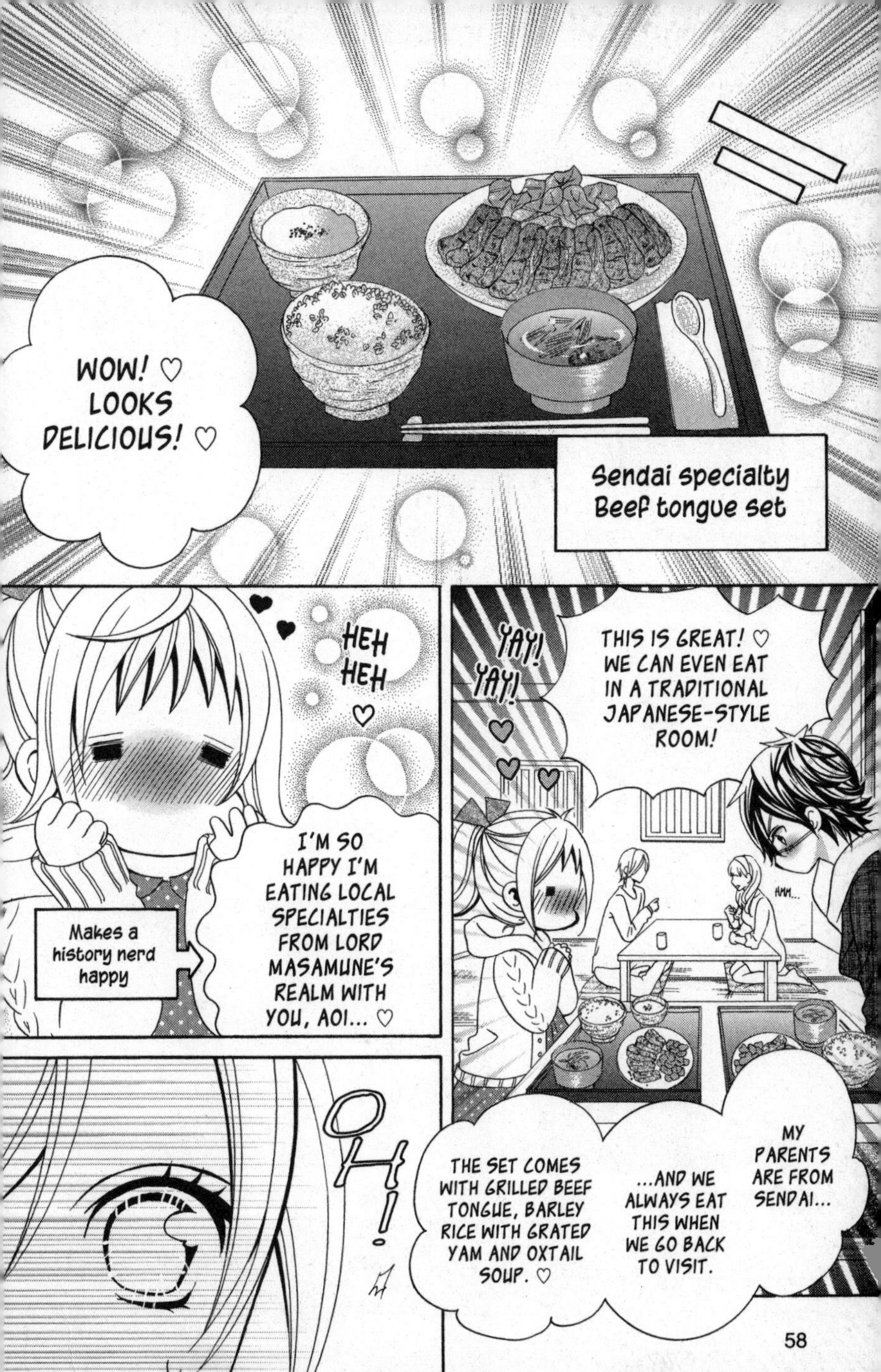

WOW! ♡ LOOKS DELICIOUS! ♡
Sendai specialty Beef tongue set
YAY! YAY!
THIS IS GREAT! ♡ WE CAN EVEN EAT IN A TRADITIONAL JAPANESE-STYLE ROOM!
HMM...
MY PARENTS ARE FROM SENDAI...
...AND WE ALWAYS EAT THIS WHEN WE GO BACK TO VISIT.
THE SET COMES WITH GRILLED BEEF TONGUE, BARLEY RICE WITH GRATED YAM AND OXTAIL SOUP. ♡
HEH HEH ♡
I'M SO HAPPY I'M EATING LOCAL SPECIALTIES FROM LORD MASAMUNE'S REALM WITH YOU, AOI... ♡
Makes a history nerd happy
OH!

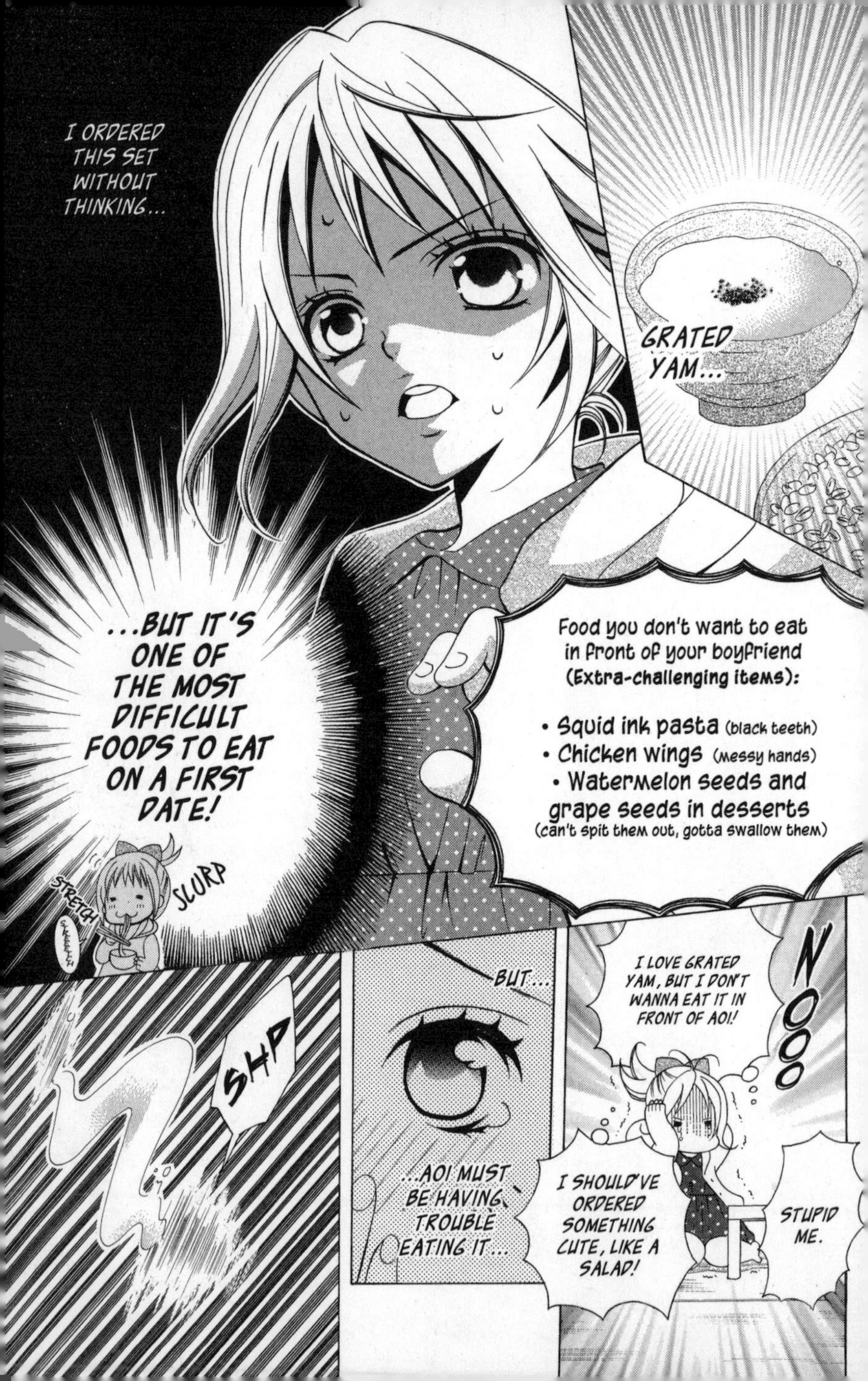
GRATED YAM...
I ORDERED THIS SET WITHOUT THINKING...
...BUT IT'S ONE OF THE MOST DIFFICULT FOODS TO EAT ON A FIRST DATE!
Food you don't want to eat in front of your boyfriend (Extra-challenging items):
• Squid ink pasta (black teeth)
• Chicken wings (messy hands)
• Watermelon seeds and grape seeds in desserts (can't spit them out, gotta swallow them)
STRETCH
SLURP
NOOO
I LOVE GRATED YAM, BUT I DON'T WANNA EAT IT IN FRONT OF AOI!
I SHOULD'VE ORDERED SOMETHING CUTE, LIKE A SALAD!
STUPID ME.
BUT...
...AOI MUST BE HAVING TROUBLE EATING IT...
SHP

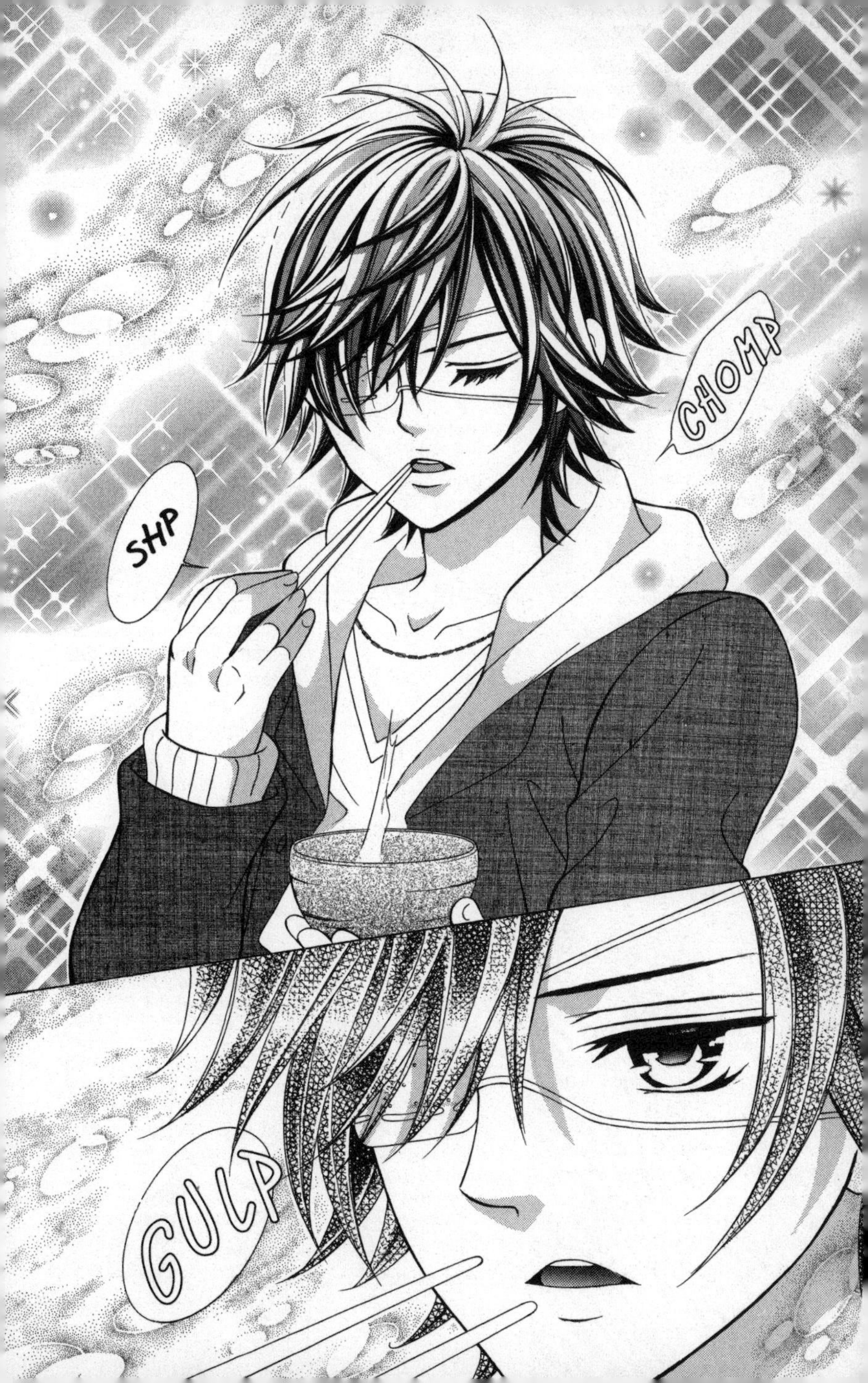
CHOMP
SHP
GULP

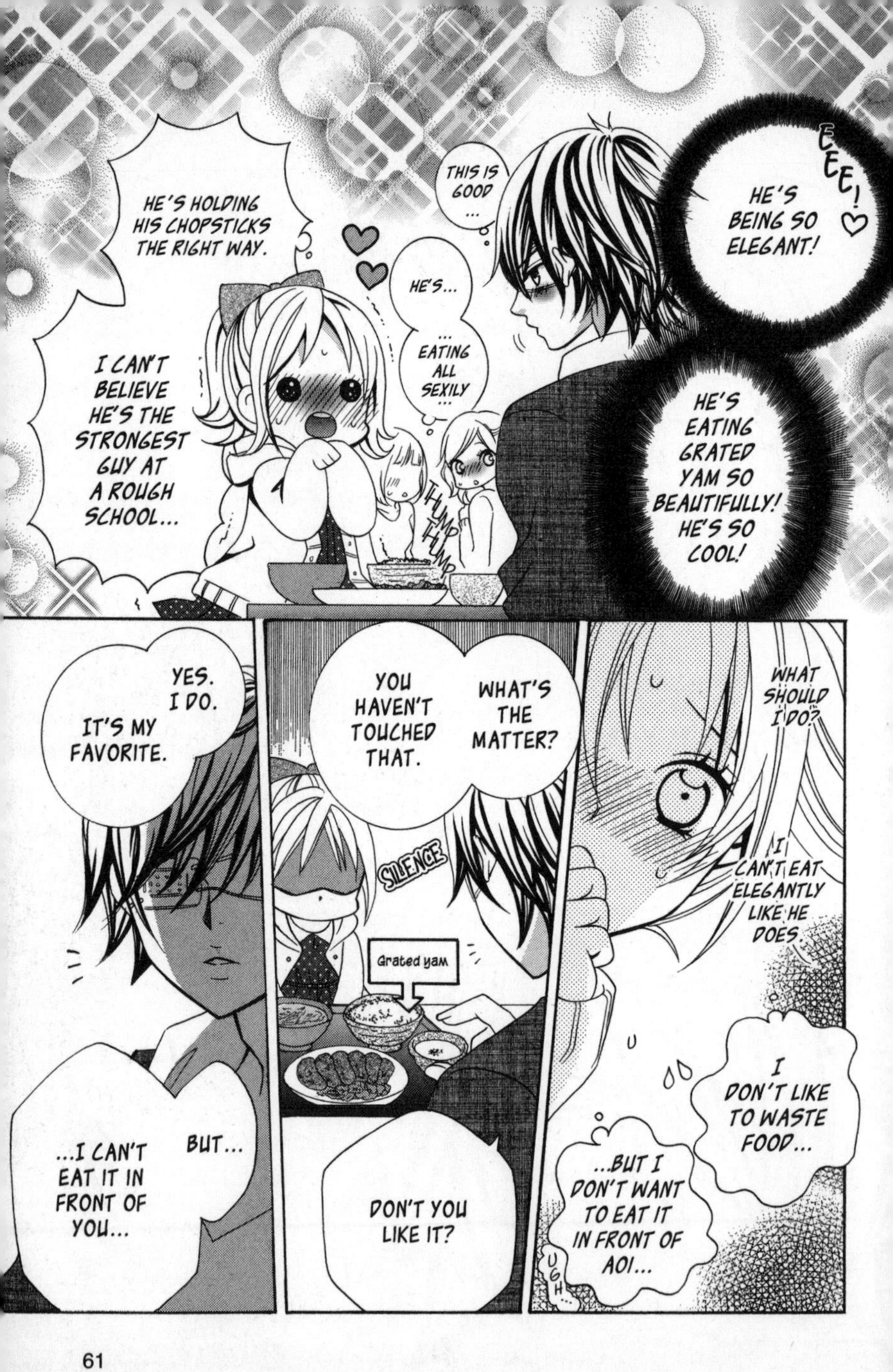
EEE! ♡
HE'S BEING SO ELEGANT!
THIS IS GOOD...
HE'S HOLDING HIS CHOPSTICKS THE RIGHT WAY.
HE'S...
...EATING ALL SEXILY...
HE'S EATING GRATED YAM SO BEAUTIFULLY! HE'S SO COOL!
I CAN'T BELIEVE HE'S THE STRONGEST GUY AT A ROUGH SCHOOL...
THUMP THUMP
WHAT SHOULD I DO?
I CAN'T EAT ELEGANTLY LIKE HE DOES.
I DON'T LIKE TO WASTE FOOD...
...BUT I DON'T WANT TO EAT IT IN FRONT OF AOI...
UGH...
WHAT'S THE MATTER?
YOU HAVEN'T TOUCHED THAT.
SILENCE
Grated yam
DON'T YOU LIKE IT?
YES. I DO.
IT'S MY FAVORITE.
BUT...
...I CAN'T EAT IT IN FRONT OF YOU...

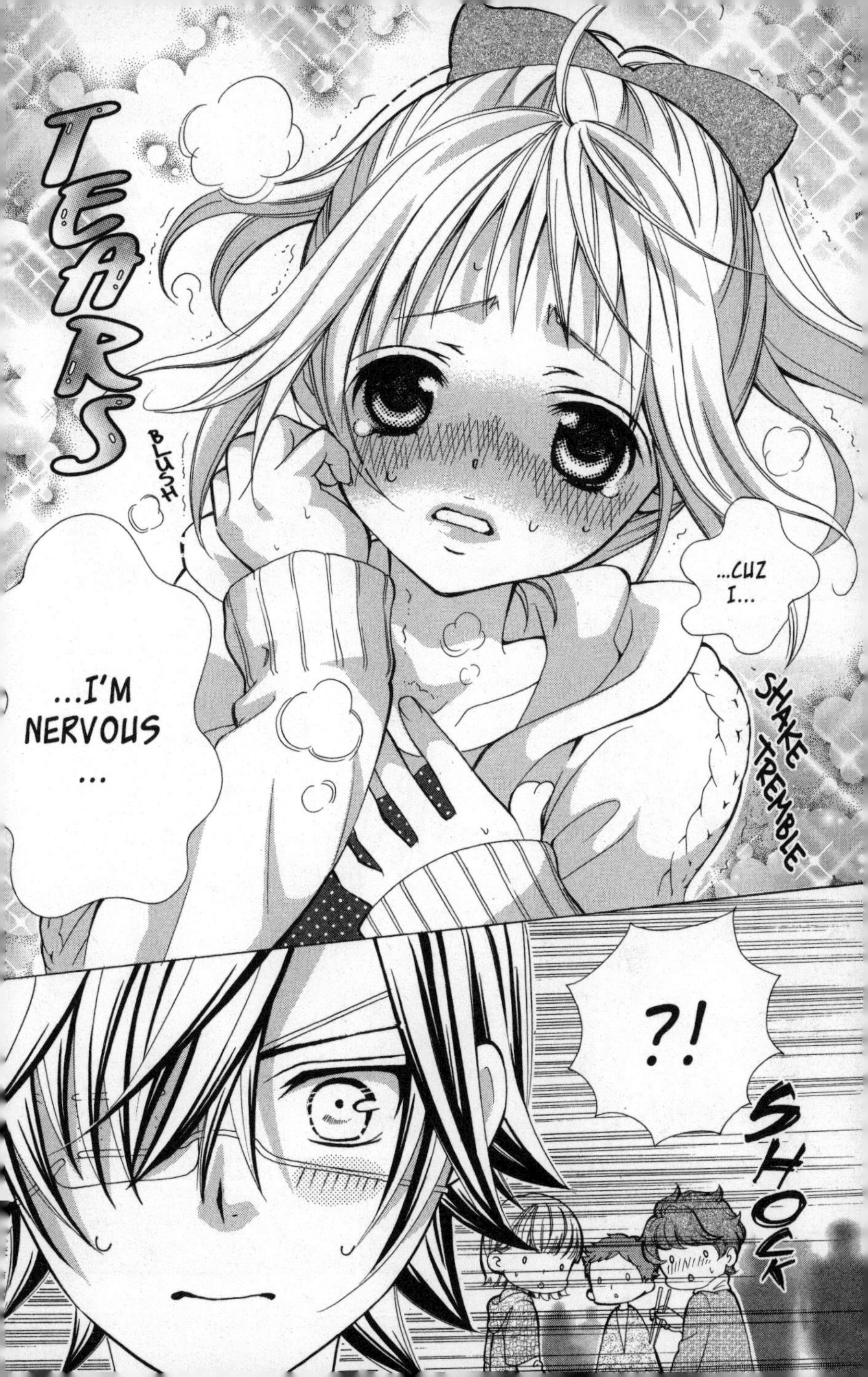
...CUZ I...
SHAKE TREMBLE
TEARS
BLUSH
...I'M NERVOUS ...
?!
SHOCK

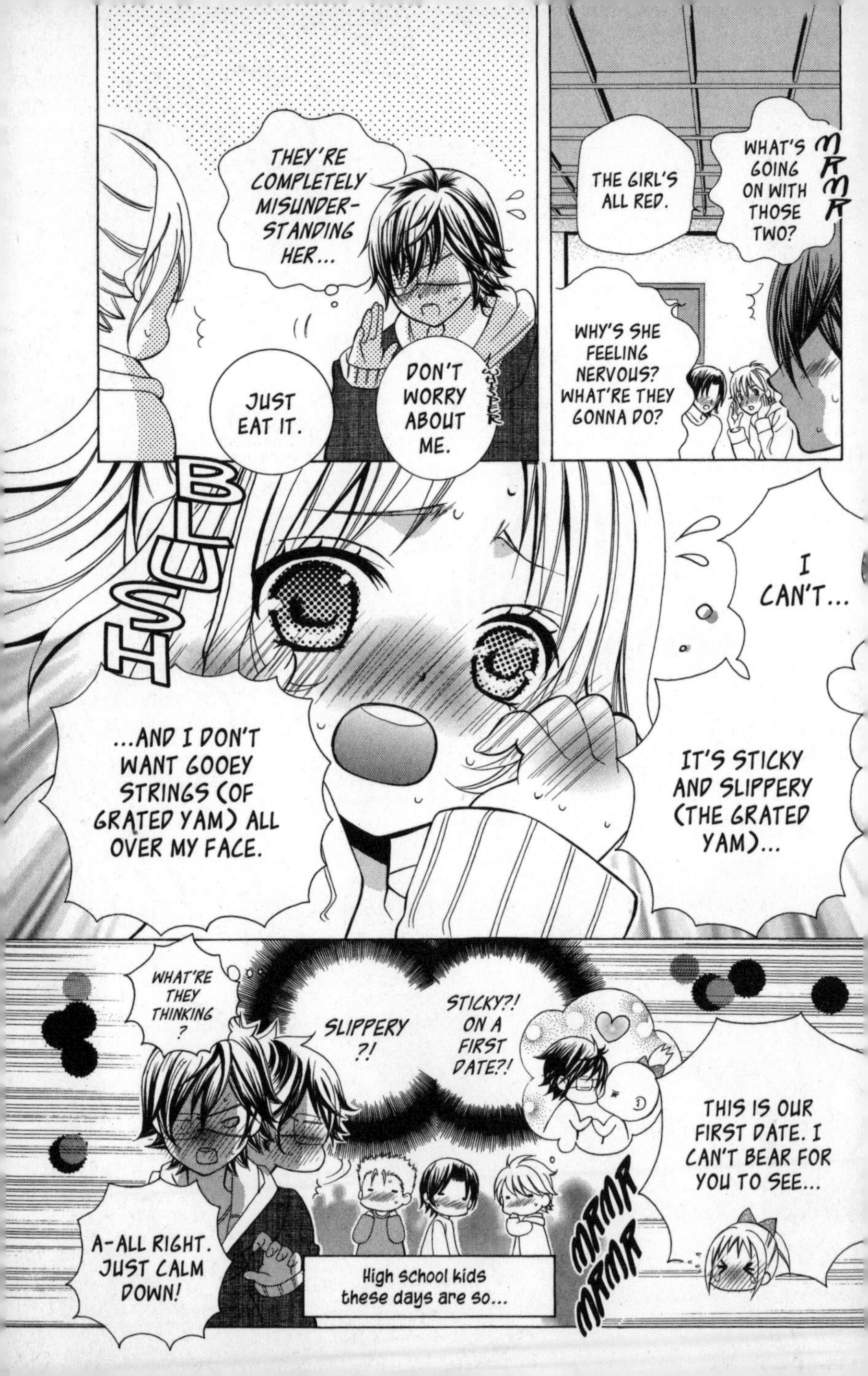
WHAT'S GOING ON WITH THOSE TWO?
MRMR
THE GIRL'S ALL RED.
WHY'S SHE FEELING NERVOUS? WHAT'RE THEY GONNA DO?
THEY'RE COMPLETELY MISUNDER-STANDING HER...
DON'T WORRY ABOUT ME.
WHISPER
JUST EAT IT.
I CAN'T...
BLUSH
IT'S STICKY AND SLIPPERY (THE GRATED YAM)...
...AND I DON'T WANT GOOEY STRINGS (OF GRATED YAM) ALL OVER MY FACE.
THIS IS OUR FIRST DATE. I CAN'T BEAR FOR YOU TO SEE...
MRMR MRMR
STICKY?! ON A FIRST DATE?!
SLIPPERY?!
WHAT'RE THEY THINKING?
High school kids these days are so...
A-ALL RIGHT. JUST CALM DOWN!

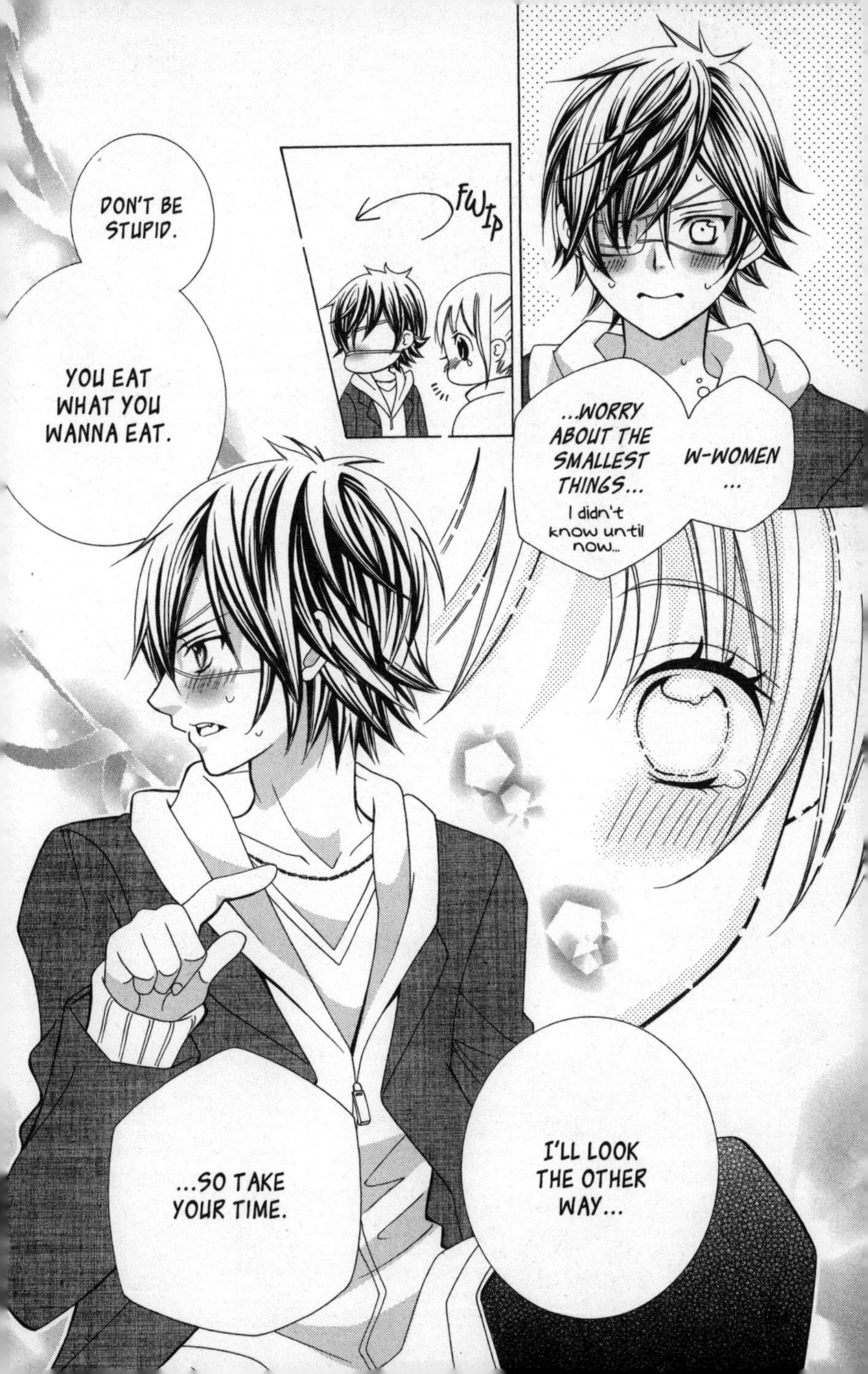
W-WOMEN ...
...WORRY ABOUT THE SMALLEST THINGS...
I didn't know until now...
FWIP
DON'T BE STUPID.
YOU EAT WHAT YOU WANNA EAT.
I'LL LOOK THE OTHER WAY...
...SO TAKE YOUR TIME.

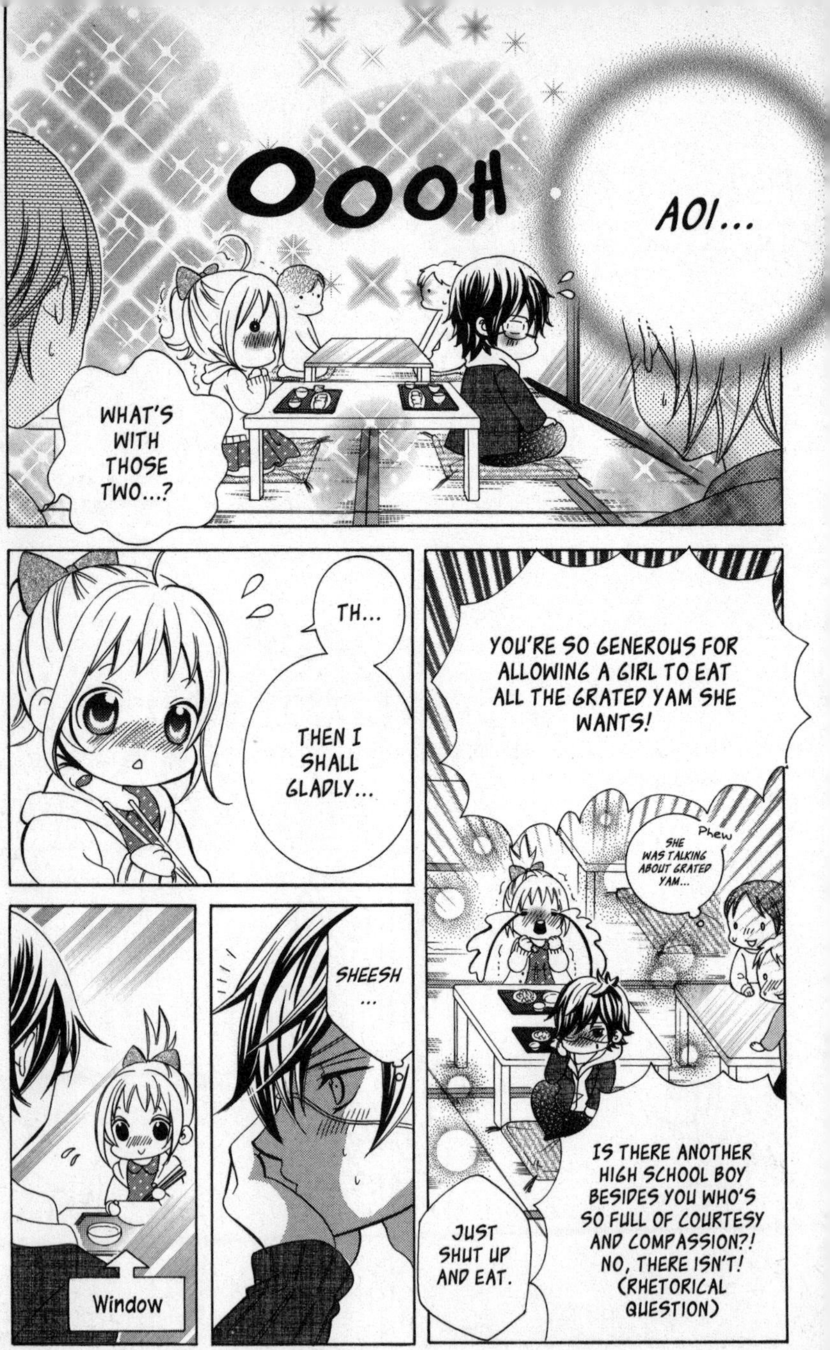
AOI...
OOOH
WHAT'S WITH THOSE TWO...?
YOU'RE SO GENEROUS FOR ALLOWING A GIRL TO EAT ALL THE GRATED YAM SHE WANTS!
Phew
SHE WAS TALKING ABOUT GRATED YAM...
IS THERE ANOTHER HIGH SCHOOL BOY BESIDES YOU WHO'S SO FULL OF COURTESY AND COMPASSION?! NO, THERE ISN'T! (RHETORICAL QUESTION)
JUST SHUT UP AND EAT.
TH...
THEN I SHALL GLADLY...
SHEESH ...
Window

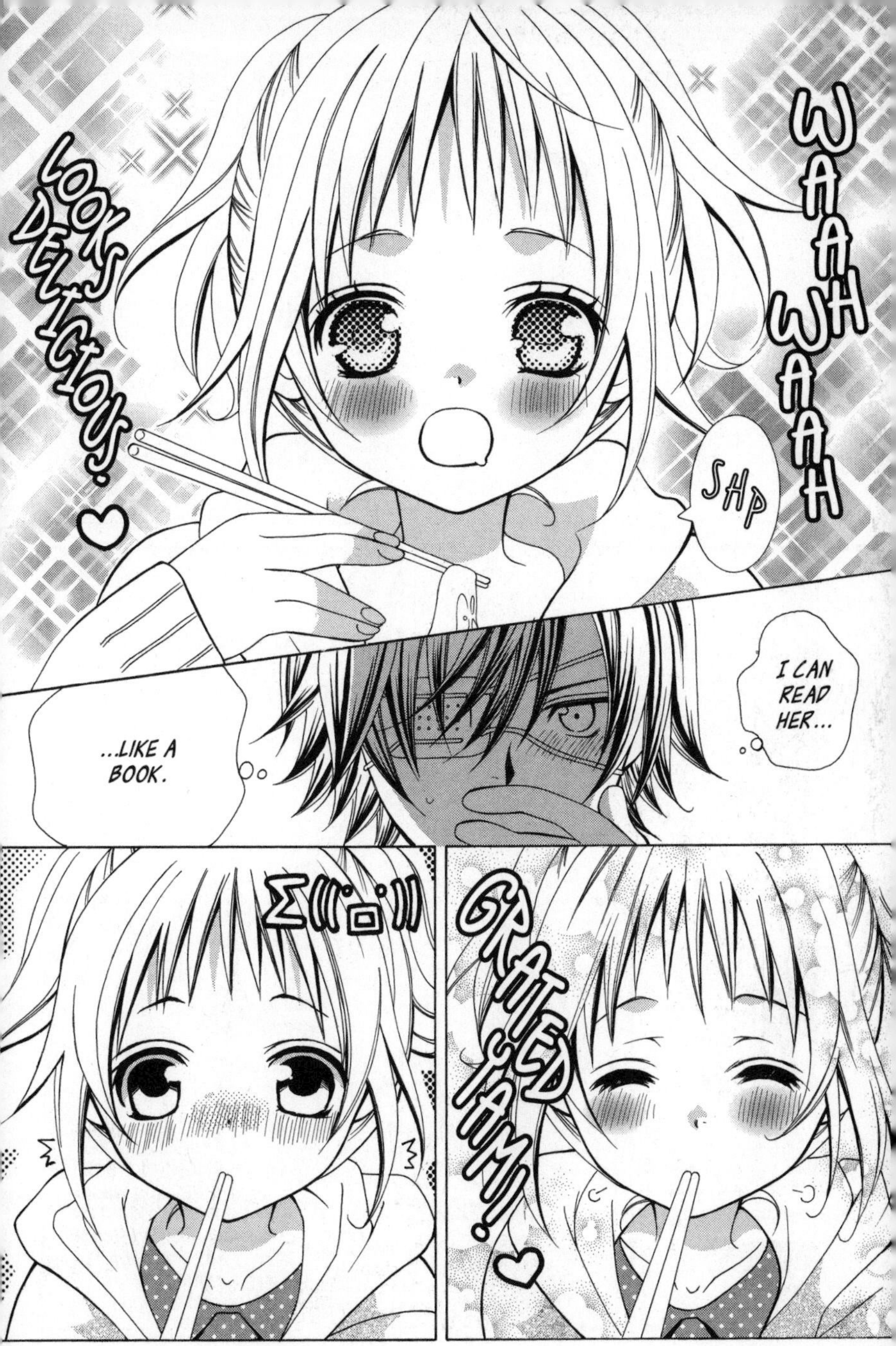
WAAH WAAH
SHP
LOOKS DELICIOUS! ♥
I CAN READ HER...
...LIKE A BOOK.
GRATED YAM! ♥
Σ(||゚□゚||)

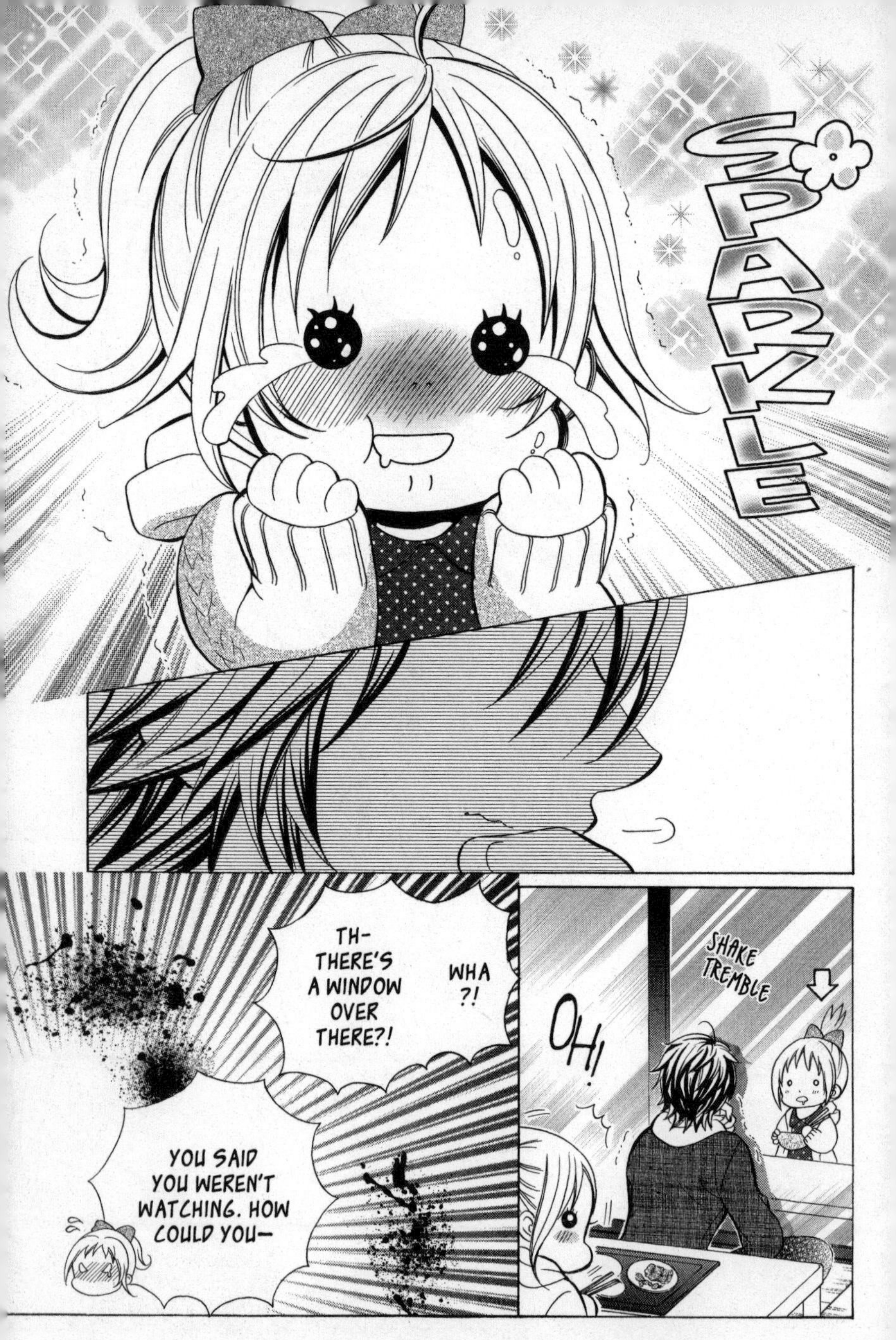
SPARKLE
SHAKE TREMBLE
OH!
WHA ?!
TH- THERE'S A WINDOW OVER THERE?!
YOU SAID YOU WEREN'T WATCHING. HOW COULD YOU—

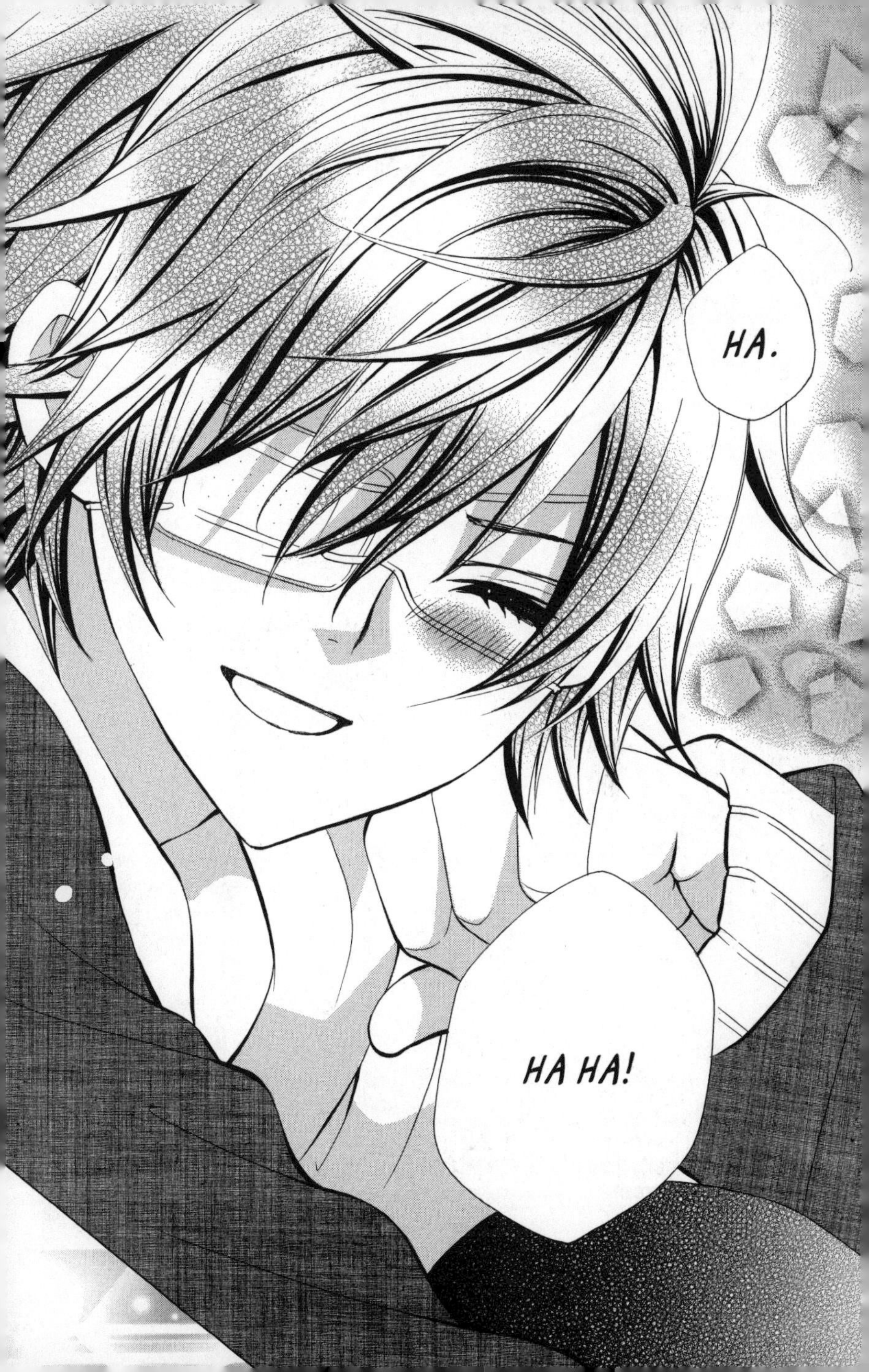
HA.
HA HA!

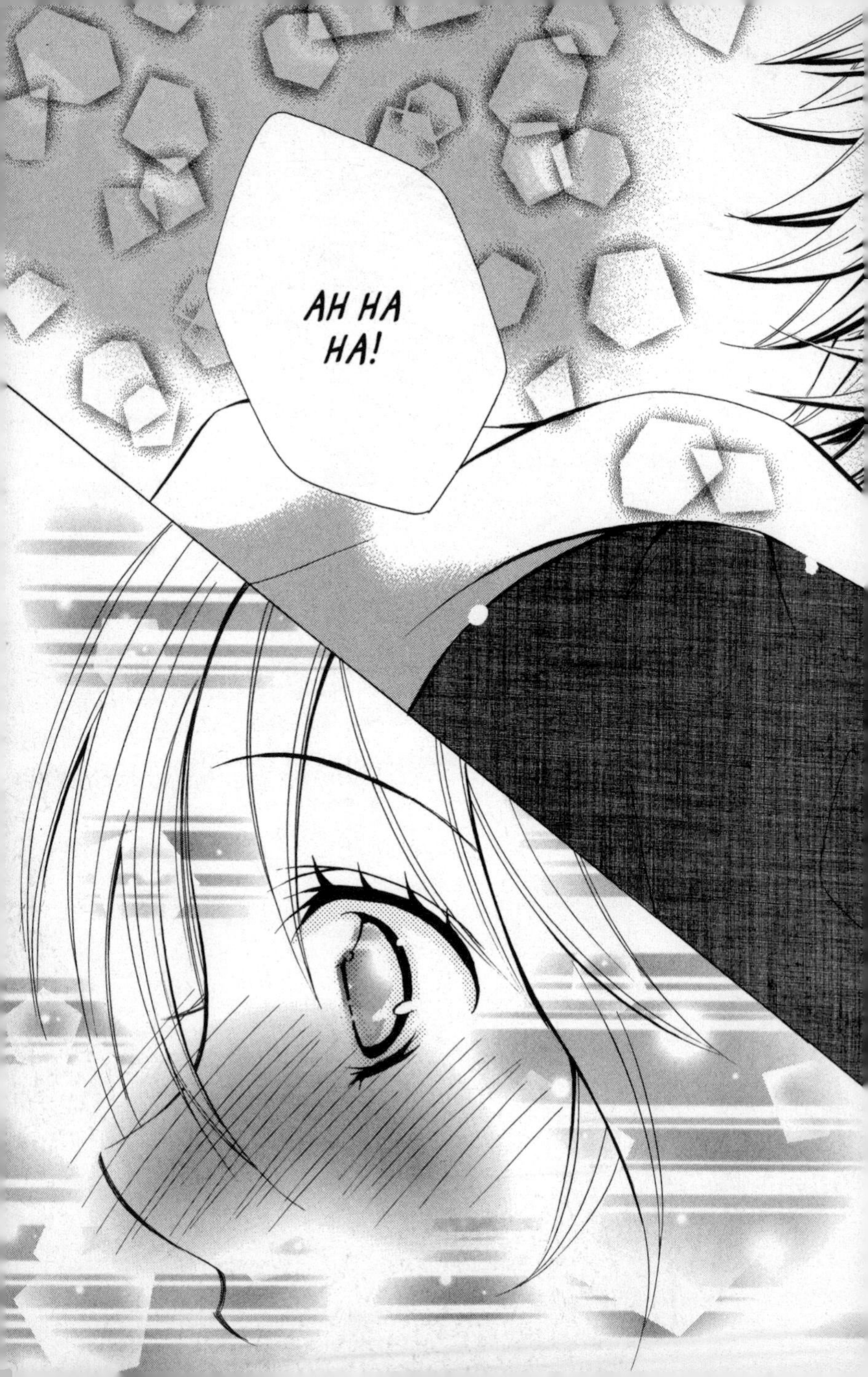
AH HA HA!

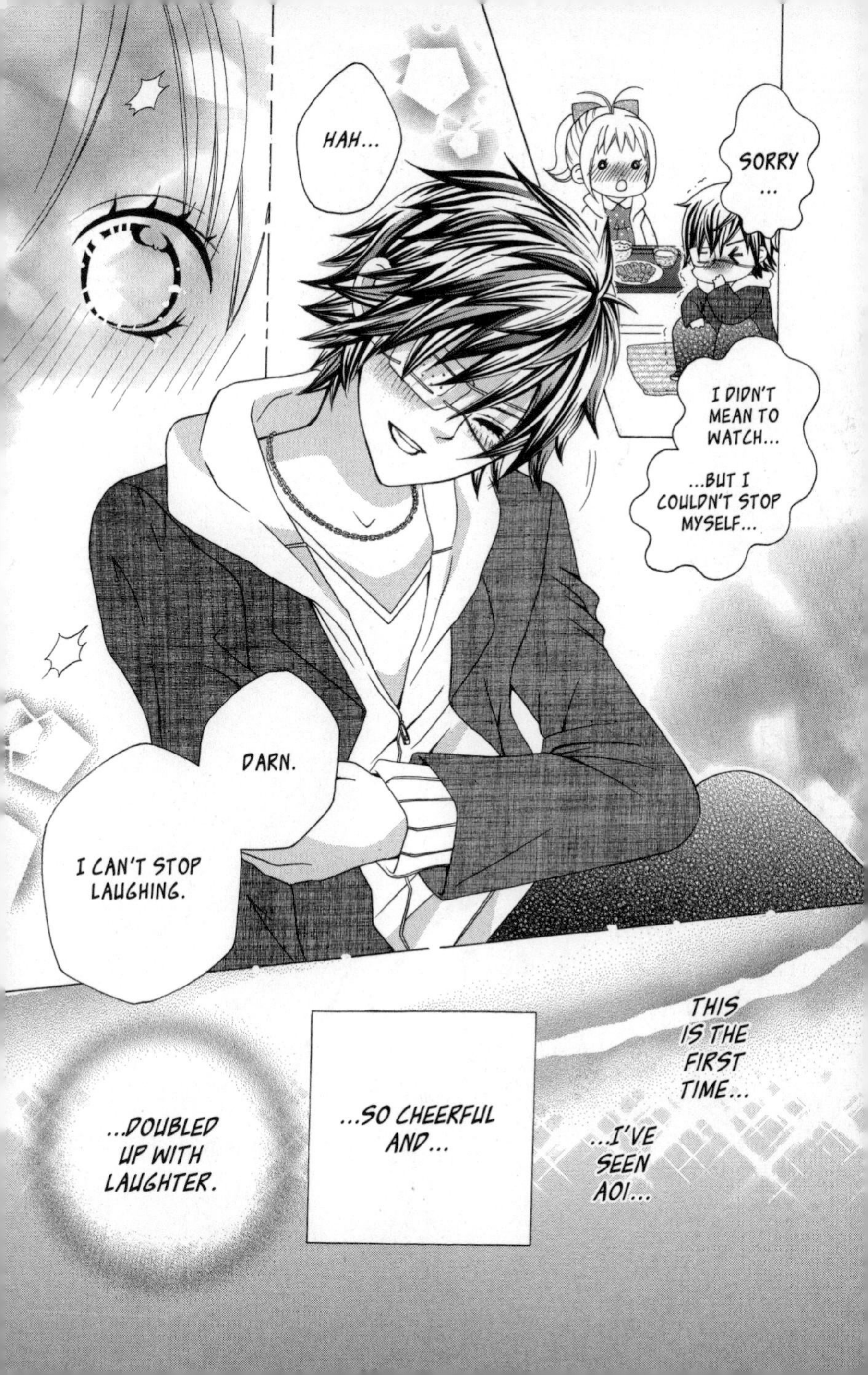
SORRY ...
I DIDN'T MEAN TO WATCH...
...BUT I COULDN'T STOP MYSELF...
HAH...
DARN.
I CAN'T STOP LAUGHING.
THIS IS THE FIRST TIME...
...I'VE SEEN AOI...
...SO CHEERFUL AND...
...DOUBLED UP WITH LAUGHTER.

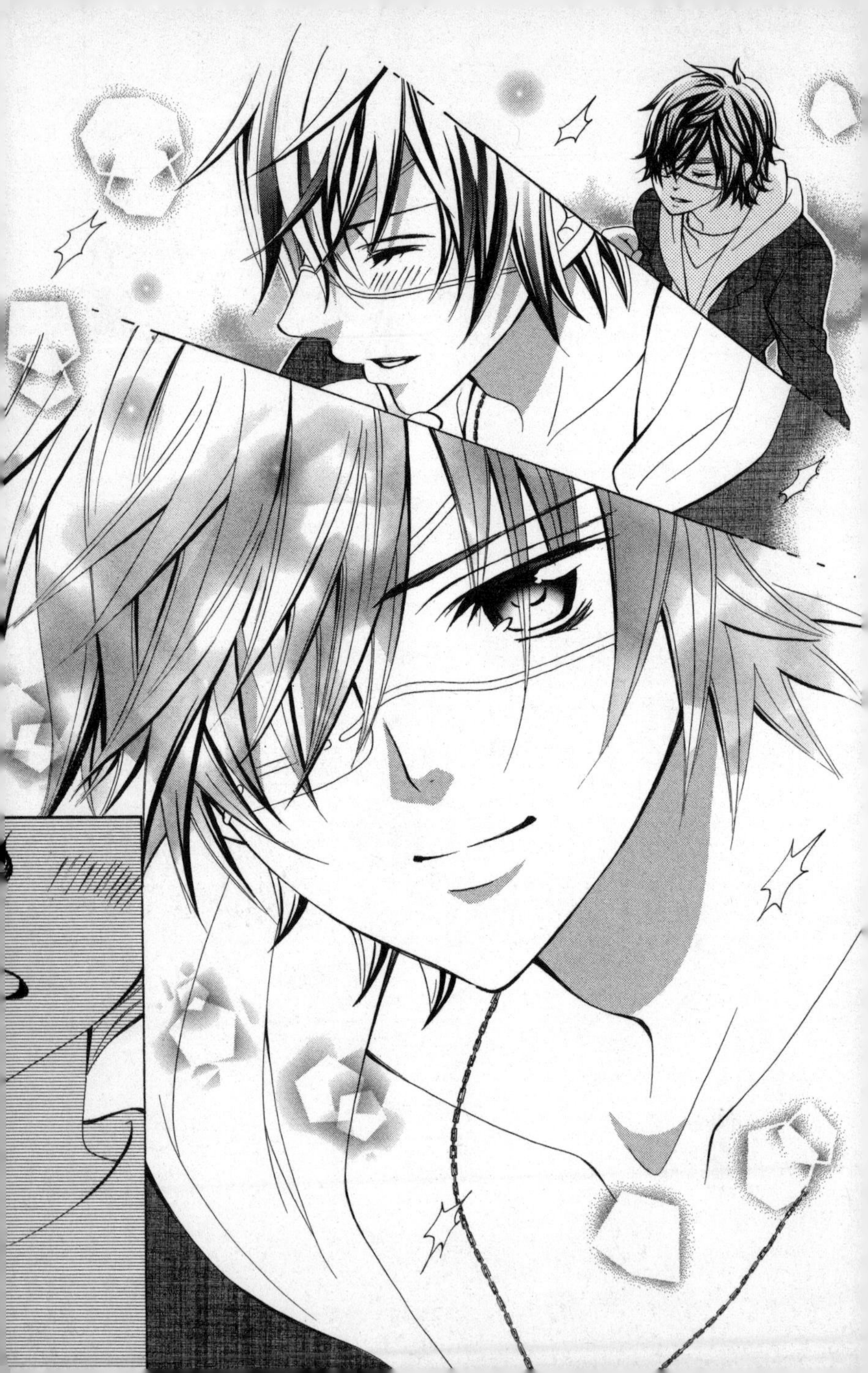

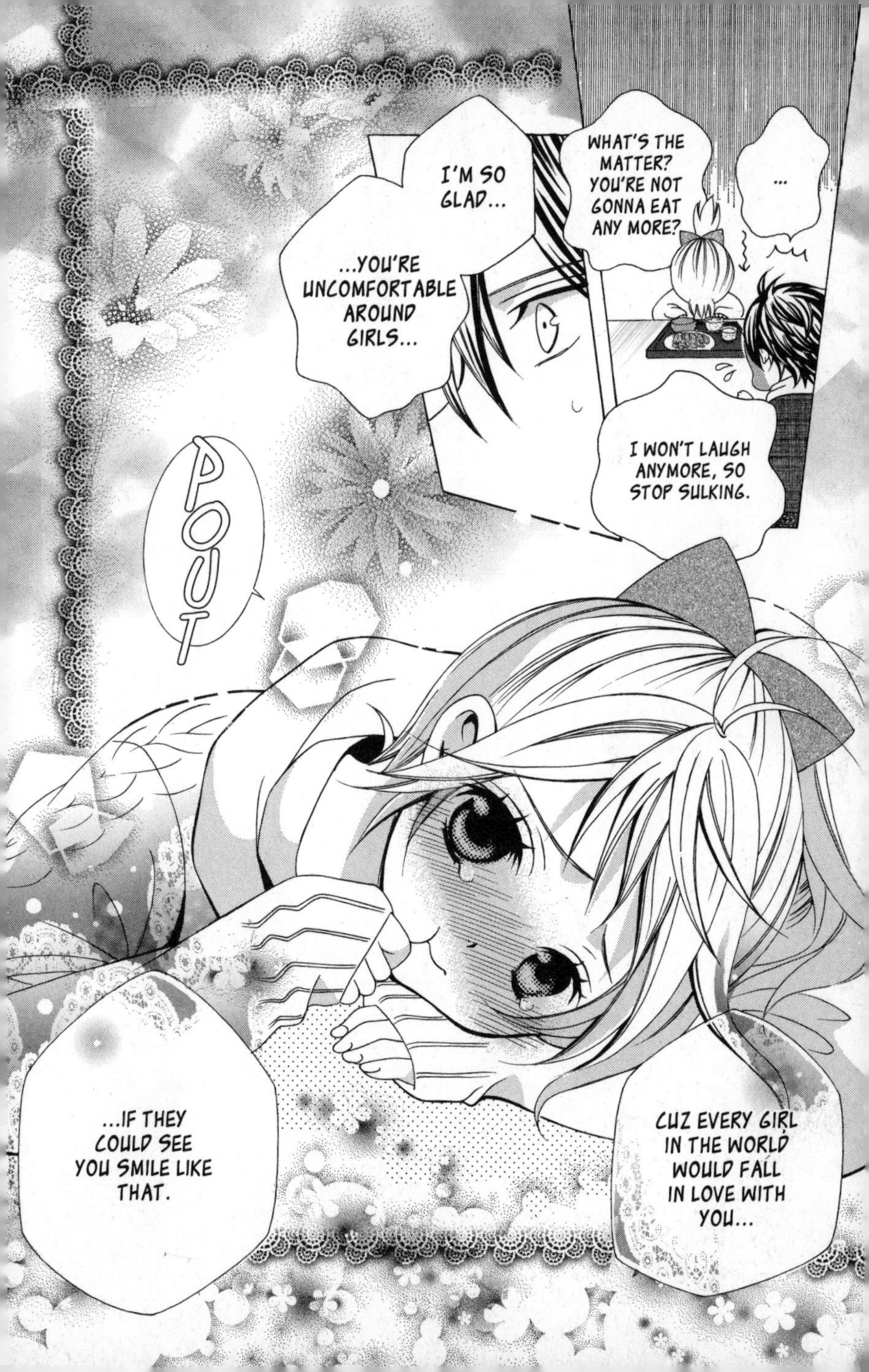
...
WHAT'S THE MATTER? YOU'RE NOT GONNA EAT ANY MORE?
I WON'T LAUGH ANYMORE, SO STOP SULKING.
I'M SO GLAD...
...YOU'RE UNCOMFORTABLE AROUND GIRLS...
POUT
CUZ EVERY GIRL IN THE WORLD WOULD FALL IN LOVE WITH YOU...
...IF THEY COULD SEE YOU SMILE LIKE THAT.

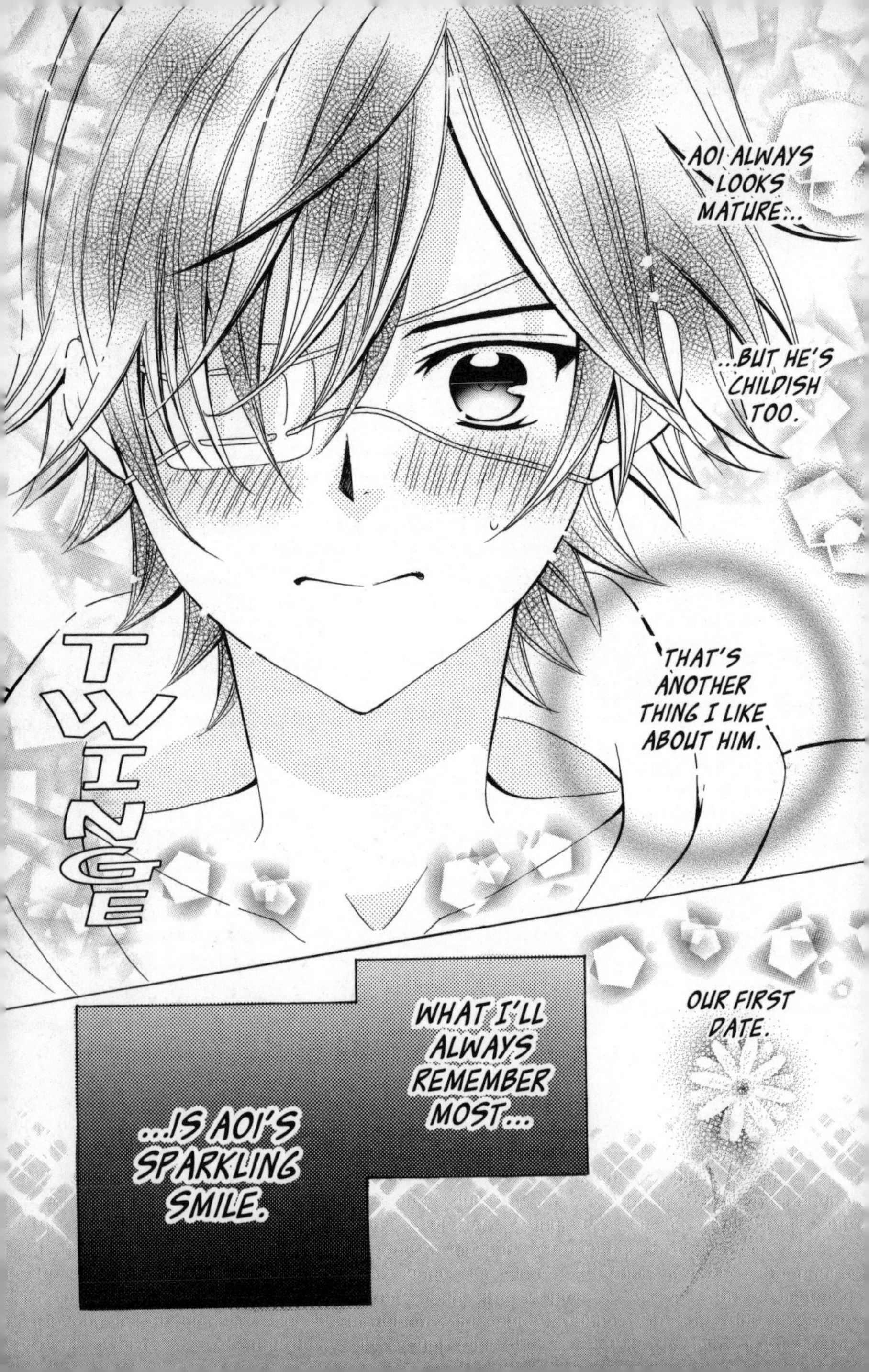
AOI ALWAYS LOOKS MATURE...
...BUT HE'S CHILDISH TOO.
THAT'S ANOTHER THING I LIKE ABOUT HIM.
TWINGE
OUR FIRST DATE.
WHAT I'LL ALWAYS REMEMBER MOST...
...IS AOI'S SPARKLING SMILE.

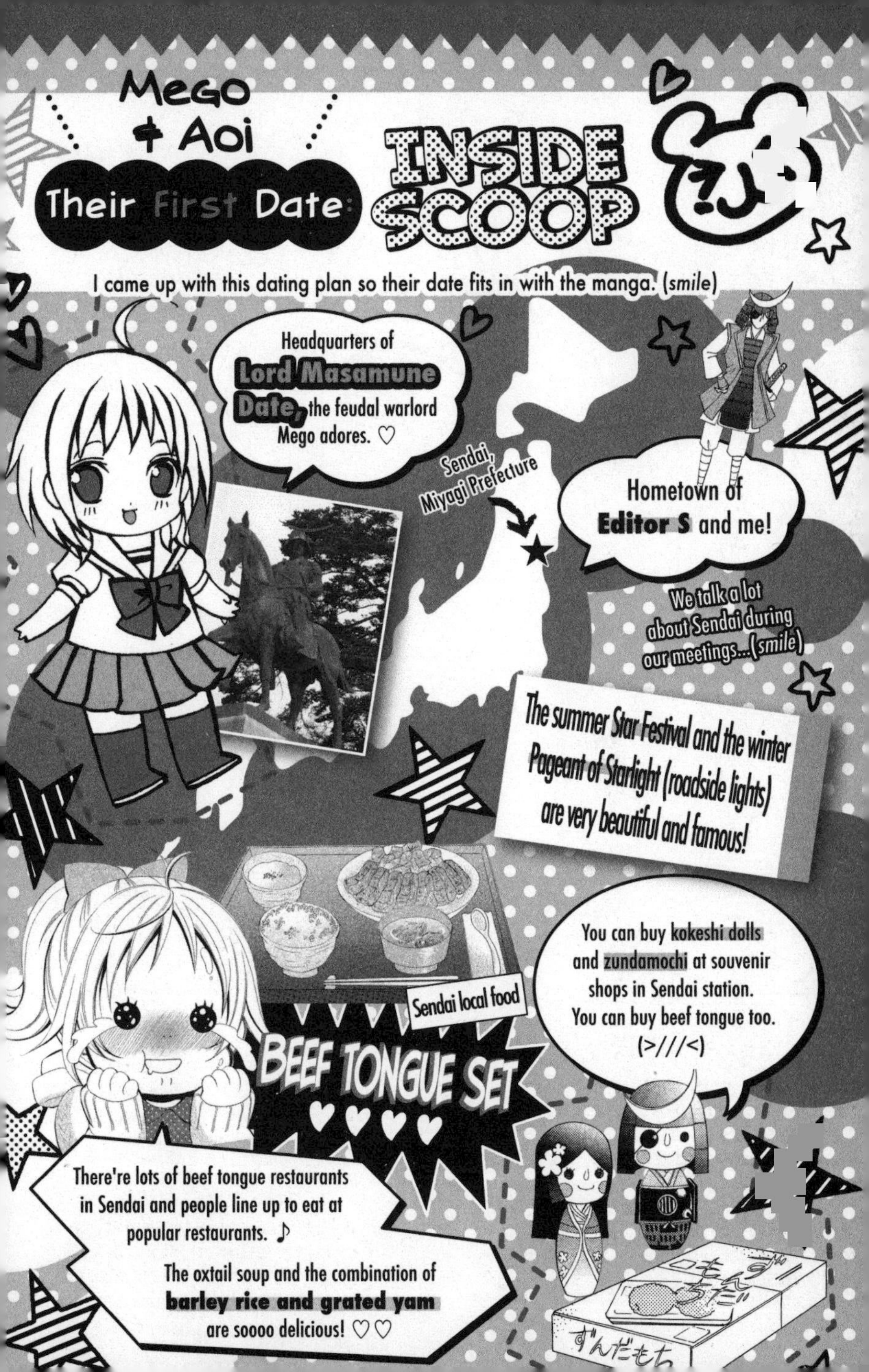
Mego & Aoi
Their First Date: INSIDE SCOOP
I came up with this dating plan so their date fits in with the manga. (*smile*)
Headquarters of **Lord Masamune Date,** the feudal warlord Mego adores. ♡
Sendai, Miyagi Prefecture
Hometown of **Editor S** and me!
We talk a lot about Sendai during our meetings... (*smile*)
The summer Star Festival and the winter Pageant of Starlight (roadside lights) are very beautiful and famous!
Sendai local food
BEEF TONGUE SET
You can buy kokeshi dolls and zundamochi at souvenir shops in Sendai station. You can buy beef tongue too. (>///<)
There're lots of beef tongue restaurants in Sendai and people line up to eat at popular restaurants. ♪
The oxtail soup and the combination of **barley rice and grated yam** are soooo delicious! ♡♡
ずんだもち

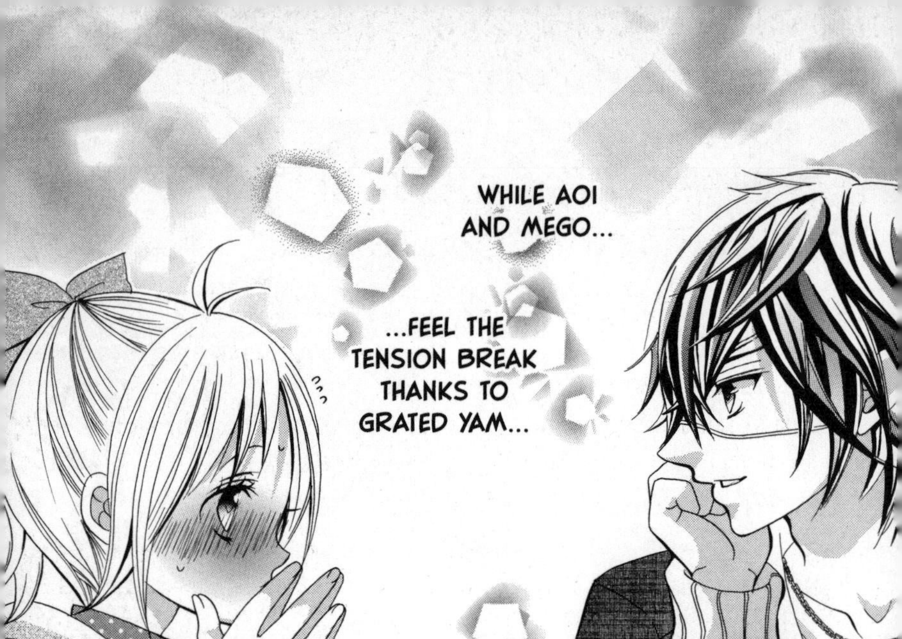
WHILE AOI AND MEGO...
...FEEL THE TENSION BREAK THANKS TO GRATED YAM...
Chapter 18

What's New.

I went to see Kis-My-Ft2 live!

I was miraculously able to get tickets (*tears*) and went to Yokohama arena with my best friend who's a Tamamori fan! All seven members were soooo good-looking! I was moved that they did four encores. (ToT) The entire venue was so excited when they sang their debut song as their last song! (^o^) The female high school student sitting next to me was also a Fujigaya fan. LOL. She was so cute and nice, and we had fun. LOL.

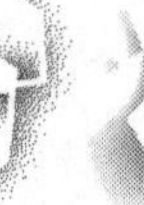

I'm watching the TV shows *Yae no sakura, Kamen Teacher, Summer Nude* and *Pintokona!* I love the *Pintokona* manga, so I'm happy it became a TV show! Yuuma-kun is so beautiful. ♡

I enjoy watching it every week and poking fun at the weird parts. LOL. I respect Loveholic-san Kento Nakajima's professionalism! I'm also looking forward to the movie version of *Bad Boys J* (^o^) !!

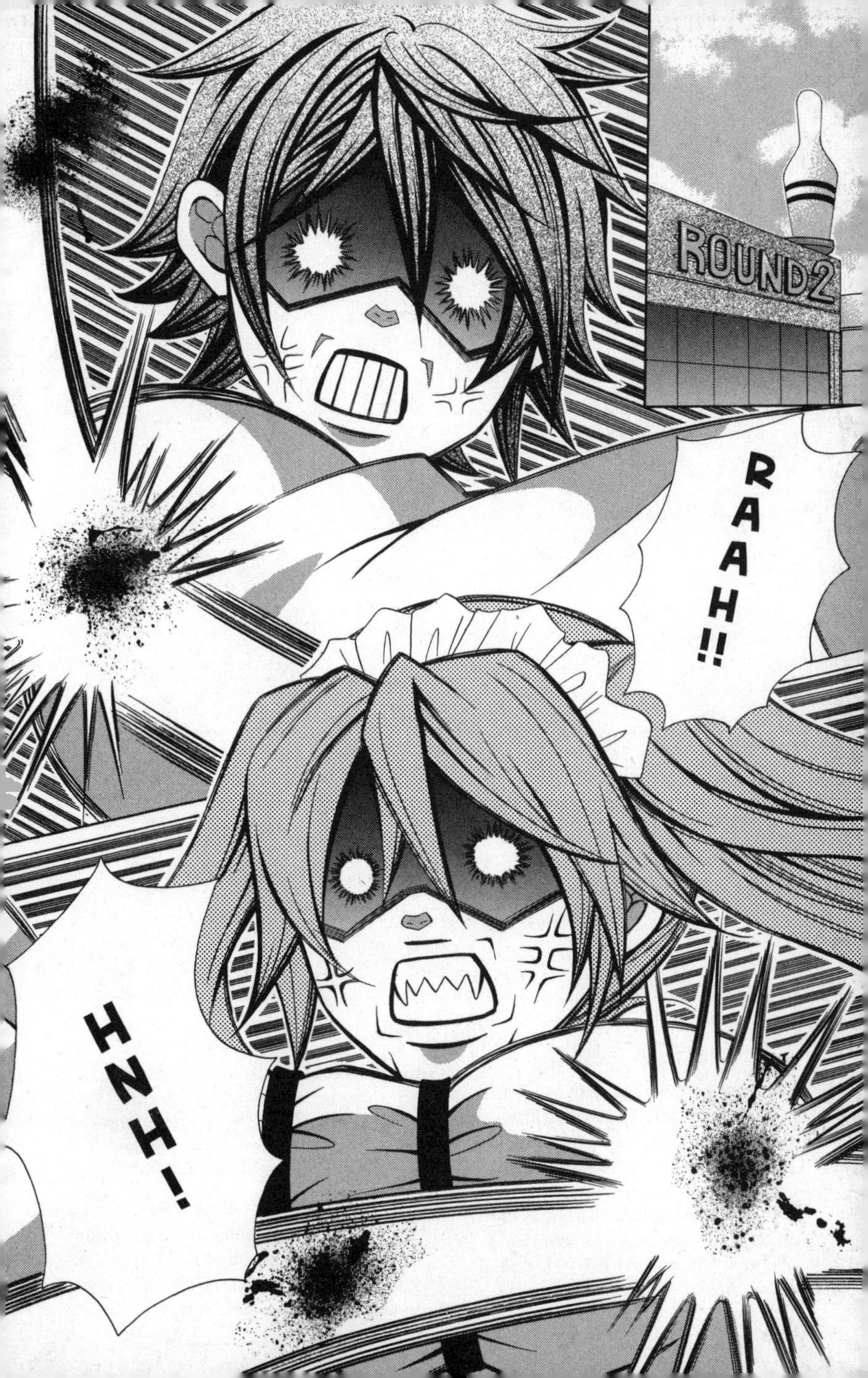
ROUND2
RAAH!!
HNH!

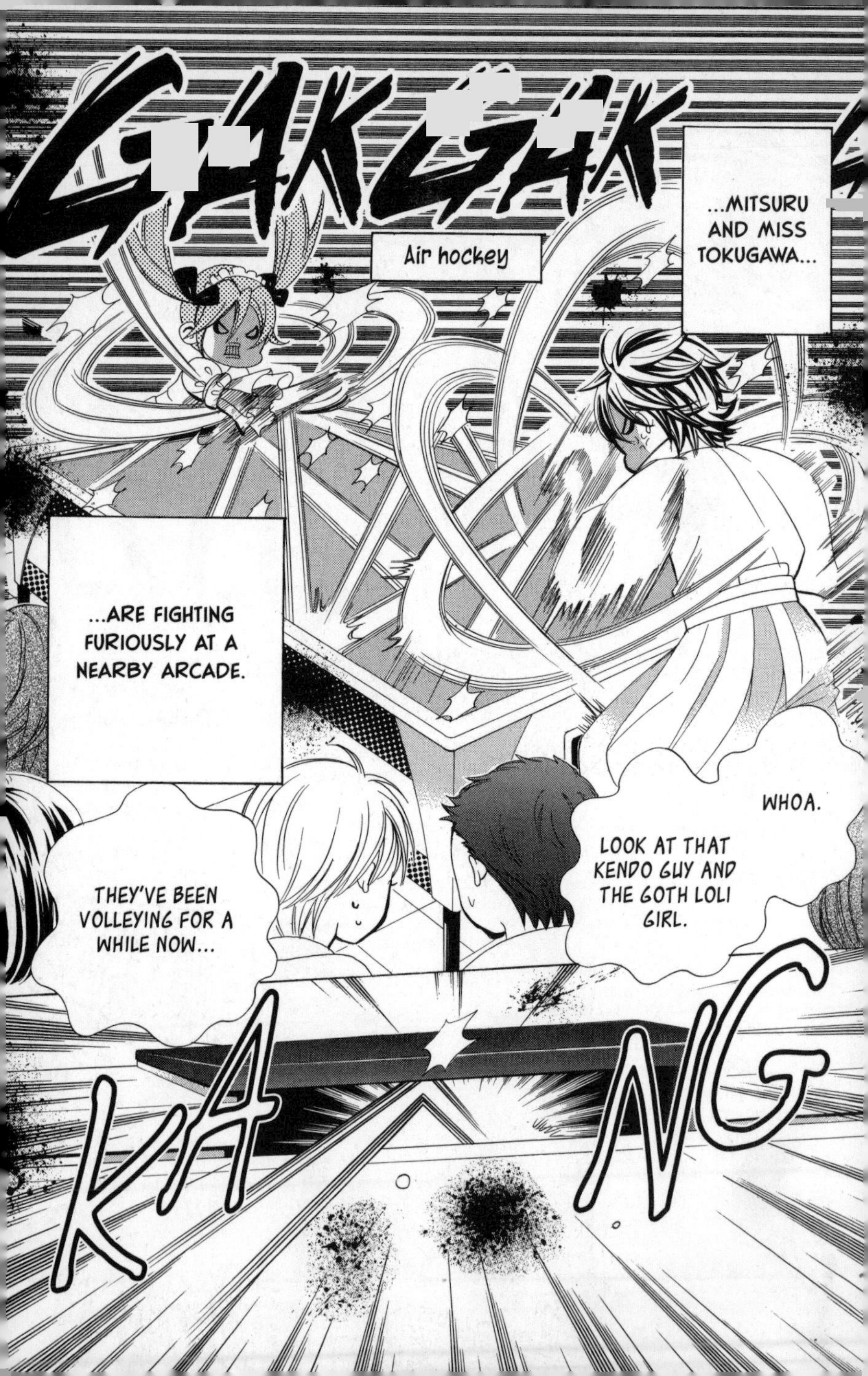
GAKGAK
...MITSURU AND MISS TOKUGAWA...
Air hockey
...ARE FIGHTING FURIOUSLY AT A NEARBY ARCADE.
WHOA.
LOOK AT THAT KENDO GUY AND THE GOTH LOLI GIRL.
THEY'VE BEEN VOLLEYING FOR A WHILE NOW...
KA NG

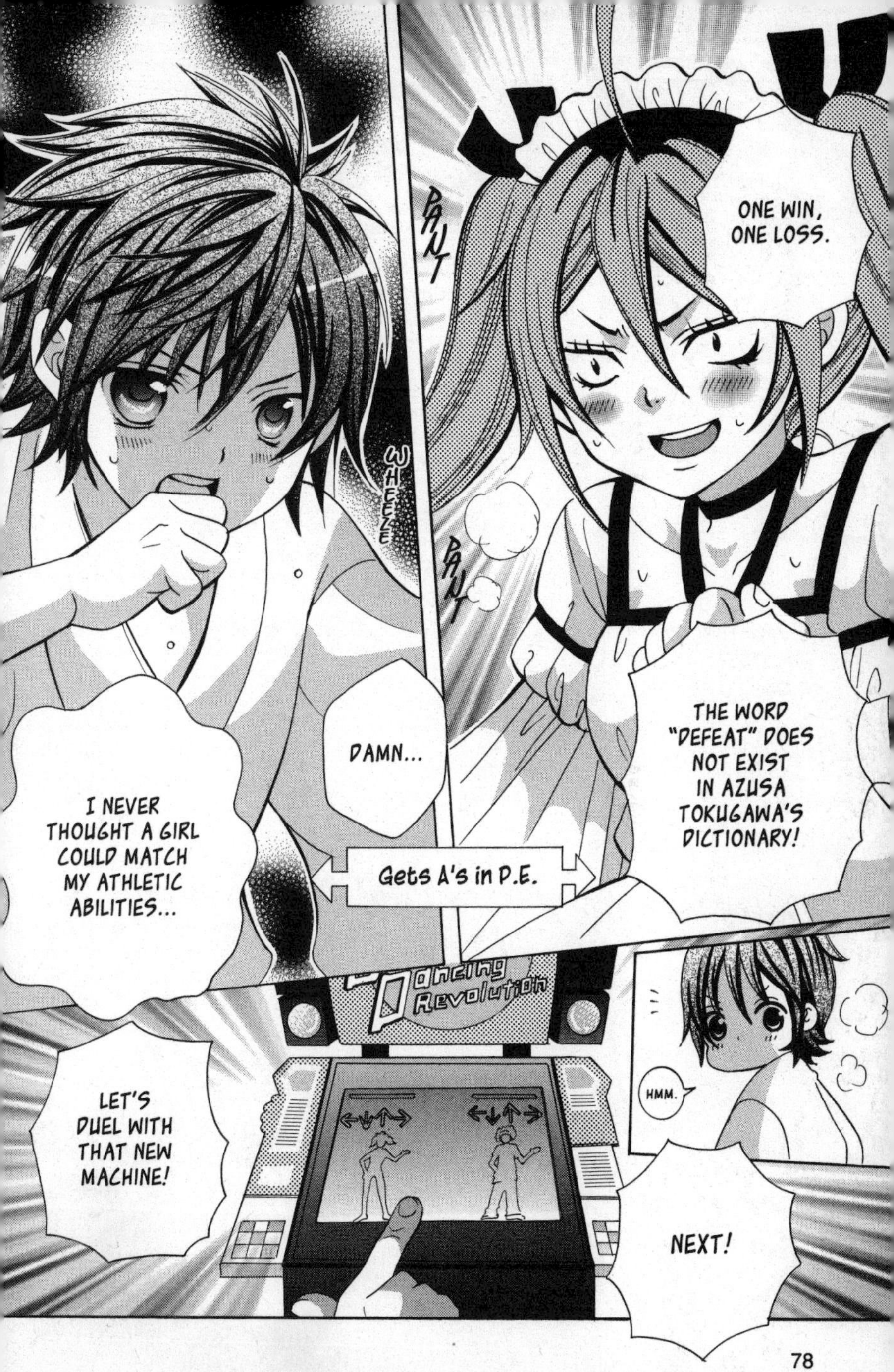
PANT
ONE WIN, ONE LOSS.
PANT
THE WORD "DEFEAT" DOES NOT EXIST IN AZUSA TOKUGAWA'S DICTIONARY!
WHEEZE
DAMN...
I NEVER THOUGHT A GIRL COULD MATCH MY ATHLETIC ABILITIES...
Gets A's in P.E.
HMM.
NEXT!
Dancing Revolution
LET'S DUEL WITH THAT NEW MACHINE!

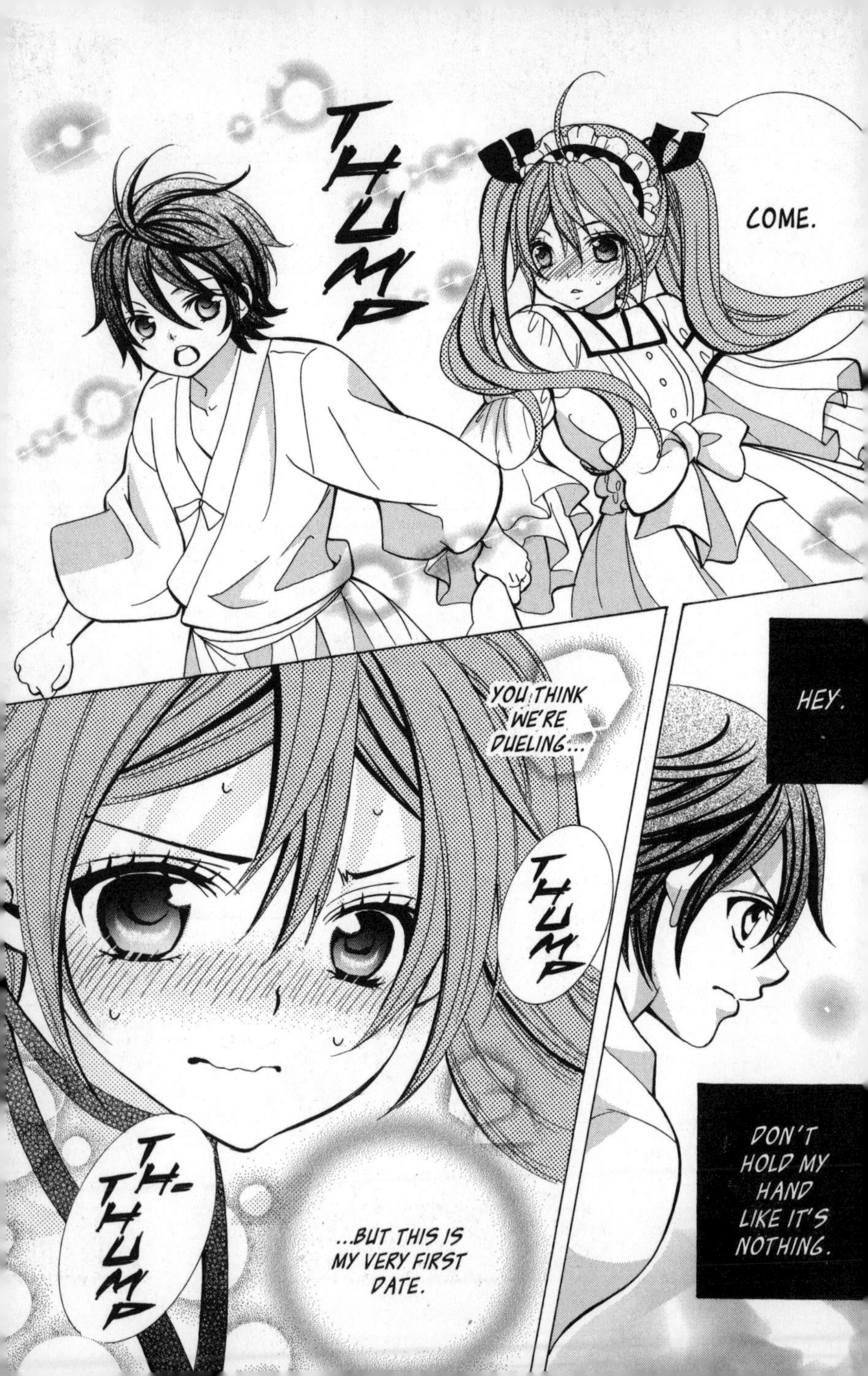
COME.
THUMP
HEY.
DON'T HOLD MY HAND LIKE IT'S NOTHING.
YOU THINK WE'RE DUELING...
THUMP
...BUT THIS IS MY VERY FIRST DATE.
TH-THUMP

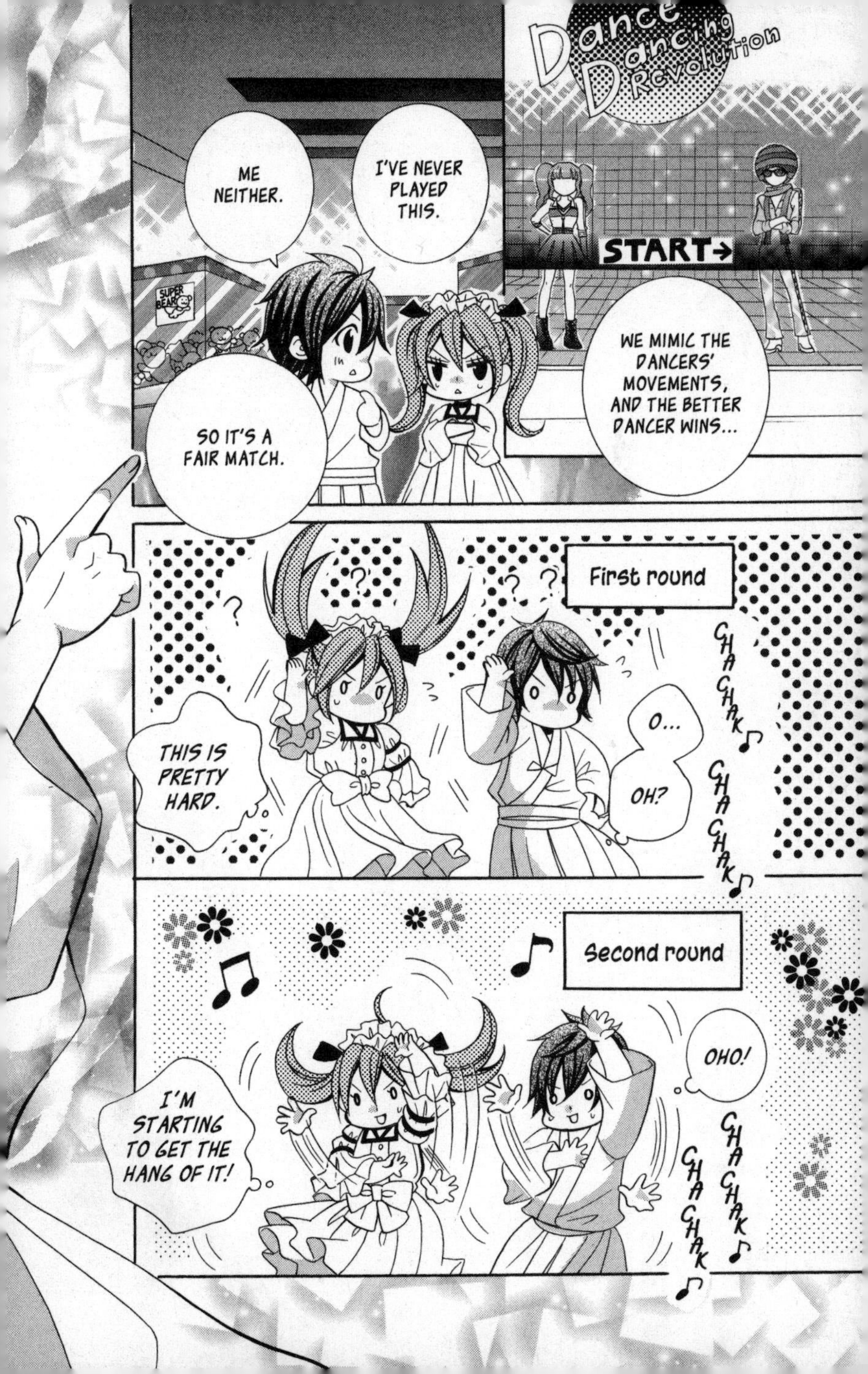
Dance Dancing Revolution
START→
WE MIMIC THE DANCERS' MOVEMENTS, AND THE BETTER DANCER WINS...
I'VE NEVER PLAYED THIS.
ME NEITHER.
SO IT'S A FAIR MATCH.
First round
CHA CHAK♪
CHA CHAK♪
O... OH?
THIS IS PRETTY HARD.
Second round
OHO!
CHA CHAK♪
CHA CHAK♪
I'M STARTING TO GET THE HANG OF IT!

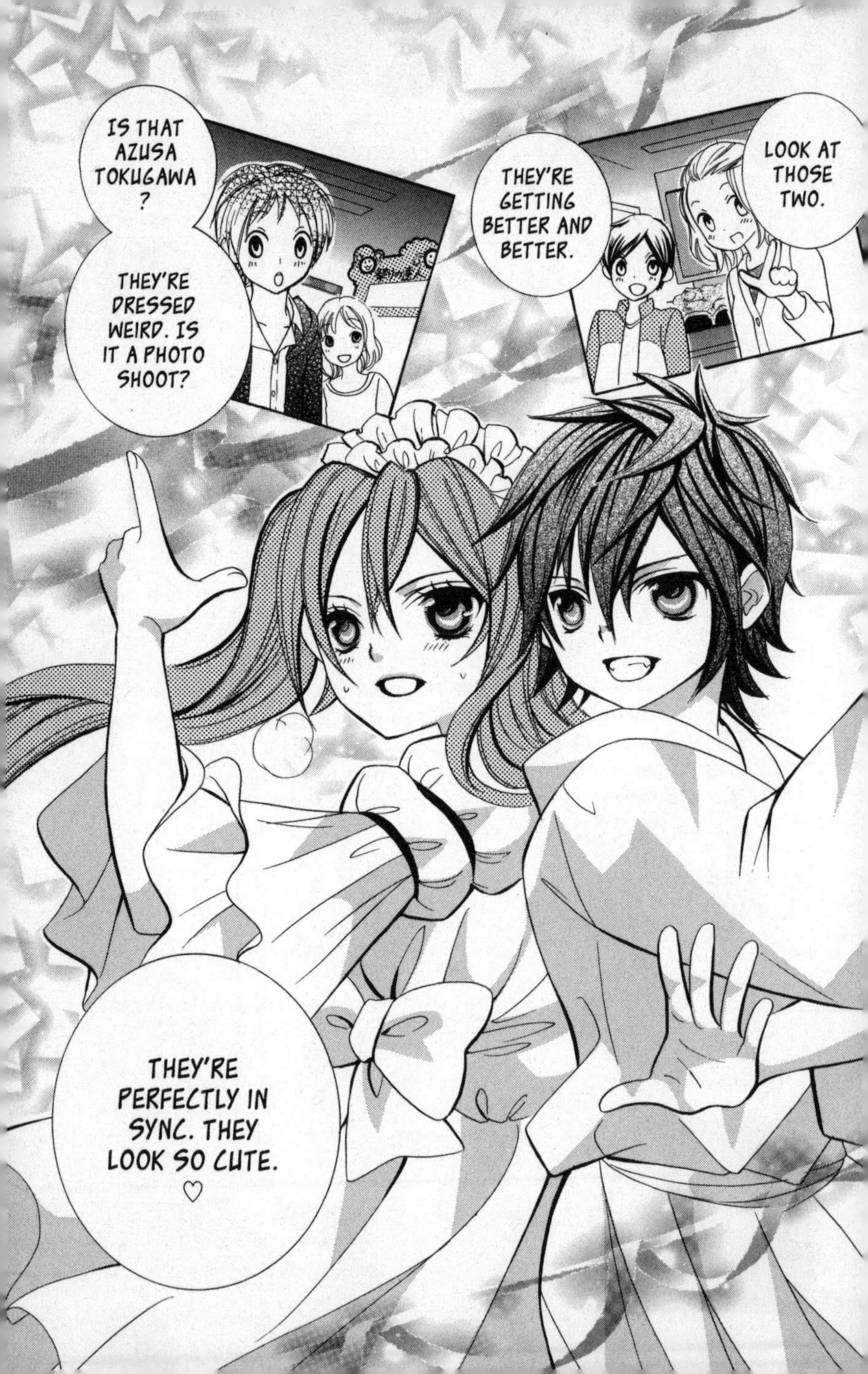
LOOK AT THOSE TWO.
THEY'RE GETTING BETTER AND BETTER.
IS THAT AZUSA TOKUGAWA?
THEY'RE DRESSED WEIRD. IS IT A PHOTO SHOOT?
THEY'RE PERFECTLY IN SYNC. THEY LOOK SO CUTE. ♡

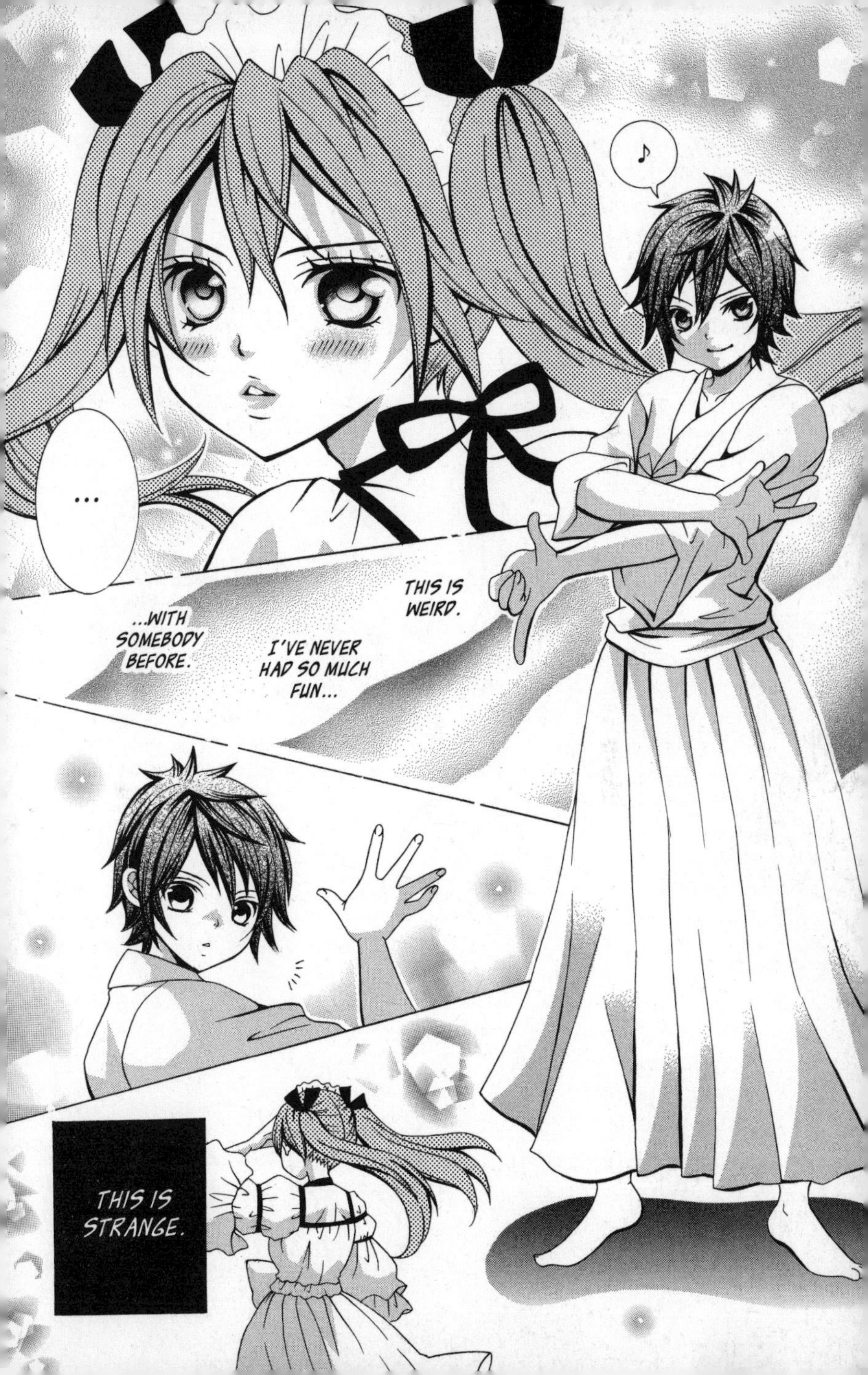
♪
...
THIS IS WEIRD.
I'VE NEVER HAD SO MUCH FUN...
...WITH SOMEBODY BEFORE.
THIS IS STRANGE.

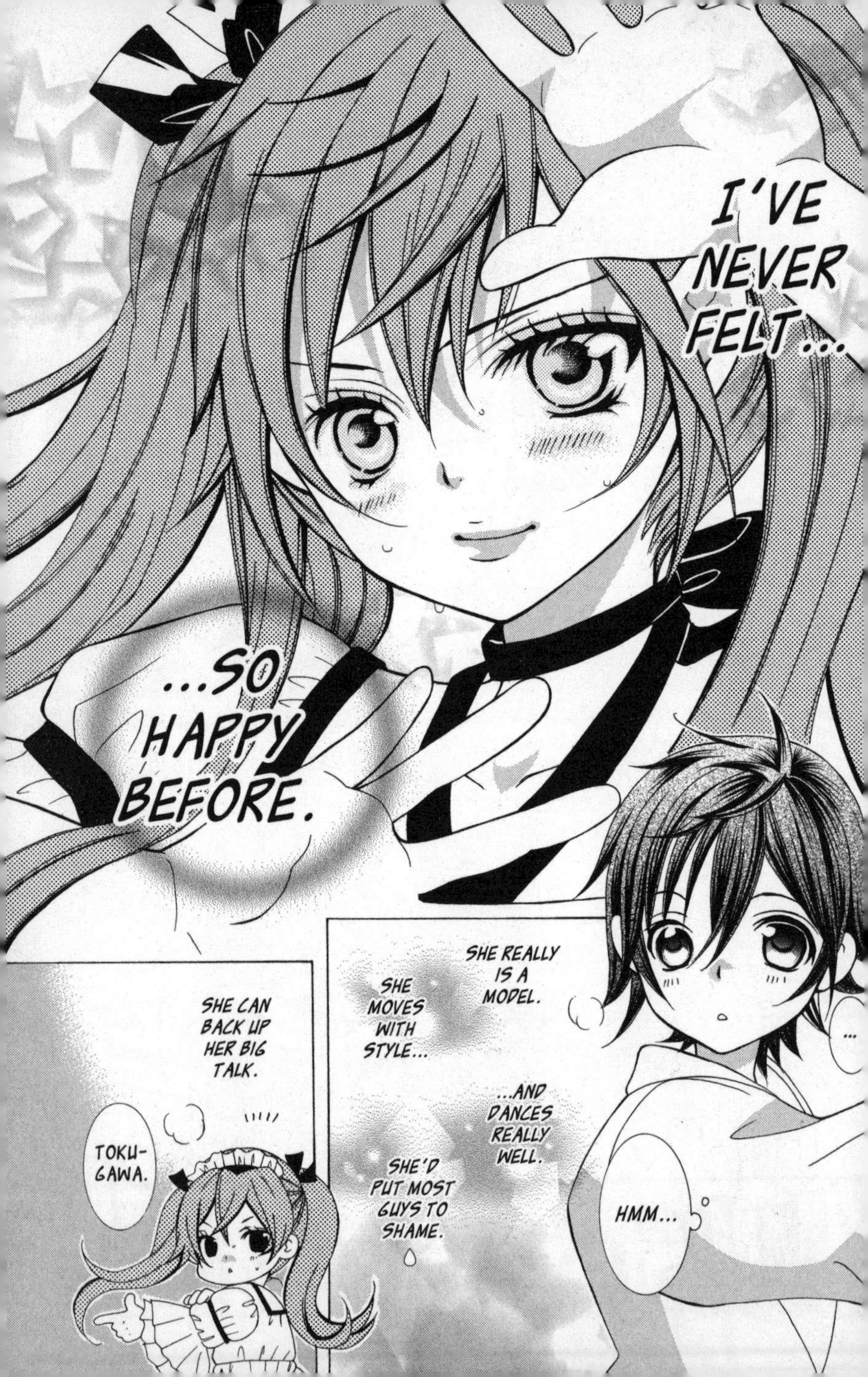
I'VE NEVER FELT...
...SO HAPPY BEFORE.
...
SHE REALLY IS A MODEL.
SHE MOVES WITH STYLE...
...AND DANCES REALLY WELL.
HMM...
SHE'D PUT MOST GUYS TO SHAME.
SHE CAN BACK UP HER BIG TALK.
TOKU-GAWA.

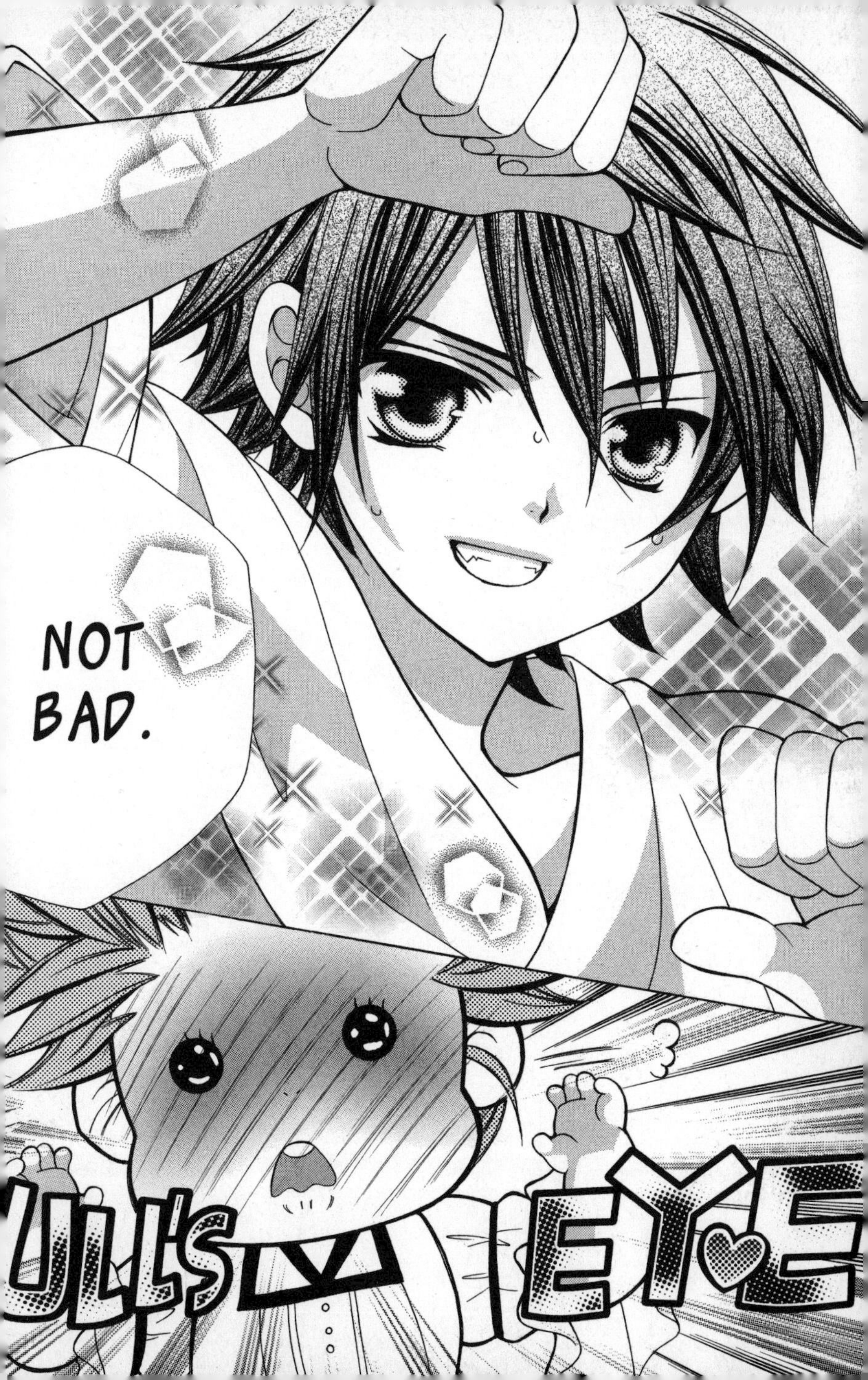
NOT BAD.
ULL'S EYE

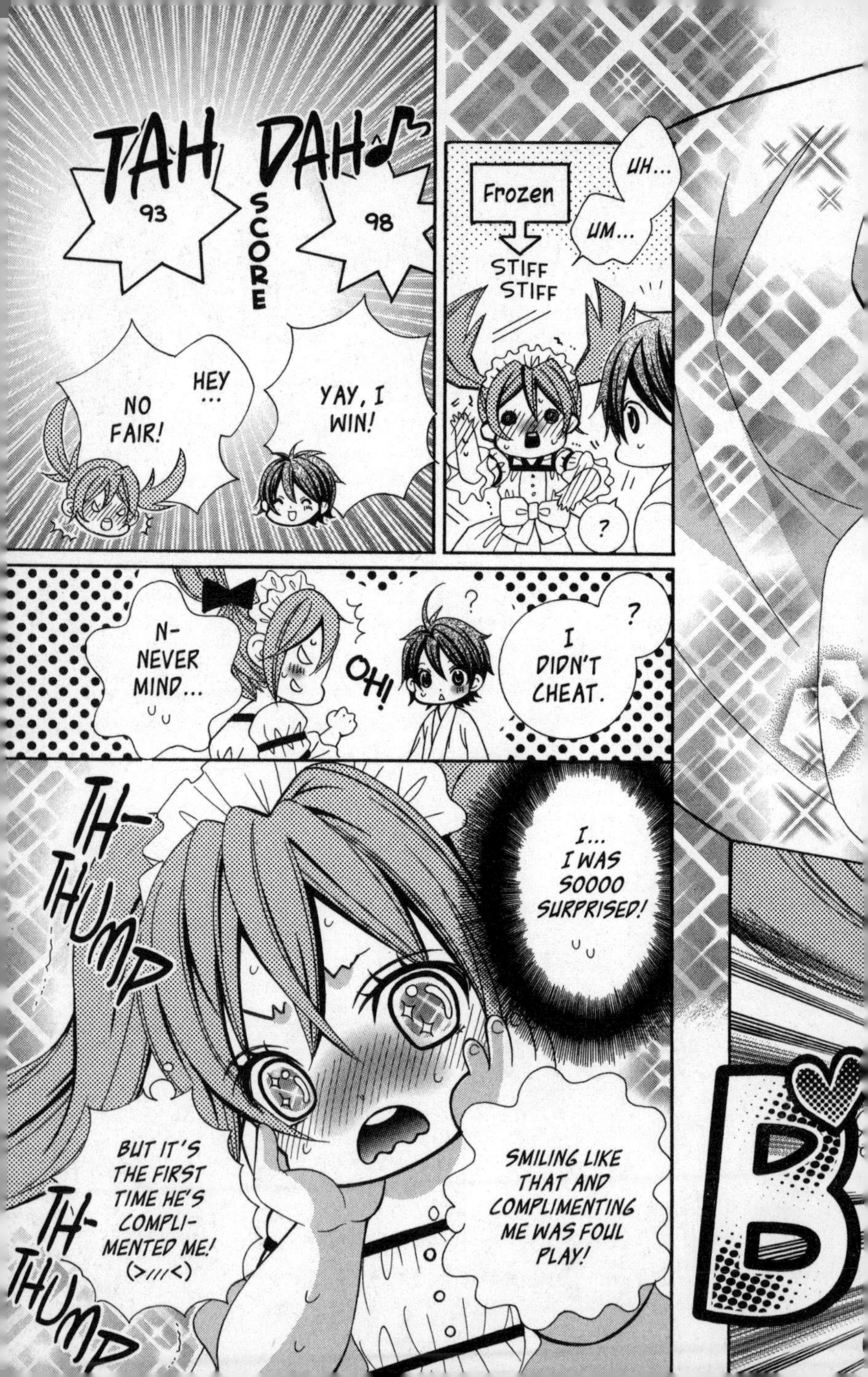

B
UH...
UM...
Frozen
STIFF STIFF
?
TAH DAH♪
SCORE
98
93
YAY, I WIN!
HEY... NO FAIR!
?
I DIDN'T CHEAT.
OH!
N- NEVER MIND...
I... I WAS SOOOO SURPRISED!
SMILING LIKE THAT AND COMPLIMENTING ME WAS FOUL PLAY!
BUT IT'S THE FIRST TIME HE'S COMPLI- MENTED ME! (>///<)
TH-THUMP
TH-THUMP

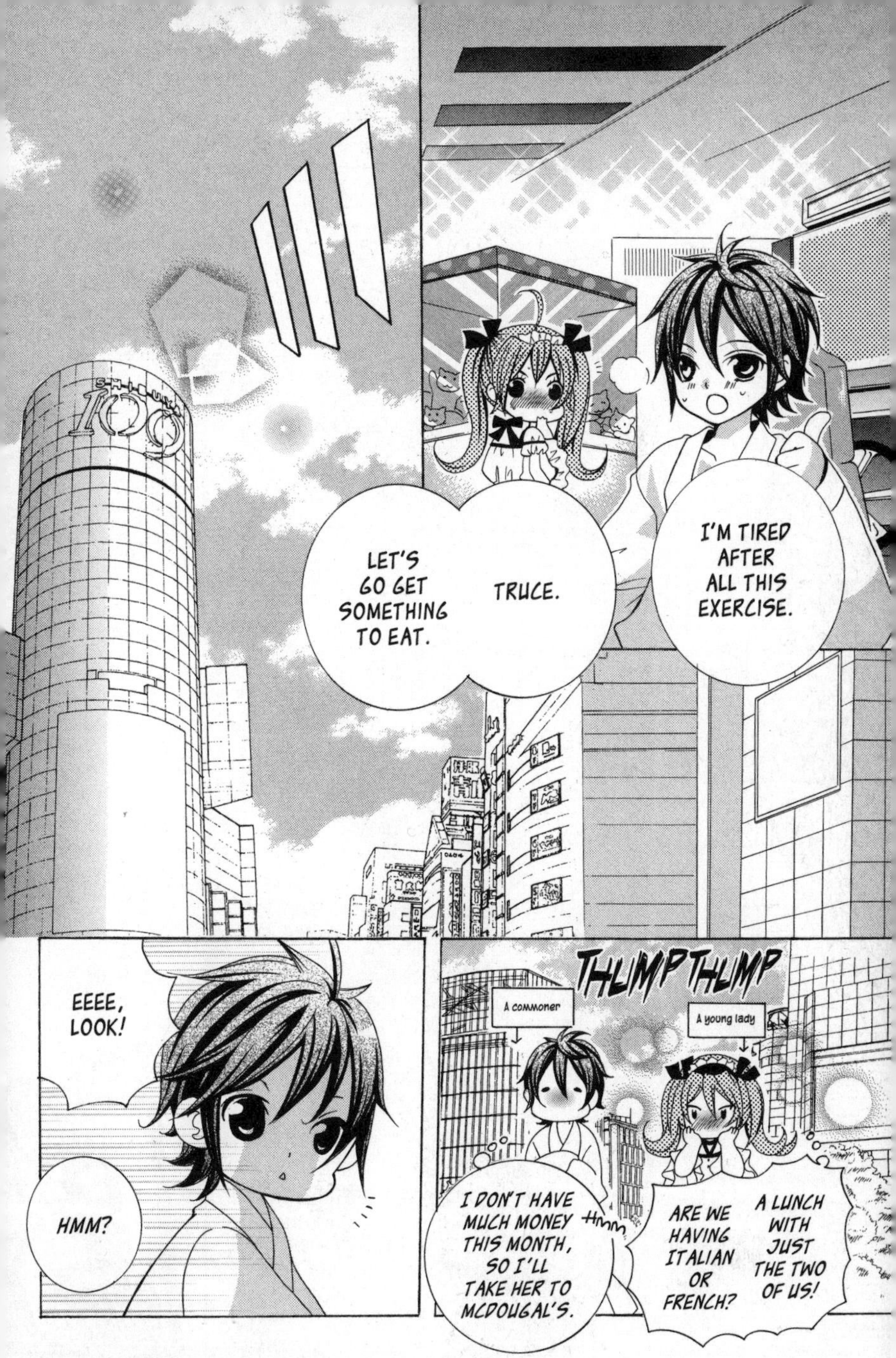
I'M TIRED AFTER ALL THIS EXERCISE.
TRUCE.
LET'S GO GET SOMETHING TO EAT.
THUMP THUMP
A young lady
A commoner
A LUNCH WITH JUST THE TWO OF US!
ARE WE HAVING ITALIAN OR FRENCH?
HMM
I DON'T HAVE MUCH MONEY THIS MONTH, SO I'LL TAKE HER TO MCDOUGAL'S.
EEEE, LOOK!
HMM?

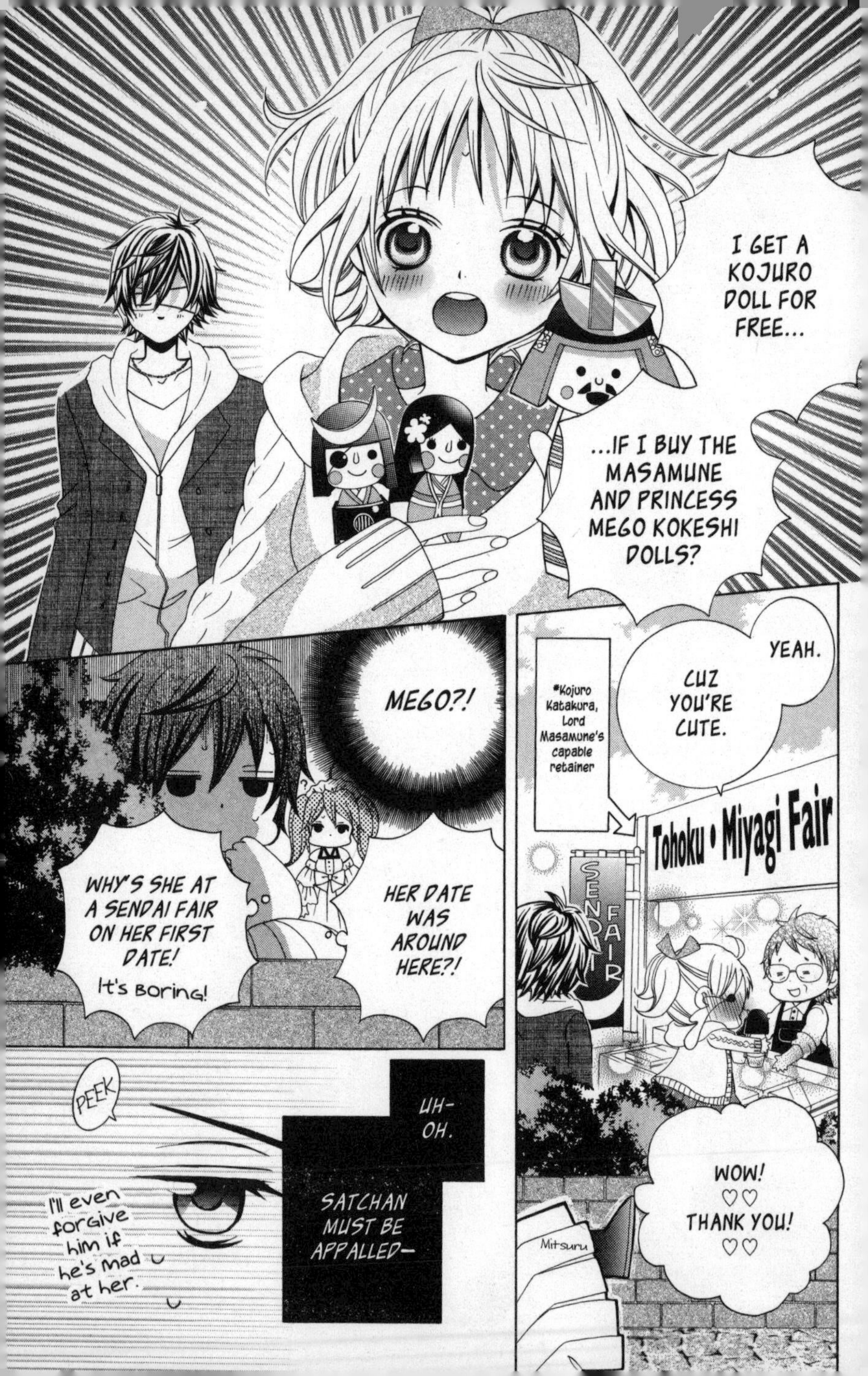
I GET A KOJURO DOLL FOR FREE...
...IF I BUY THE MASAMUNE AND PRINCESS MEGO KOKESHI DOLLS?
YEAH.
CUZ YOU'RE CUTE.
*Kojuro Katakura, Lord Masamune's capable retainer
Tohoku • Miyagi Fair
SENDAI FAIR
WOW! ♡♡ THANK YOU! ♡♡
Mitsuru
MEGO?!
HER DATE WAS AROUND HERE?!
WHY'S SHE AT A SENDAI FAIR ON HER FIRST DATE!
It's boring!
UH-OH.
SATCHAN MUST BE APPALLED—
PEEK
I'll even forgive him if he's mad at her.

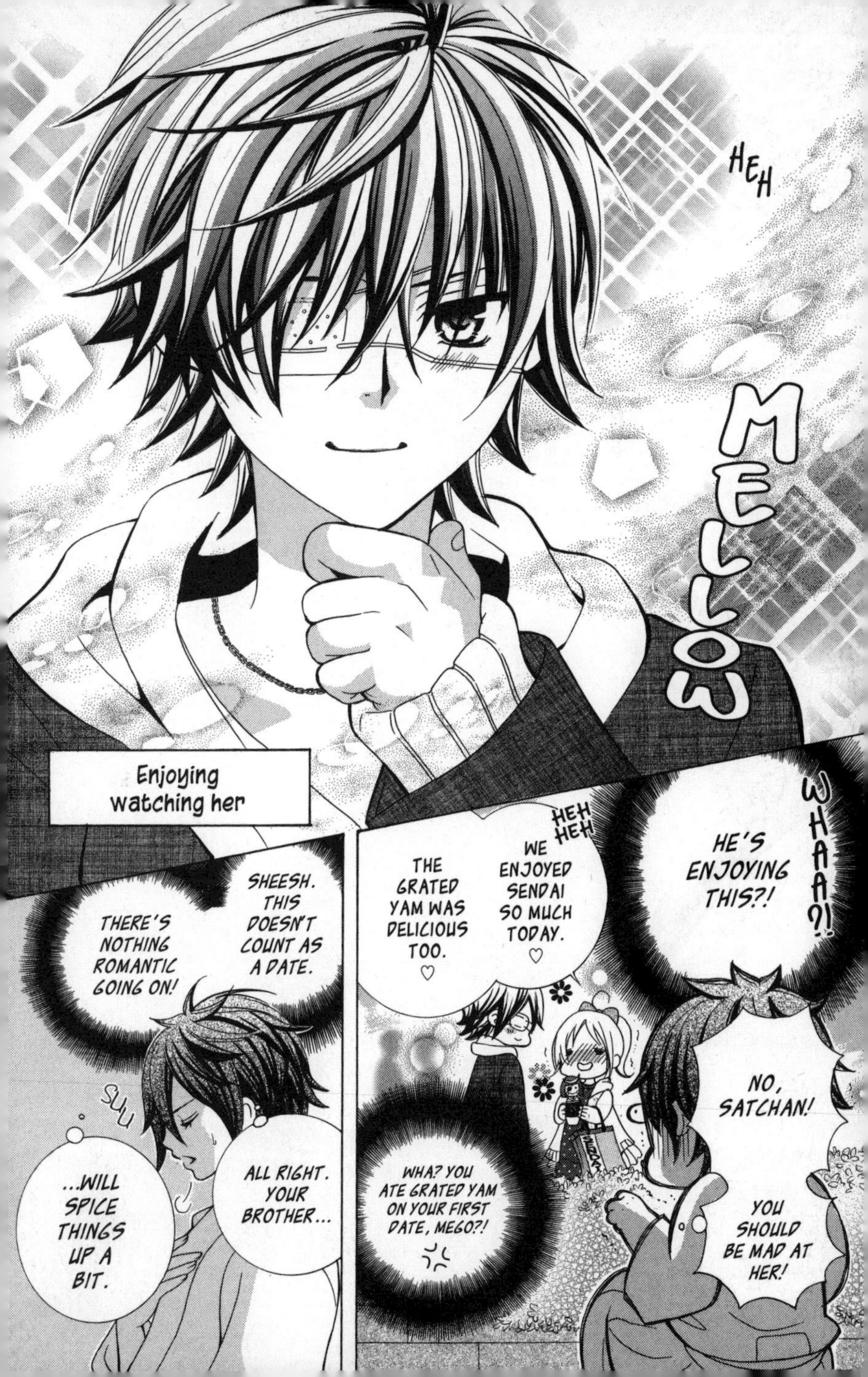
HEH
MELLOW
Enjoying watching her
WHAAA?!
HE'S ENJOYING THIS?!
HEH HEH
WE ENJOYED SENDAI SO MUCH TODAY. ♡
THE GRATED YAM WAS DELICIOUS TOO. ♡
NO, SATCHAN!
YOU SHOULD BE MAD AT HER!
WHA? YOU ATE GRATED YAM ON YOUR FIRST DATE, MEGO?!
SHEESH. THIS DOESN'T COUNT AS A DATE.
THERE'S NOTHING ROMANTIC GOING ON!
SUU
ALL RIGHT. YOUR BROTHER...
...WILL SPICE THINGS UP A BIT.

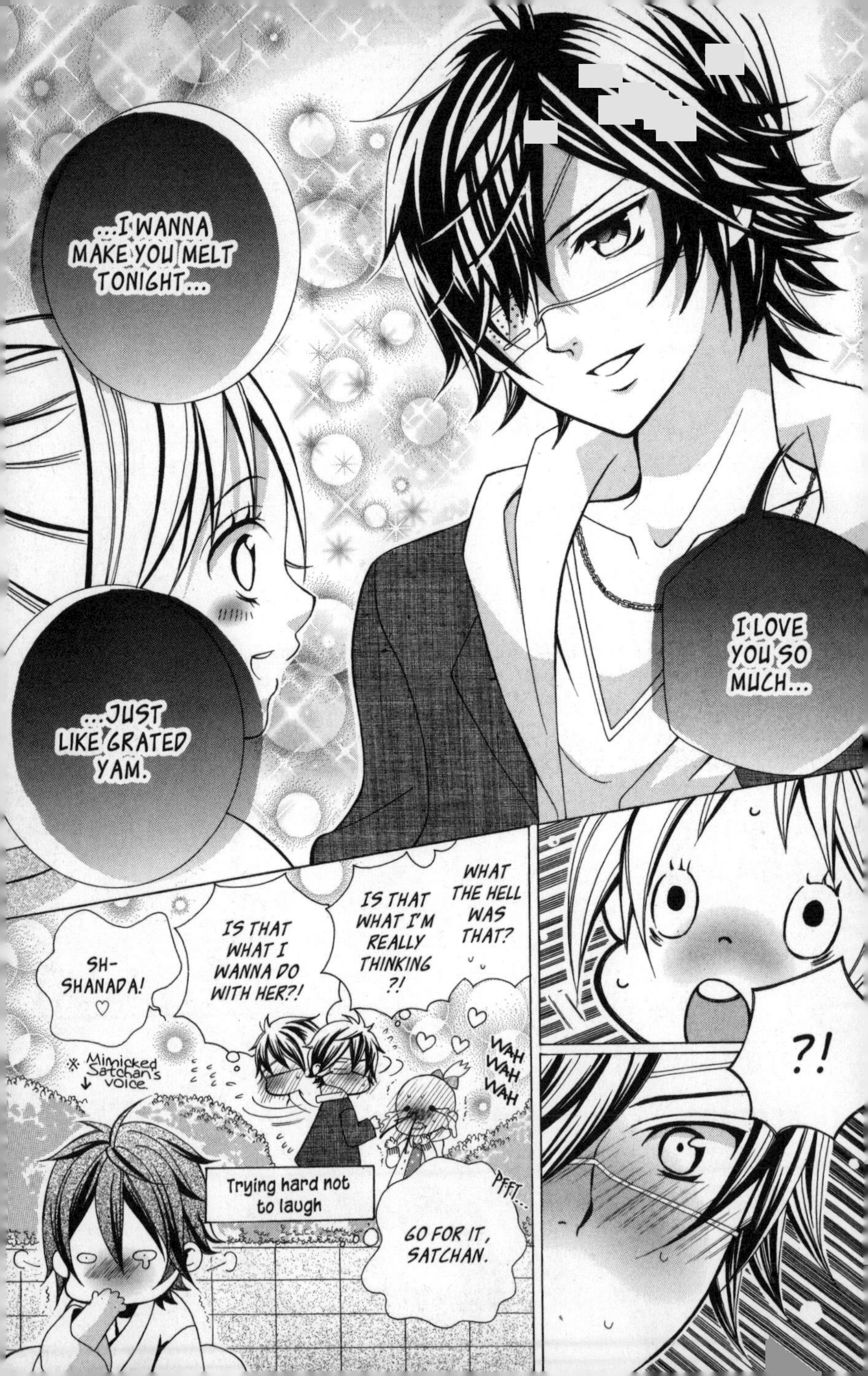
I LOVE YOU SO MUCH...
...I WANNA MAKE YOU MELT TONIGHT...
...JUST LIKE GRATED YAM.
?!
WHAT THE HELL WAS THAT?
IS THAT WHAT I'M REALLY THINKING?!
IS THAT WHAT I WANNA DO WITH HER?!
SH-SHANADA! ♡
※ Mimicked Satchan's voice
WAH WAH WAH
PFFT...
GO FOR IT, SATCHAN.
Trying hard not to laugh

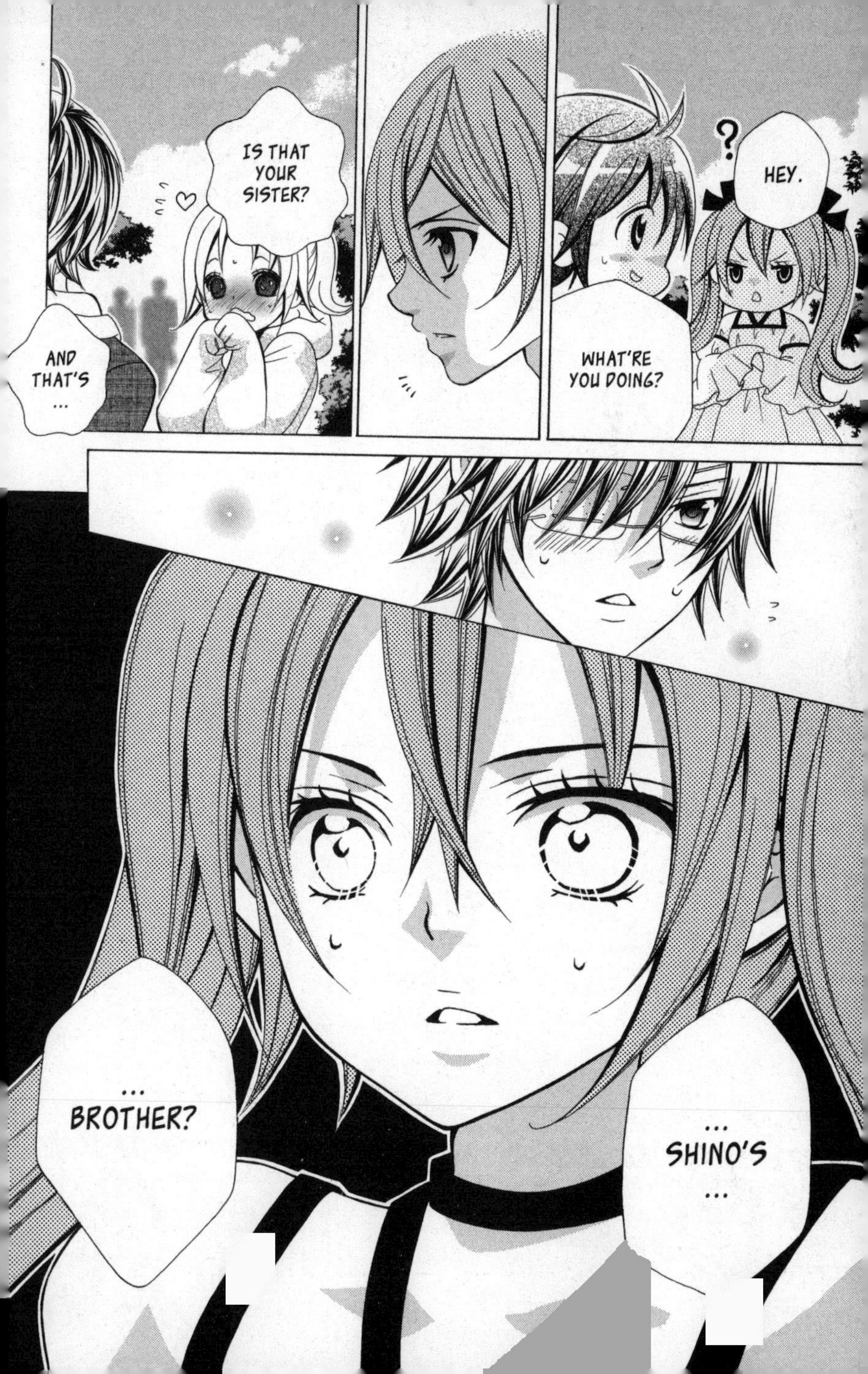
HEY.
WHAT'RE YOU DOING?
IS THAT YOUR SISTER?
AND THAT'S ...
... SHINO'S ...
... BROTHER?

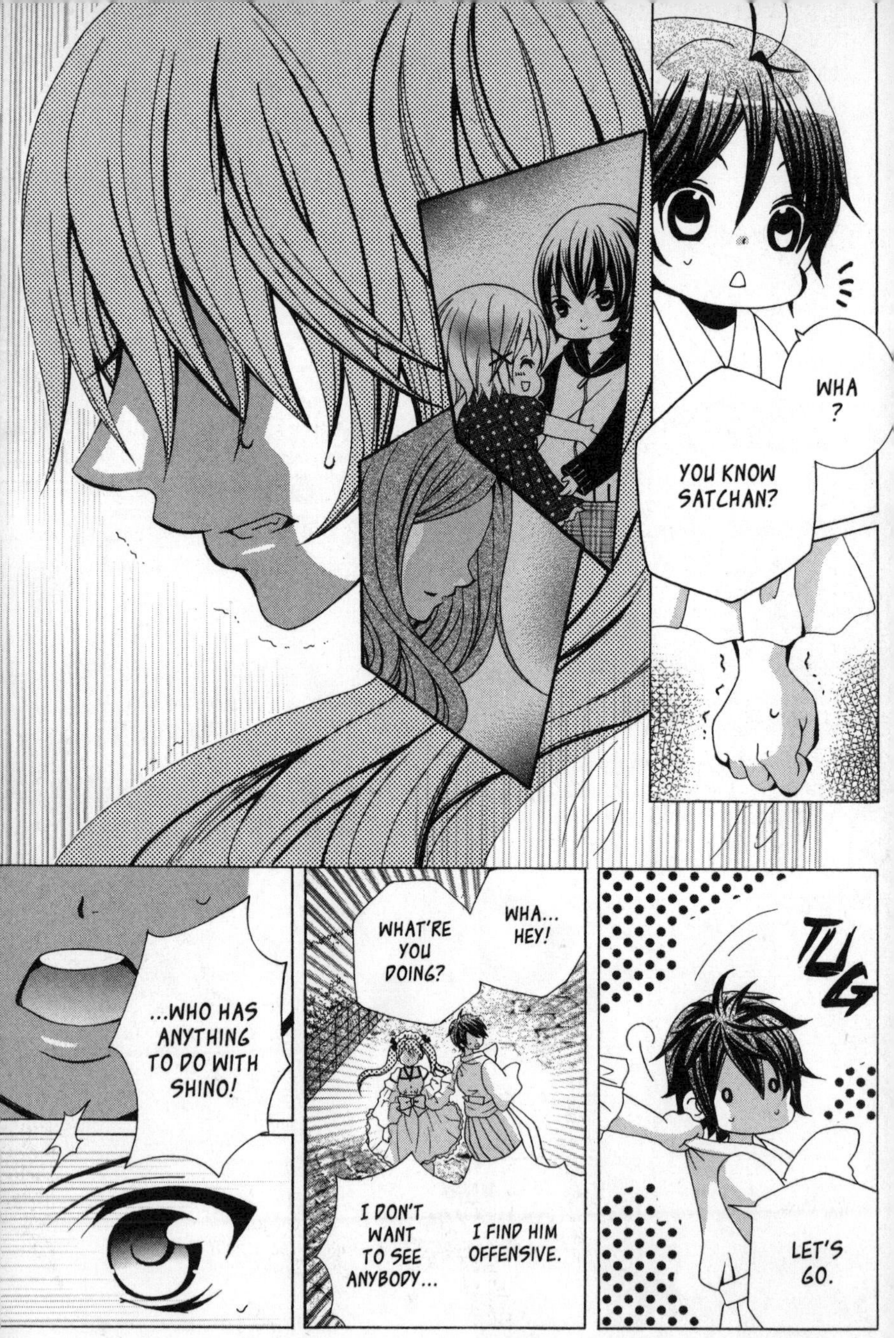
WHA ?
YOU KNOW SATCHAN?
TUG
LET'S GO.
WHA... HEY!
WHAT'RE YOU DOING?
I FIND HIM OFFENSIVE.
I DON'T WANT TO SEE ANYBODY...
...WHO HAS ANYTHING TO DO WITH SHINO!

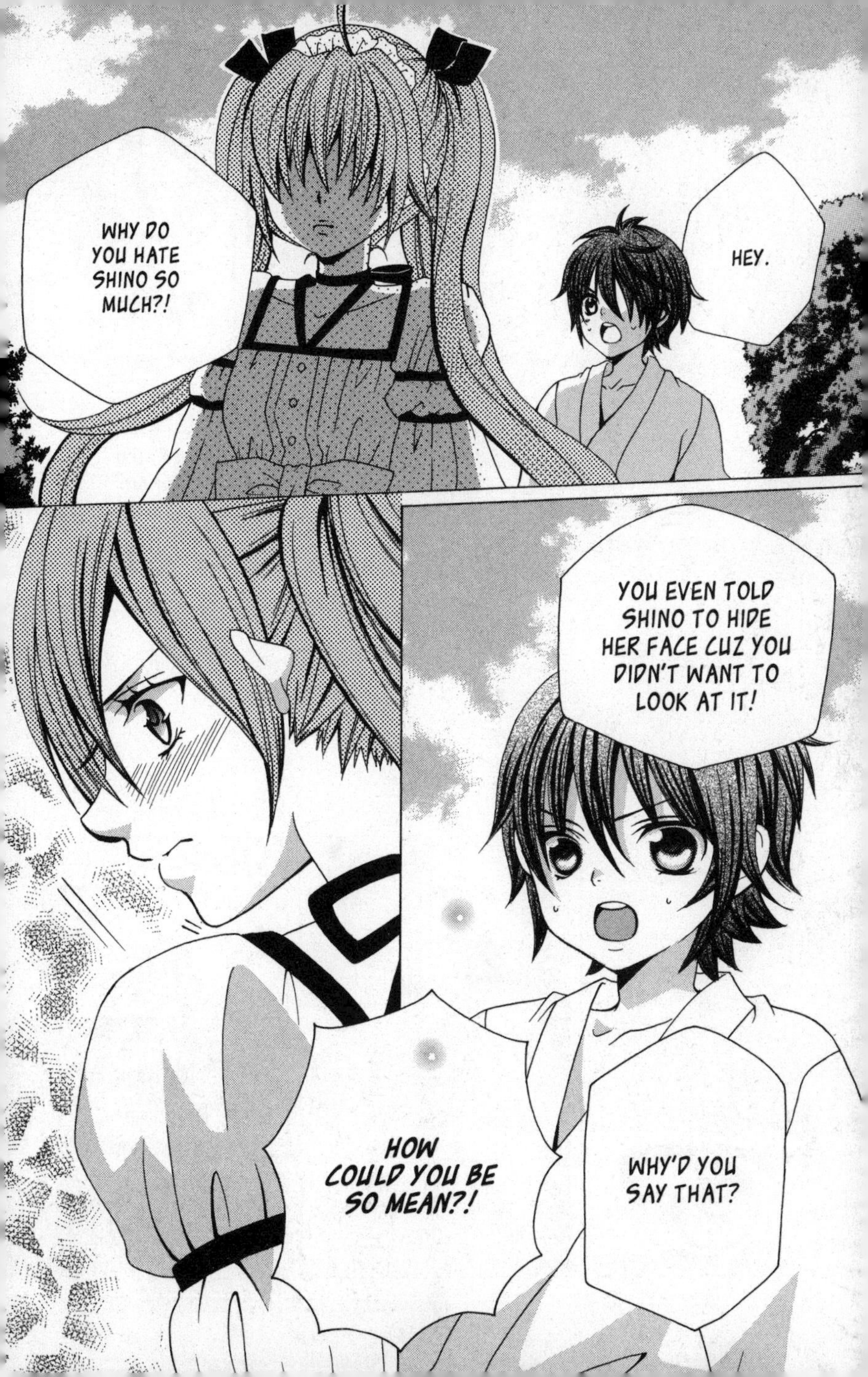
HEY.
WHY DO YOU HATE SHINO SO MUCH?!
YOU EVEN TOLD SHINO TO HIDE HER FACE CUZ YOU DIDN'T WANT TO LOOK AT IT!
WHY'D YOU SAY THAT?
HOW COULD YOU BE SO MEAN?!

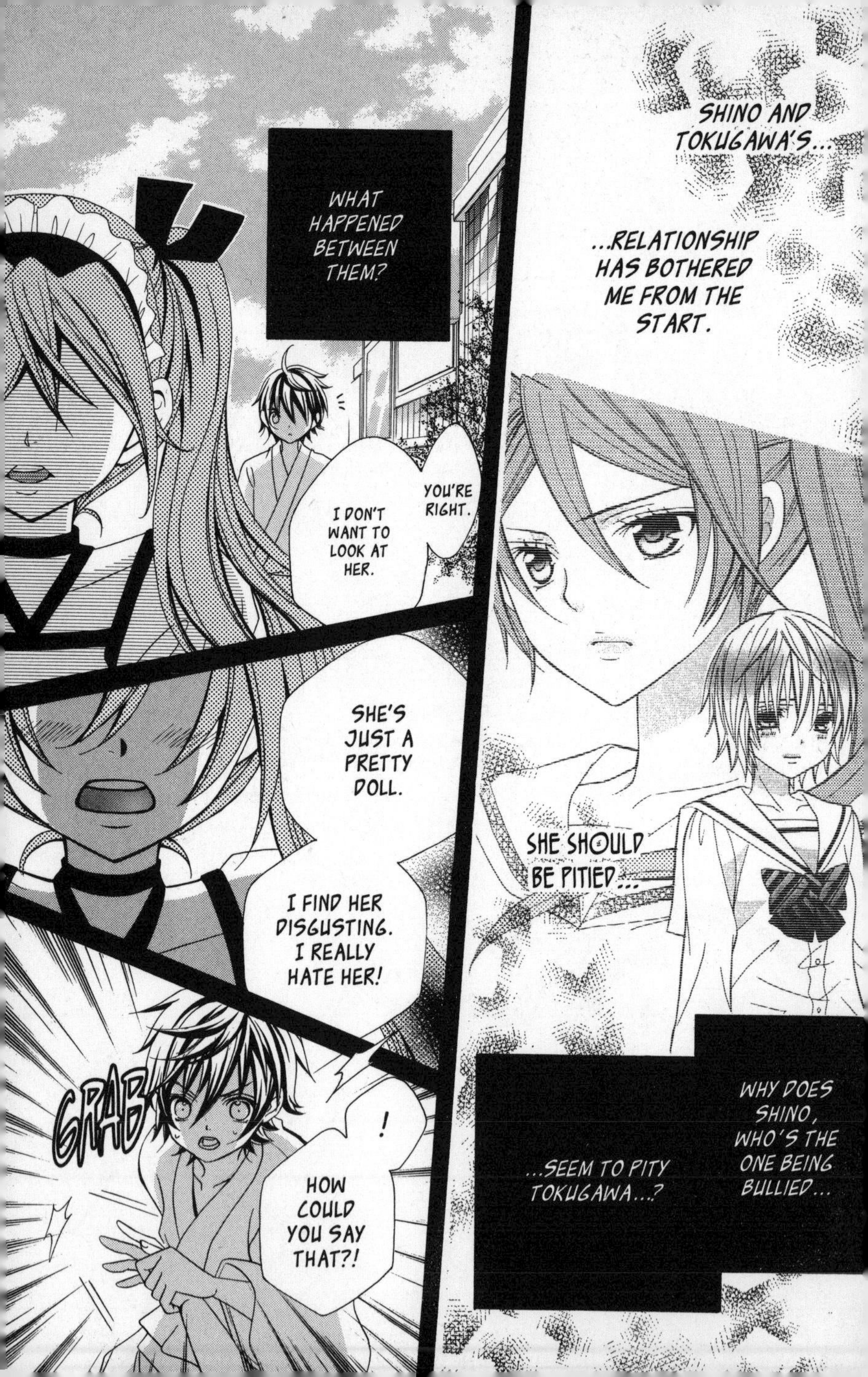

SHINO AND TOKUGAWA'S...
...RELATIONSHIP HAS BOTHERED ME FROM THE START.
SHE SHOULD BE PITIED...
WHY DOES SHINO, WHO'S THE ONE BEING BULLIED...
...SEEM TO PITY TOKUGAWA...?
WHAT HAPPENED BETWEEN THEM?
YOU'RE RIGHT.
I DON'T WANT TO LOOK AT HER.
SHE'S JUST A PRETTY DOLL.
I FIND HER DISGUSTING. I REALLY HATE HER!
GRAB
!
HOW COULD YOU SAY THAT?!

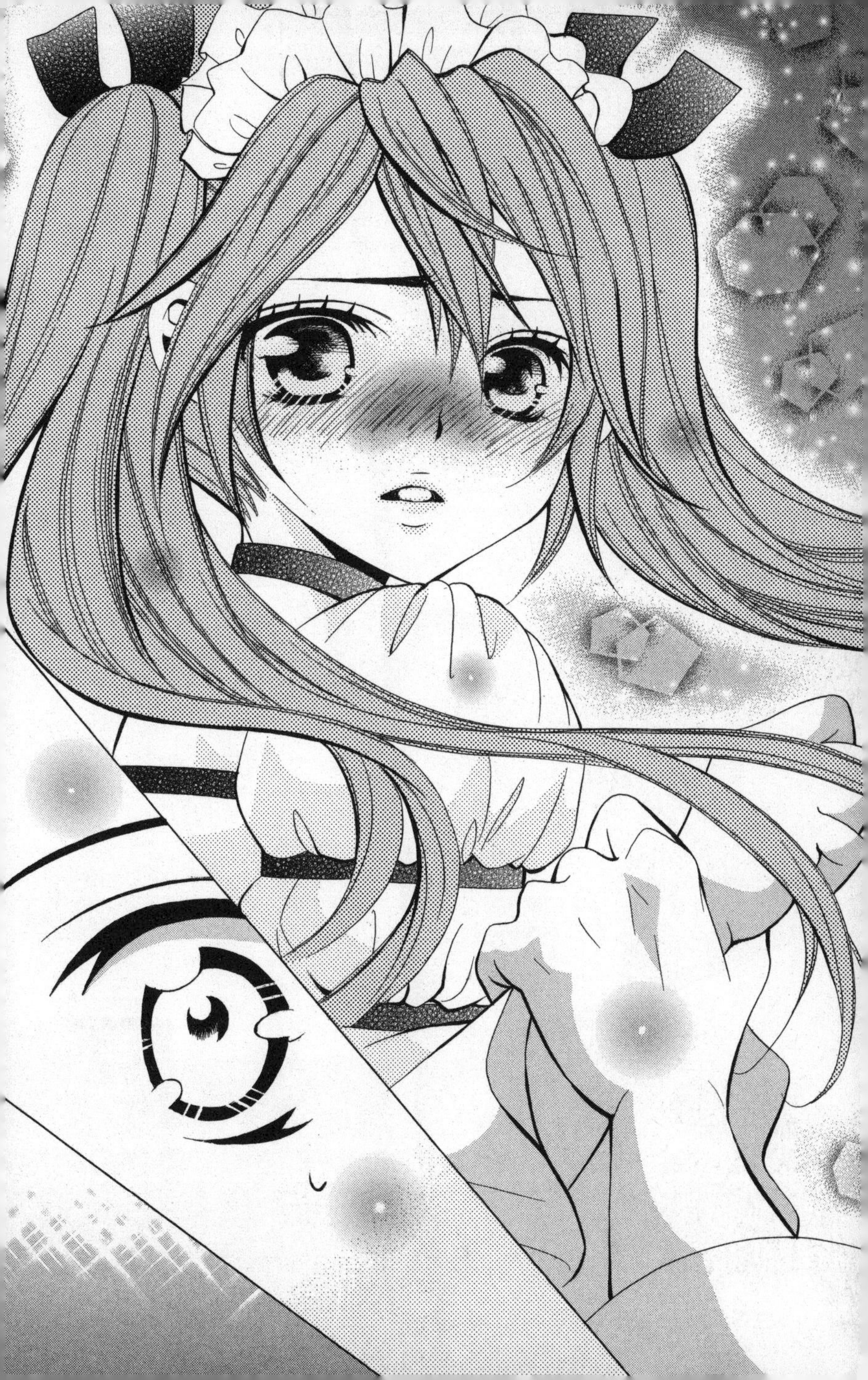

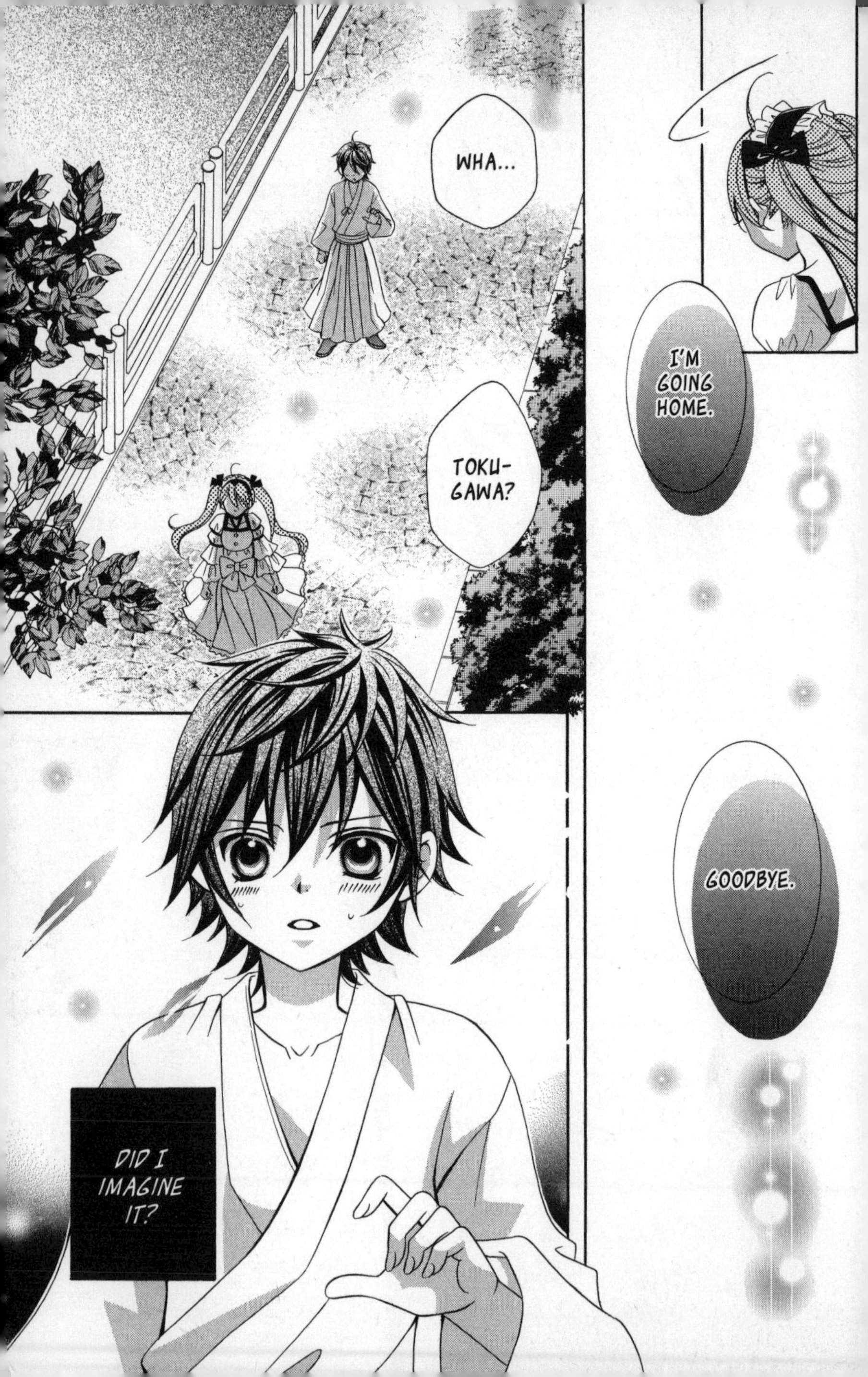
I'M GOING HOME.
GOODBYE.
WHA...
TOKU-GAWA?
DID I IMAGINE IT?

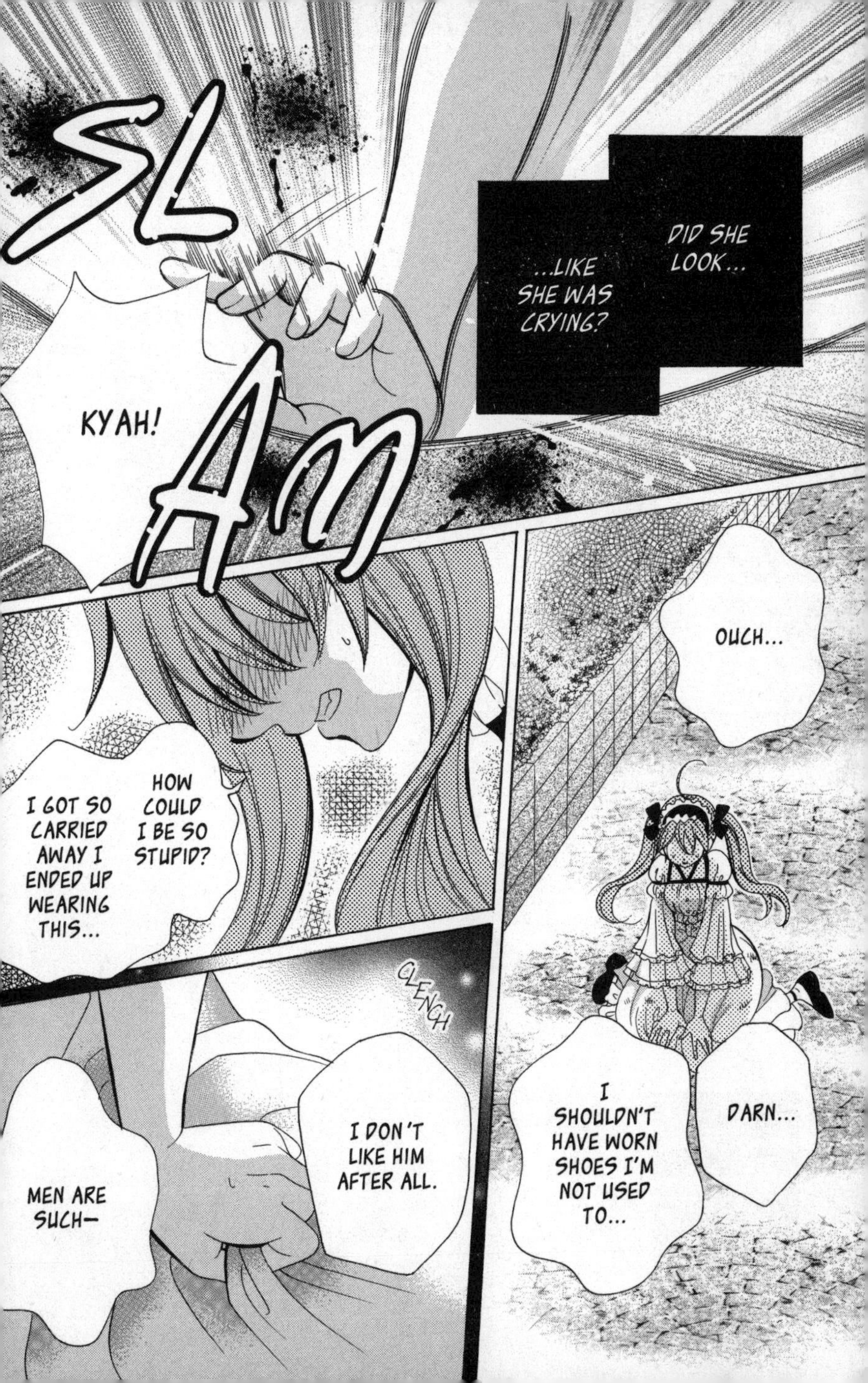
DID SHE LOOK...
...LIKE SHE WAS CRYING?
SLAM
KYAH!
OUCH...
DARN...
I SHOULDN'T HAVE WORN SHOES I'M NOT USED TO...
HOW COULD I BE SO STUPID?
I GOT SO CARRIED AWAY I ENDED UP WEARING THIS...
CLENCH
I DON'T LIKE HIM AFTER ALL.
MEN ARE SUCH—

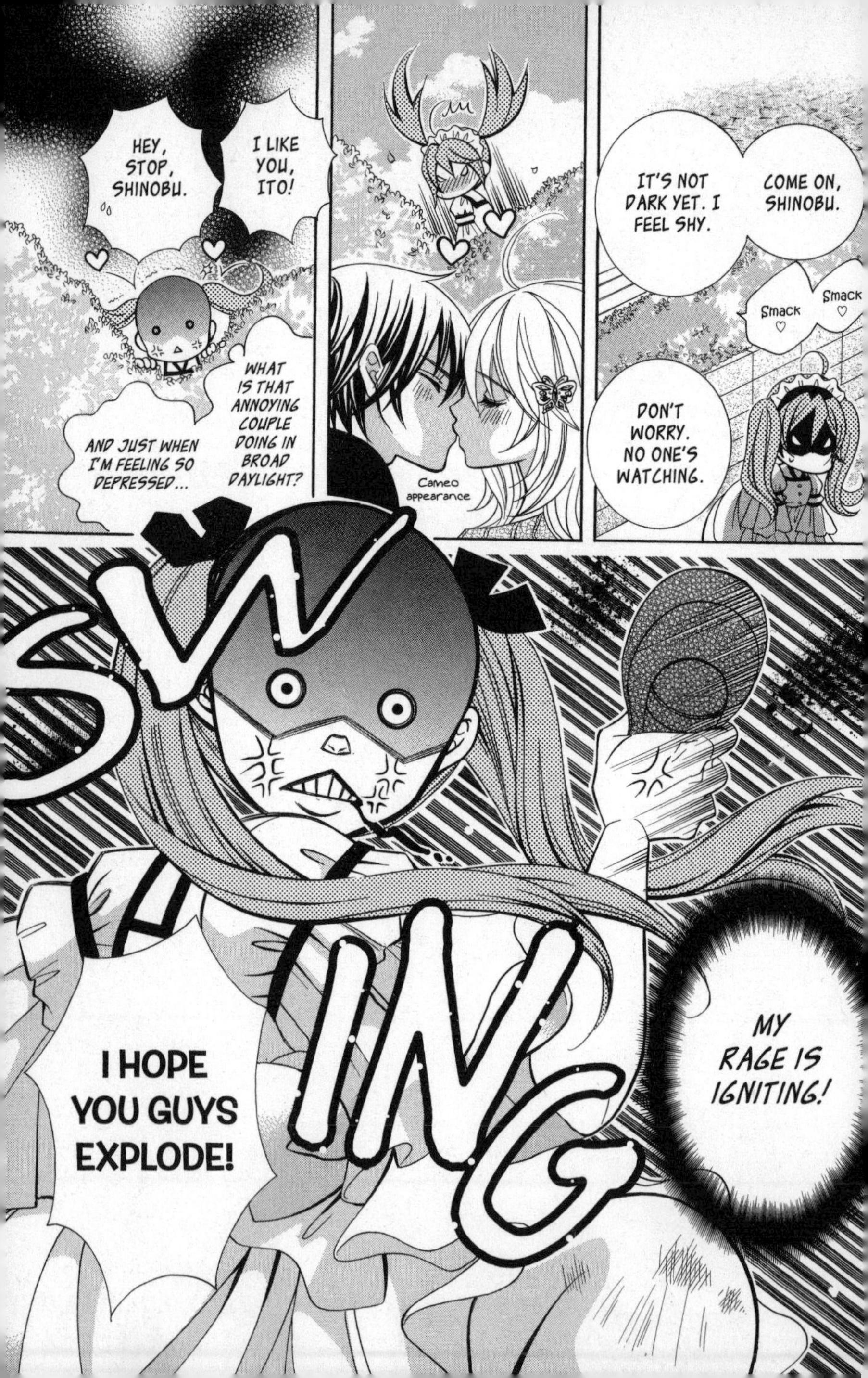
COME ON, SHINOBU.
IT'S NOT DARK YET. I FEEL SHY.
Smack ♡
Smack ♡
DON'T WORRY. NO ONE'S WATCHING.
Cameo appearance
I LIKE YOU, ITO!
HEY, STOP, SHINOBU.
WHAT IS THAT ANNOYING COUPLE DOING IN BROAD DAYLIGHT?
AND JUST WHEN I'M FEELING SO DEPRESSED...
MY RAGE IS IGNITING!
SWING
I HOPE YOU GUYS EXPLODE!

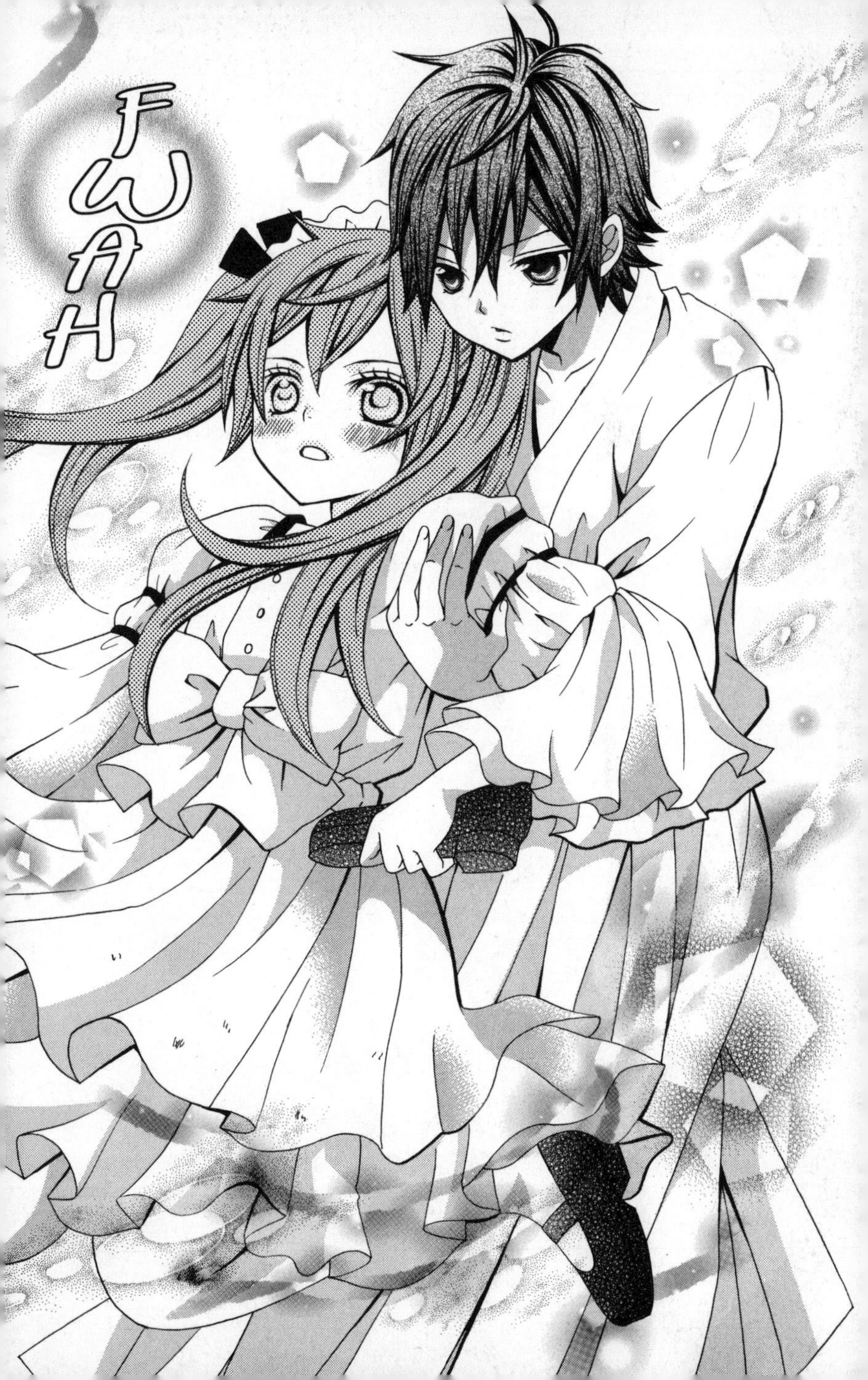
FWAH

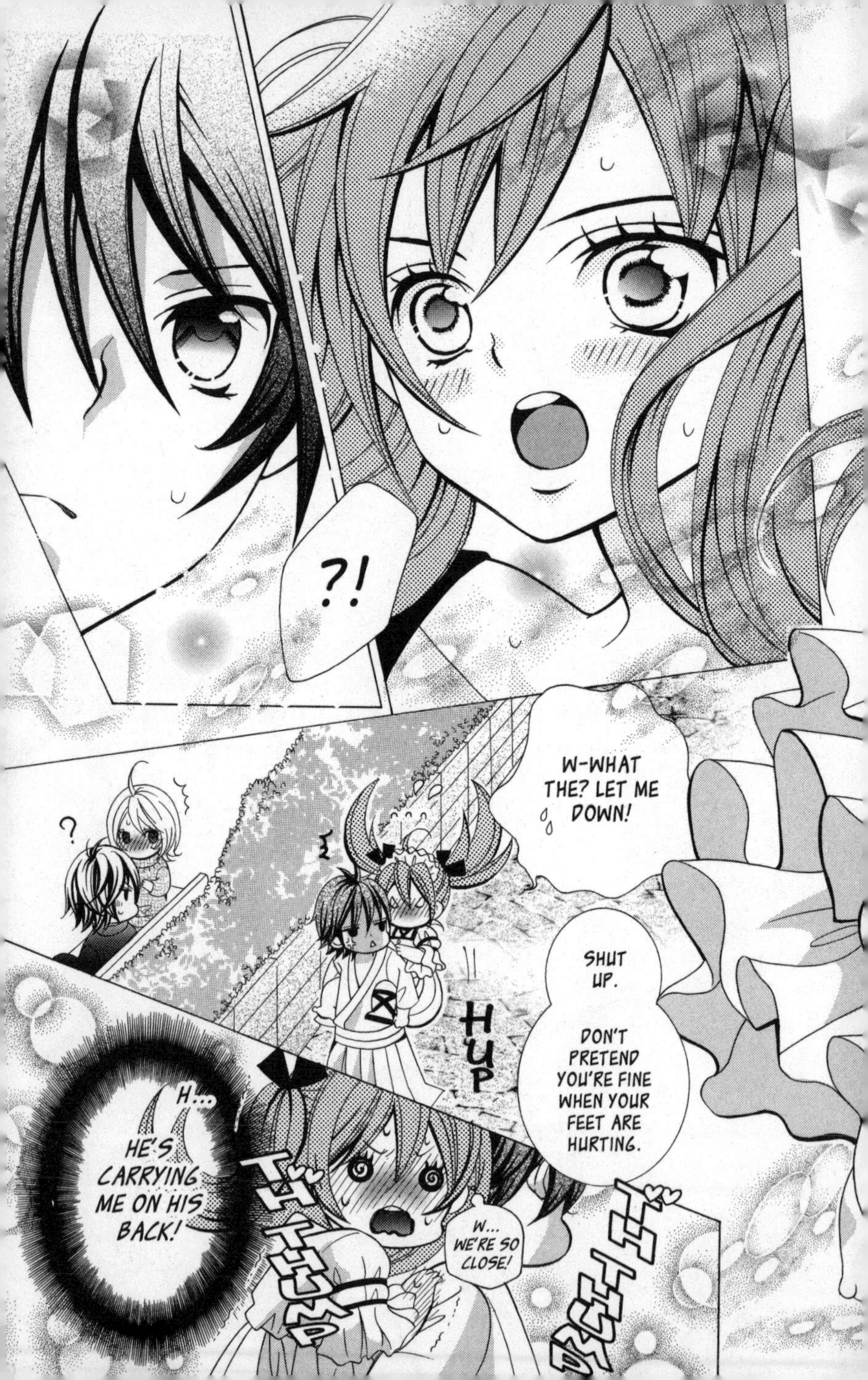
?!
W-WHAT THE? LET ME DOWN!
SHUT UP.
DON'T PRETEND YOU'RE FINE WHEN YOUR FEET ARE HURTING.
HUP
?
TH THUMP
W... WE'RE SO CLOSE!
TH THUMP
H...
HE'S CARRYING ME ON HIS BACK!

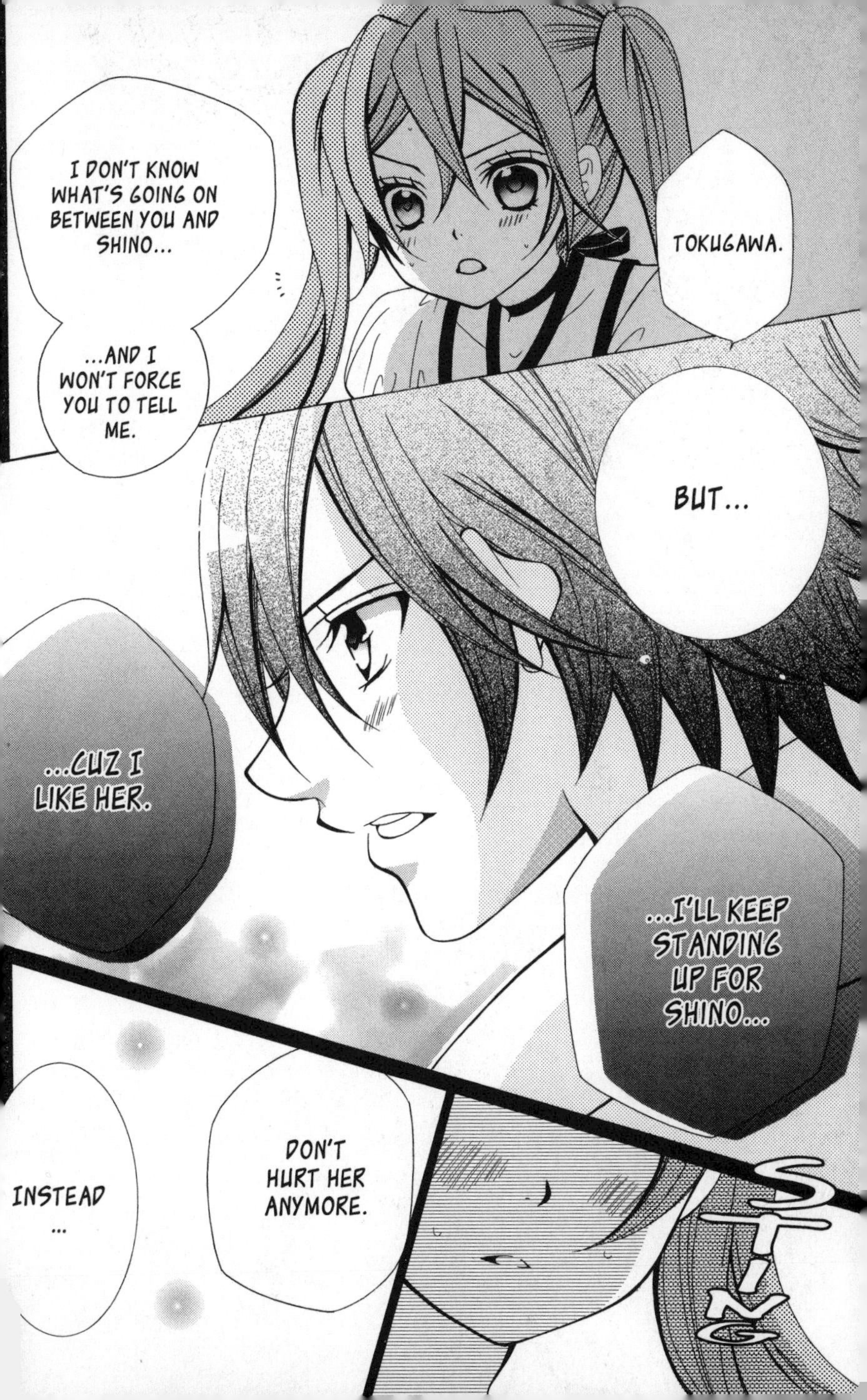
TOKUGAWA.
I DON'T KNOW WHAT'S GOING ON BETWEEN YOU AND SHINO...
...AND I WON'T FORCE YOU TO TELL ME.
BUT...
...I'LL KEEP STANDING UP FOR SHINO...
...CUZ I LIKE HER.
STING
DON'T HURT HER ANYMORE.
INSTEAD ...

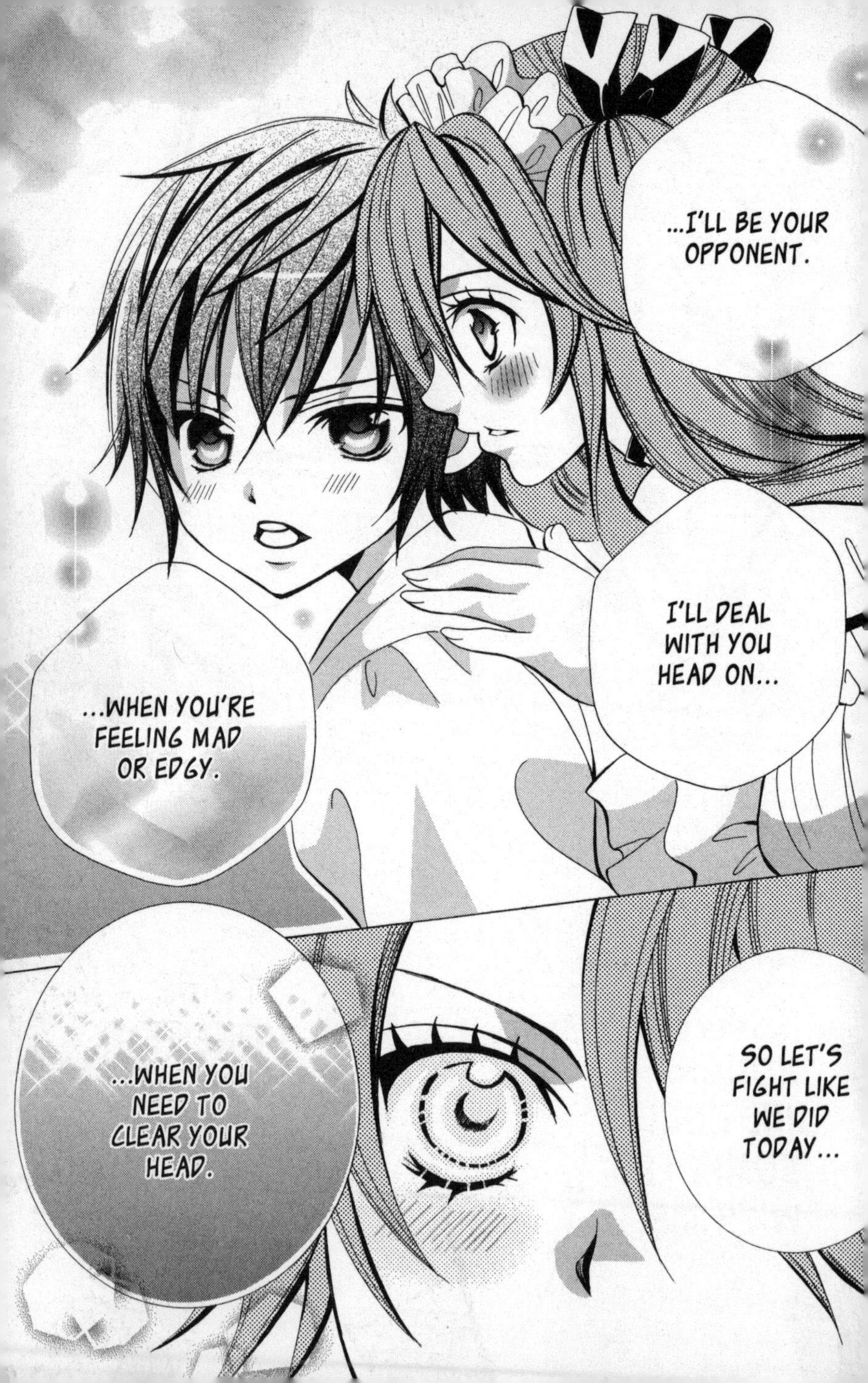
...I'LL BE YOUR OPPONENT.
I'LL DEAL WITH YOU HEAD ON...
...WHEN YOU'RE FEELING MAD OR EDGY.
SO LET'S FIGHT LIKE WE DID TODAY...
...WHEN YOU NEED TO CLEAR YOUR HEAD.

TO BE HONEST, I HAD FUN TODAY!
I NEVER THOUGHT A GIRL COULD COMPETE WITH ME.

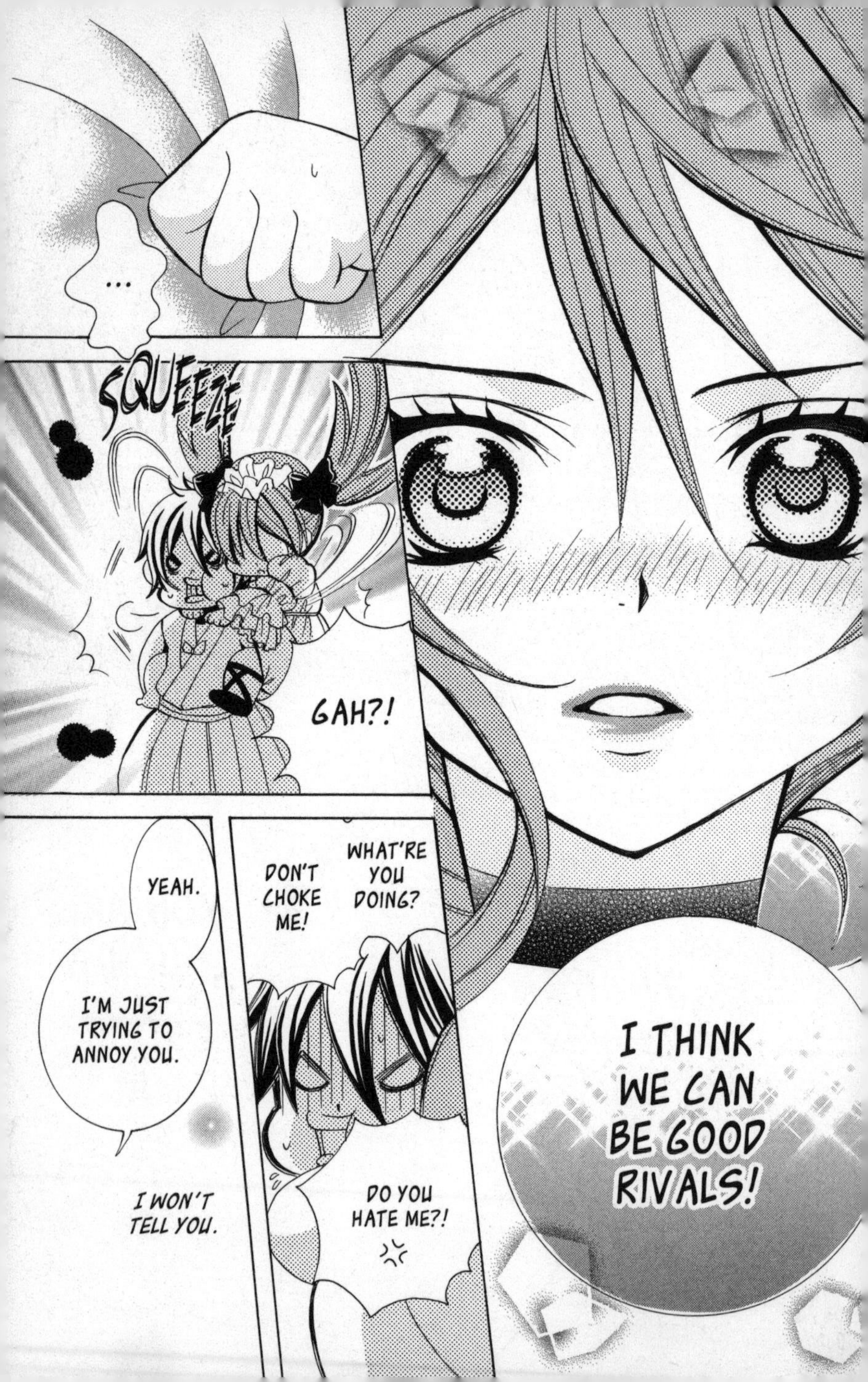
I THINK WE CAN BE GOOD RIVALS!
...
SQUEEZE
GAH?!
WHAT'RE YOU DOING?
DON'T CHOKE ME!
DO YOU HATE ME?!
YEAH.
I'M JUST TRYING TO ANNOY YOU.
I WON'T TELL YOU.

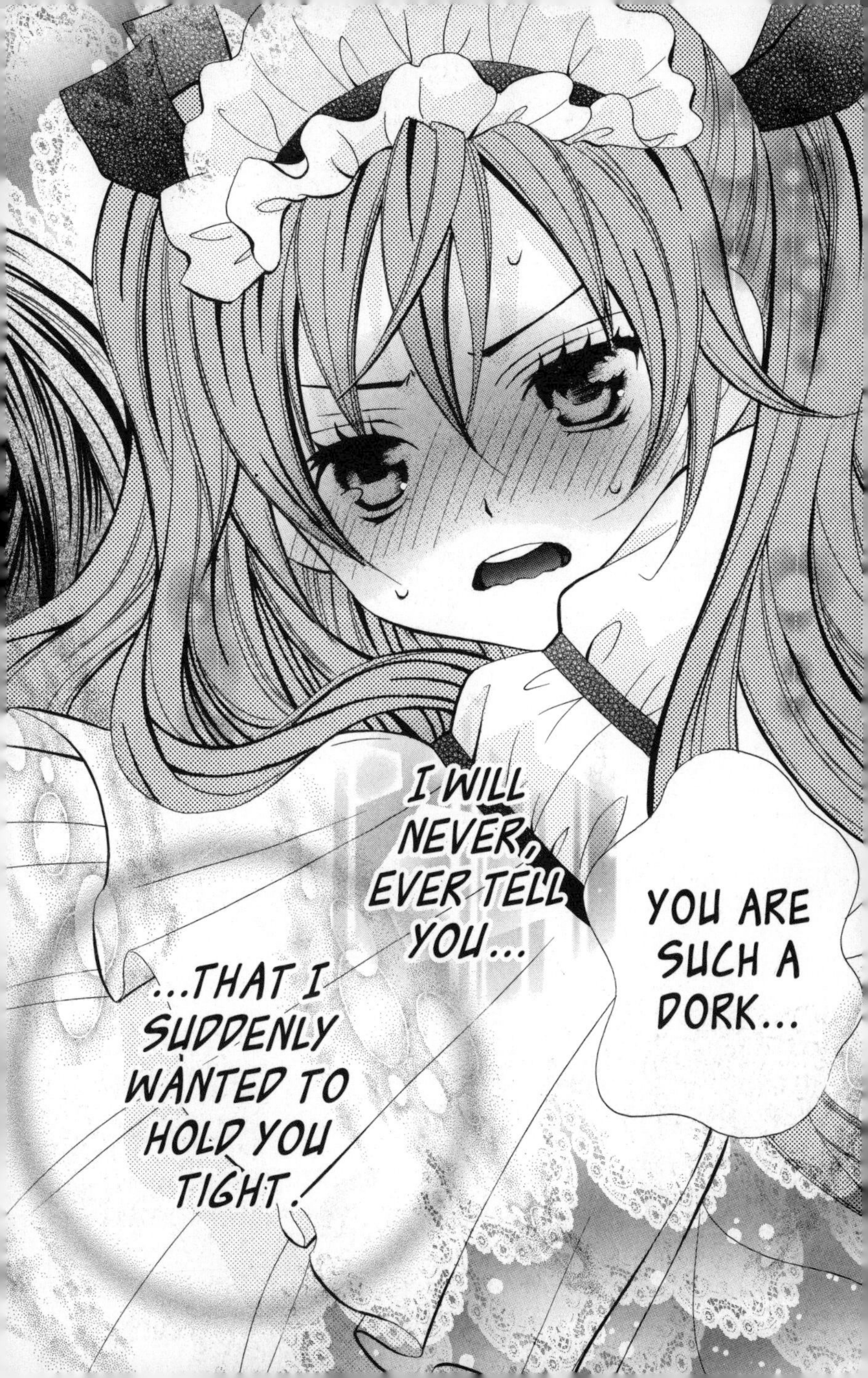
YOU ARE SUCH A DORK...
I WILL NEVER, EVER TELL YOU...
...THAT I SUDDENLY WANTED TO HOLD YOU TIGHT.

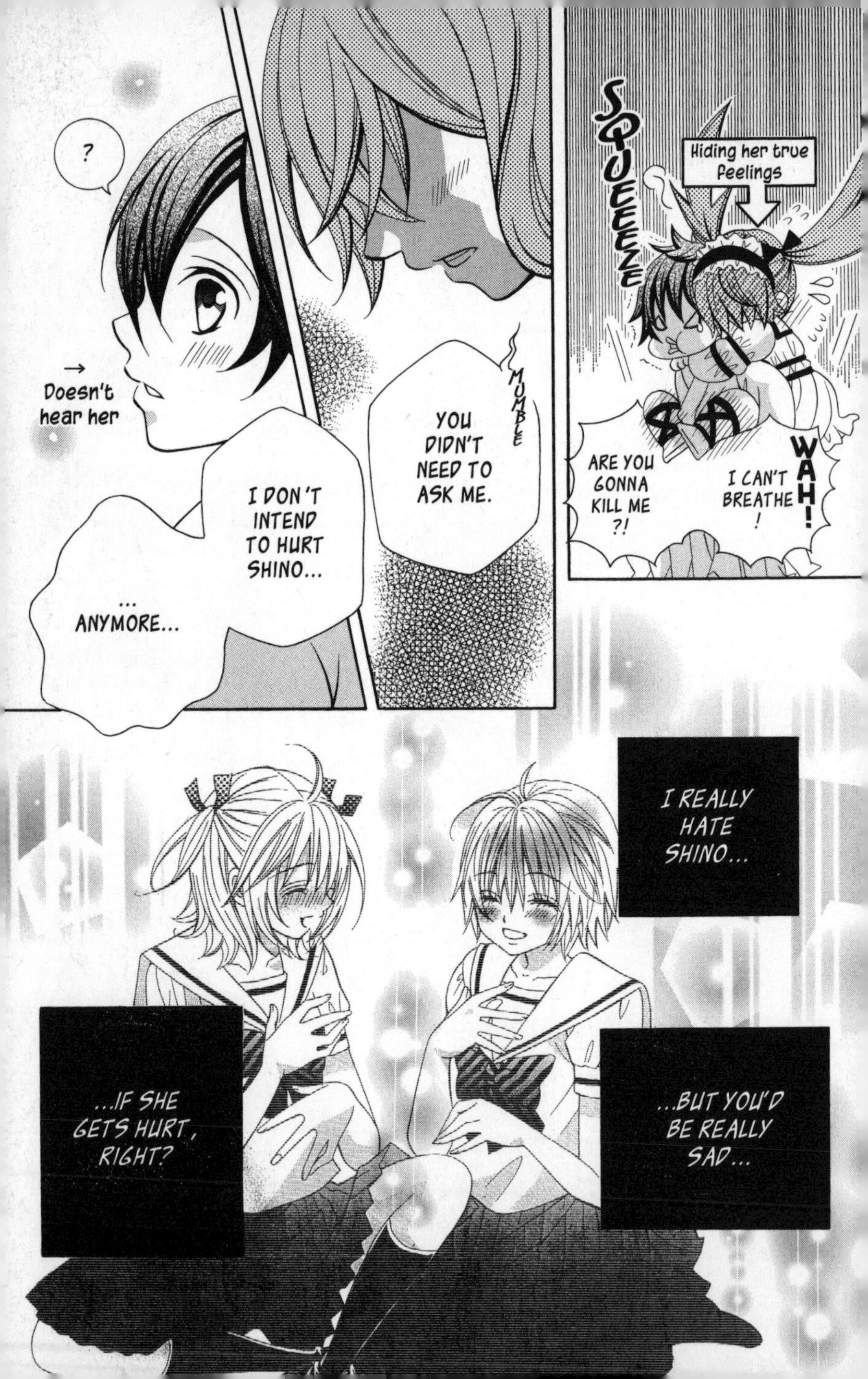
SQUEEEEZE
Hiding her true feelings
WAH!
I CAN'T BREATHE!
ARE YOU GONNA KILL ME?!
MUMBLE
YOU DIDN'T NEED TO ASK ME.
?
I DON'T INTEND TO HURT SHINO...
→ Doesn't hear her
... ANYMORE...
I REALLY HATE SHINO...
...BUT YOU'D BE REALLY SAD...
...IF SHE GETS HURT, RIGHT?

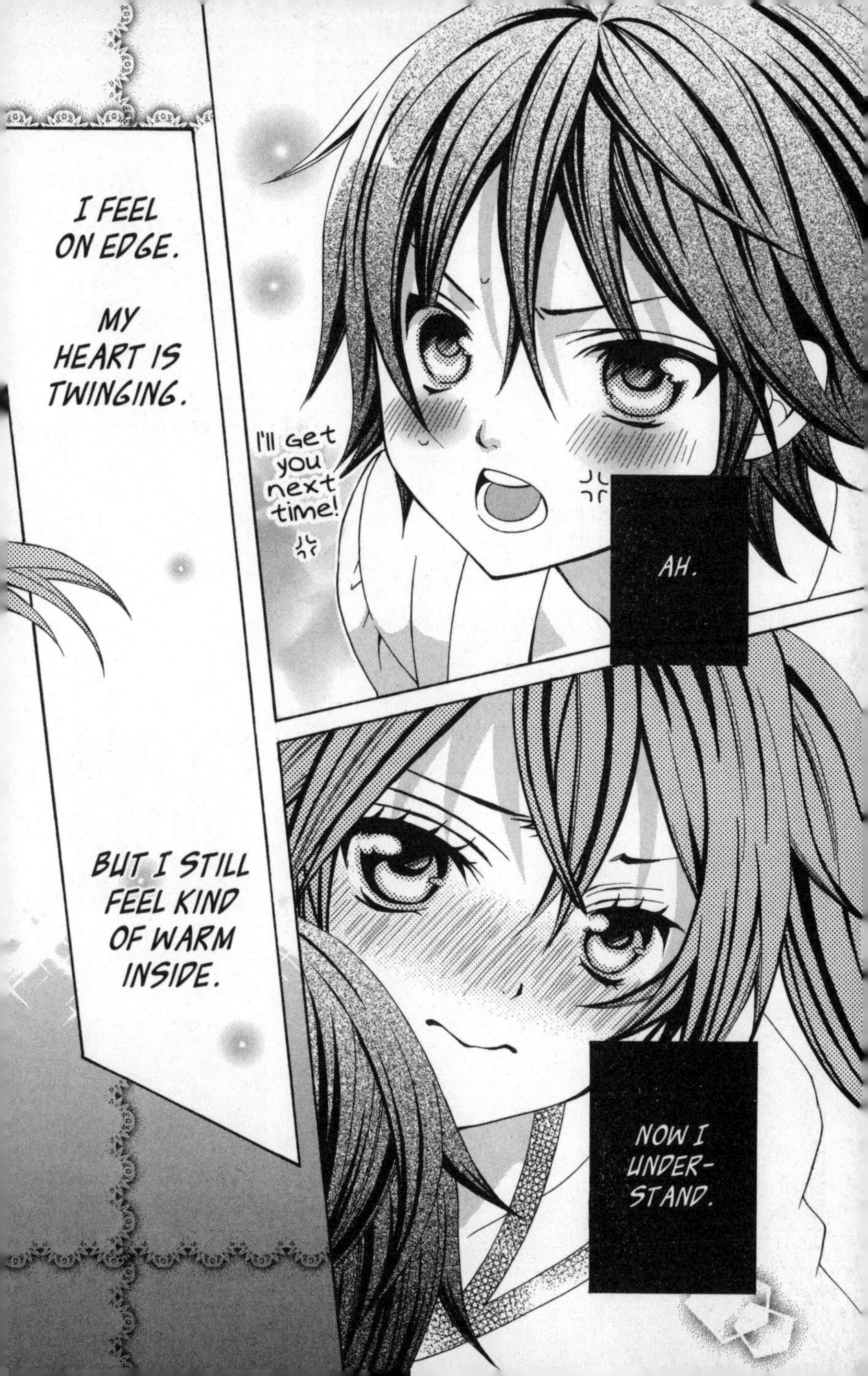
I'll get you next time!
AH.
NOW I UNDER-STAND.
I FEEL ON EDGE.
MY HEART IS TWINGING.
BUT I STILL FEEL KIND OF WARM INSIDE.

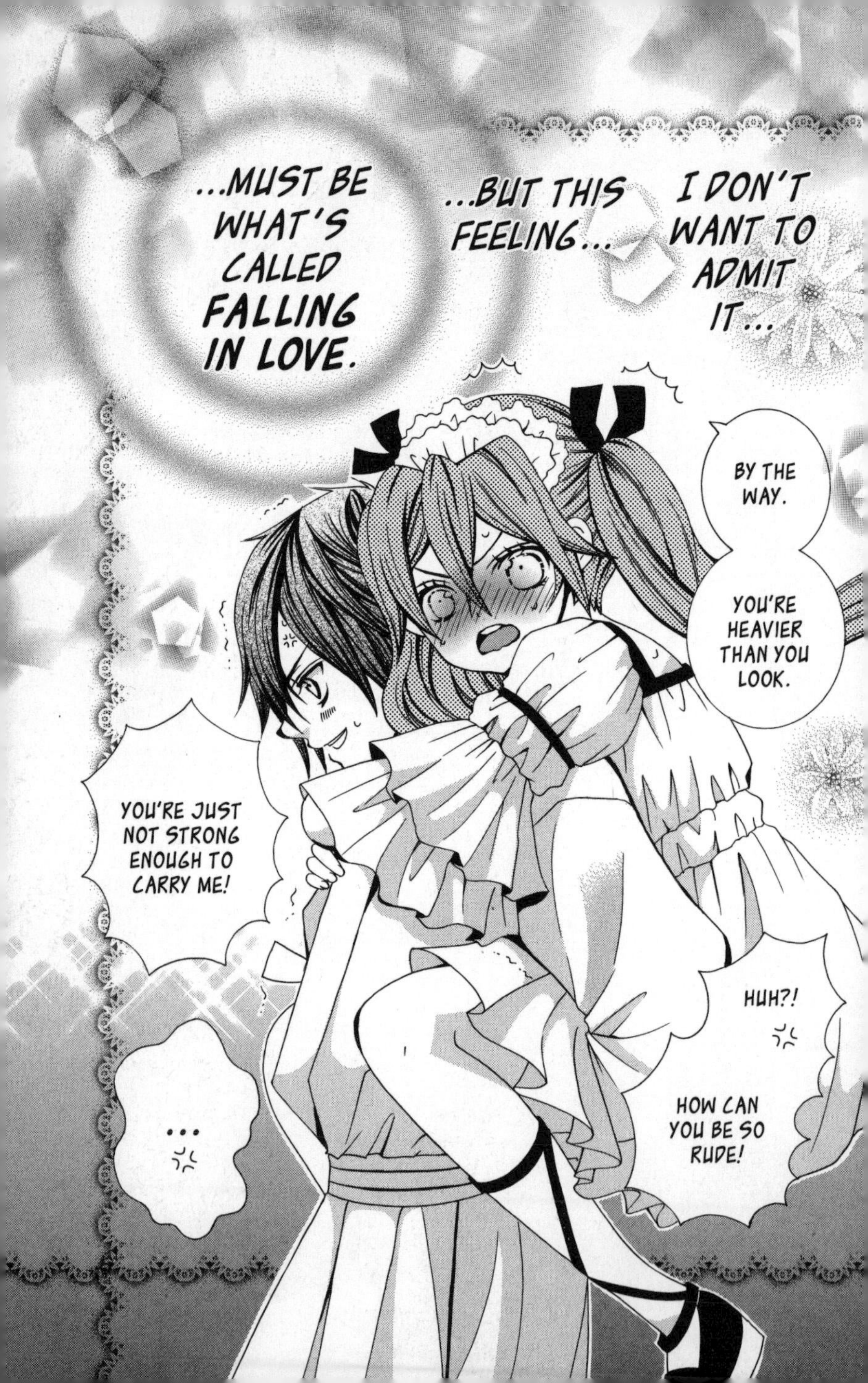
I DON'T WANT TO ADMIT IT...
...BUT THIS FEELING...
...MUST BE WHAT'S CALLED FALLING IN LOVE.
BY THE WAY.
YOU'RE HEAVIER THAN YOU LOOK.
YOU'RE JUST NOT STRONG ENOUGH TO CARRY ME!
HUH?!
HOW CAN YOU BE SO RUDE!
...

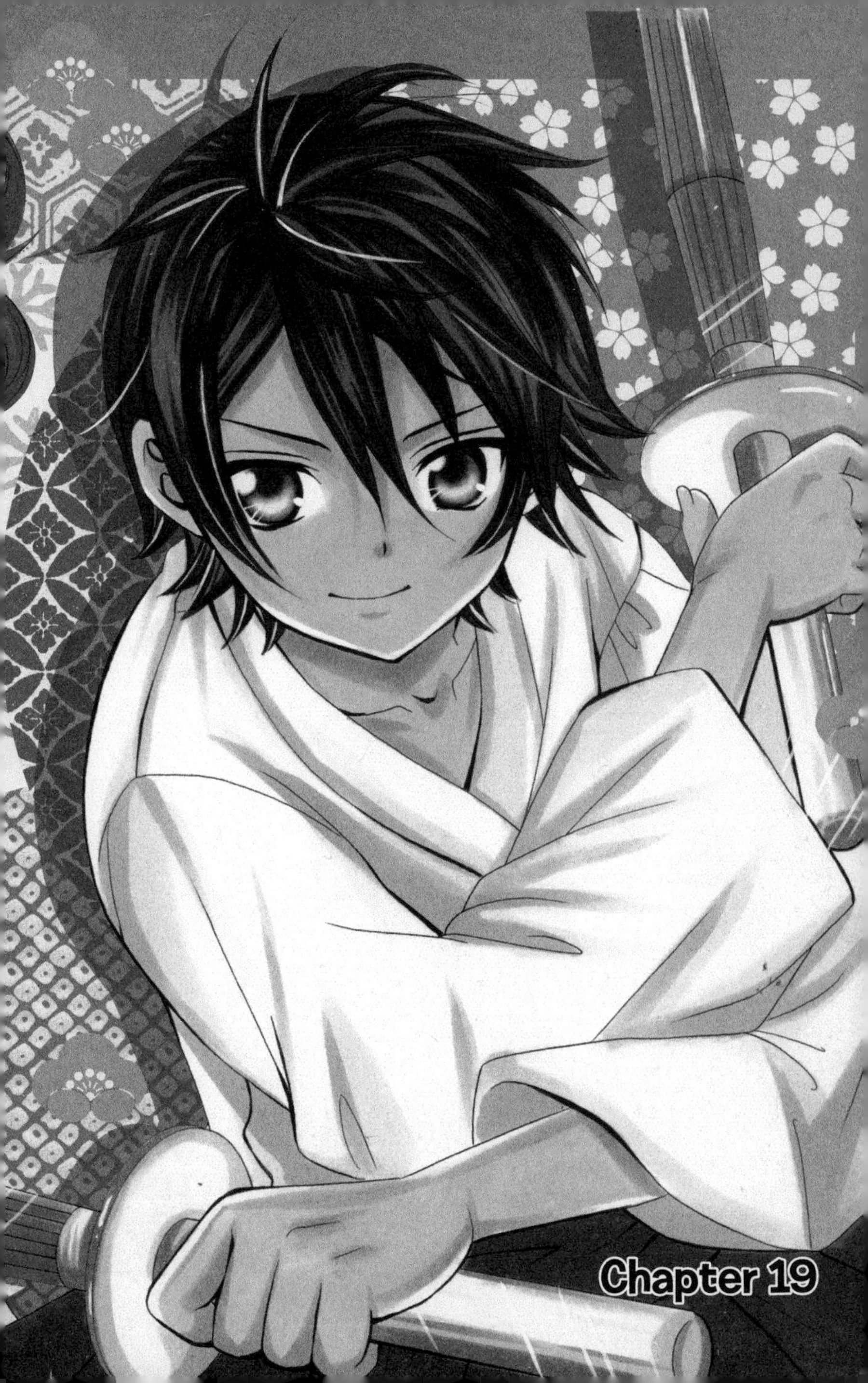
Chapter 19

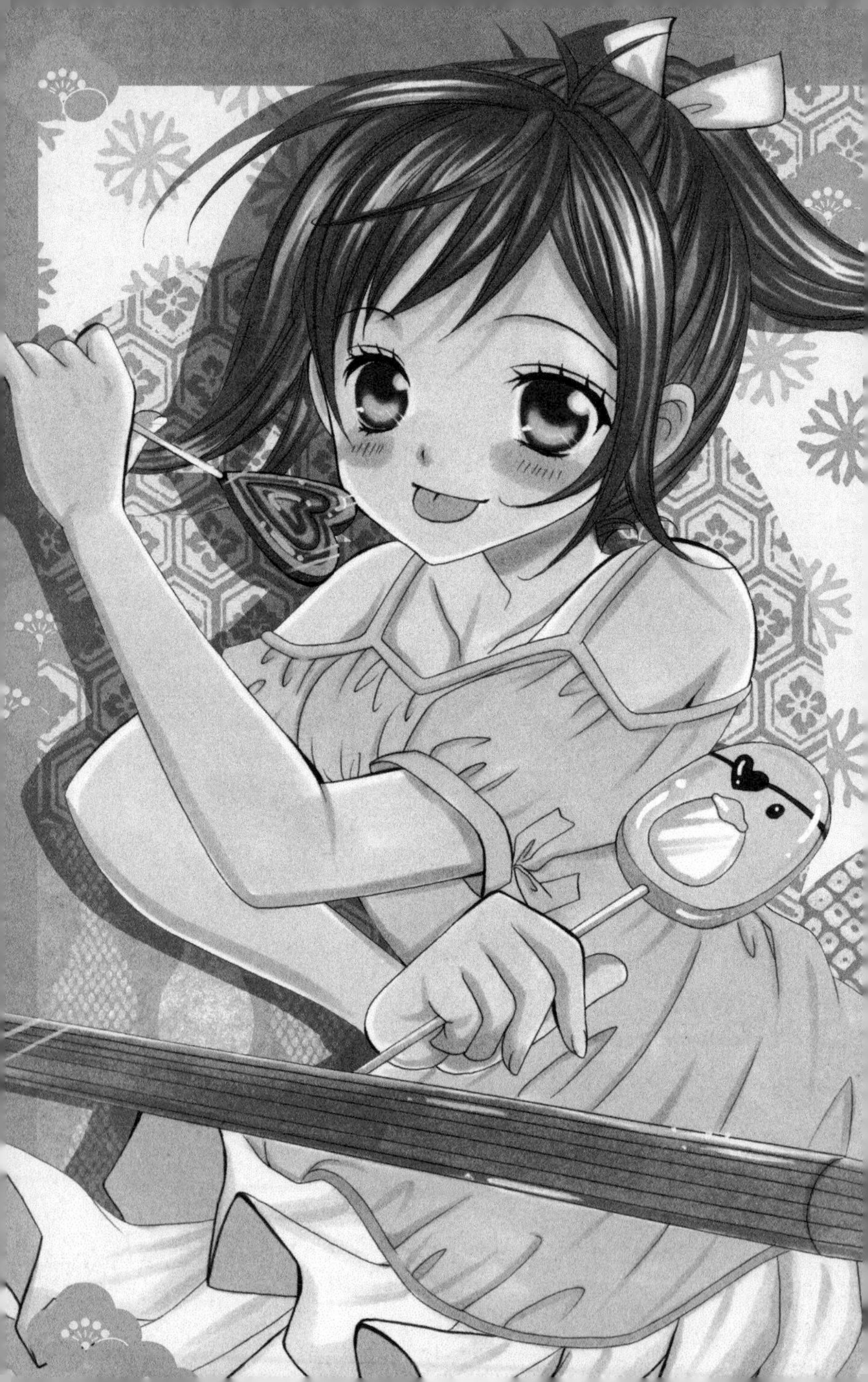

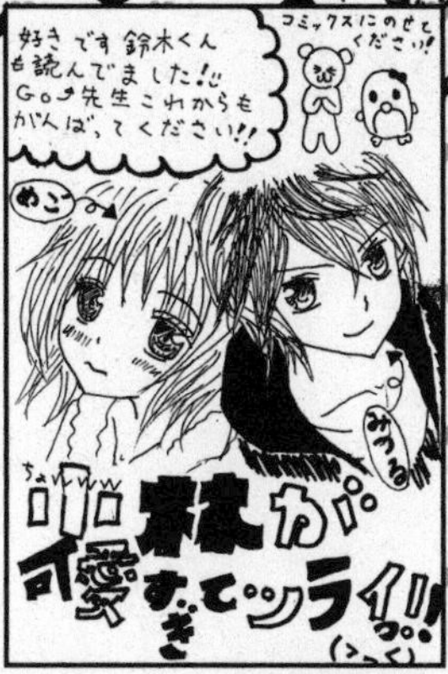

好きです鈴木くんも読んでました!! Go先生これからもがんばってください!!
コミックスにのせてください!!
めごーみ
みつる
小林が可愛すぎてツライ!!

Aachan (Aichi)
←
Editor: *So Cute!* is doing great thanks to all of you. ♪

Shiho Hoshino (Fukuoka) →
Editor: M-Mego's wearing an eye patch?! ((;゚Д゚) Woo.

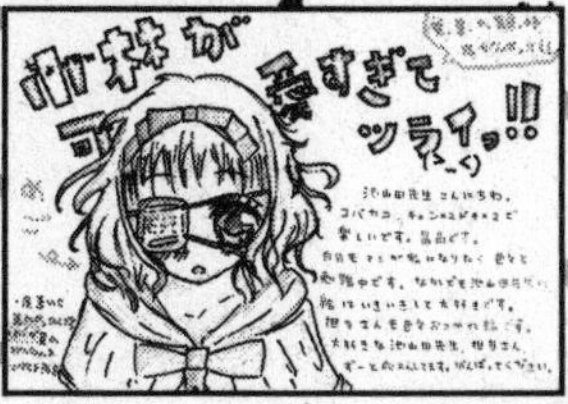

小林が可愛すぎてツライっ!!

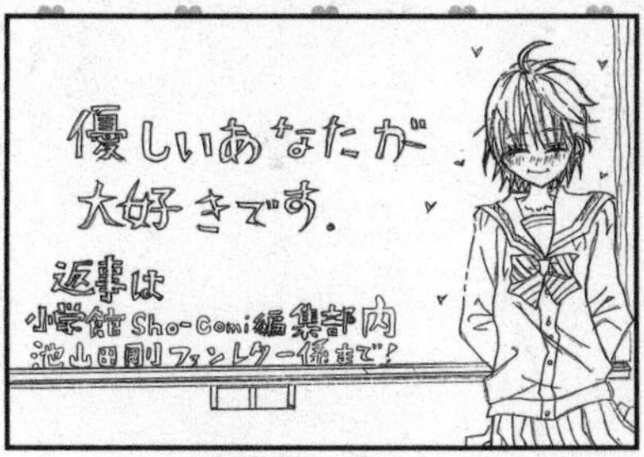

優しいあなたが大好きです。
返事は
小学館Sho-Comi編集部内
池山田剛ファンレター係まで!

Tomomi Ishii (Hyogo) ↑
Editor: The great scene when Shino's and Mitsuru's hearts touch! Shino's such a nice girl...(T_T)

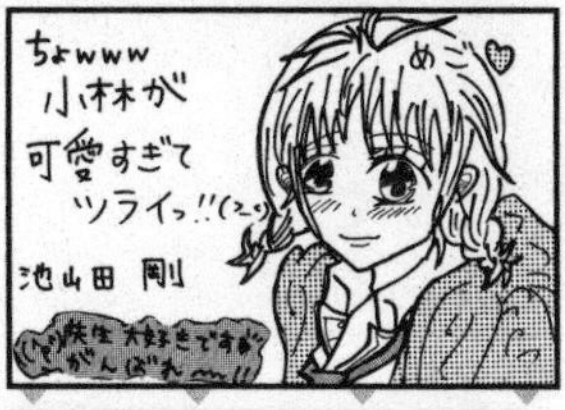

ちょwww
小林が可愛すぎてツライっ!!
めご
池山田 剛

Yuika Matsuda (Nara)
←
Editor: Mego looks cute in braids too!!

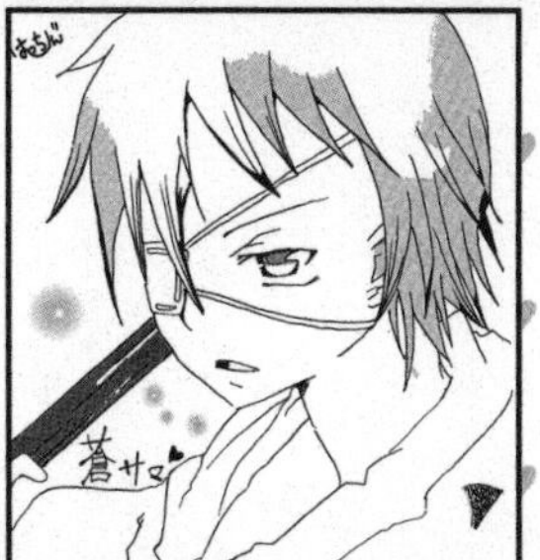

蒼サマ
Go先生
Go先生のかく男の子がカッコ良すぎて大好きです
Go先生これからも頑張って下さい!

↑ Haru Aoki (Hokkaido)
Editor: Here's Aoi holding a bamboo sword!!!! Just as you'd expect from Akechi High's #1!

↓ Kuuchan (Kyoto)
Editor: Mitsuru needs red ribbons when he's cross-dressed. ♪

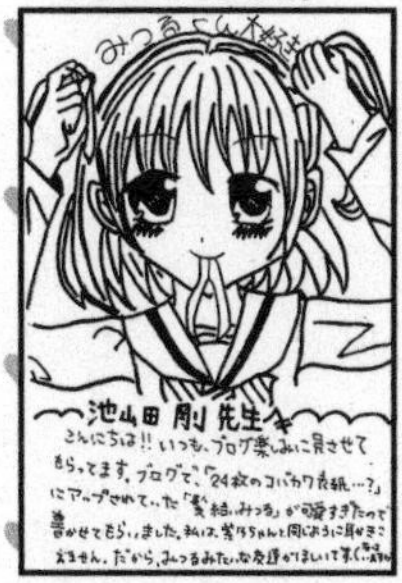

池山田剛先生

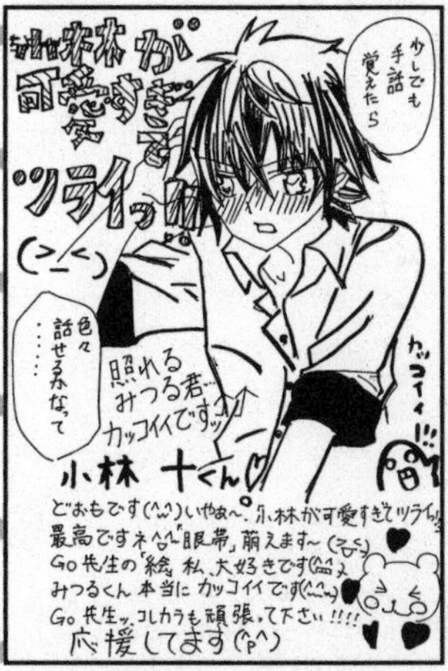

小林が可愛すぎてツライっ
少しでも手話覚えたら
色々話せるかなって
照れるみつる君カッコイイです
カッコイイ!!!
小林 十くん
Go先生っ、コレカラも頑張って下さい!!!!
応援してます

↑ Yurika (><) (Kanagawa)
Editor: Mitsuru looks great even when he's bashful!! For sure!!

Send your fan mail to:

Go Ikeyamada
c/o Shojo Beat
VIZ Media, LLC
P.O. Box 77010
San Francisco, CA
94107

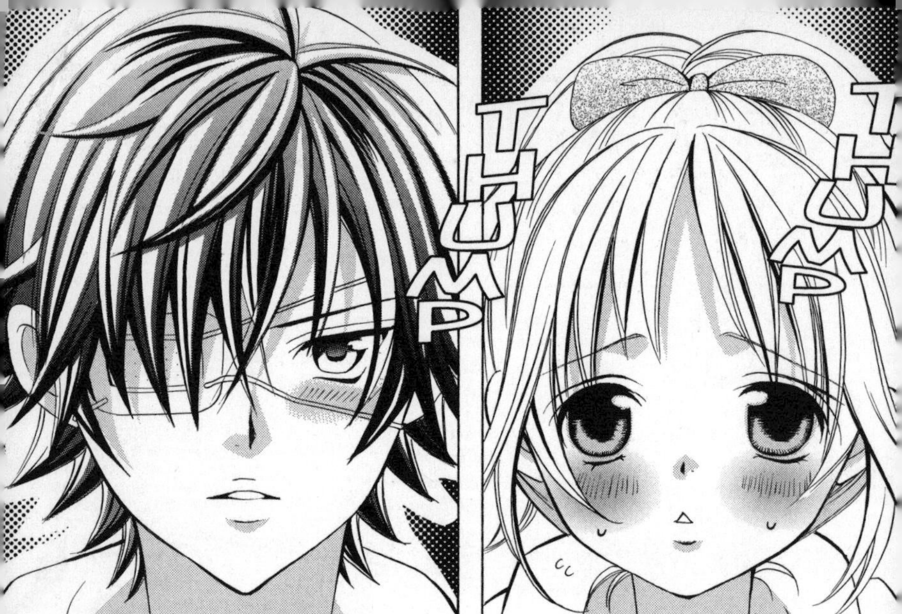
THUMP
SANADA ...
YOU REALLY DON'T MIND?
THUMP
I'M FINE.
IF IT'S WHAT YOU WANT...

Manga and Anime

My older brother and my best friend Yuka-san love *Attack on Titan*, so I read the first ten volumes in one sitting. The manga is so very intriguing! I kept being drawn into it. It's compelling and like watching a movie! Levi is so cool! LOL. I'm looking forward to the *Silver Spoon* anime every week as well. ♡♡

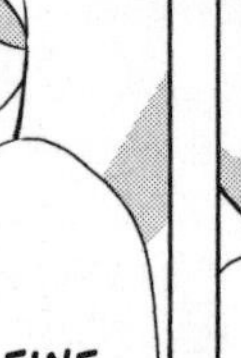

I love the new *Inazuma Eleven GO! Galaxy* anime and the third season of *Vanguard* ♪♪
I'm wondering what'll happen to Kai-kun. (>_<)
Ren-sama is so cool!
And the details about *Sengoku BASARA 4* have finally been announced!
I'm looking forward to playing the game as Sakon-san, one of the new characters who is soooo good-looking. ♡♡ I'm also happy Masamune-sama, my #1 favorite, seems to be the lead once again. ♡♡
Looking at the official site makes me so excited. LOL. ♪♪

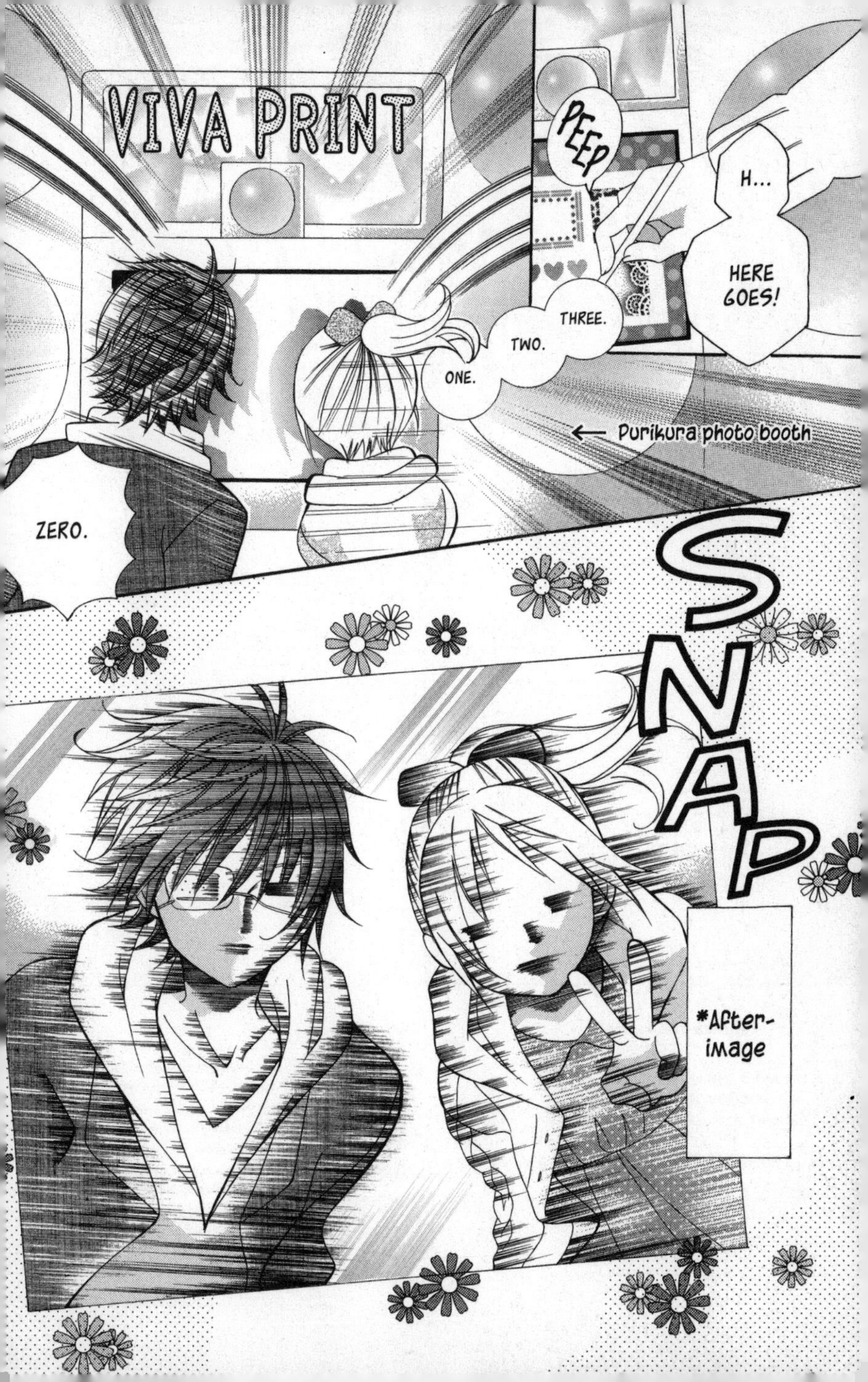
PEEP
H... HERE GOES!
THREE.
TWO.
ONE.
← Purikura photo booth
VIVA PRINT
ZERO.
SNAP
*After-image

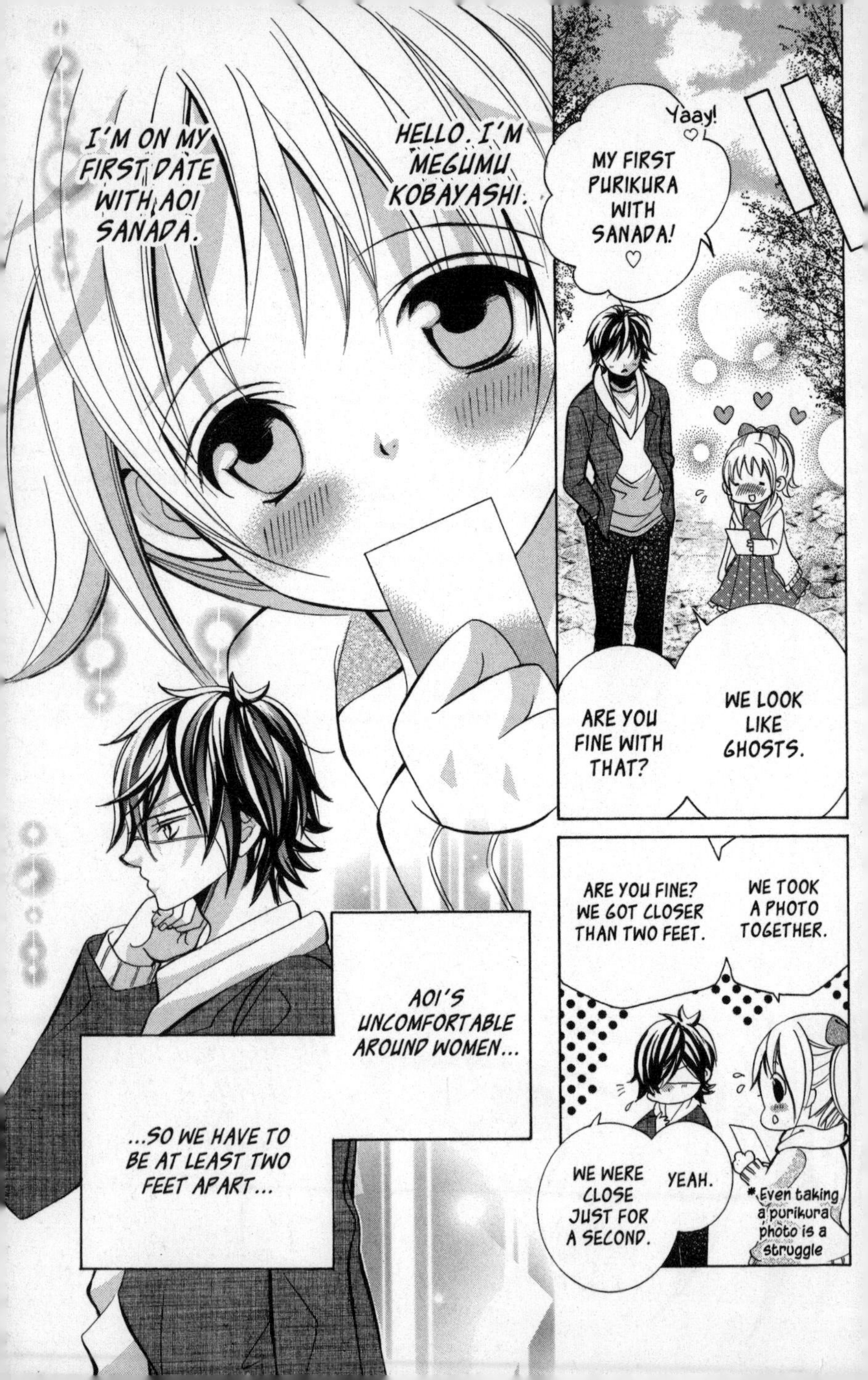

Yaay!
MY FIRST PURIKURA WITH SANADA!
WE LOOK LIKE GHOSTS.
ARE YOU FINE WITH THAT?
WE TOOK A PHOTO TOGETHER.
ARE YOU FINE? WE GOT CLOSER THAN TWO FEET.
YEAH.
WE WERE CLOSE JUST FOR A SECOND.
*Even taking a purikura photo is a struggle
HELLO. I'M MEGUMU KOBAYASHI.
I'M ON MY FIRST DATE WITH AOI SANADA.
AOI'S UNCOMFORTABLE AROUND WOMEN...
...SO WE HAVE TO BE AT LEAST TWO FEET APART...

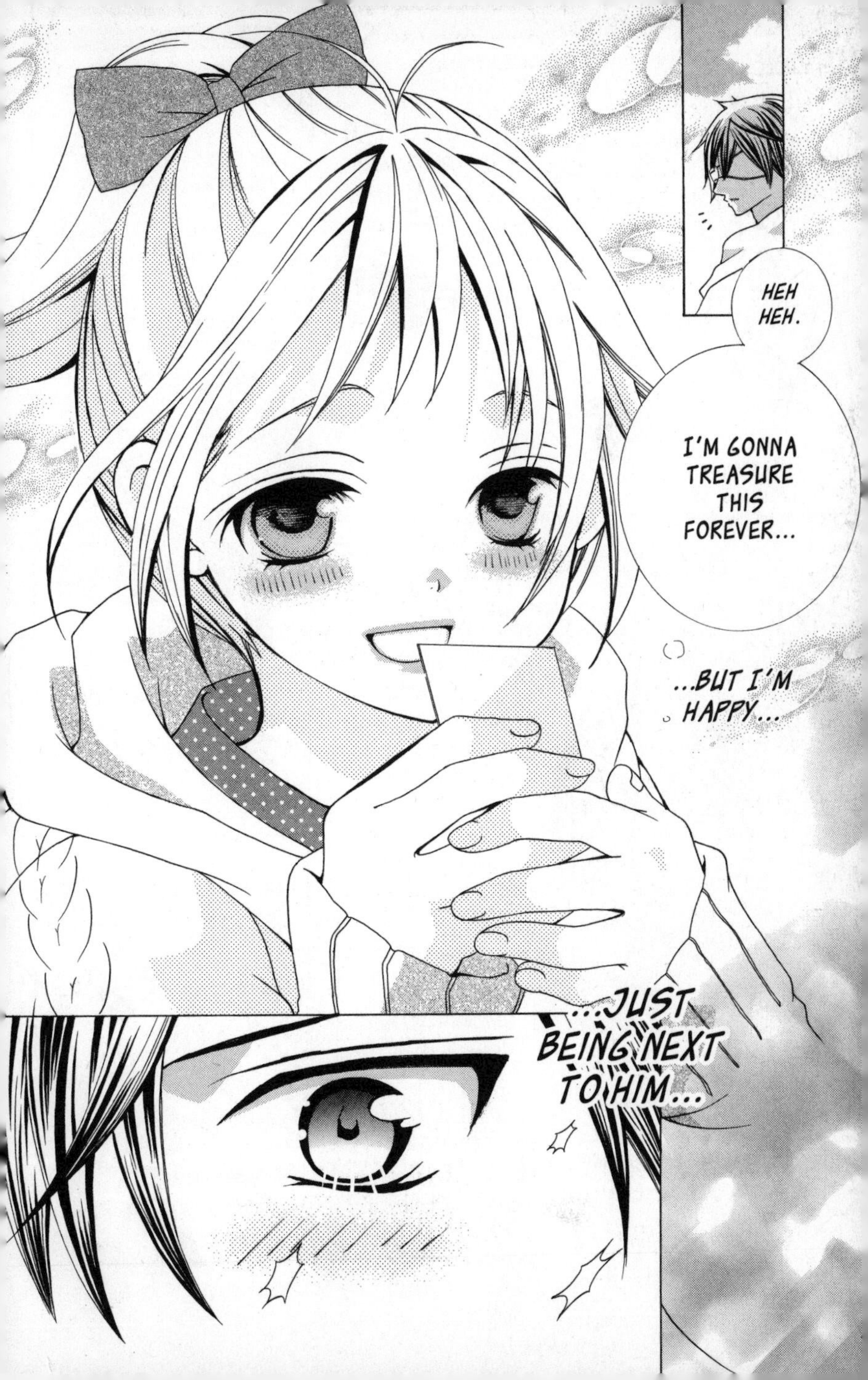
HEH HEH.
I'M GONNA TREASURE THIS FOREVER...
...BUT I'M HAPPY...
...JUST BEING NEXT TO HIM...

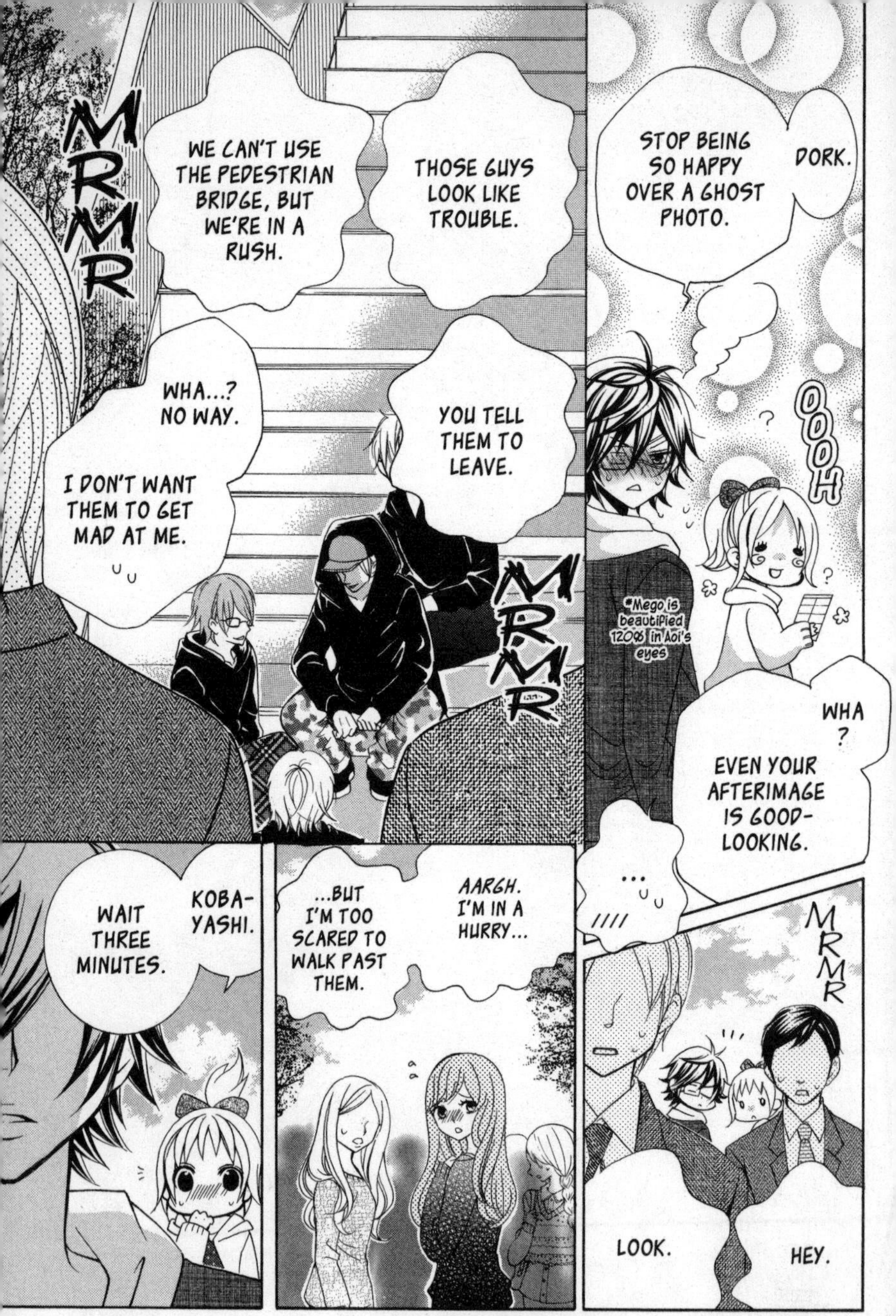
DORK.
STOP BEING SO HAPPY OVER A GHOST PHOTO.
OOOH
*Mego is beautified 120% in Aoi's eyes
WHA?
EVEN YOUR AFTERIMAGE IS GOOD-LOOKING.
THOSE GUYS LOOK LIKE TROUBLE.
WE CAN'T USE THE PEDESTRIAN BRIDGE, BUT WE'RE IN A RUSH.
MRMR
YOU TELL THEM TO LEAVE.
WHA...? NO WAY.
I DON'T WANT THEM TO GET MAD AT ME.
MRMR
...
MRMR
HEY.
LOOK.
AARGH. I'M IN A HURRY...
...BUT I'M TOO SCARED TO WALK PAST THEM.
KOBAYASHI.
WAIT THREE MINUTES.

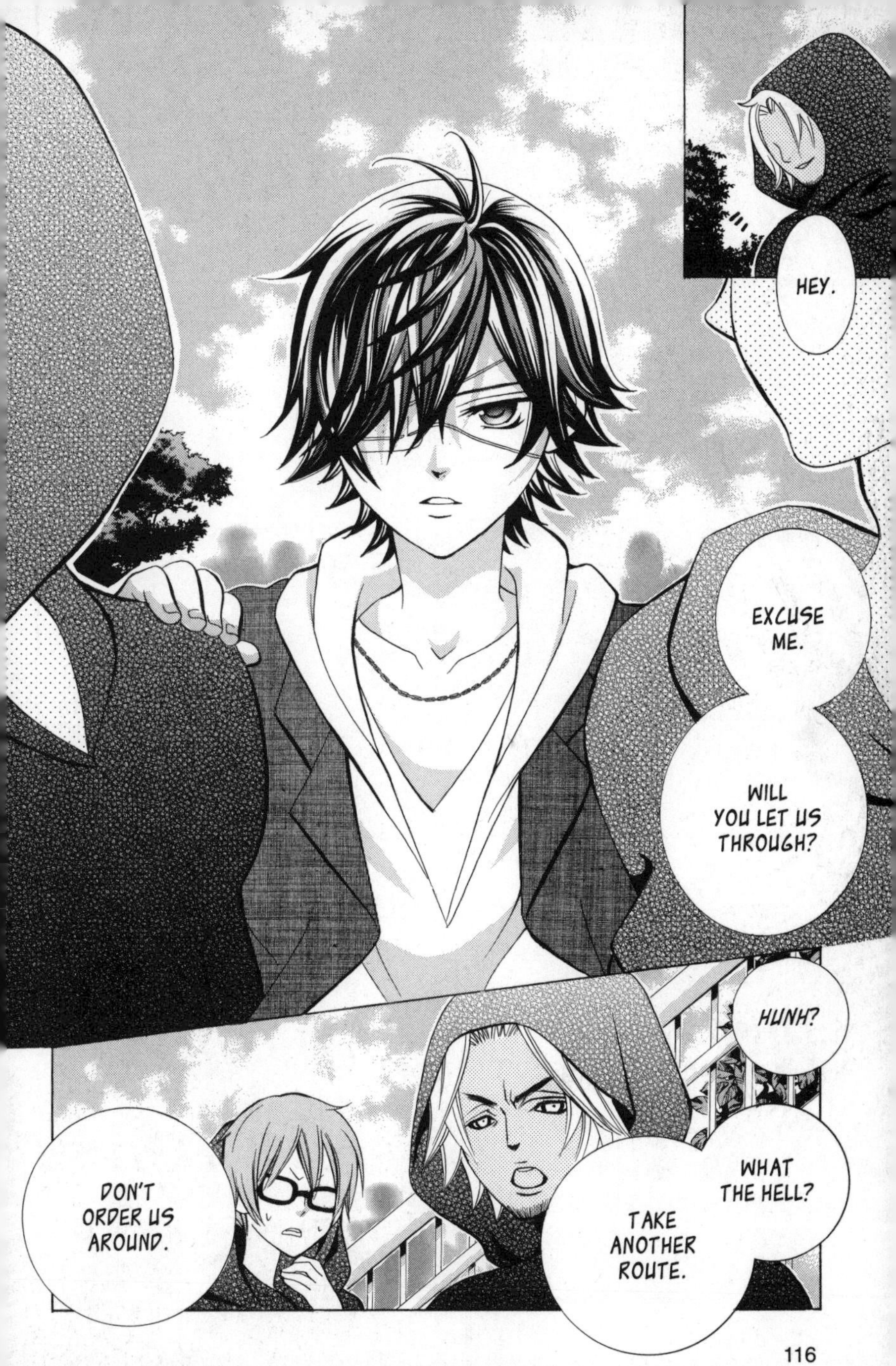
HEY.
EXCUSE ME.
WILL YOU LET US THROUGH?
HUNH?
WHAT THE HELL?
TAKE ANOTHER ROUTE.
DON'T ORDER US AROUND.

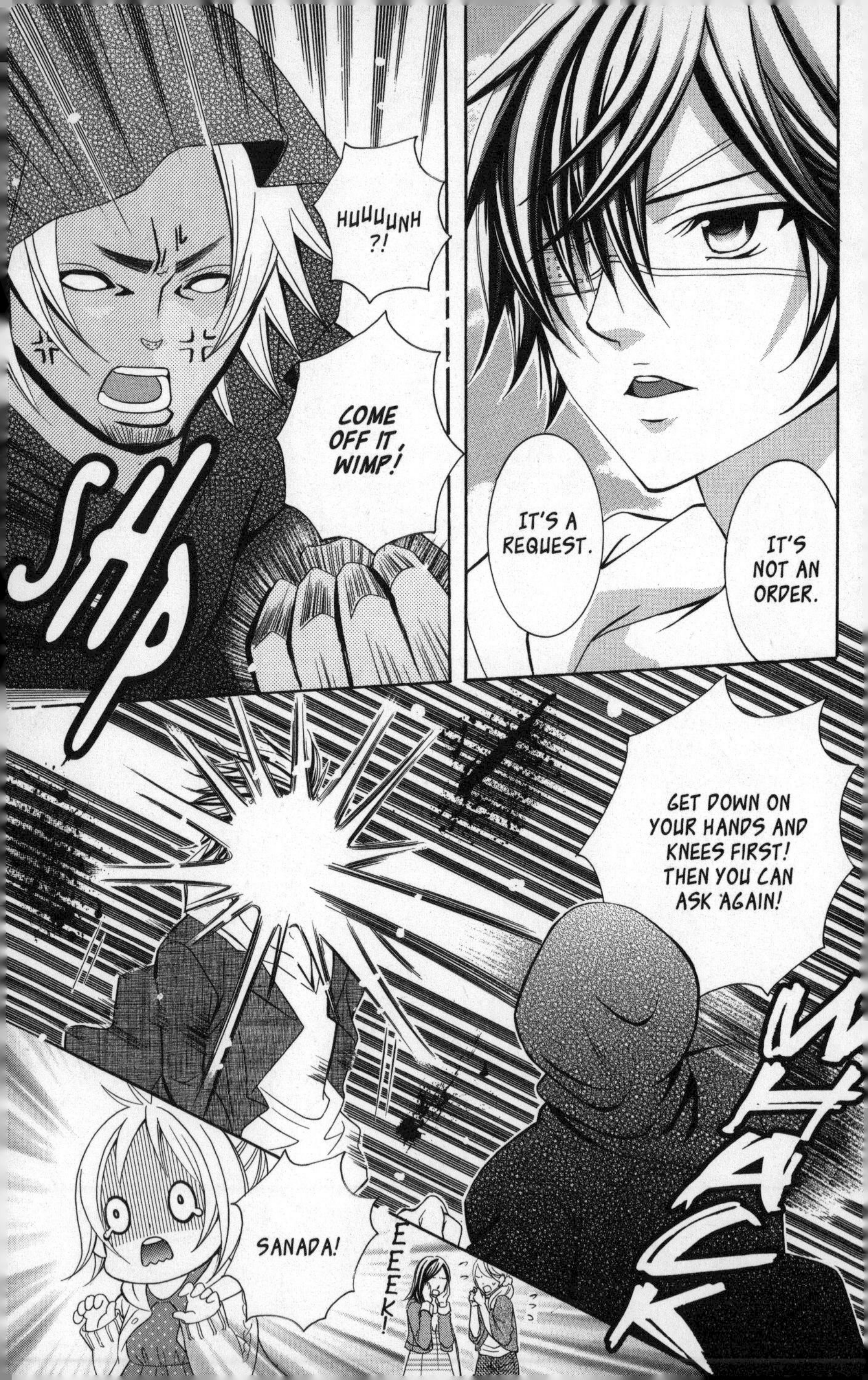
IT'S NOT AN ORDER.
IT'S A REQUEST.
HUUUUNH ?!
COME OFF IT, WIMP!
SHP
GET DOWN ON YOUR HANDS AND KNEES FIRST! THEN YOU CAN ASK AGAIN!
WHACK
EEEEK!
SANADA!

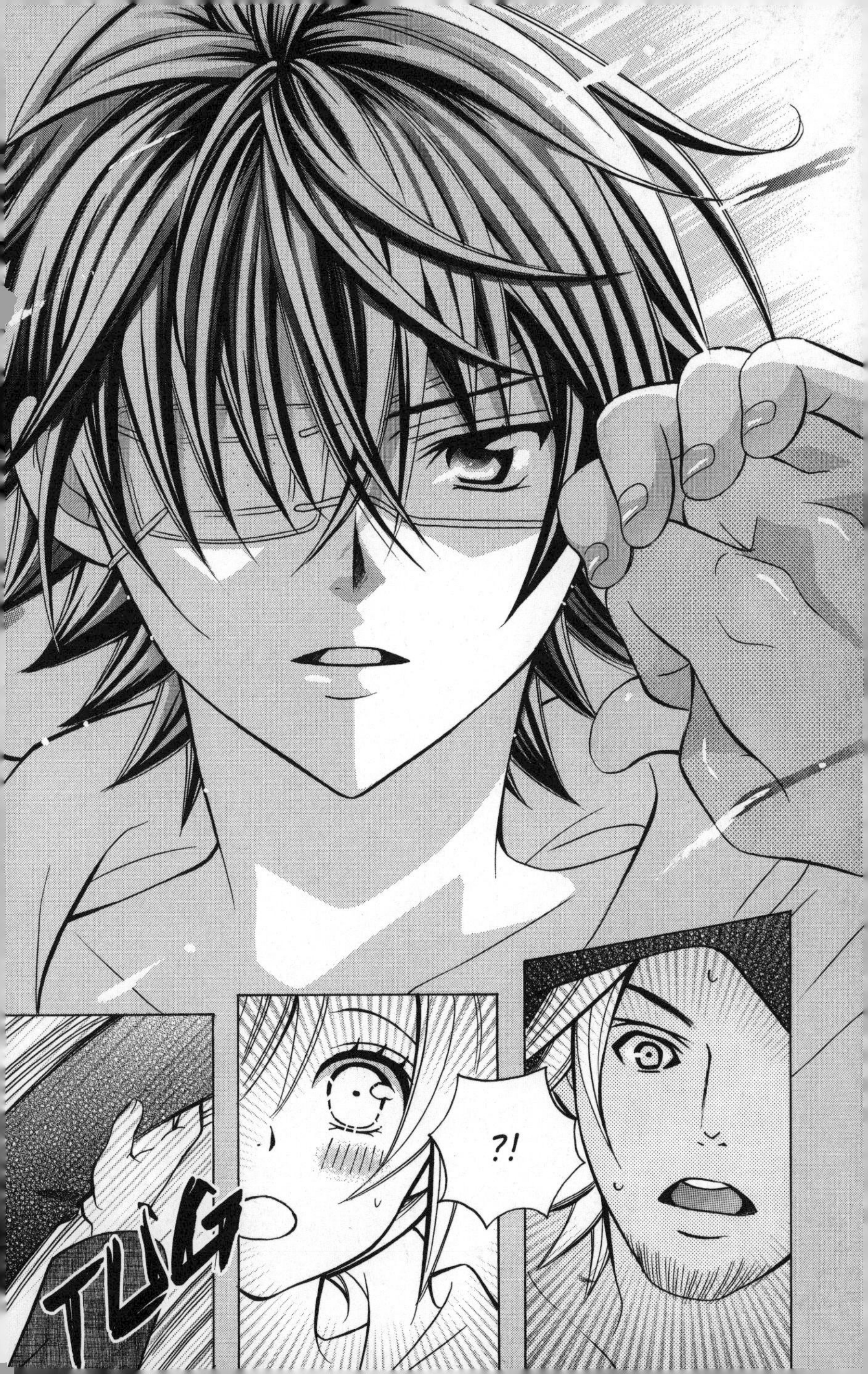
?!
TUG

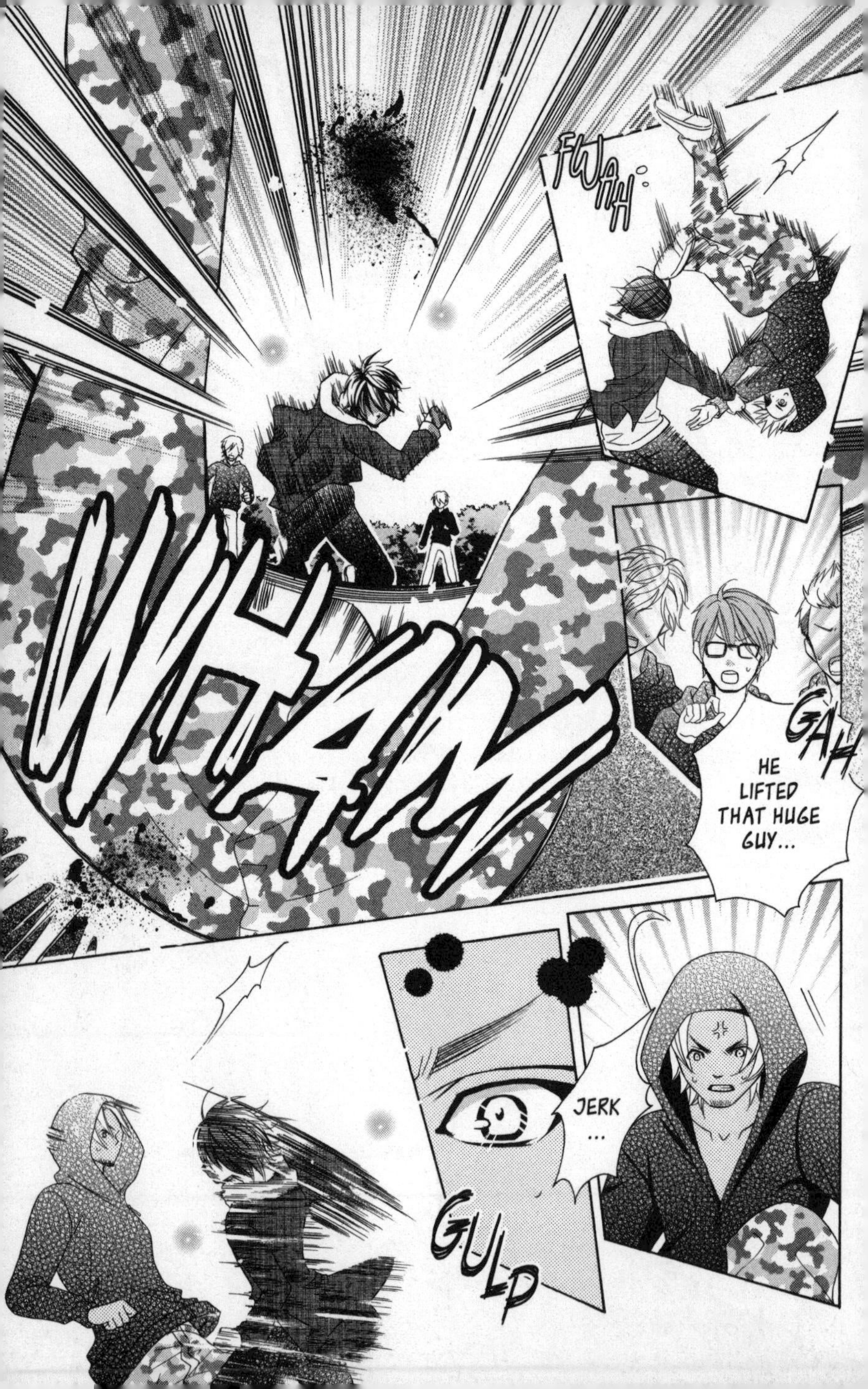
FWAH
GAH
HE LIFTED THAT HUGE GUY...
WHAM
JERK...
GULP

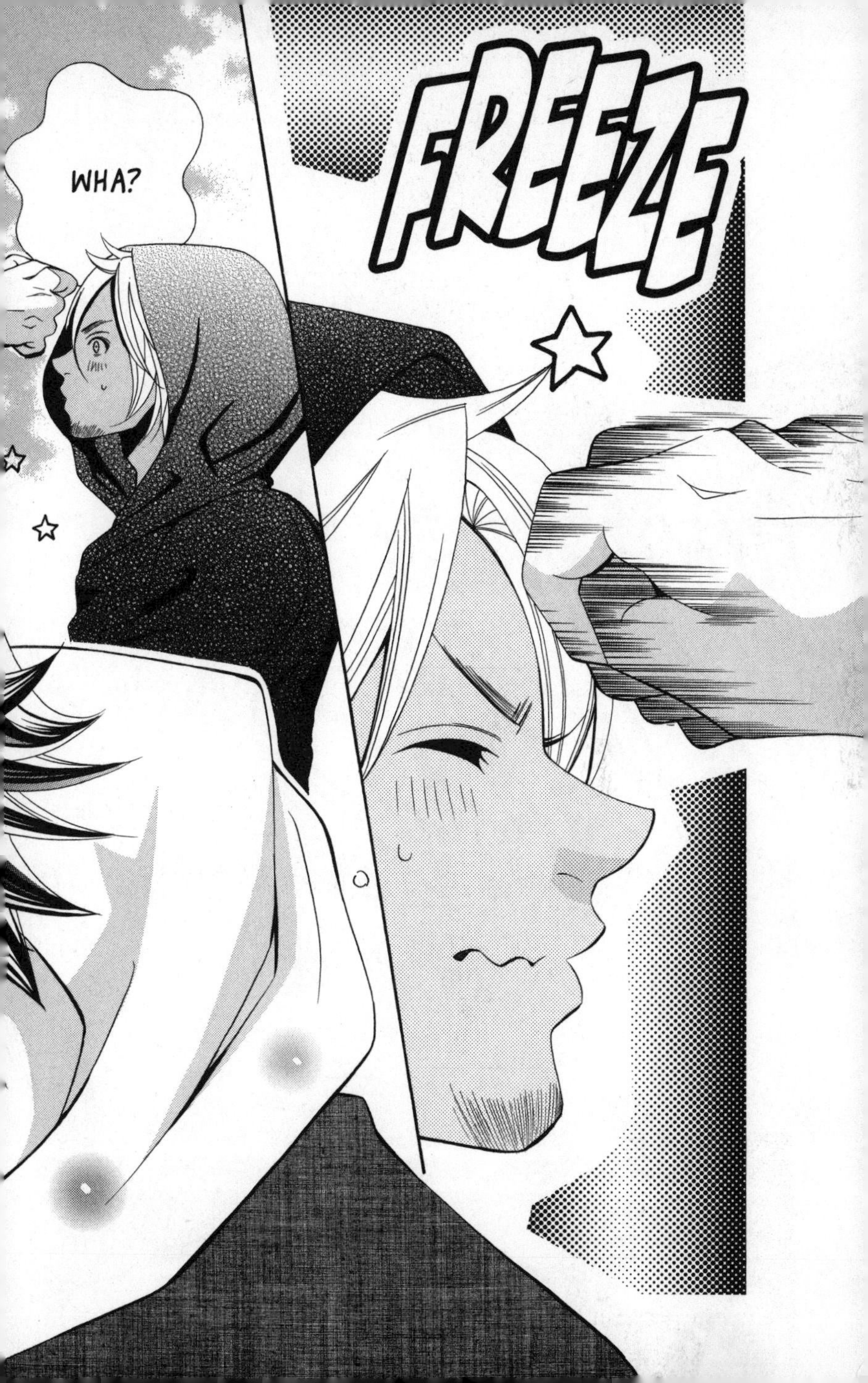
FREEZE
WHA?

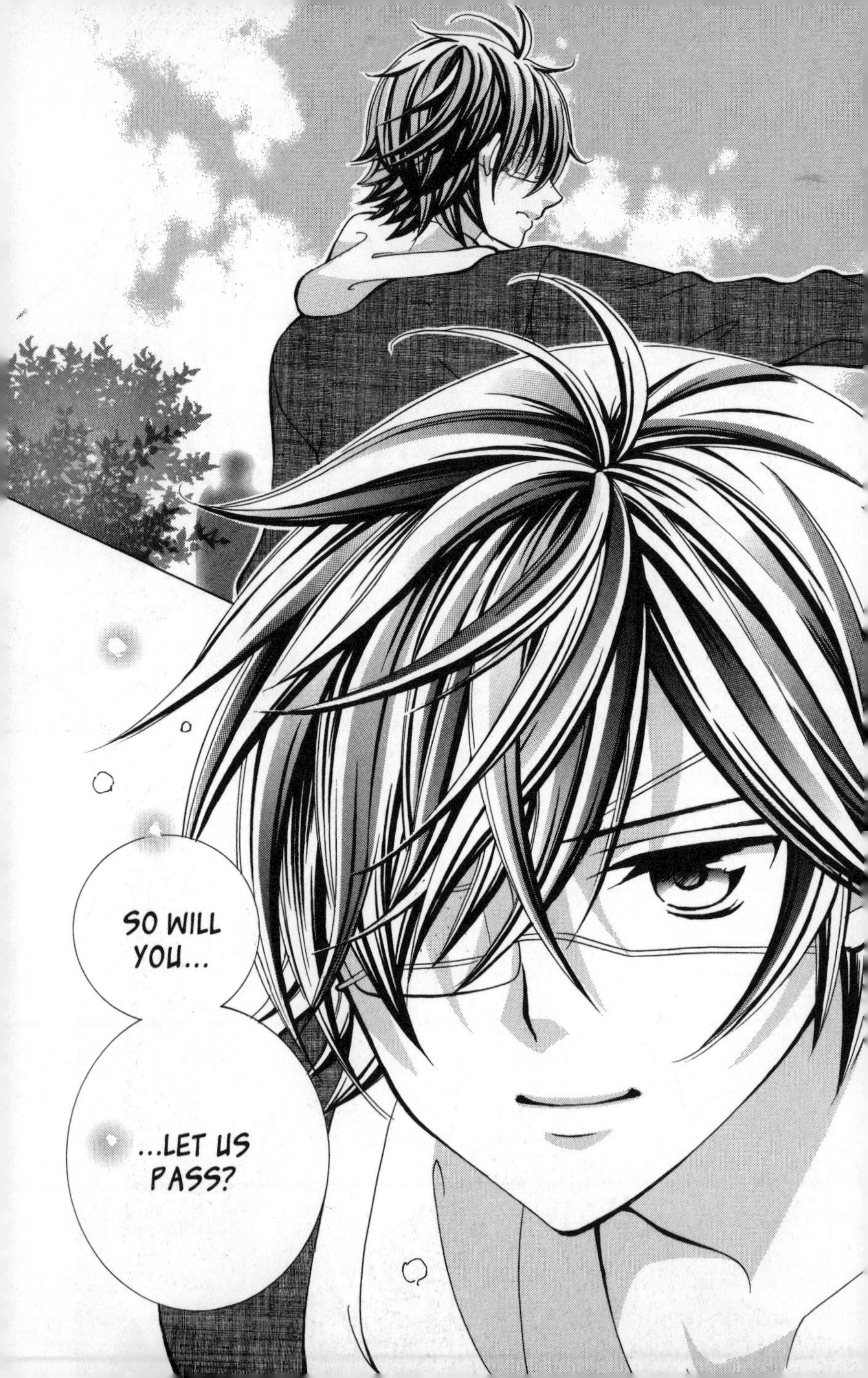
SO WILL YOU...
...LET US PASS?

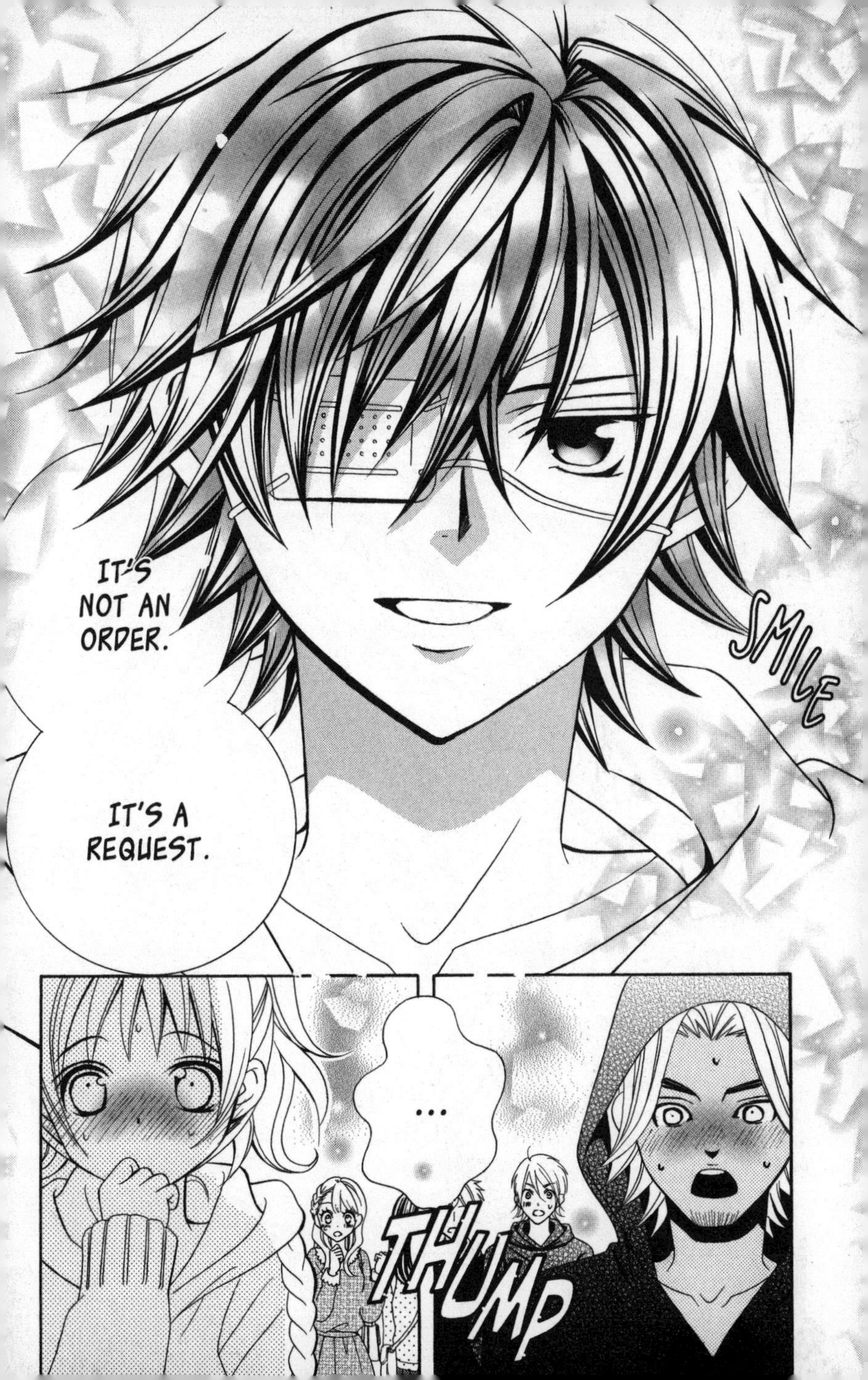
IT'S NOT AN ORDER.
IT'S A REQUEST.
SMILE
...
THUMP

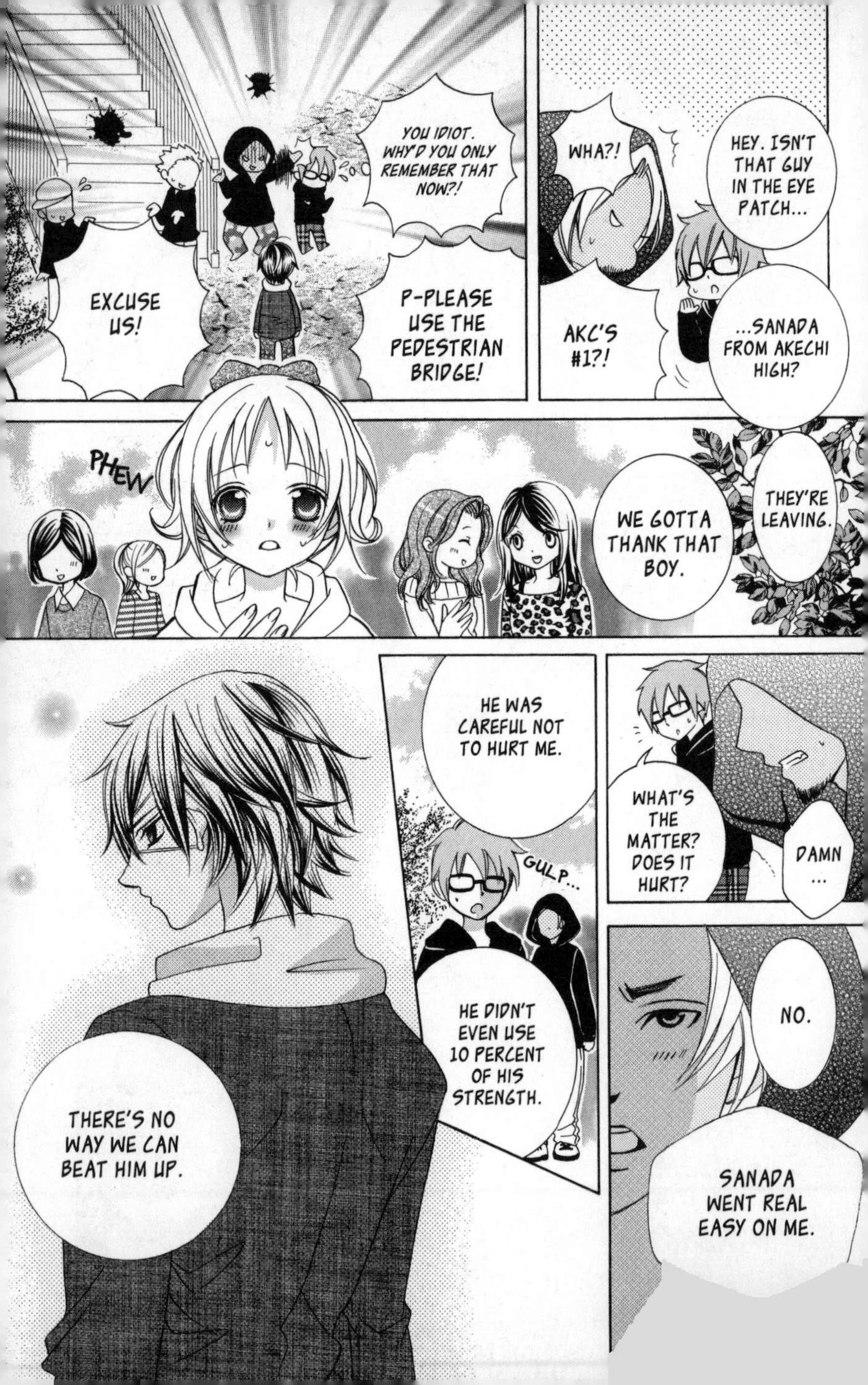
HEY. ISN'T THAT GUY IN THE EYE PATCH...
WHA?!
...SANADA FROM AKECHI HIGH?
AKC'S #1?!
YOU IDIOT. WHY'D YOU ONLY REMEMBER THAT NOW?!
P-PLEASE USE THE PEDESTRIAN BRIDGE!
EXCUSE US!
THEY'RE LEAVING.
WE GOTTA THANK THAT BOY.
PHEW
DAMN ...
WHAT'S THE MATTER? DOES IT HURT?
NO.
SANADA WENT REAL EASY ON ME.
HE WAS CAREFUL NOT TO HURT ME.
GULP...
HE DIDN'T EVEN USE 10 PERCENT OF HIS STRENGTH.
THERE'S NO WAY WE CAN BEAT HIM UP.

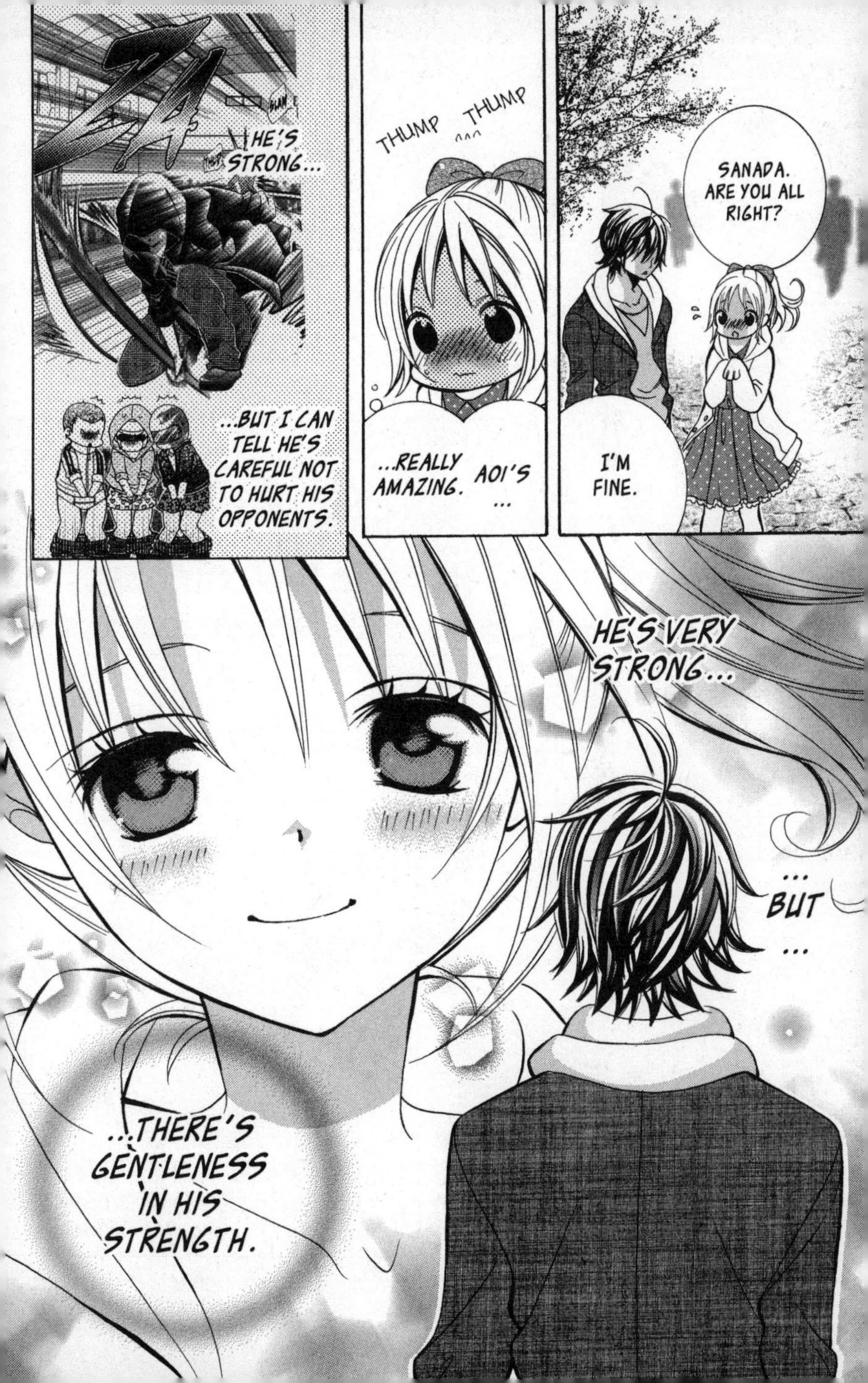
SANADA. ARE YOU ALL RIGHT?
I'M FINE.
THUMP THUMP
AOI'S ...
...REALLY AMAZING.
ZA
SLAM
HE'S STRONG...
...BUT I CAN TELL HE'S CAREFUL NOT TO HURT HIS OPPONENTS.
HE'S VERY STRONG...
...BUT...
...THERE'S GENTLENESS IN HIS STRENGTH.

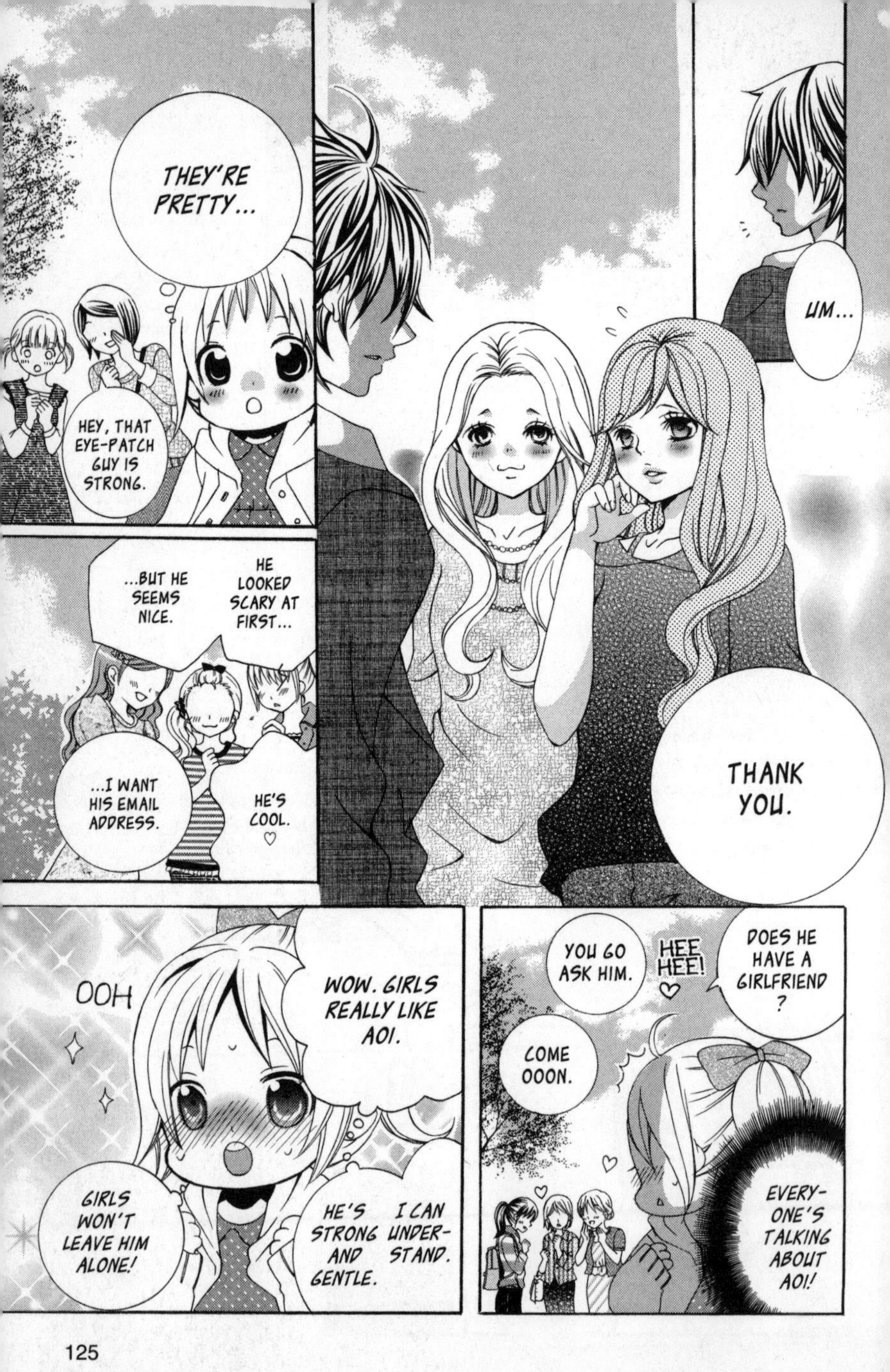
UM...
THANK YOU.
THEY'RE PRETTY...
HEY, THAT EYE-PATCH GUY IS STRONG.
HE LOOKED SCARY AT FIRST...
...BUT HE SEEMS NICE.
HE'S COOL. ♡
...I WANT HIS EMAIL ADDRESS.
DOES HE HAVE A GIRLFRIEND?
HEE HEE! ♡
YOU GO ASK HIM.
COME OOON.
EVERY-ONE'S TALKING ABOUT AOI!
WOW. GIRLS REALLY LIKE AOI.
OOH
I CAN UNDER-STAND.
HE'S STRONG AND GENTLE.
GIRLS WON'T LEAVE HIM ALONE!

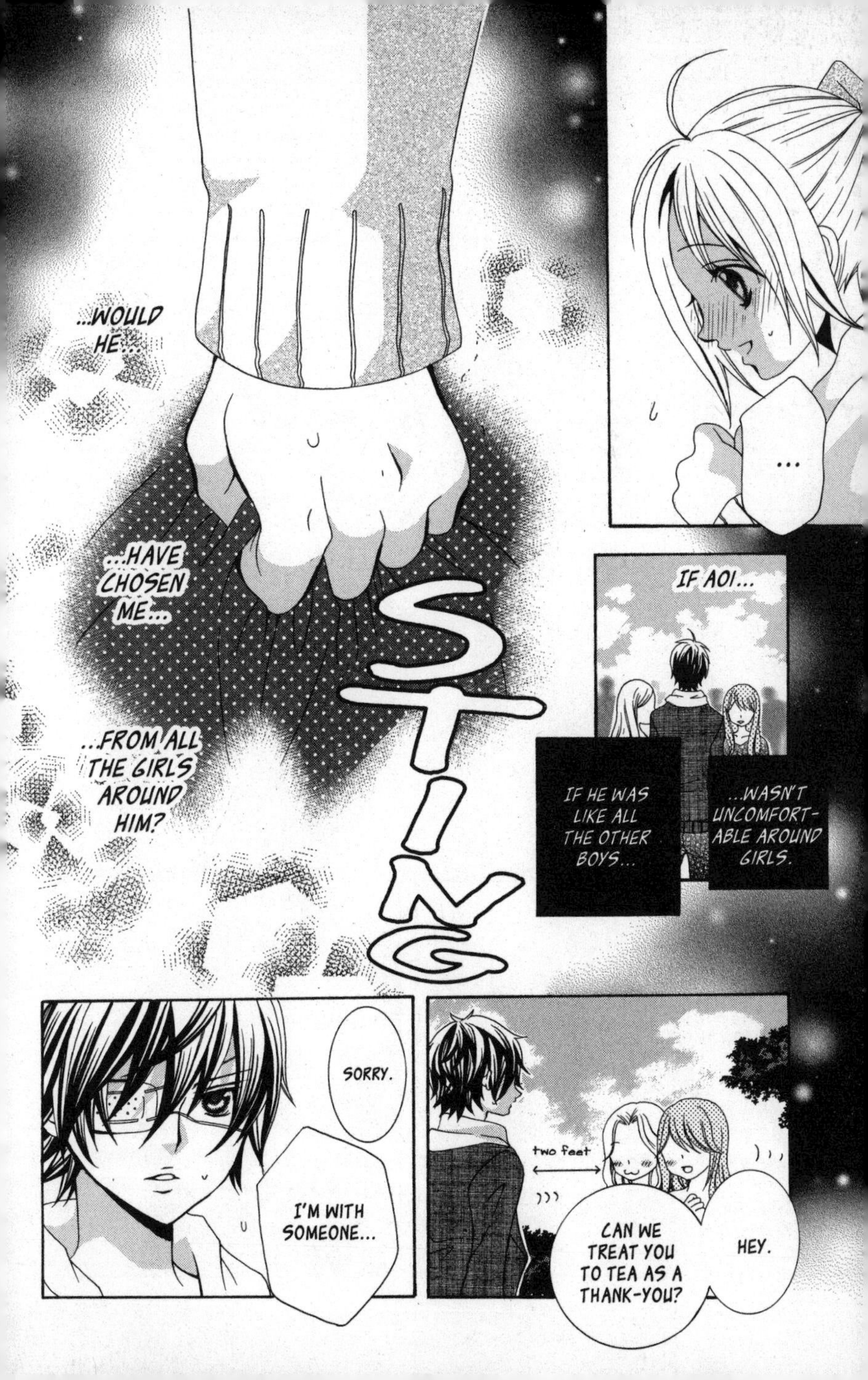
...
IF AOI...
...WASN'T UNCOMFORTABLE AROUND GIRLS.
IF HE WAS LIKE ALL THE OTHER BOYS...
...WOULD HE...
...HAVE CHOSEN ME...
...FROM ALL THE GIRLS AROUND HIM?
STING
HEY.
CAN WE TREAT YOU TO TEA AS A THANK-YOU?
two feet
SORRY.
I'M WITH SOMEONE...

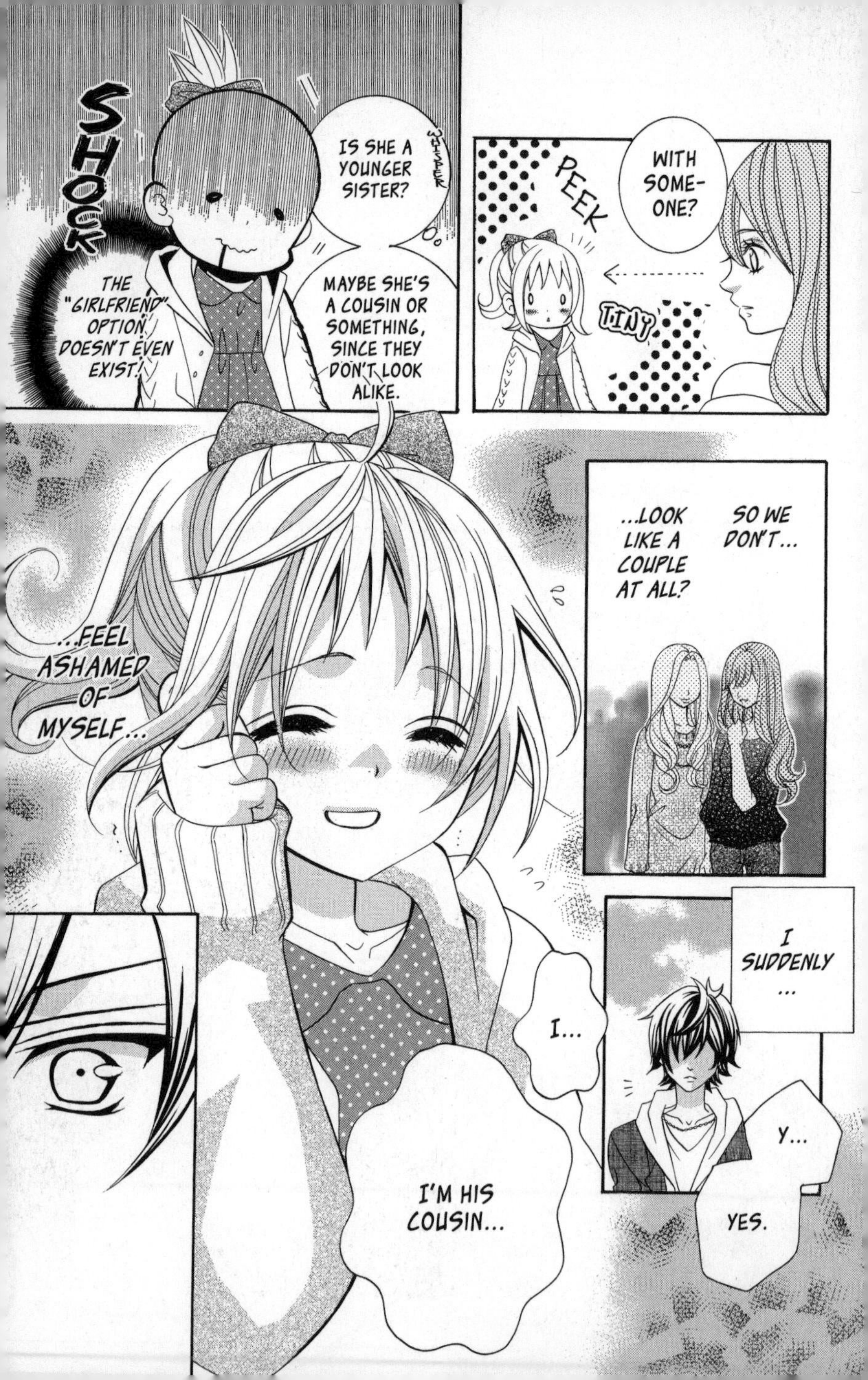
WITH SOME-ONE?
PEEK
TINY
IS SHE A YOUNGER SISTER?
WHISPER
MAYBE SHE'S A COUSIN OR SOMETHING, SINCE THEY DON'T LOOK ALIKE.
SHOCK
THE "GIRLFRIEND" OPTION DOESN'T EVEN EXIST!
SO WE DON'T...
...LOOK LIKE A COUPLE AT ALL?
I SUDDENLY ...
...FEEL ASHAMED OF MYSELF...
I...
I'M HIS COUSIN...
Y...
YES.

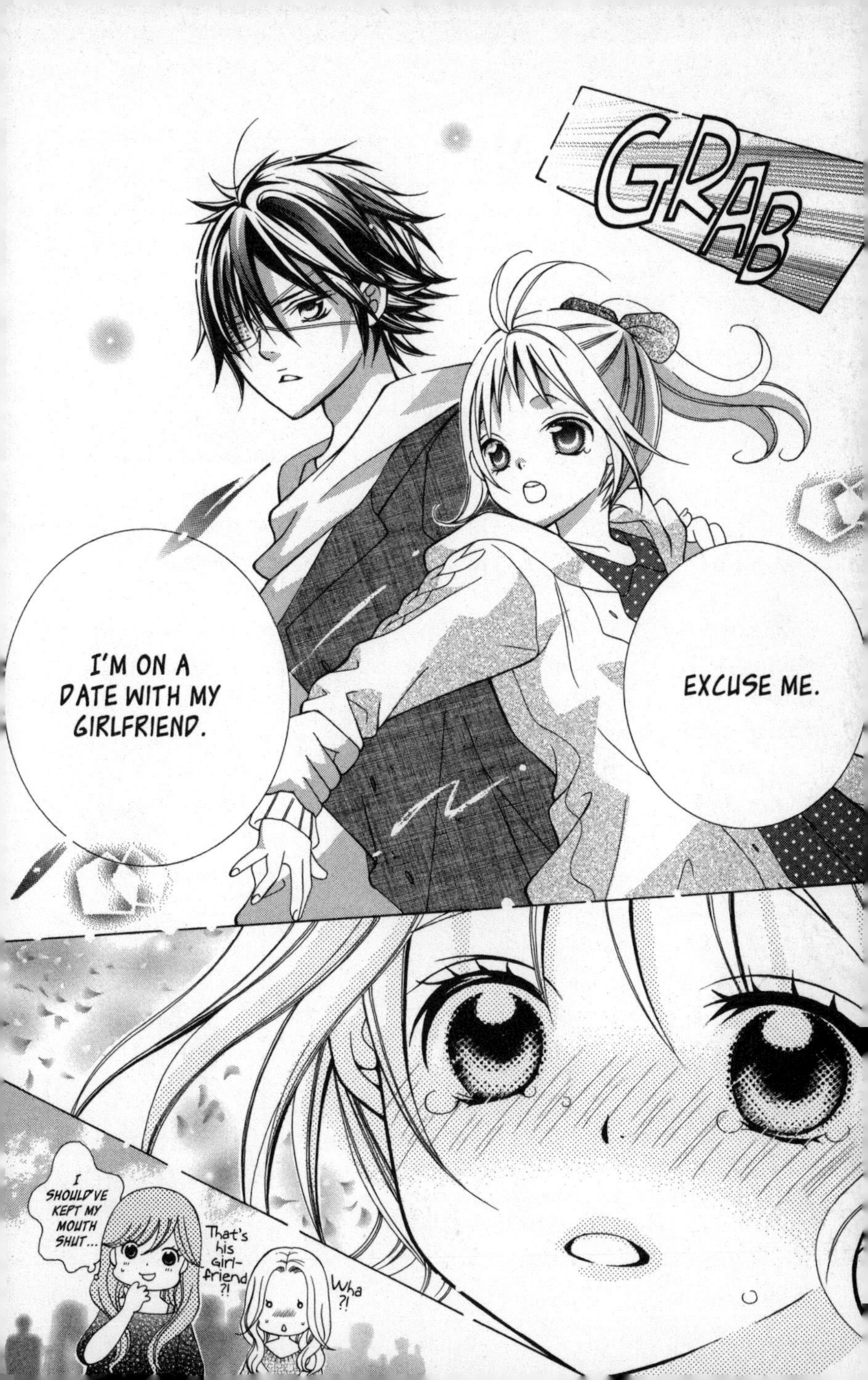
GRAB
EXCUSE ME.
I'M ON A DATE WITH MY GIRLFRIEND.
Wha ?!
That's his girl-friend ?!
I SHOULD'VE KEPT MY MOUTH SHUT...

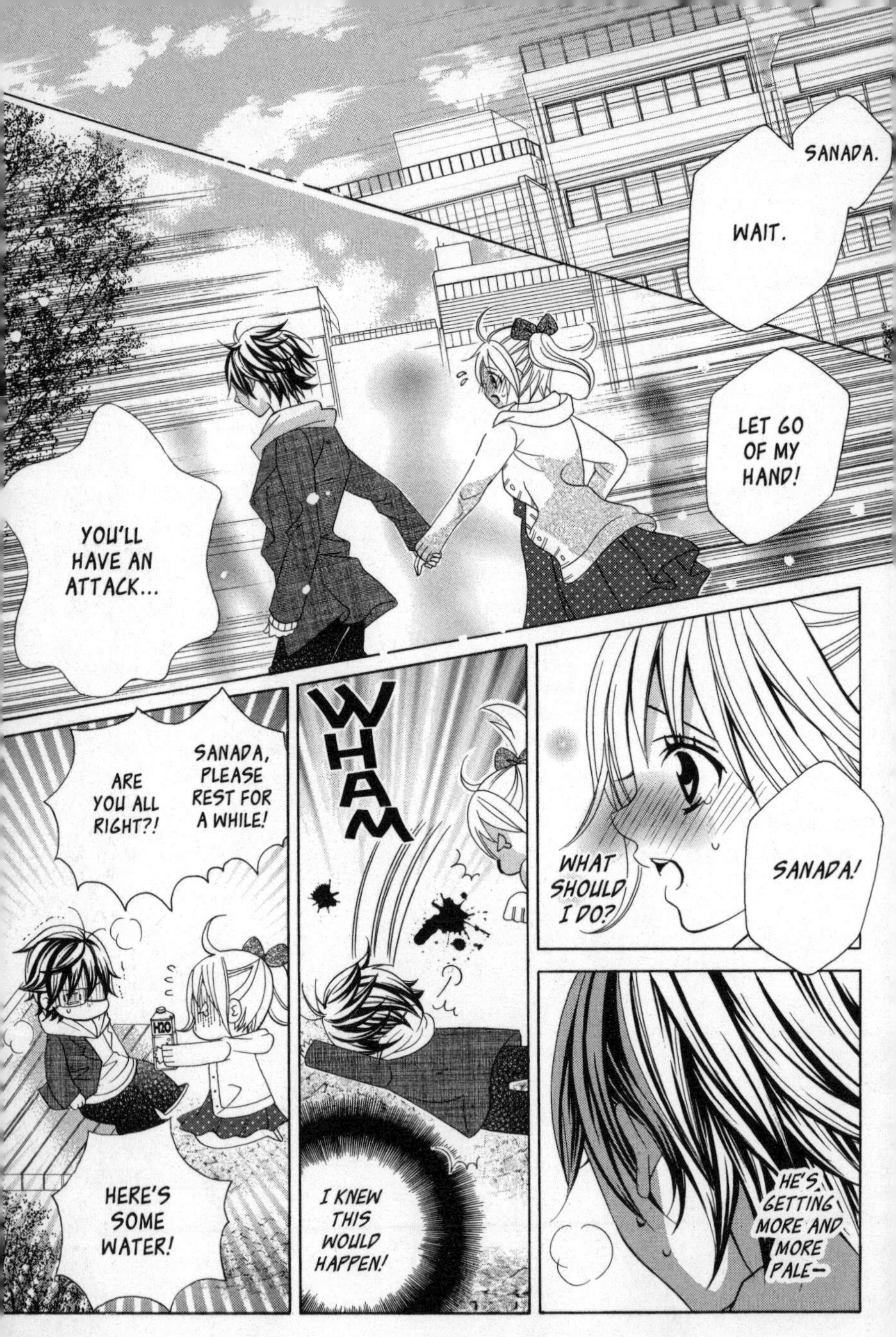
SANADA.
WAIT.
LET GO OF MY HAND!
YOU'LL HAVE AN ATTACK...
SANADA!
WHAT SHOULD I DO?
HE'S GETTING MORE AND MORE PALE—
WHAM
I KNEW THIS WOULD HAPPEN!
SANADA, PLEASE REST FOR A WHILE!
ARE YOU ALL RIGHT?!
H2O
HERE'S SOME WATER!

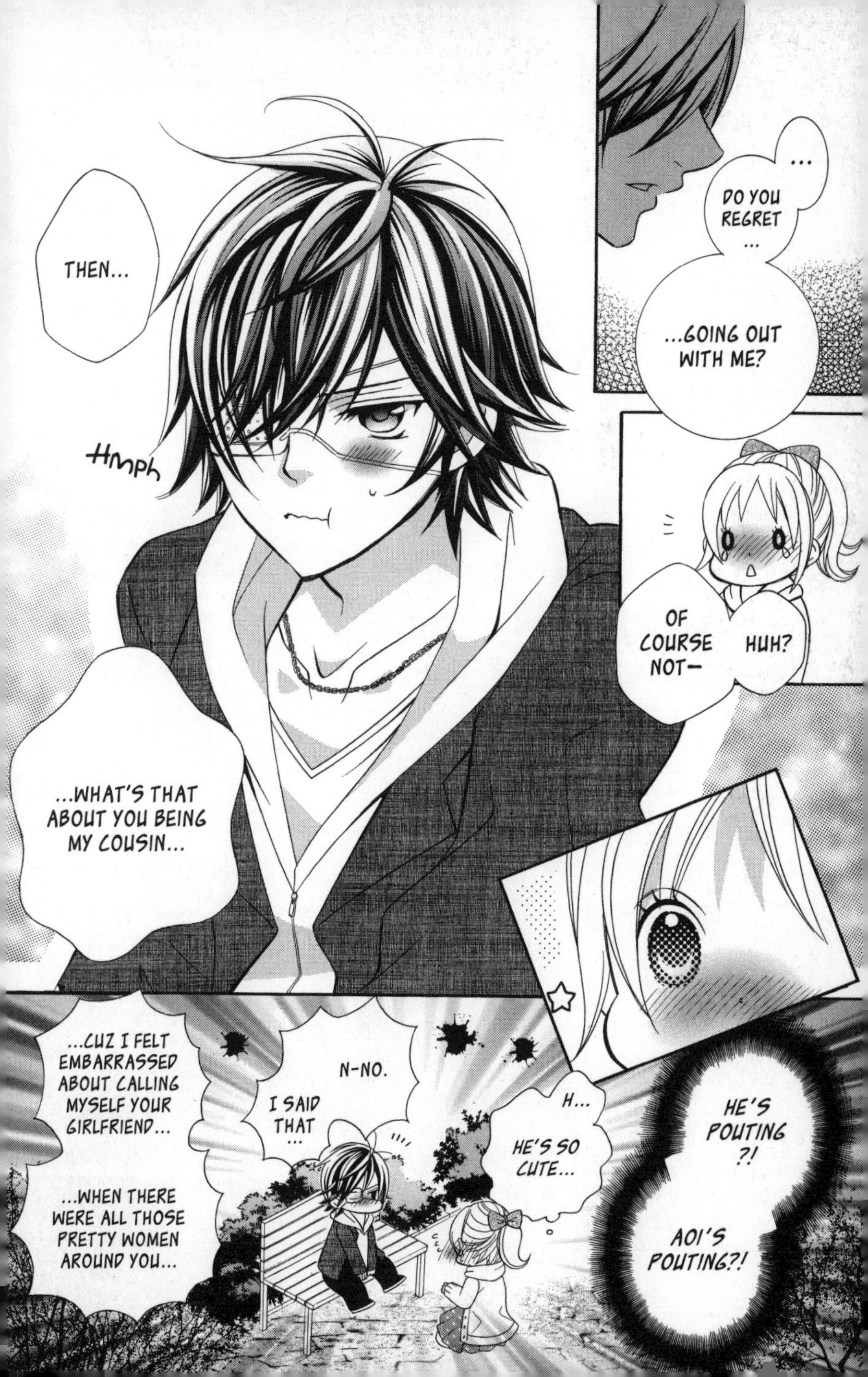

...
DO YOU REGRET ...
...GOING OUT WITH ME?
HUH?
OF COURSE NOT—
THEN...
...WHAT'S THAT ABOUT YOU BEING MY COUSIN...
Hmph
HE'S POUTING?!
AOI'S POUTING?!
H... HE'S SO CUTE...
N-NO.
I SAID THAT ...
...CUZ I FELT EMBARRASSED ABOUT CALLING MYSELF YOUR GIRLFRIEND...
...WHEN THERE WERE ALL THOSE PRETTY WOMEN AROUND YOU...

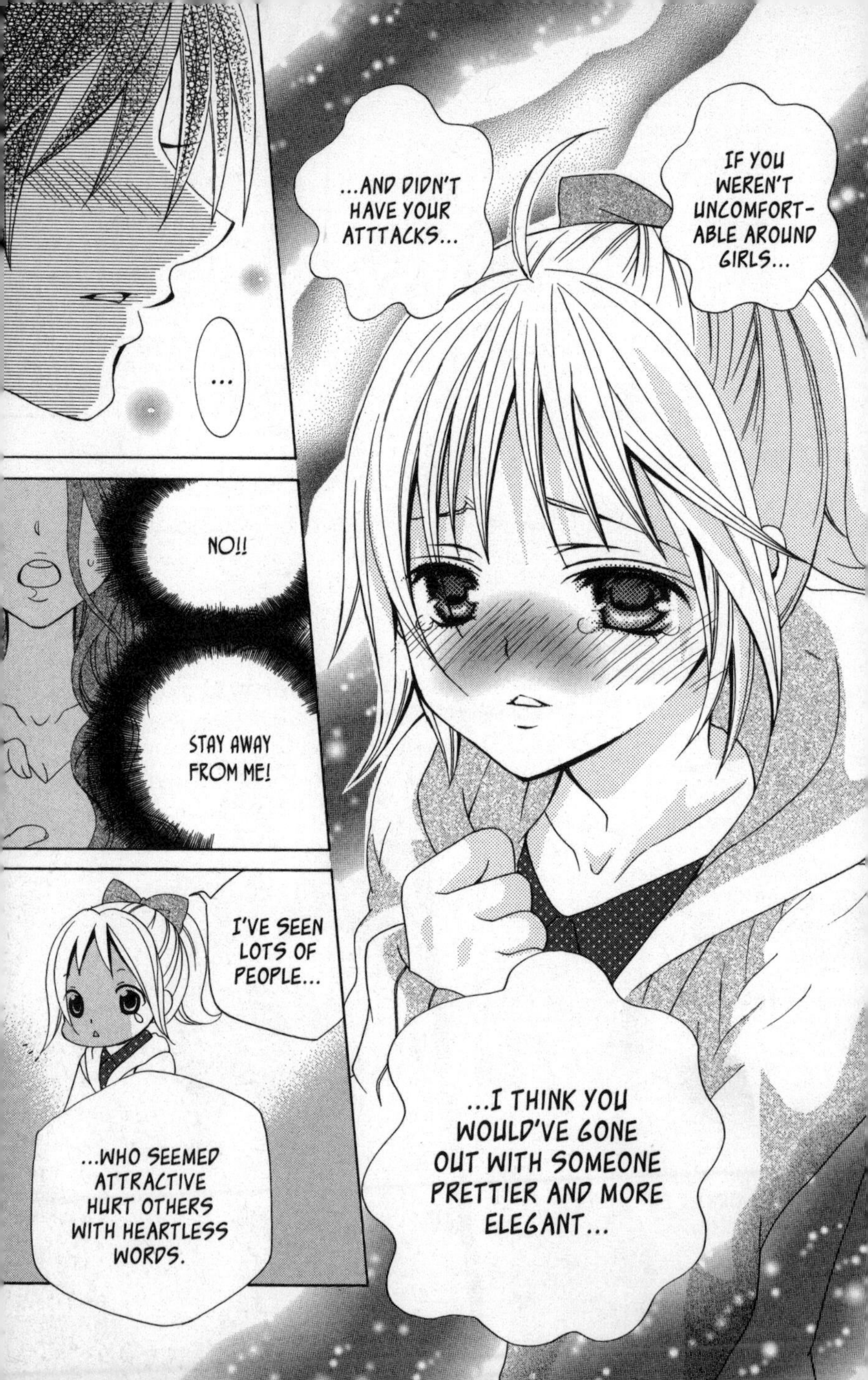
IF YOU WEREN'T UNCOMFORT-ABLE AROUND GIRLS...
...AND DIDN'T HAVE YOUR ATTTACKS...
...I THINK YOU WOULD'VE GONE OUT WITH SOMEONE PRETTIER AND MORE ELEGANT...
...
NO!!
STAY AWAY FROM ME!
I'VE SEEN LOTS OF PEOPLE...
...WHO SEEMED ATTRACTIVE HURT OTHERS WITH HEARTLESS WORDS.

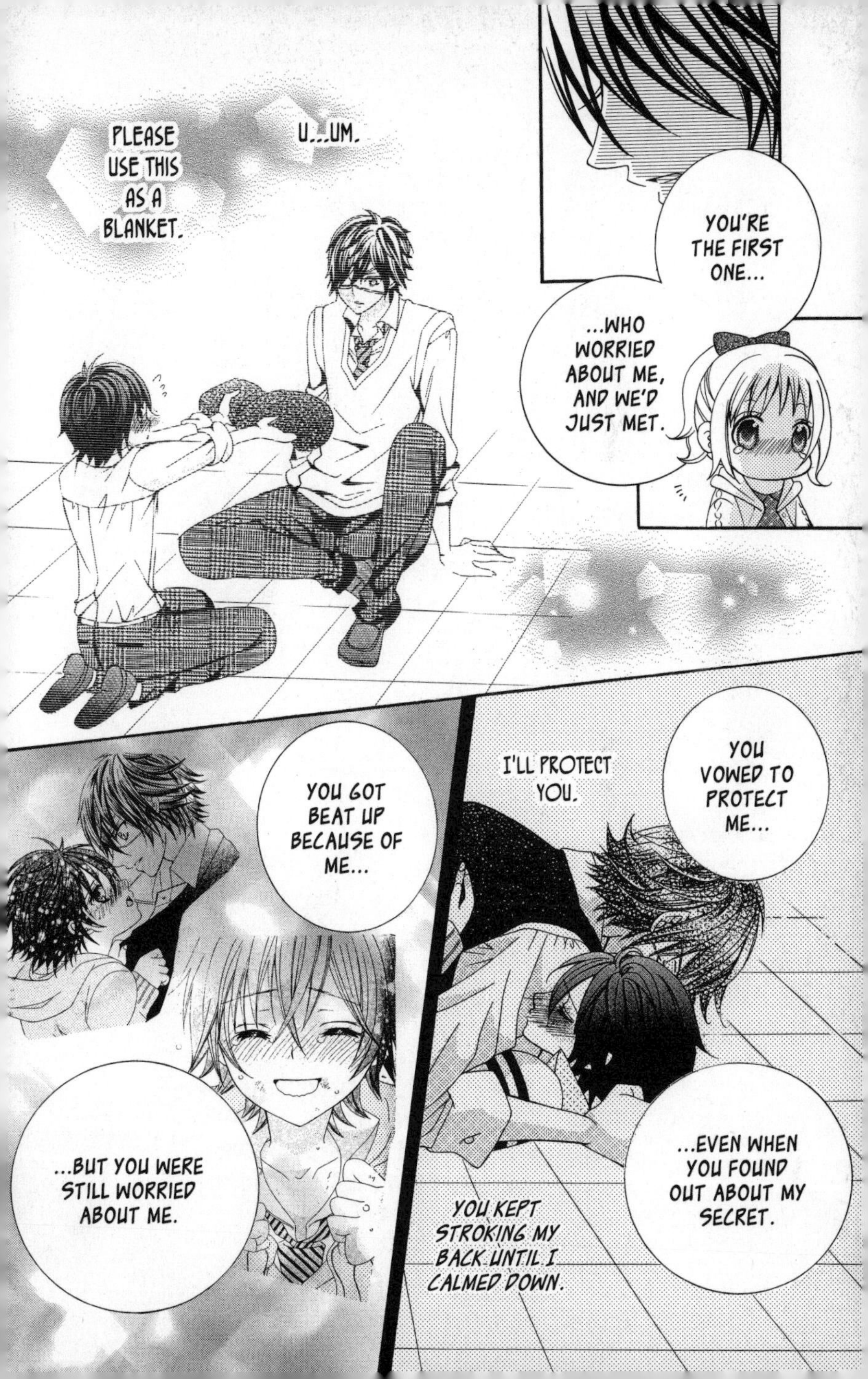
YOU'RE THE FIRST ONE...
...WHO WORRIED ABOUT ME, AND WE'D JUST MET.
U...UM.
PLEASE USE THIS AS A BLANKET.
YOU VOWED TO PROTECT ME...
I'LL PROTECT YOU.
...EVEN WHEN YOU FOUND OUT ABOUT MY SECRET.
YOU KEPT STROKING MY BACK UNTIL I CALMED DOWN.
YOU GOT BEAT UP BECAUSE OF ME...
...BUT YOU WERE STILL WORRIED ABOUT ME.

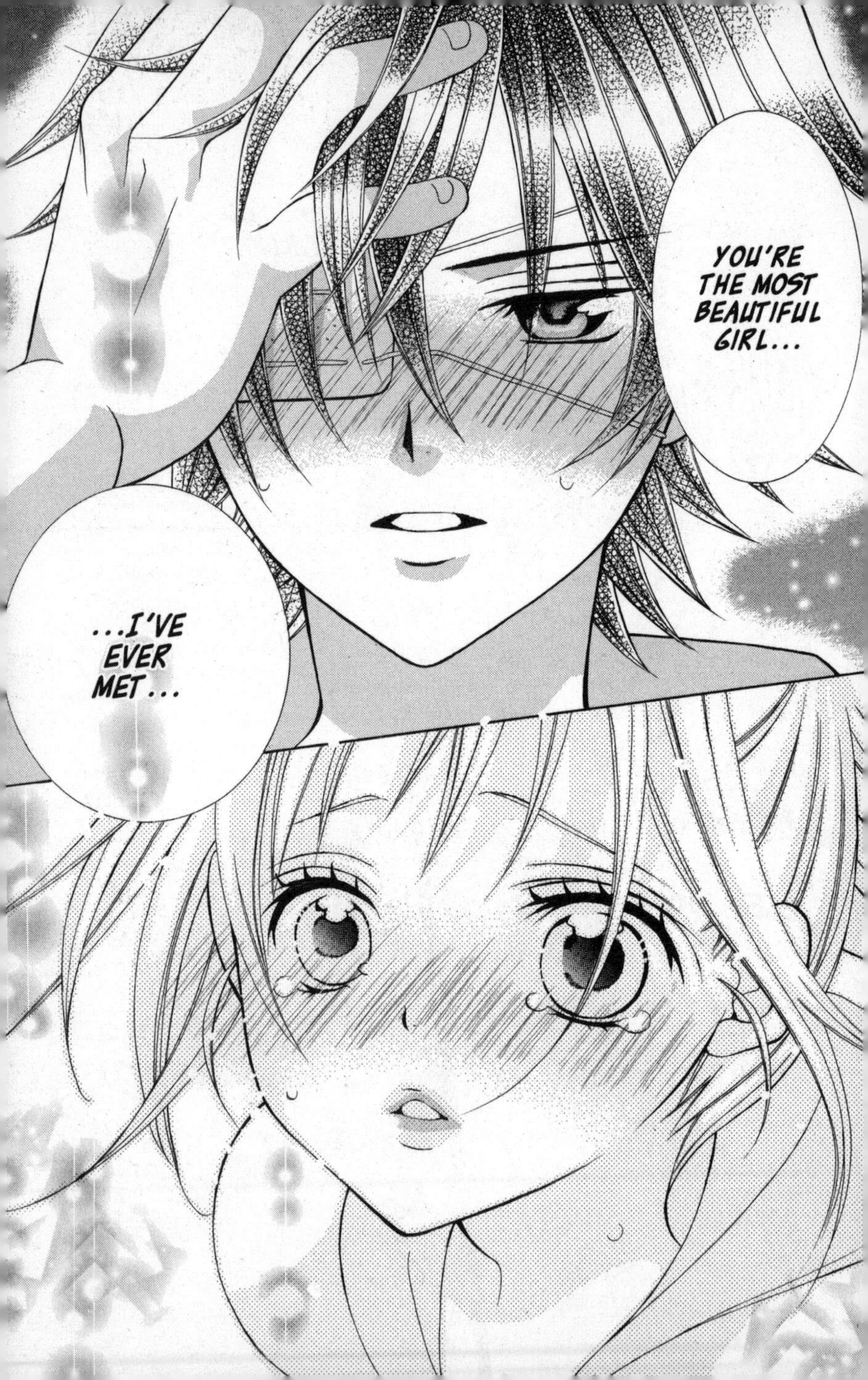
YOU'RE THE MOST BEAUTIFUL GIRL...
...I'VE EVER MET...

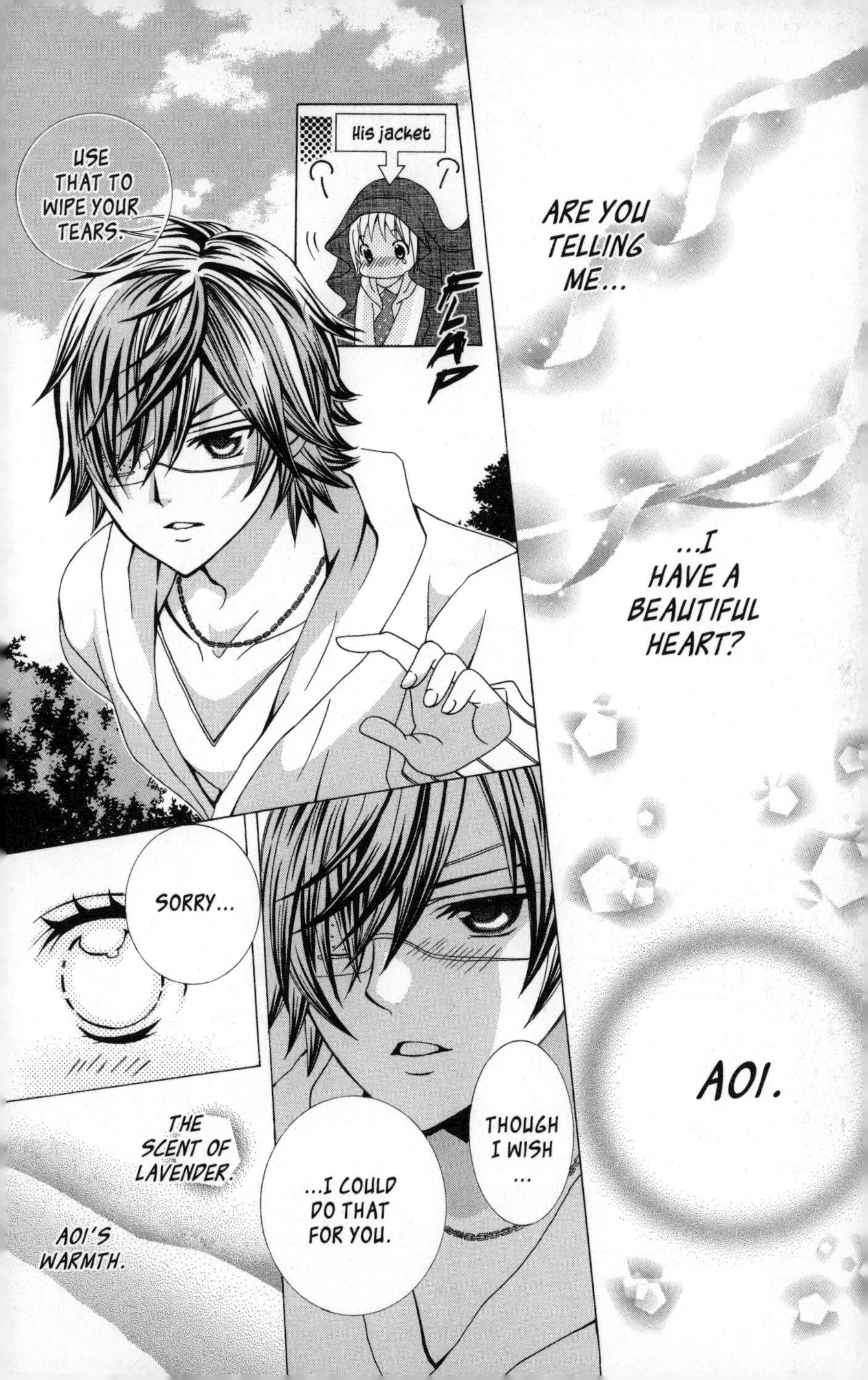
ARE YOU TELLING ME...
...I HAVE A BEAUTIFUL HEART?
AOI.
His jacket
FLAP
USE THAT TO WIPE YOUR TEARS.
THOUGH I WISH ...
...I COULD DO THAT FOR YOU.
SORRY...
THE SCENT OF LAVENDER.
AOI'S WARMTH.

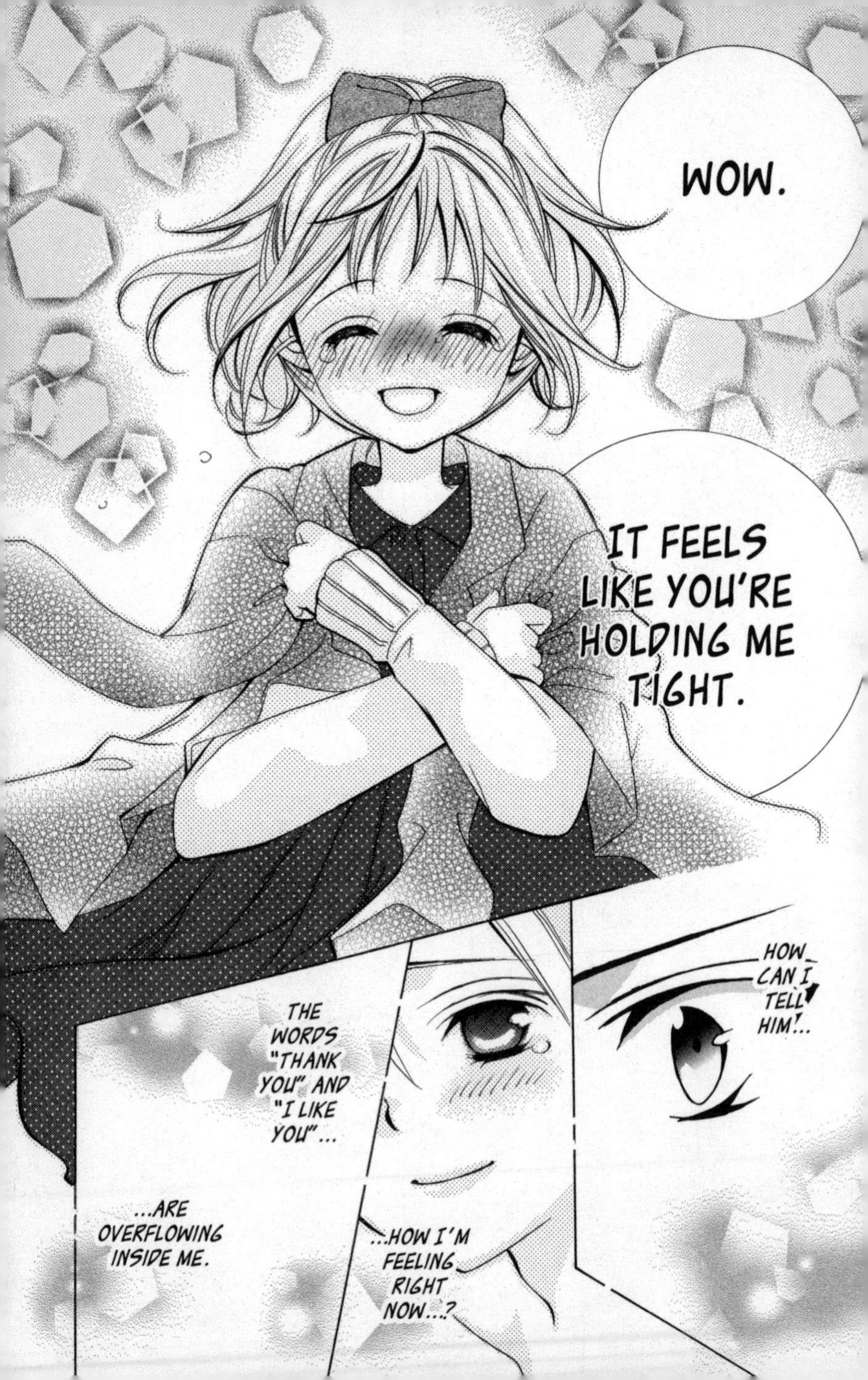
WOW.
IT FEELS LIKE YOU'RE HOLDING ME TIGHT.
HOW CAN I TELL HIM...
...HOW I'M FEELING RIGHT NOW...?
THE WORDS "THANK YOU" AND "I LIKE YOU"...
...ARE OVERFLOWING INSIDE ME.

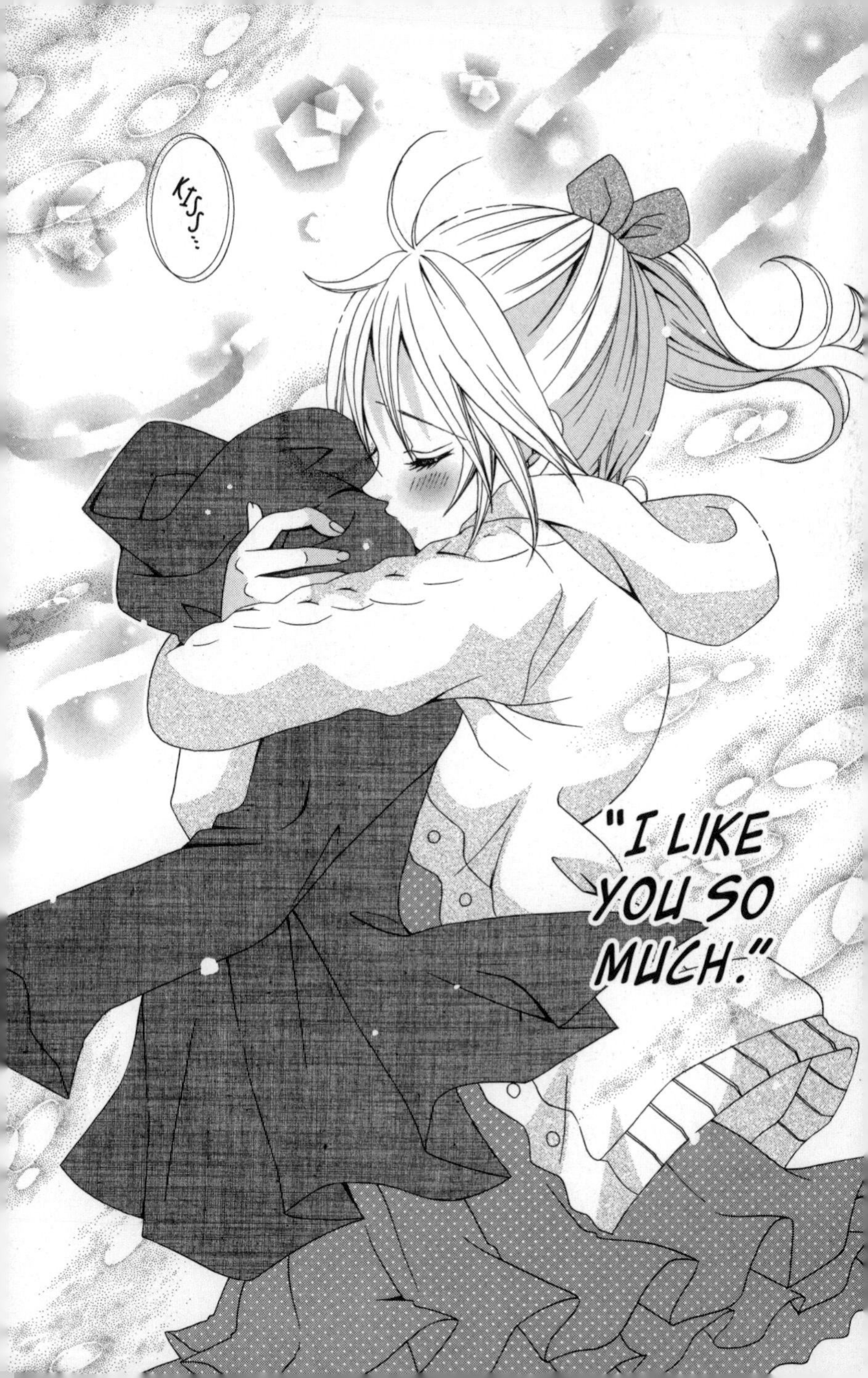
Kiss...
"I LIKE YOU SO MUCH."

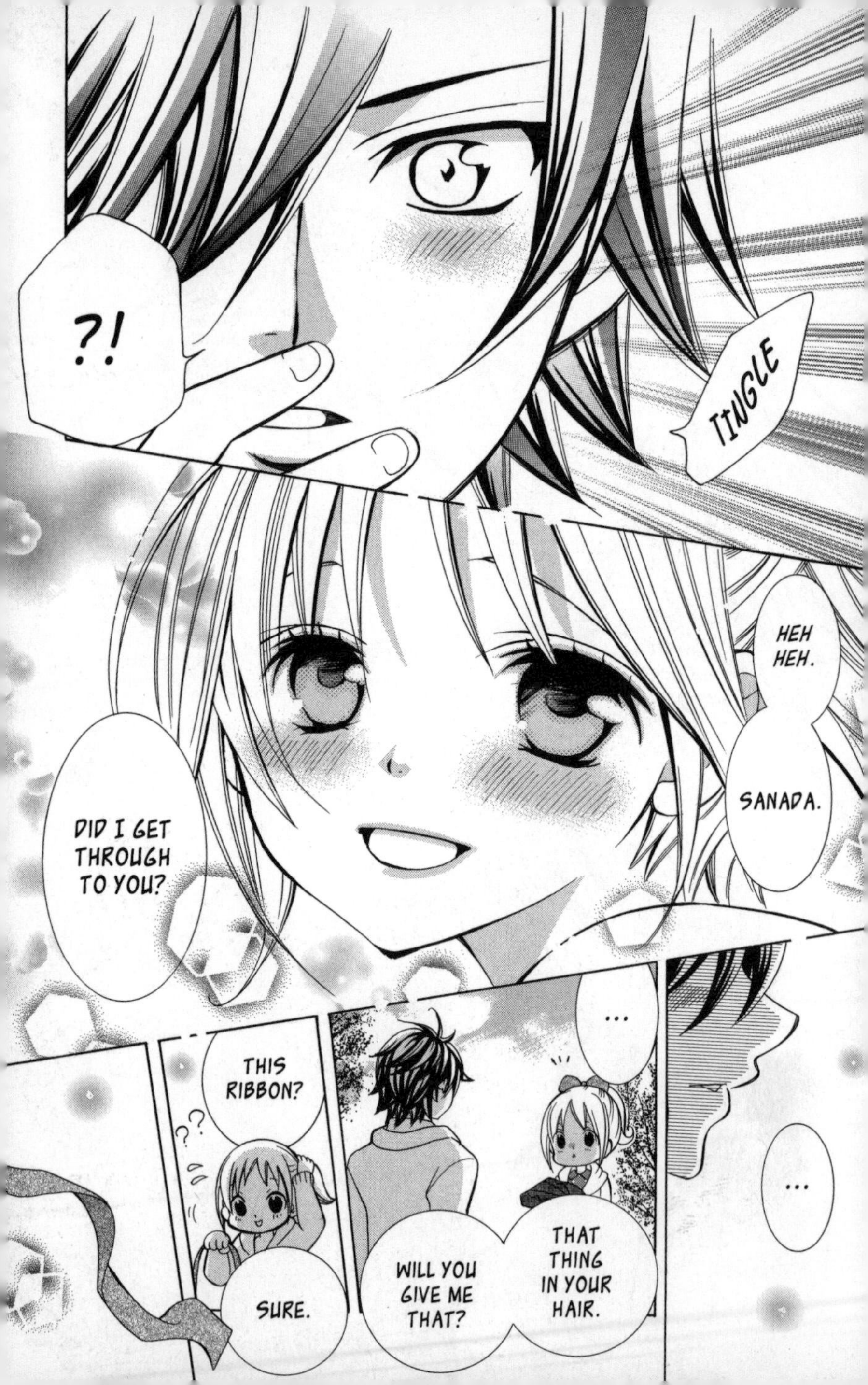
TINGLE
?!
HEH HEH.
SANADA.
DID I GET THROUGH TO YOU?
...
...
THAT THING IN YOUR HAIR.
WILL YOU GIVE ME THAT?
THIS RIBBON?
SURE.

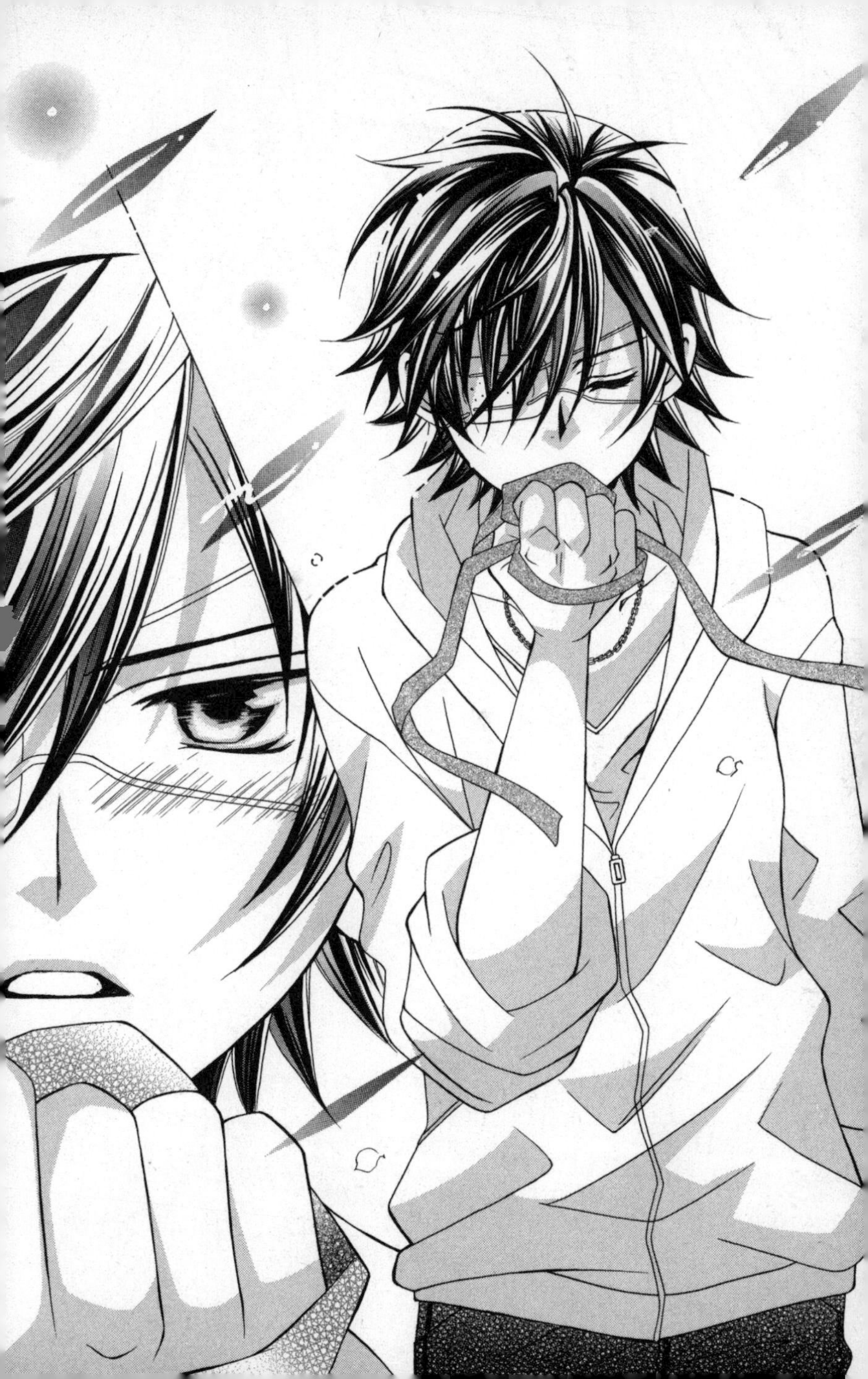

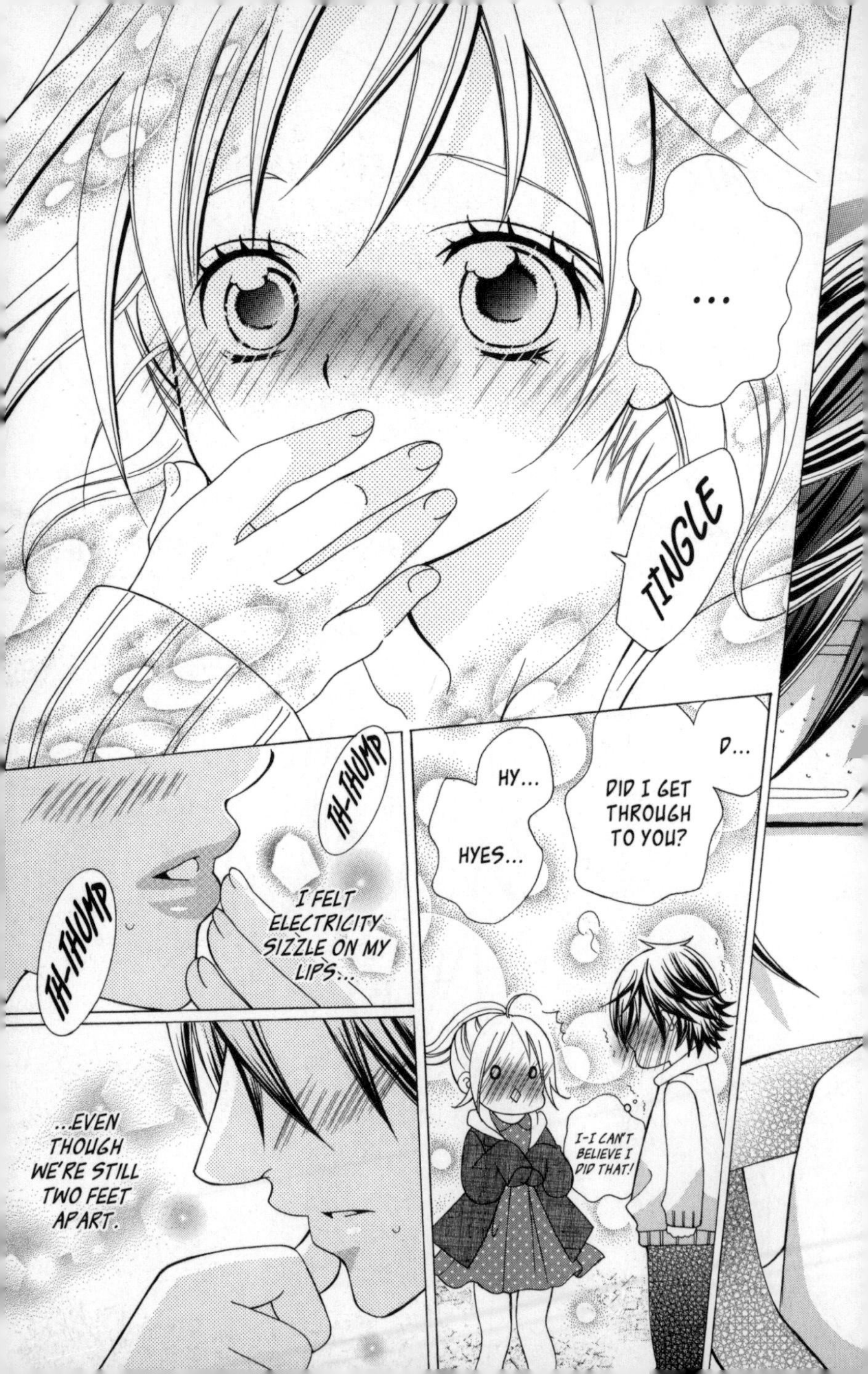
...
TINGLE
D...
DID I GET THROUGH TO YOU?
HY...
HYES...
I-I CAN'T BELIEVE I DID THAT!
TH-THUMP
I FELT ELECTRICITY SIZZLE ON MY LIPS...
TH-THUMP
...EVEN THOUGH WE'RE STILL TWO FEET APART.

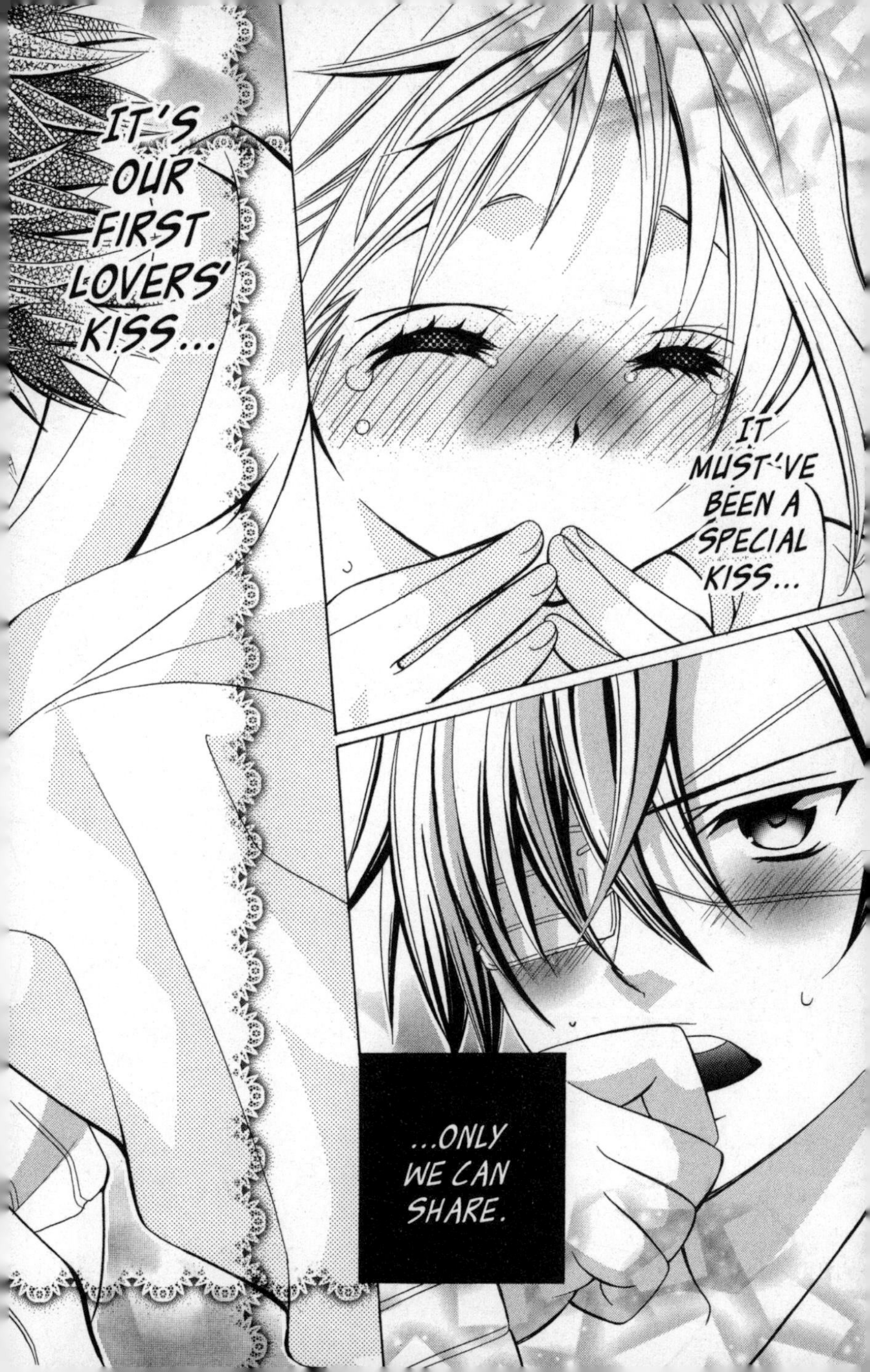
IT MUST'VE BEEN A SPECIAL KISS...
...ONLY WE CAN SHARE.
IT'S OUR FIRST LOVERS' KISS...

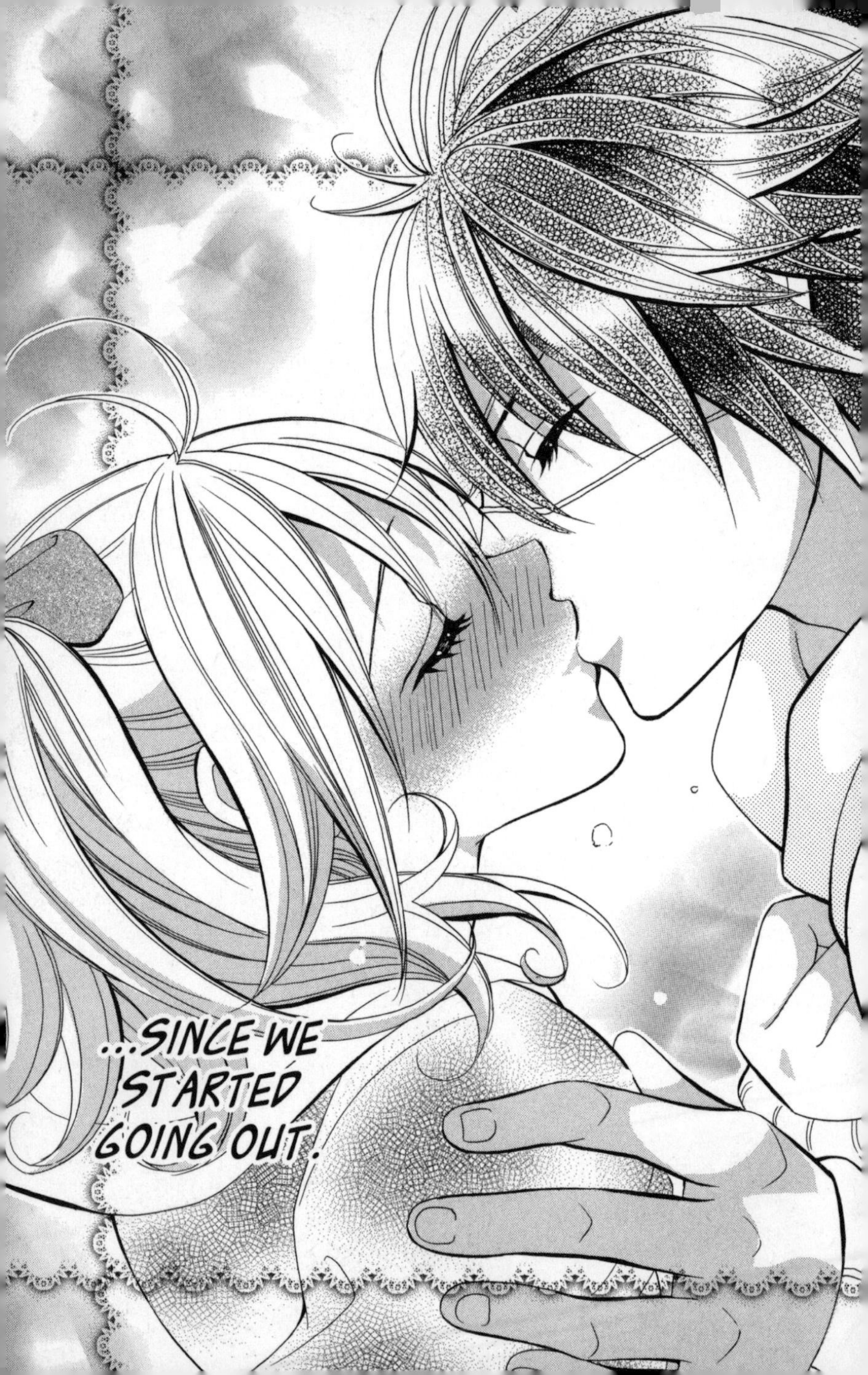
...SINCE WE STARTED GOING OUT.

Chapter 20

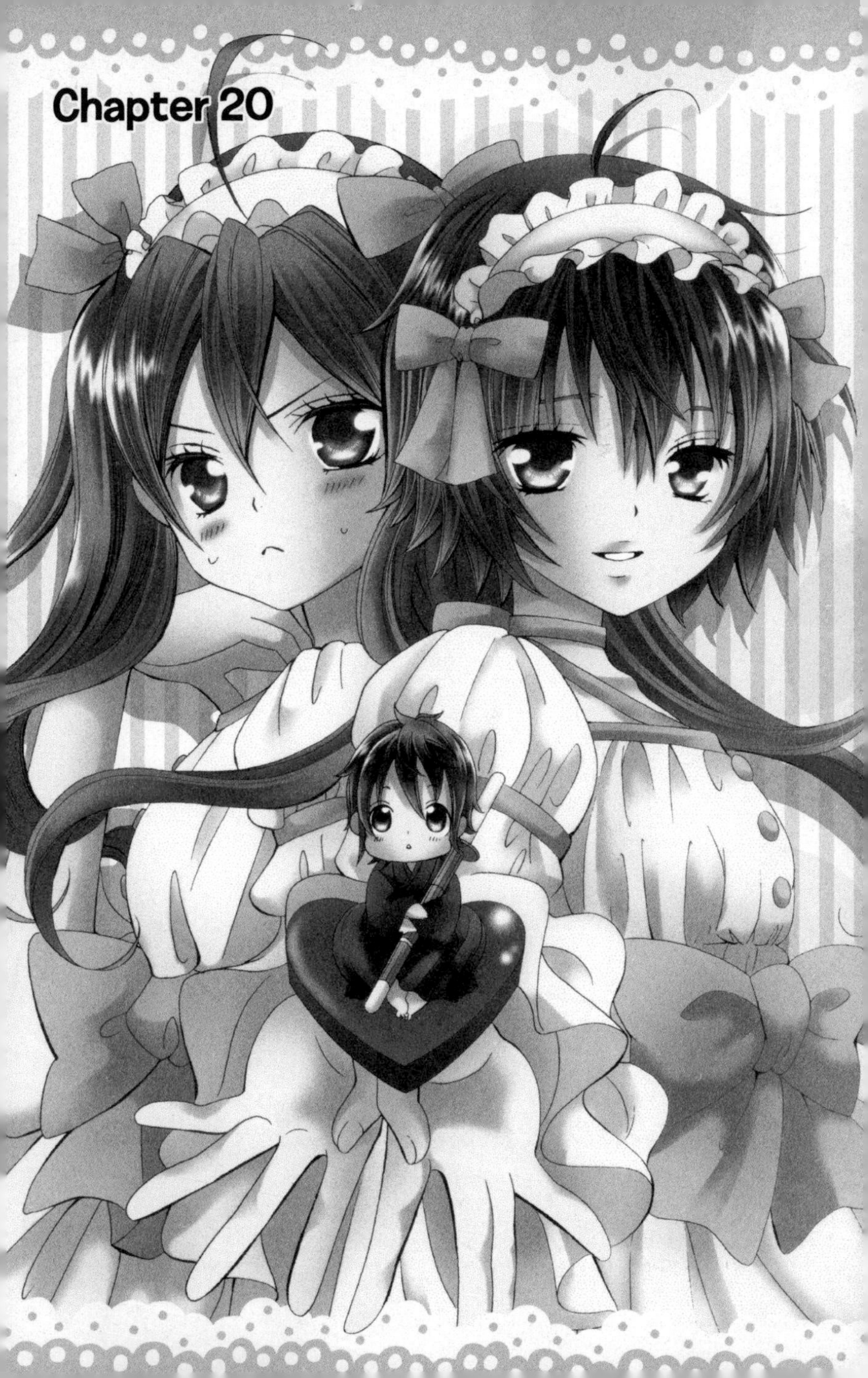

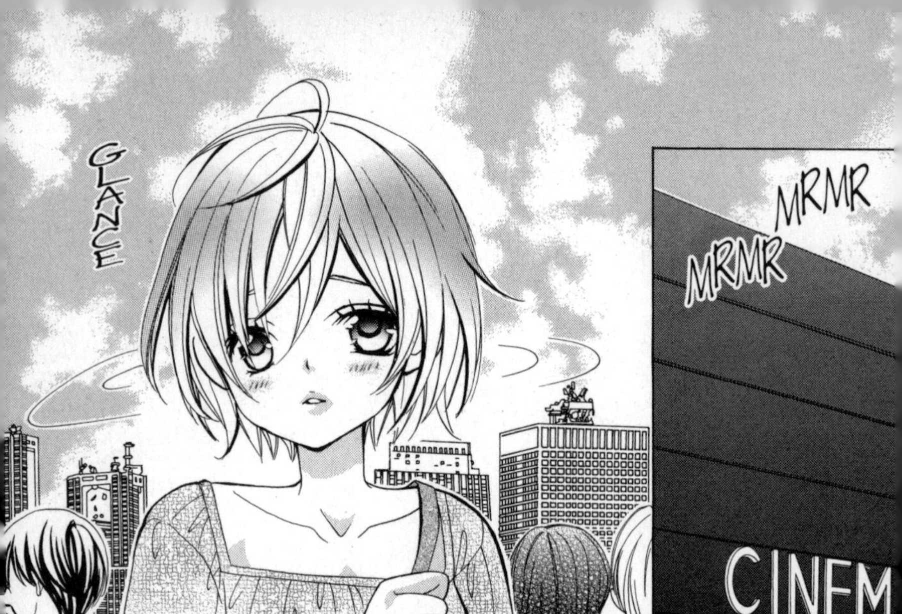
MRMR
MRMR
CINEM
GLANCE

It's a bit early, but this is the afterword. Thank you for reading volume 4 of *So Cute!* ♡ Did you enjoy Mego and Aoi's first date? I agonized a lot over how to make the love scene moving when the two can't get closer than two feet (*smile*), but I found it very novel since I've never drawn a relationship like this before. (*So Cute!* is the most "pure love" story I've ever drawn.)

Mitsuru's love undergoes a dramatic upheaval and finally reaches the critical moment in volume 5. (I'm nervous about the reactions of readers who are rooting for Azusa and those who are rooting for Shino (*sweat*). The second story arc will also begin in volume 5. Look forward to it, as all sorts of secrets will be revealed! (^o^) ♡♡

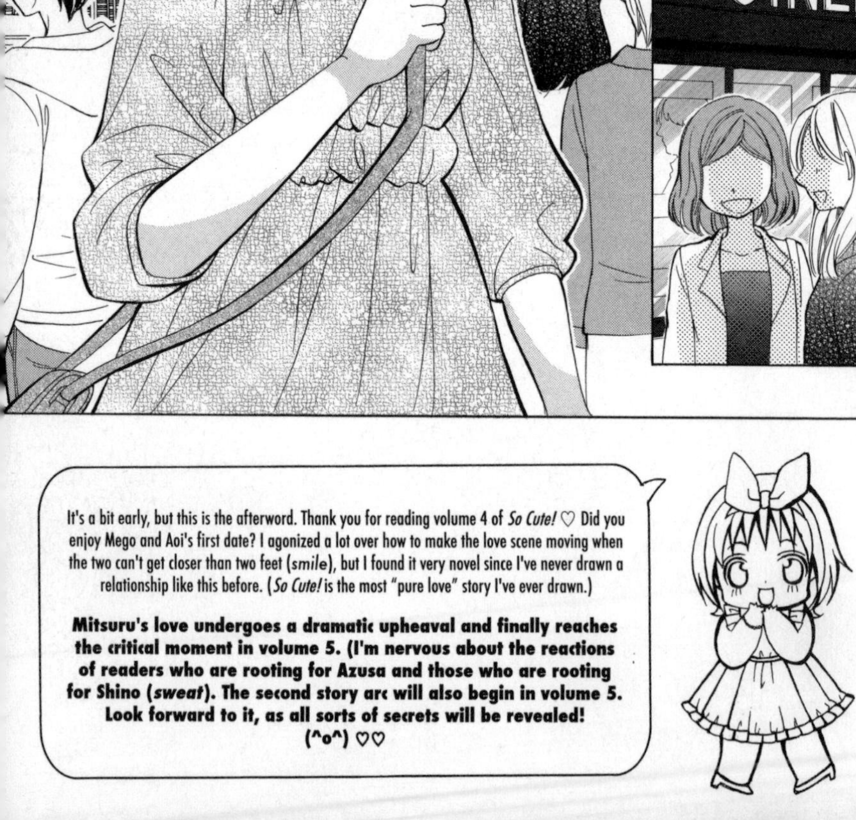

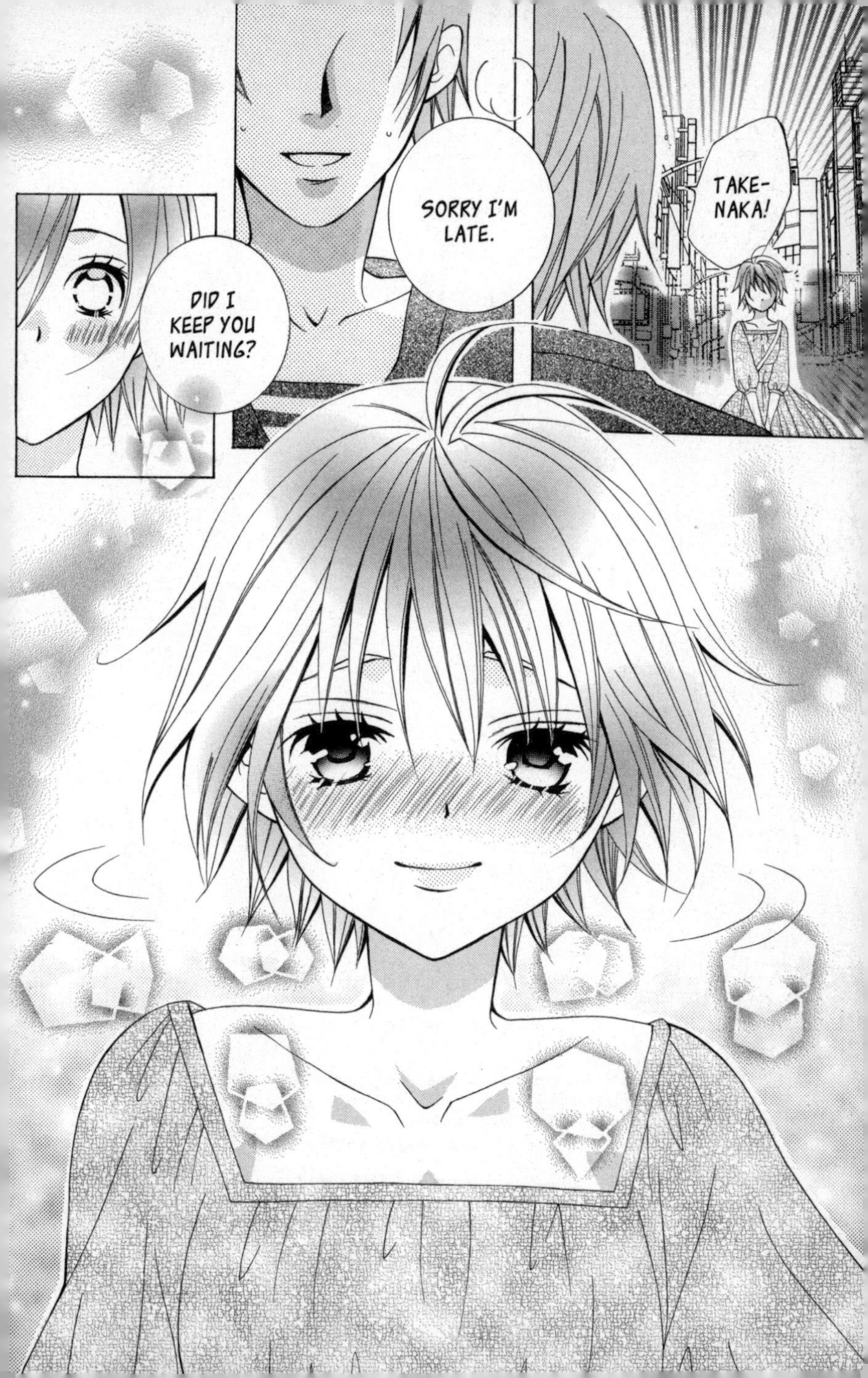
TAKE-NAKA!
SORRY I'M LATE.
DID I KEEP YOU WAITING?

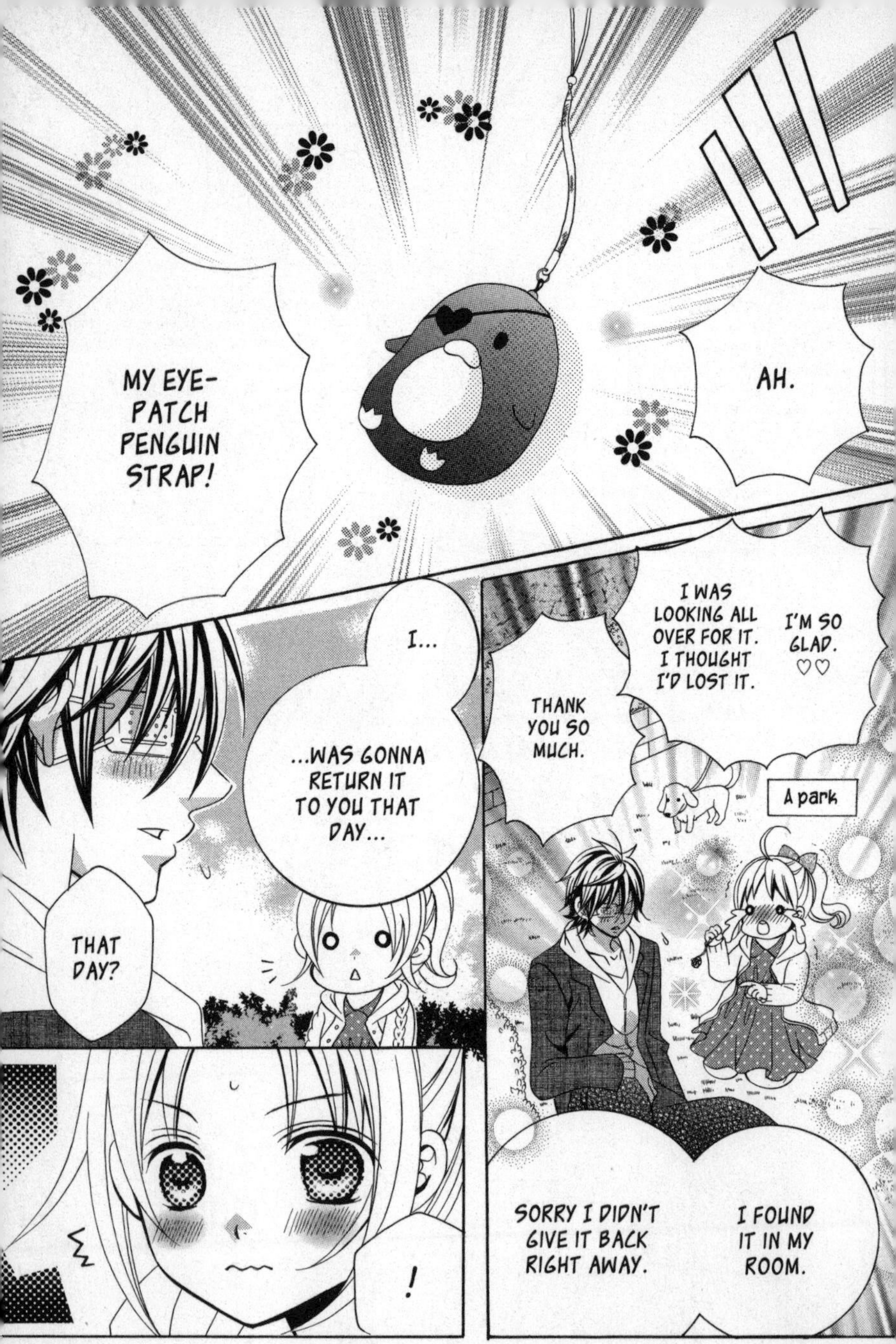
AH.
MY EYE-PATCH PENGUIN STRAP!
I'M SO GLAD. ♡♡
I WAS LOOKING ALL OVER FOR IT. I THOUGHT I'D LOST IT.
THANK YOU SO MUCH.
A park
I FOUND IT IN MY ROOM.
SORRY I DIDN'T GIVE IT BACK RIGHT AWAY.
I...
...WAS GONNA RETURN IT TO YOU THAT DAY...
THAT DAY?
!

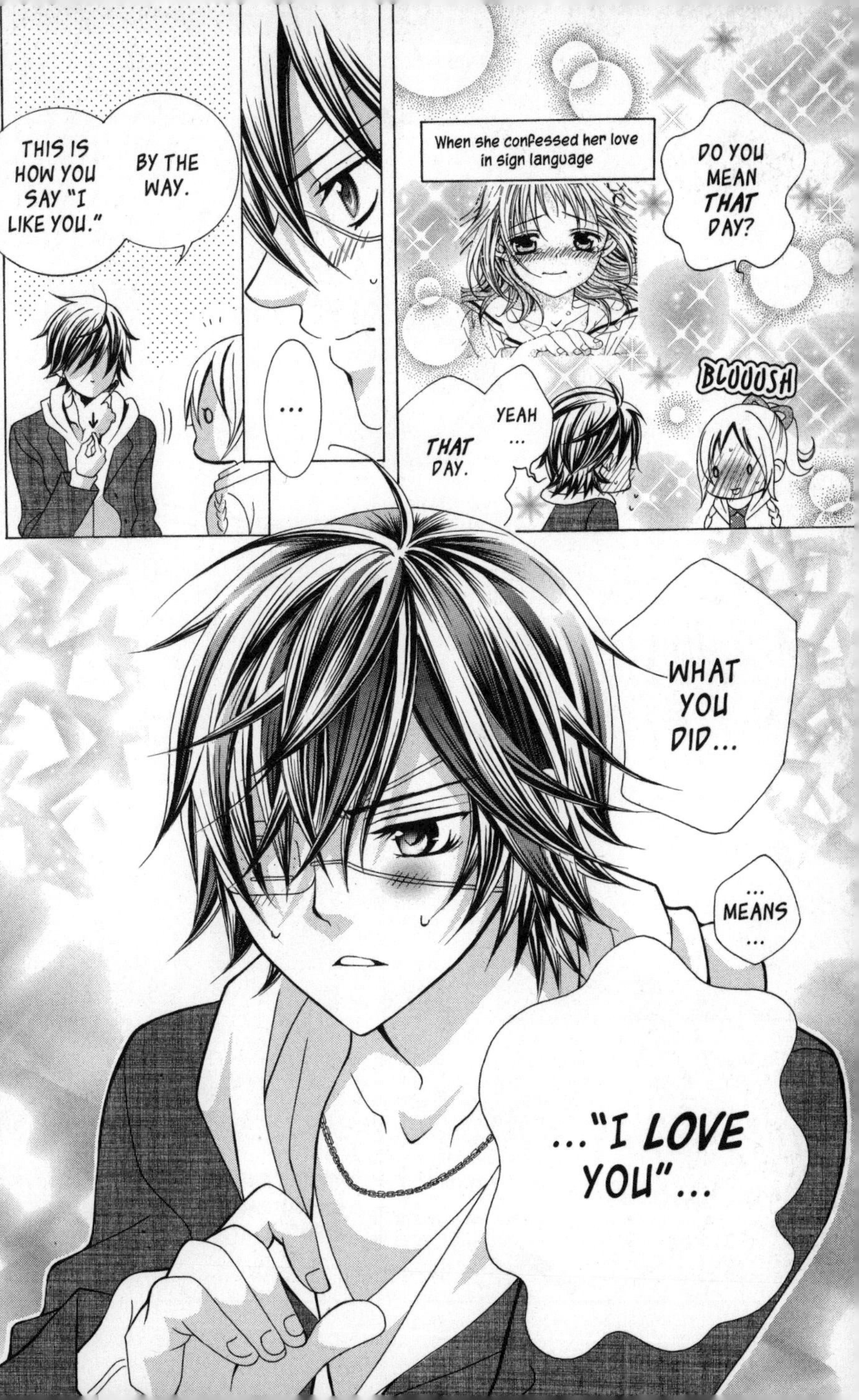
DO YOU MEAN *THAT* DAY?
When she confessed her love in sign language
BLUUUSH
YEAH ...
THAT DAY.
...
BY THE WAY.
THIS IS HOW YOU SAY "I LIKE YOU."
WHAT YOU DID...
... MEANS ...
..."I *LOVE* YOU"...

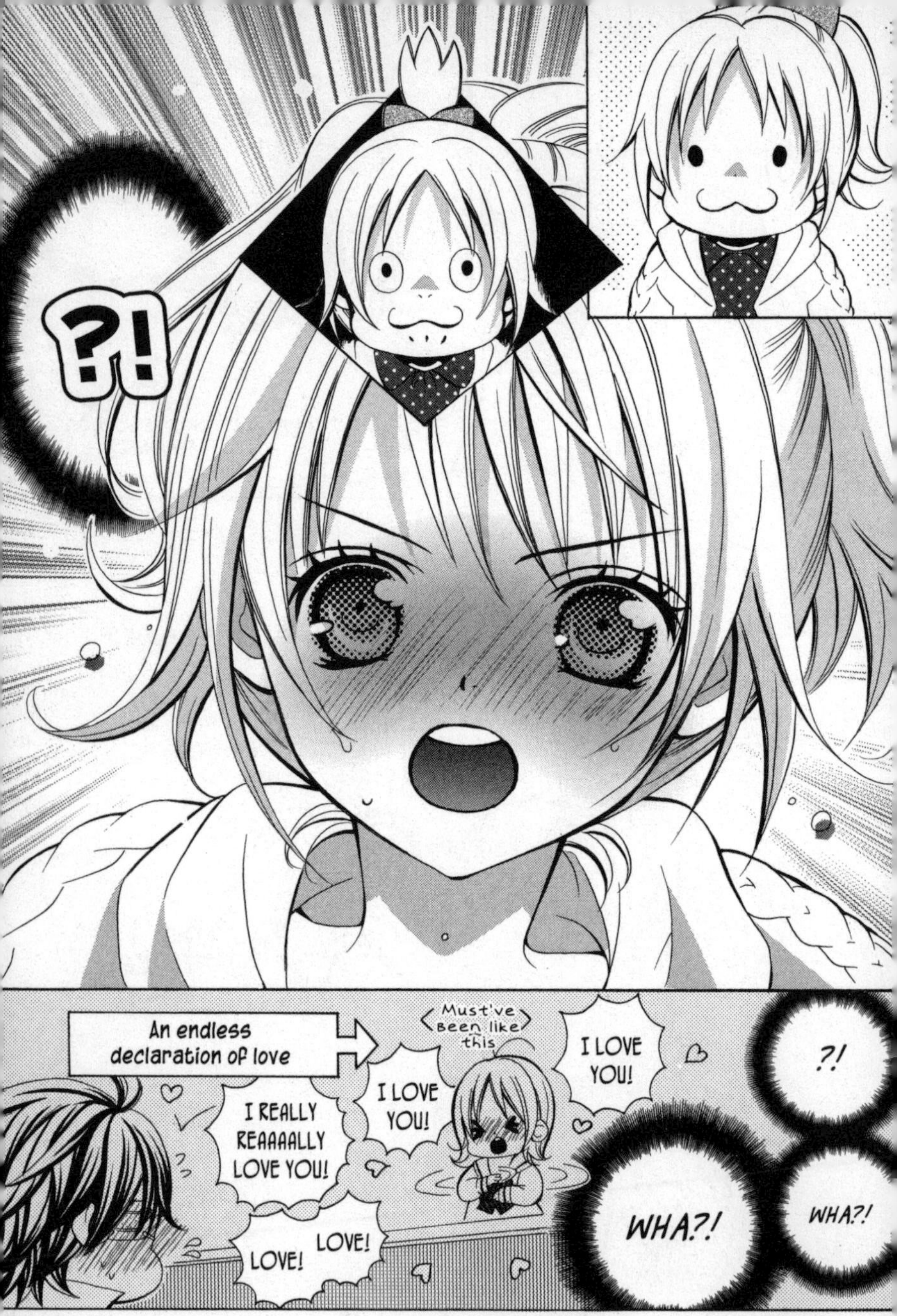
?!
?!
WHA?!
WHA?!
I LOVE YOU!
Must've been like this
I LOVE YOU!
An endless declaration of love
I REALLY REAAAALLY LOVE YOU!
LOVE!
LOVE!

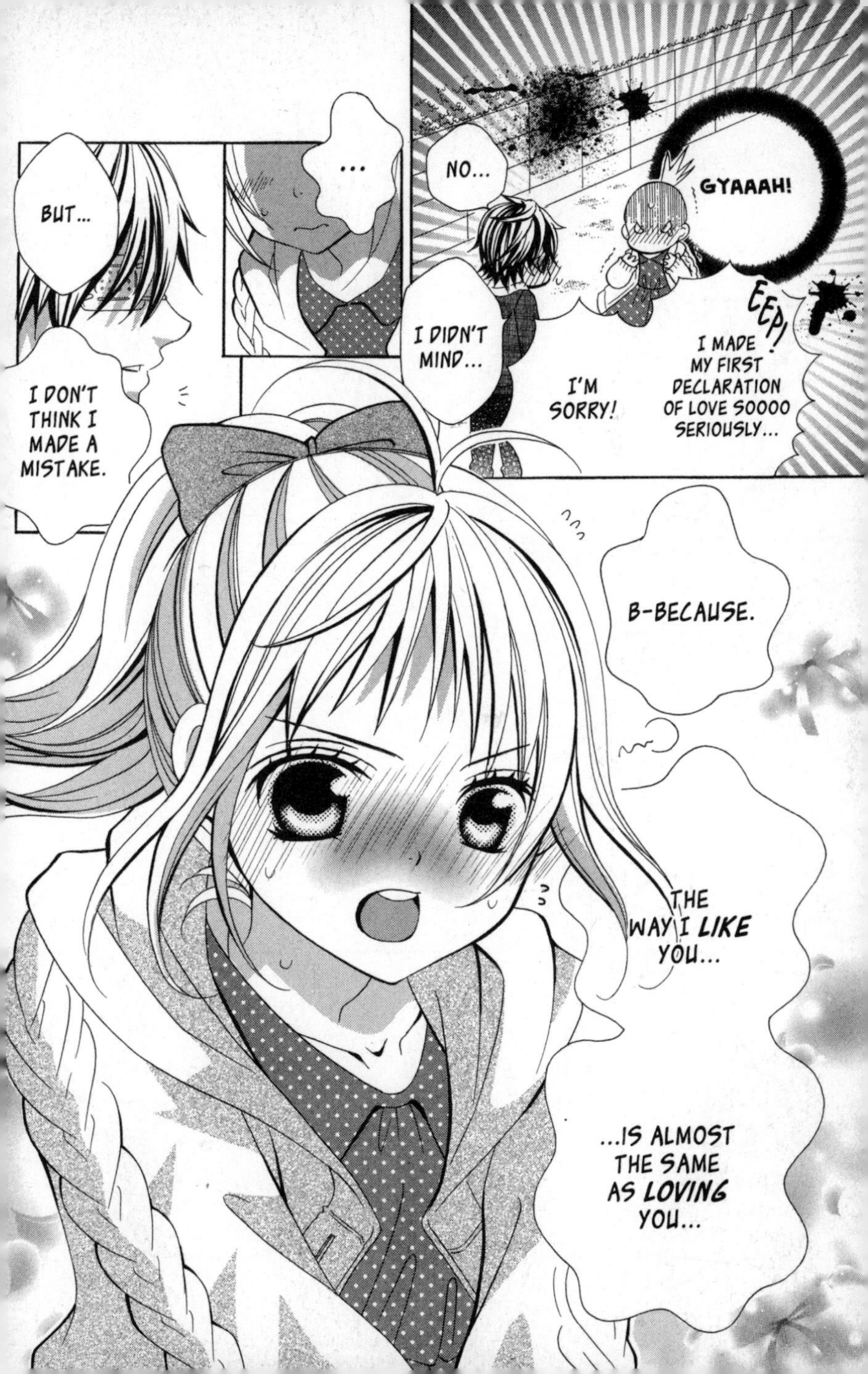
GYAAAH!
EEP!
I MADE MY FIRST DECLARATION OF LOVE SOOOO SERIOUSLY...
I'M SORRY!
NO...
I DIDN'T MIND...
...
BUT...
I DON'T THINK I MADE A MISTAKE.
B-BECAUSE.
THE WAY I LIKE YOU...
...IS ALMOST THE SAME AS LOVING YOU...

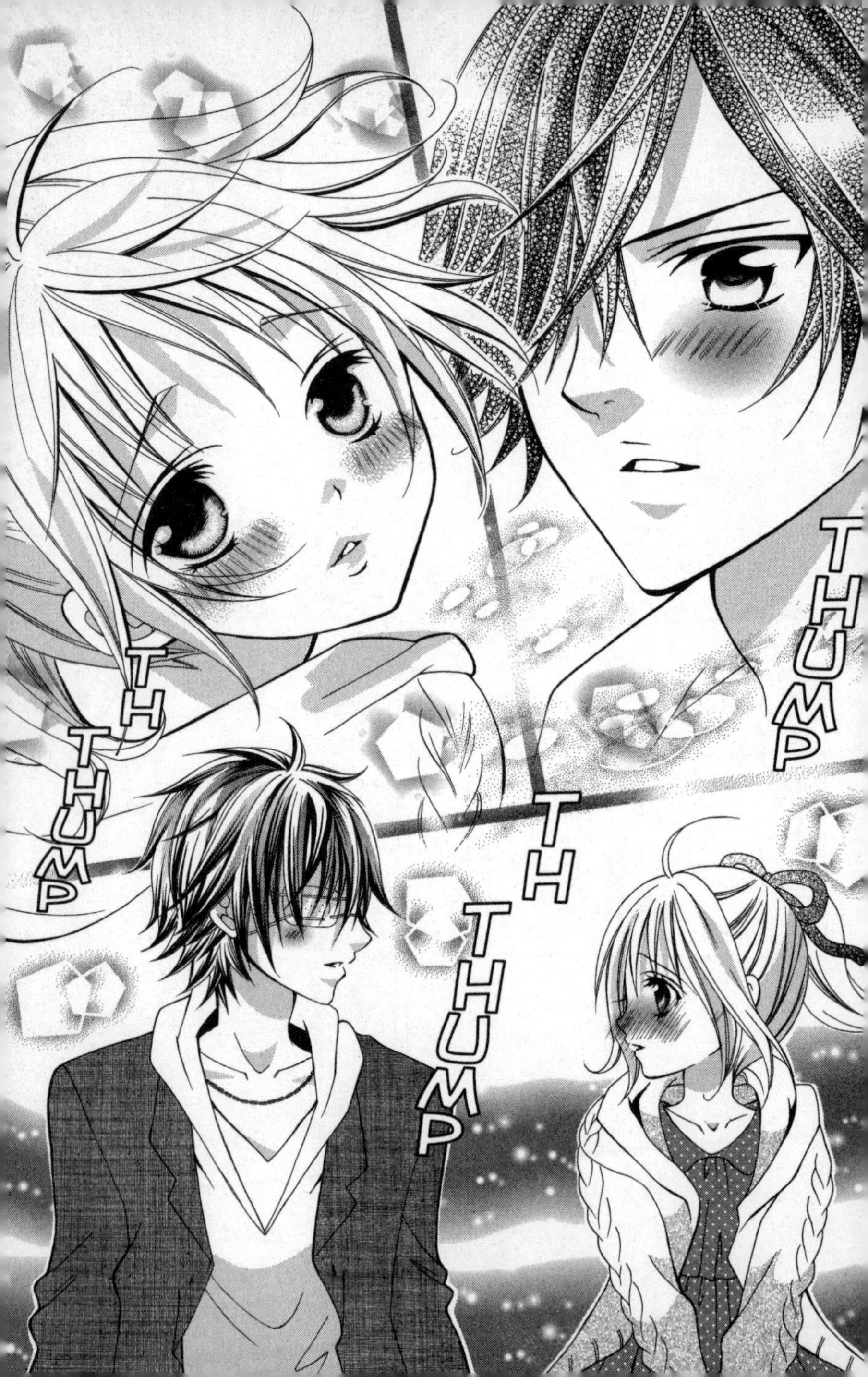
THUMP
TH
THUMP
TH
THUMP

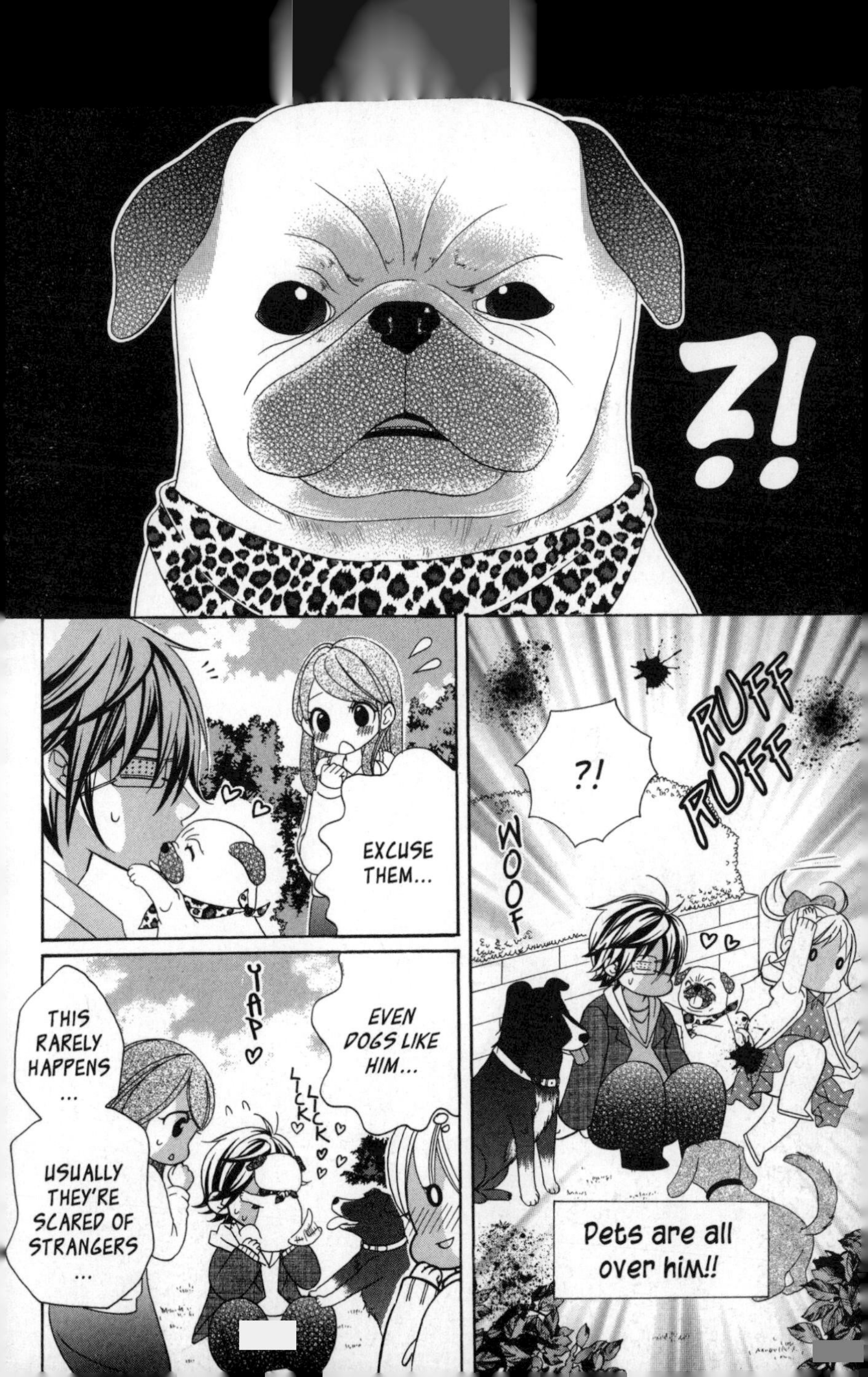
?!
?!
RUFF RUFF
WOOF
Pets are all over him!!
EXCUSE THEM...
EVEN DOGS LIKE HIM...
YAP
LICK LICK
THIS RARELY HAPPENS ...
USUALLY THEY'RE SCARED OF STRANGERS ...

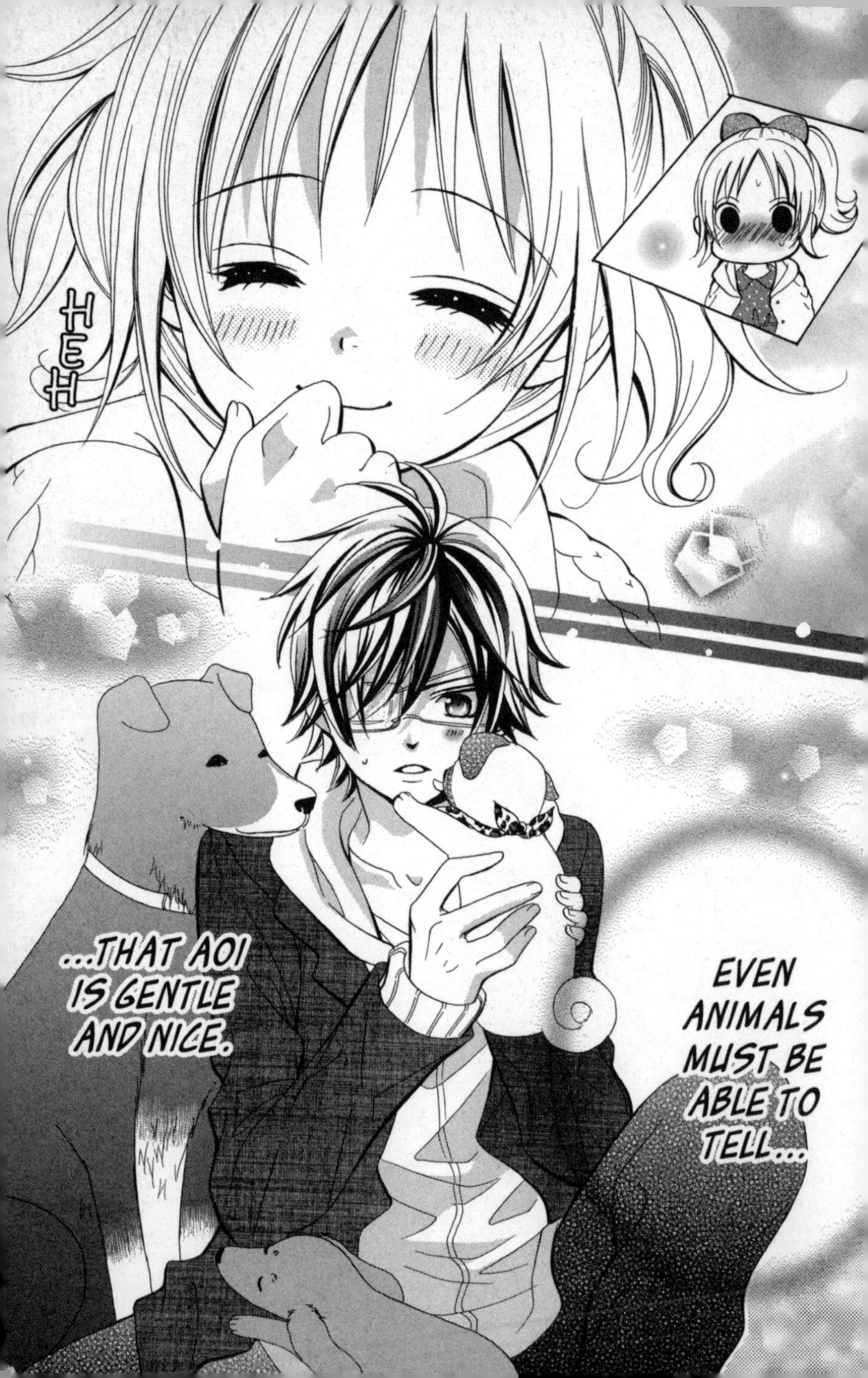
EVEN ANIMALS MUST BE ABLE TO TELL...
...THAT AOI IS GENTLE AND NICE.
HEH

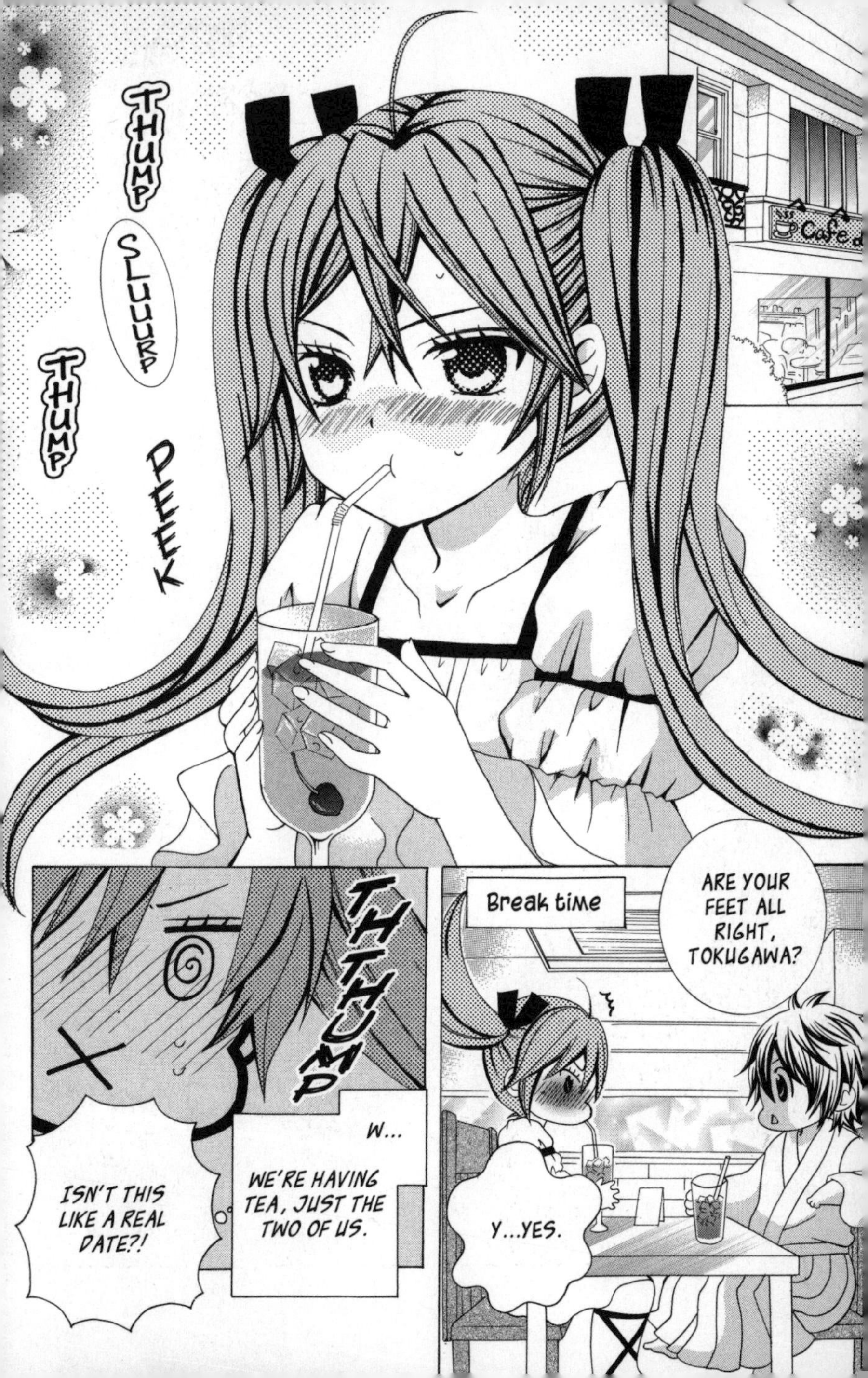
THUMP
SLUUUURP
THUMP
PEEEK
ARE YOUR FEET ALL RIGHT, TOKUGAWA?
Break time
Y...YES.
THTHUMP
W...
WE'RE HAVING TEA, JUST THE TWO OF US.
ISN'T THIS LIKE A REAL DATE?!

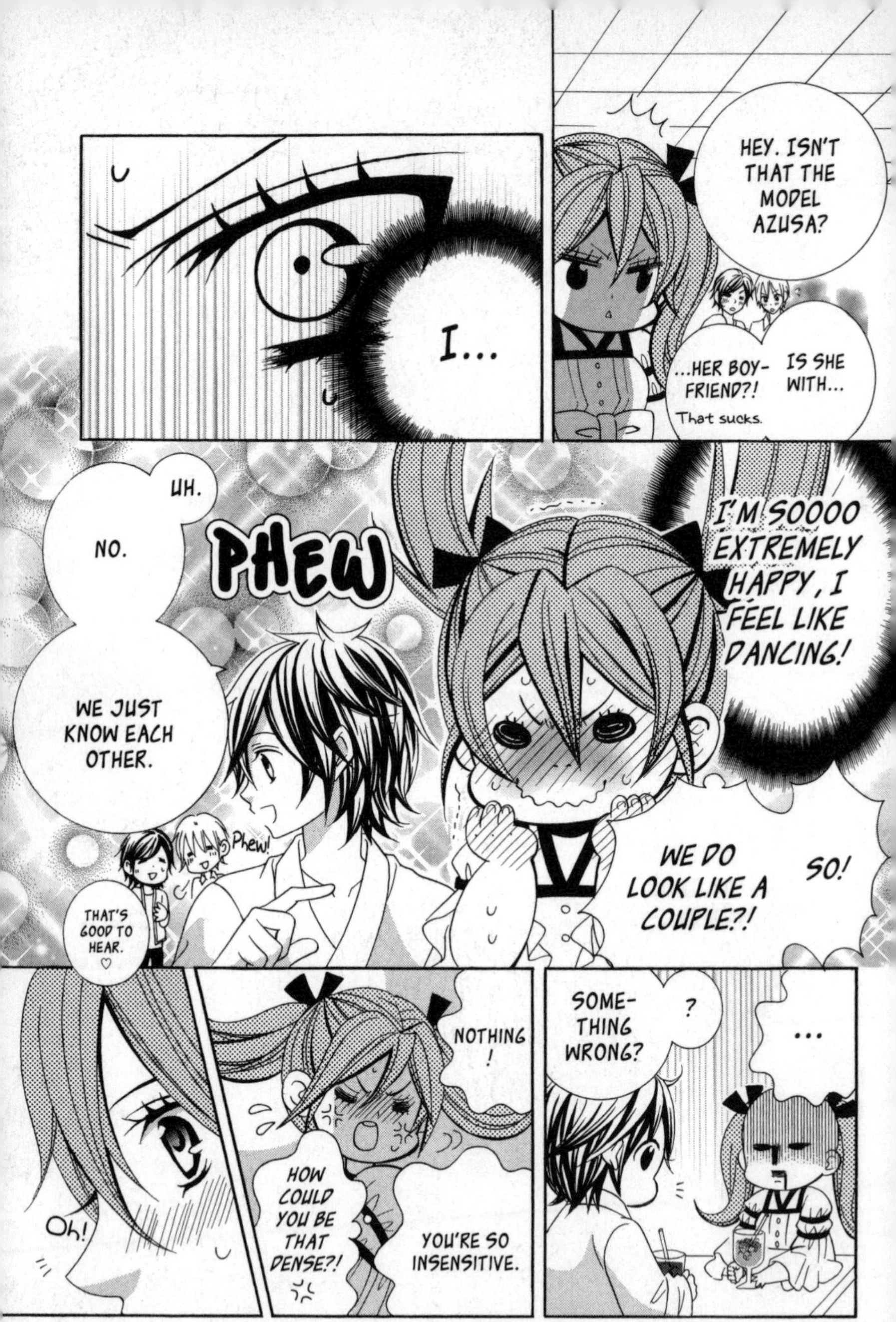
HEY. ISN'T THAT THE MODEL AZUSA?
IS SHE WITH...
...HER BOY-FRIEND?!
That sucks.
I...
I'M SOOOO EXTREMELY HAPPY, I FEEL LIKE DANCING!
SO!
WE DO LOOK LIKE A COUPLE?!
PHEW
UH.
NO.
WE JUST KNOW EACH OTHER.
Phew!
THAT'S GOOD TO HEAR. ♡
...
?
SOME-THING WRONG?
NOTHING!
YOU'RE SO INSENSITIVE.
HOW COULD YOU BE THAT DENSE?!
Oh!

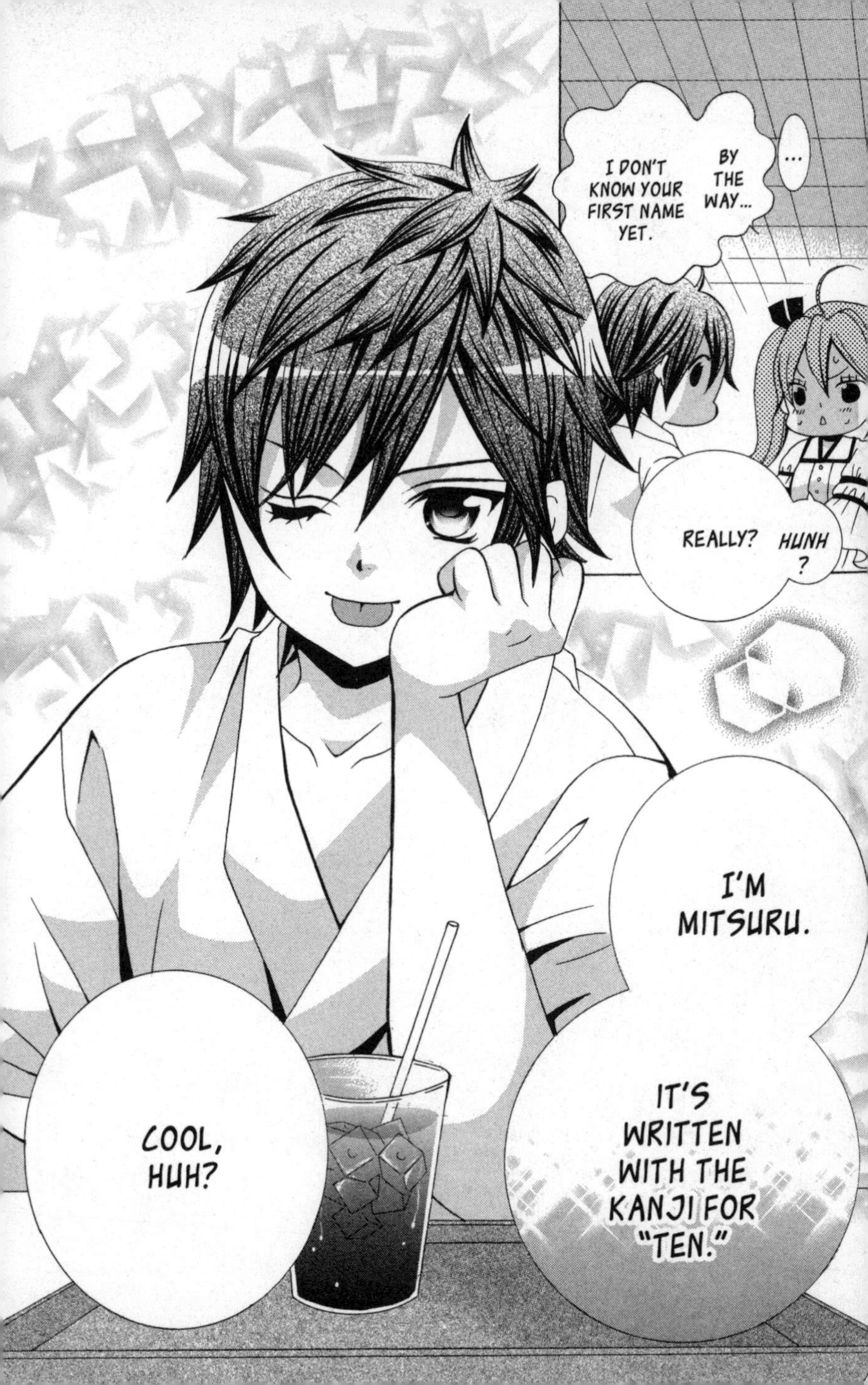
...
BY THE WAY...
I DON'T KNOW YOUR FIRST NAME YET.
HUNH?
REALLY?
I'M MITSURU.
IT'S WRITTEN WITH THE KANJI FOR "TEN."
COOL, HUH?

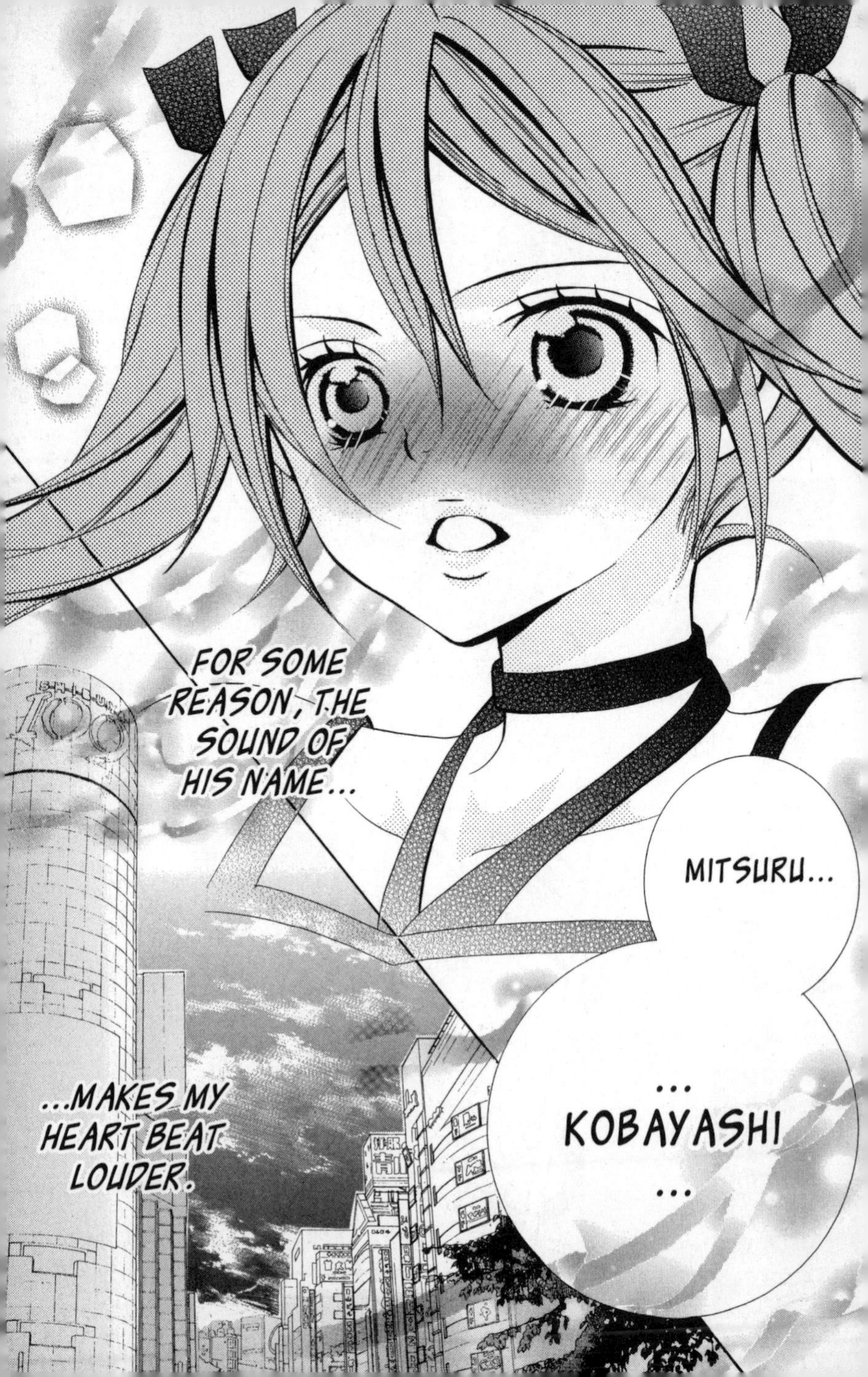
MITSURU...
... KOBAYASHI ...
FOR SOME REASON, THE SOUND OF HIS NAME...
...MAKES MY HEART BEAT LOUDER.

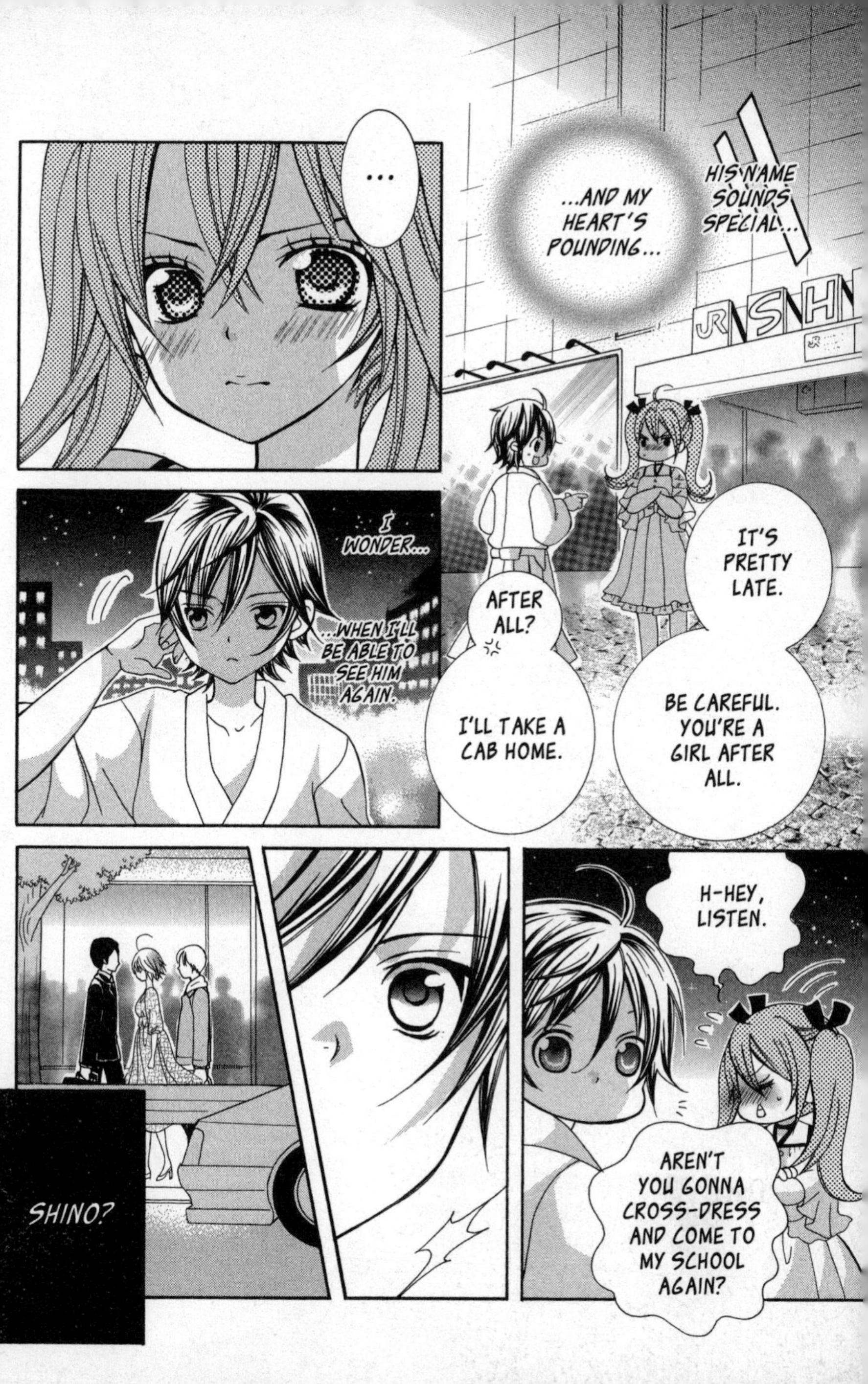
HIS NAME SOUNDS SPECIAL...
...AND MY HEART'S POUNDING...
IT'S PRETTY LATE.
BE CAREFUL. YOU'RE A GIRL AFTER ALL.
AFTER ALL?
I'LL TAKE A CAB HOME.
...
I WONDER...
...WHEN I'LL BE ABLE TO SEE HIM AGAIN.
H-HEY, LISTEN.
AREN'T YOU GONNA CROSS-DRESS AND COME TO MY SCHOOL AGAIN?
SHINO?

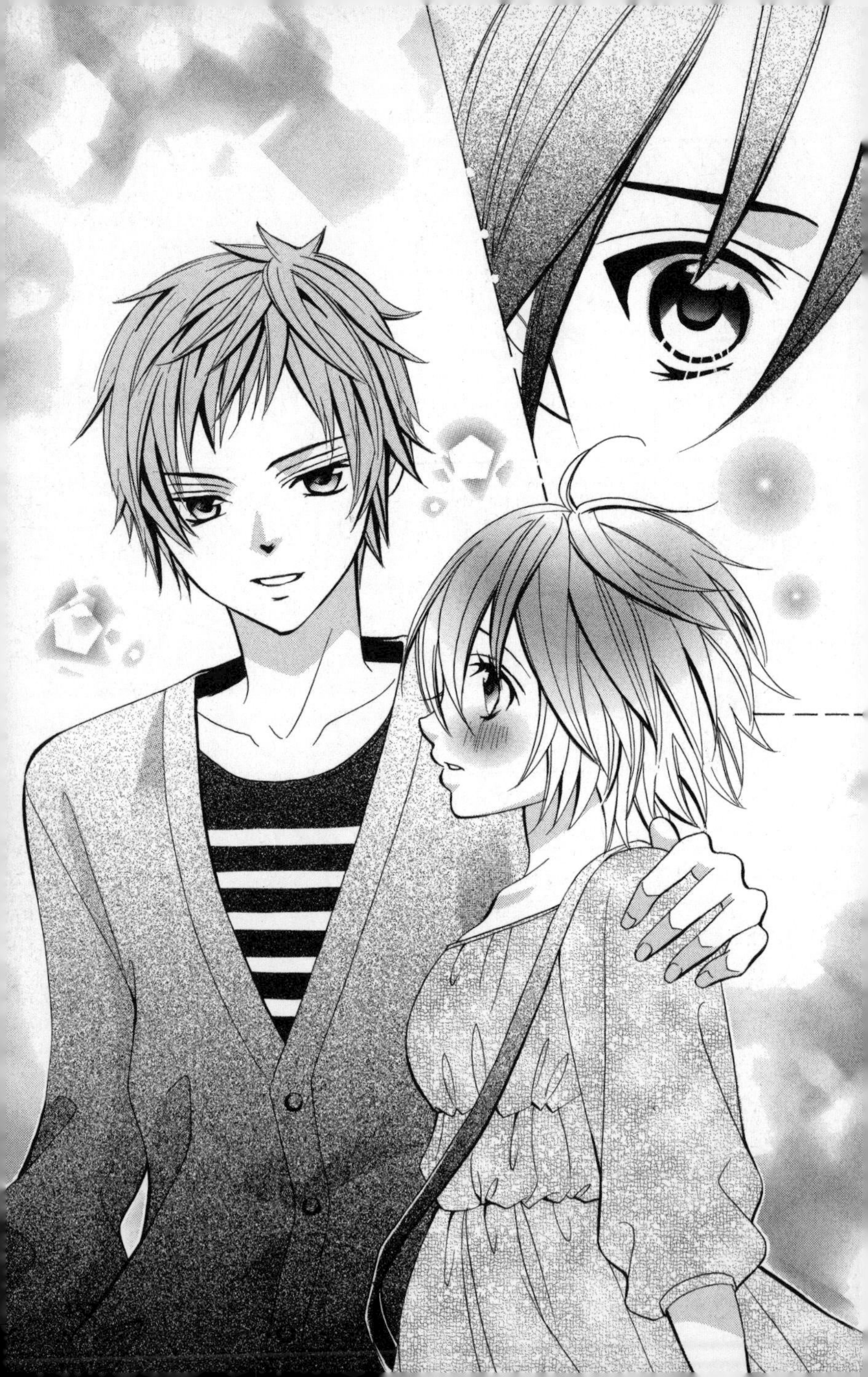

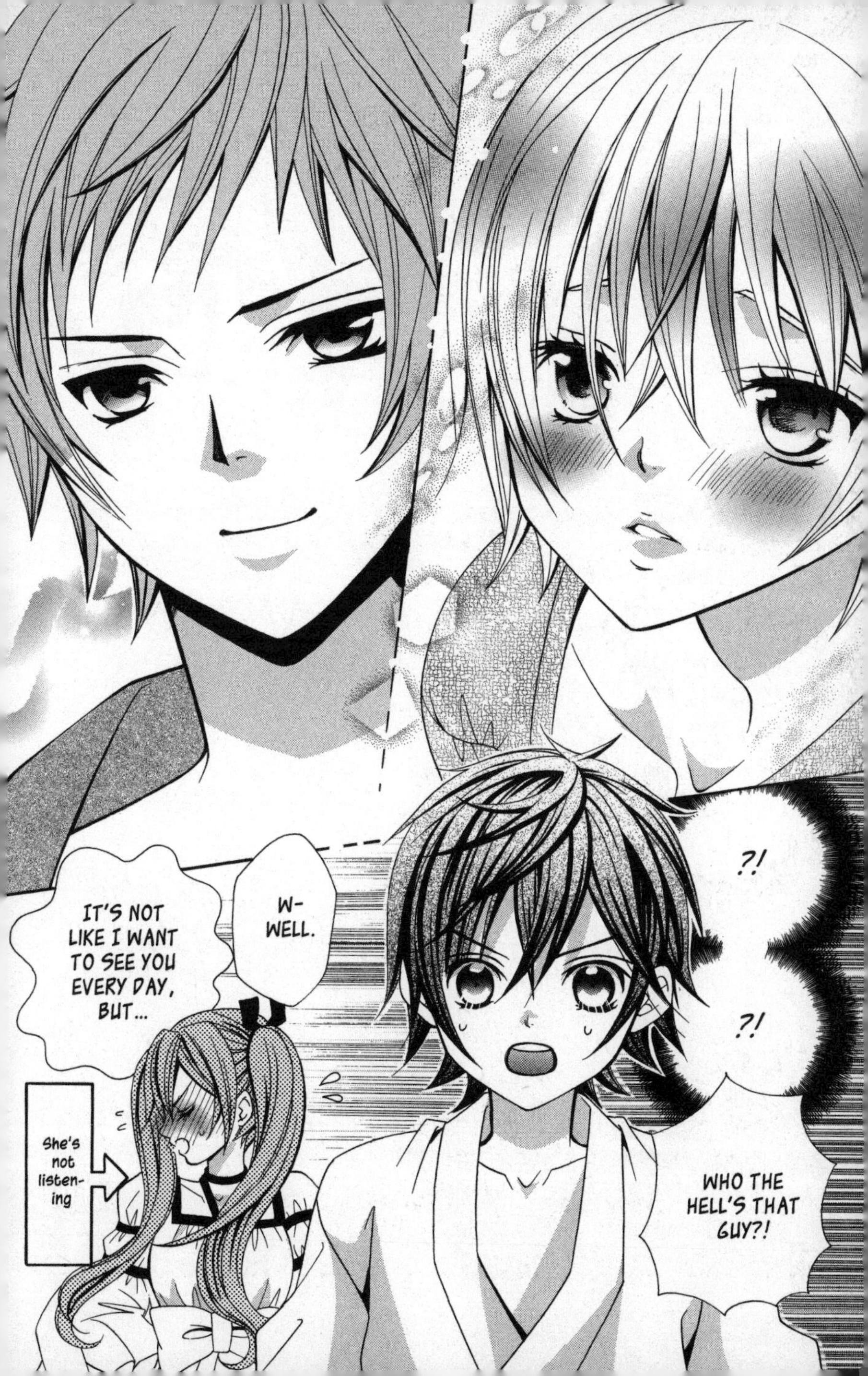
?!
?!
WHO THE HELL'S THAT GUY?!
W-WELL.
IT'S NOT LIKE I WANT TO SEE YOU EVERY DAY, BUT...
She's not listening

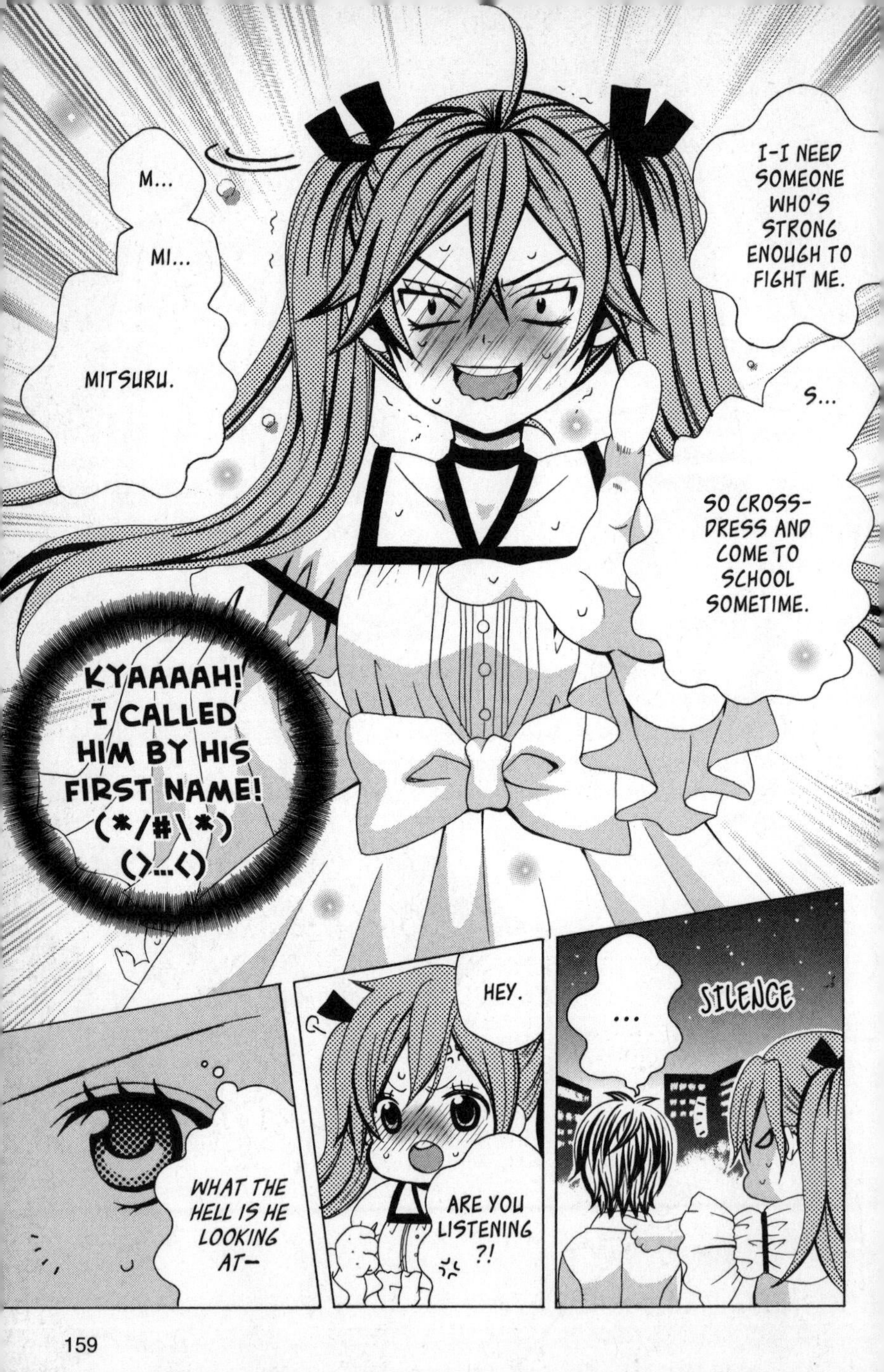
I-I NEED SOMEONE WHO'S STRONG ENOUGH TO FIGHT ME.
M...
MI...
MITSURU.
S...
SO CROSS-DRESS AND COME TO SCHOOL SOMETIME.
KYAAAAH! I CALLED HIM BY HIS FIRST NAME! (*/#*) (>...<)
...
SILENCE
HEY.
ARE YOU LISTENING ?!
WHAT THE HELL IS HE LOOKING AT—

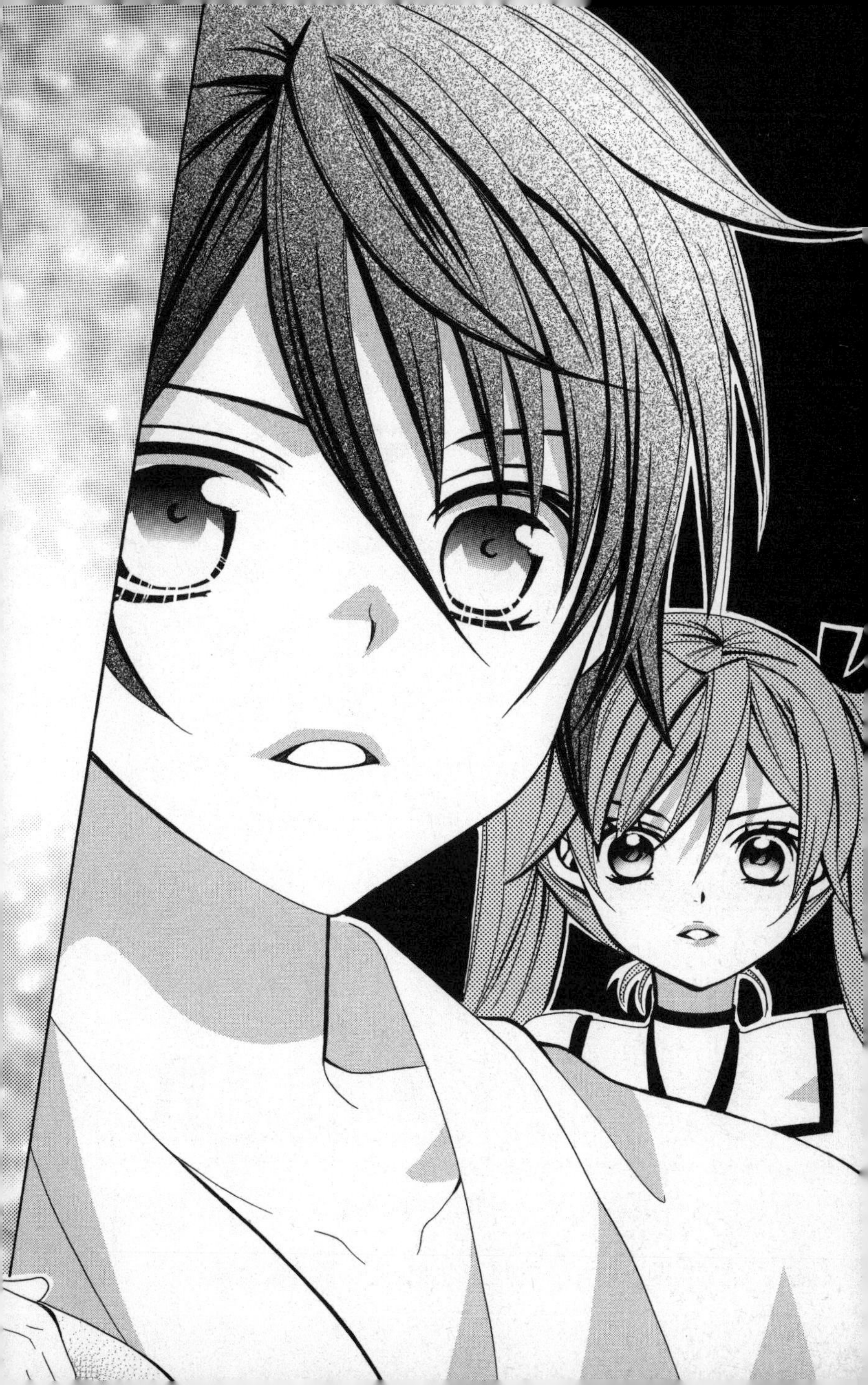

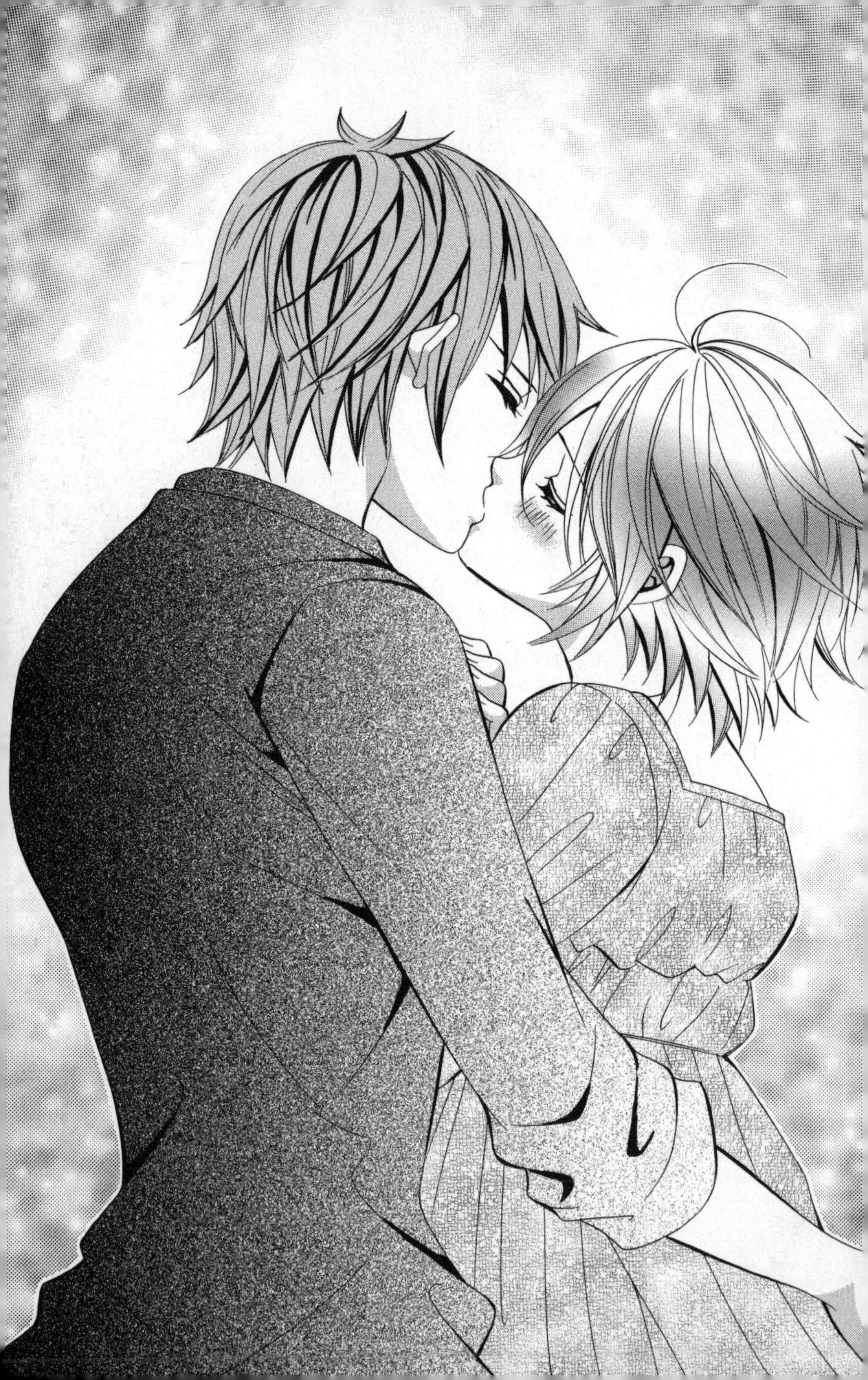

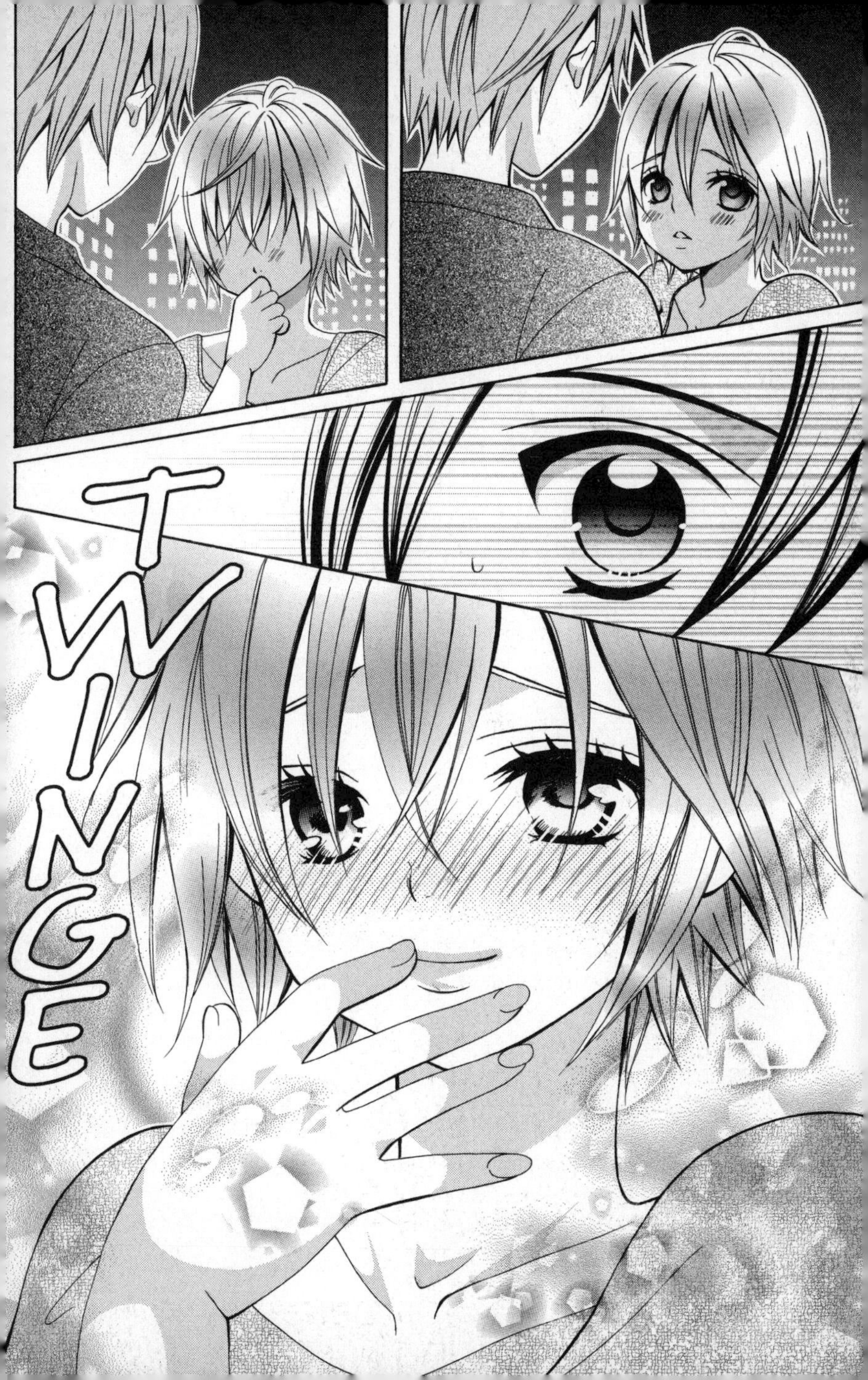
TWINGE

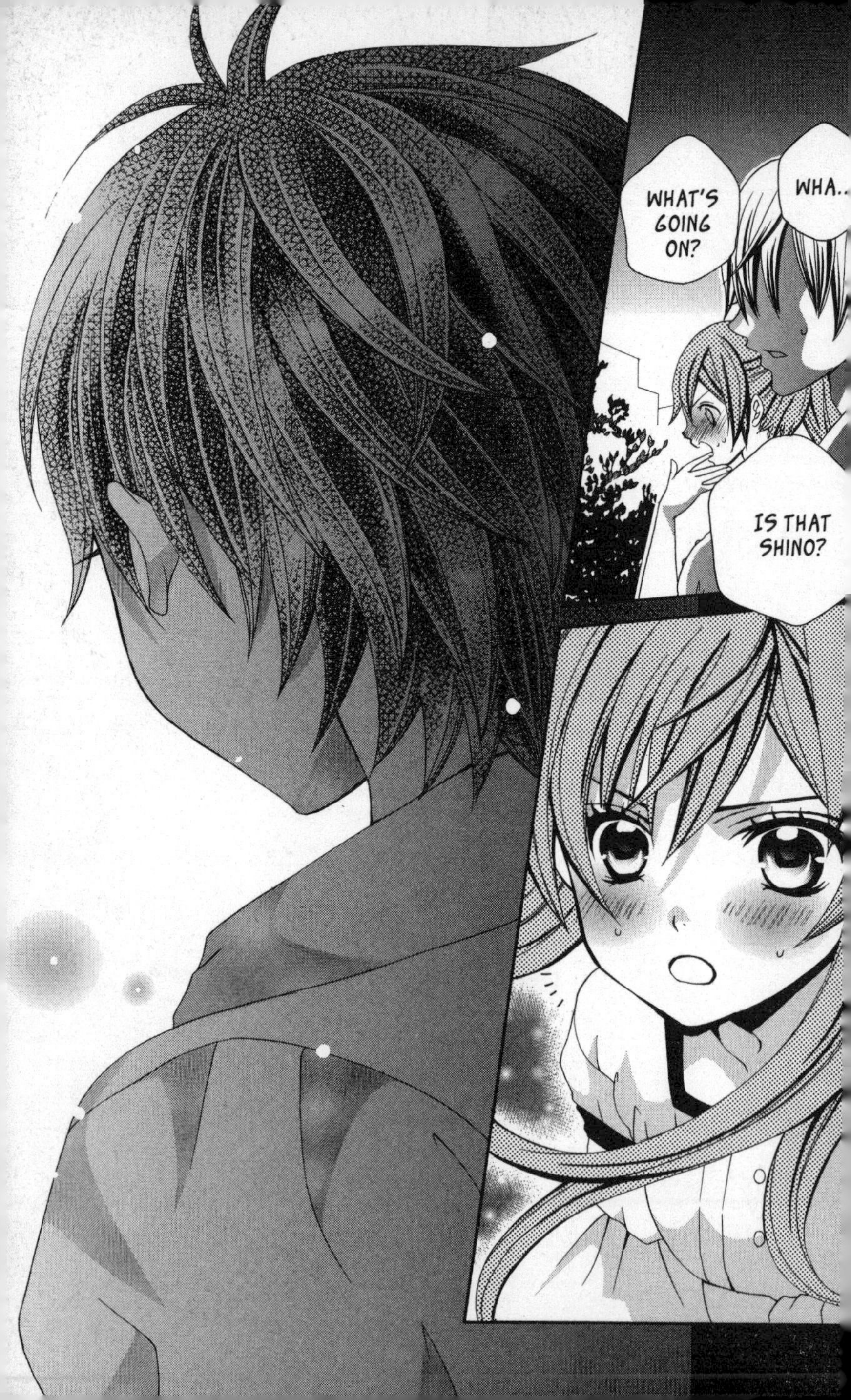
WHA..
WHAT'S GOING ON?
IS THAT SHINO?

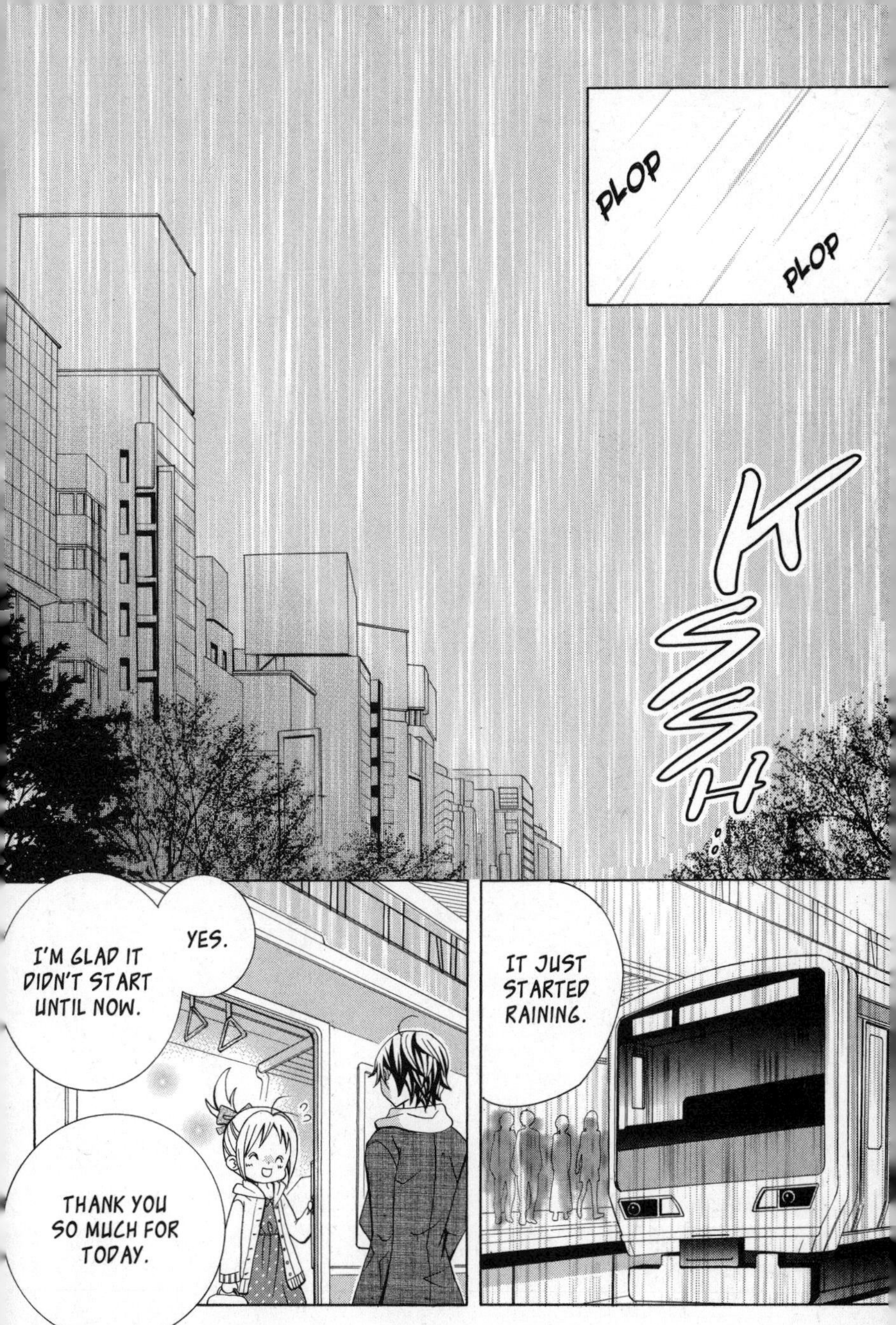
PLOP
PLOP
KSSH...
IT JUST STARTED RAINING.
YES.
I'M GLAD IT DIDN'T START UNTIL NOW.
THANK YOU SO MUCH FOR TODAY.

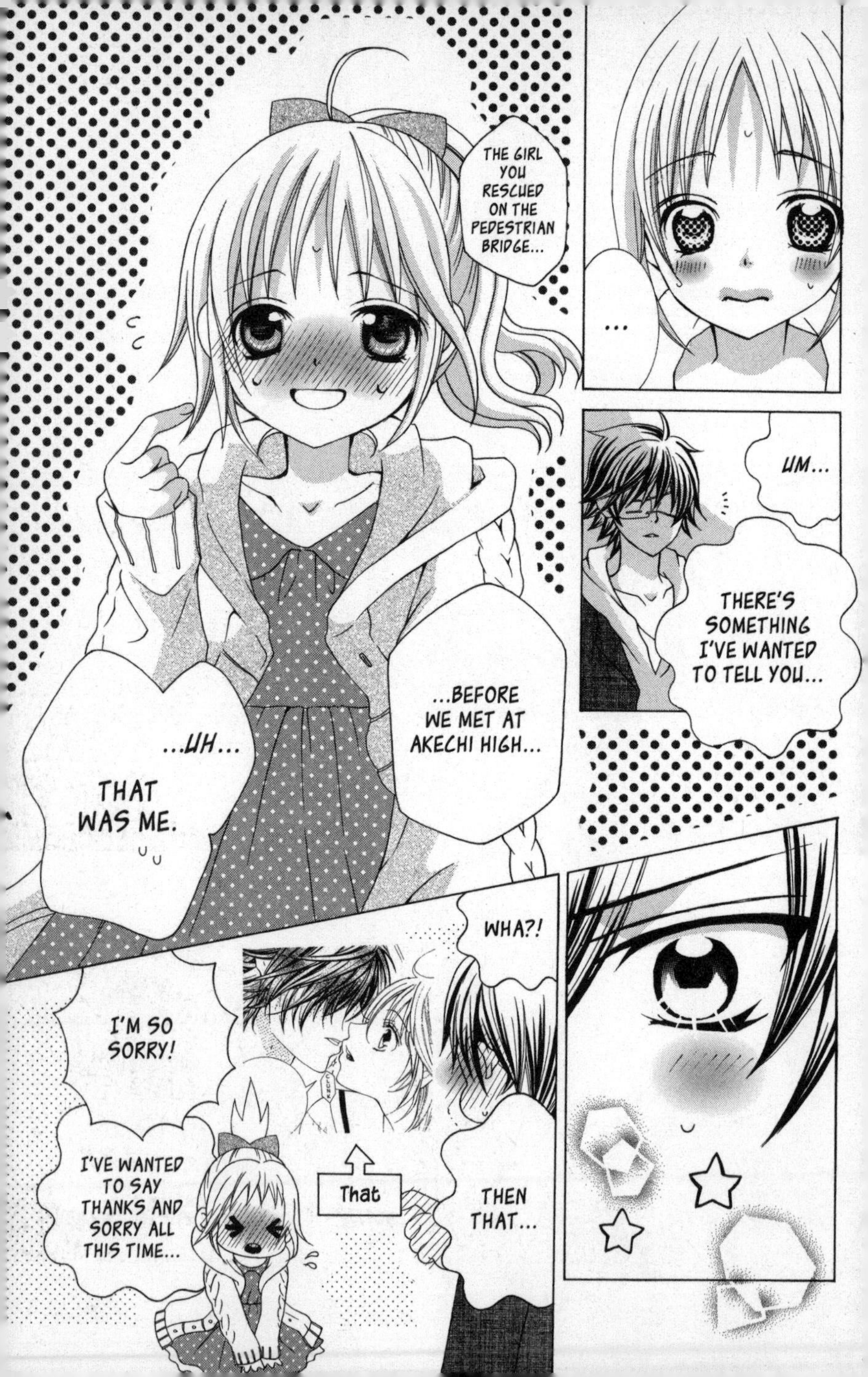
...
UM...
THERE'S SOMETHING I'VE WANTED TO TELL YOU...
THE GIRL YOU RESCUED ON THE PEDESTRIAN BRIDGE...
...BEFORE WE MET AT AKECHI HIGH...
...UH...
THAT WAS ME.
WHA?!
THEN THAT...
That
I'M SO SORRY!
I'VE WANTED TO SAY THANKS AND SORRY ALL THIS TIME...

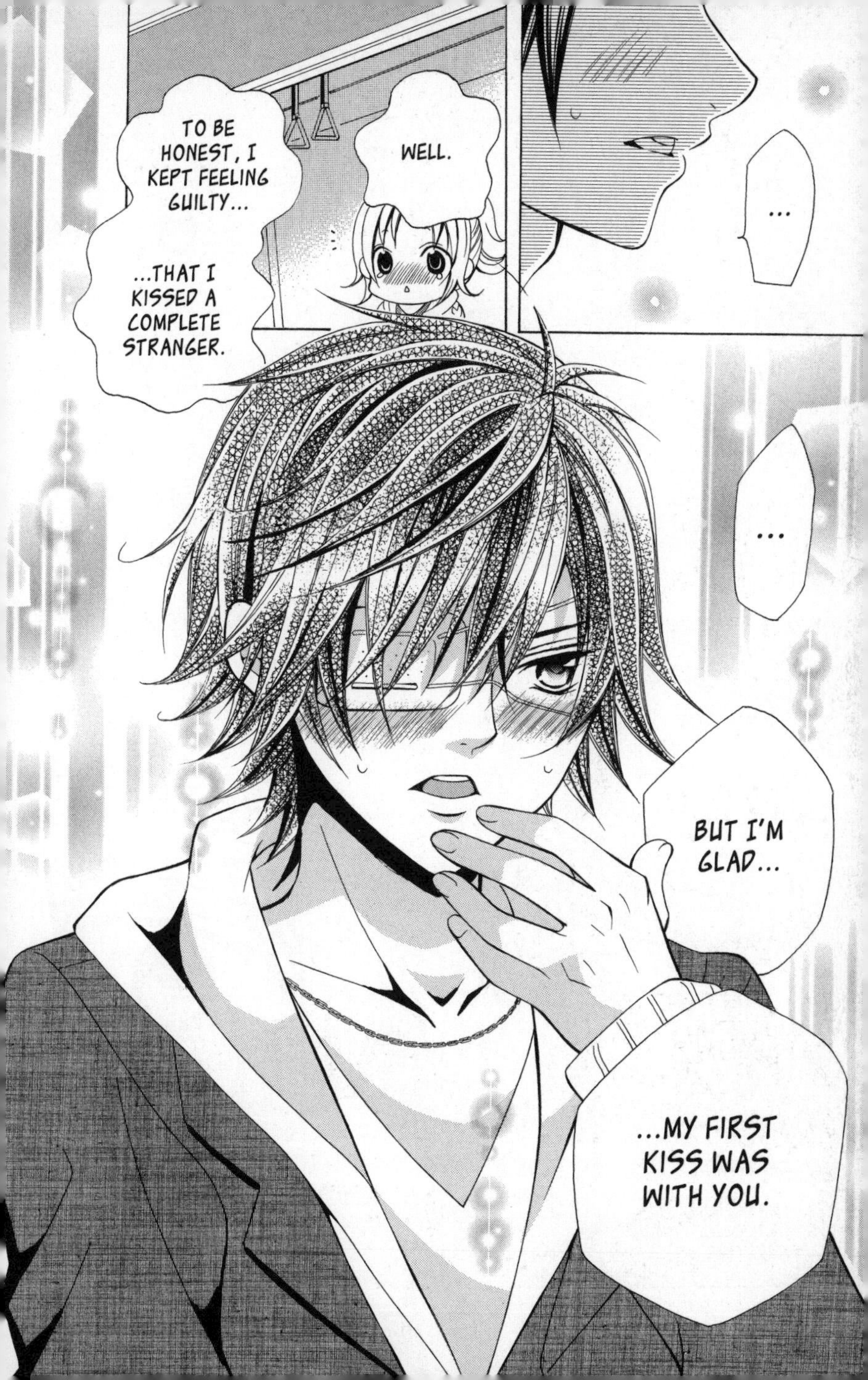
...
WELL.
TO BE HONEST, I KEPT FEELING GUILTY...
...THAT I KISSED A COMPLETE STRANGER.
...
BUT I'M GLAD...
...MY FIRST KISS WAS WITH YOU.

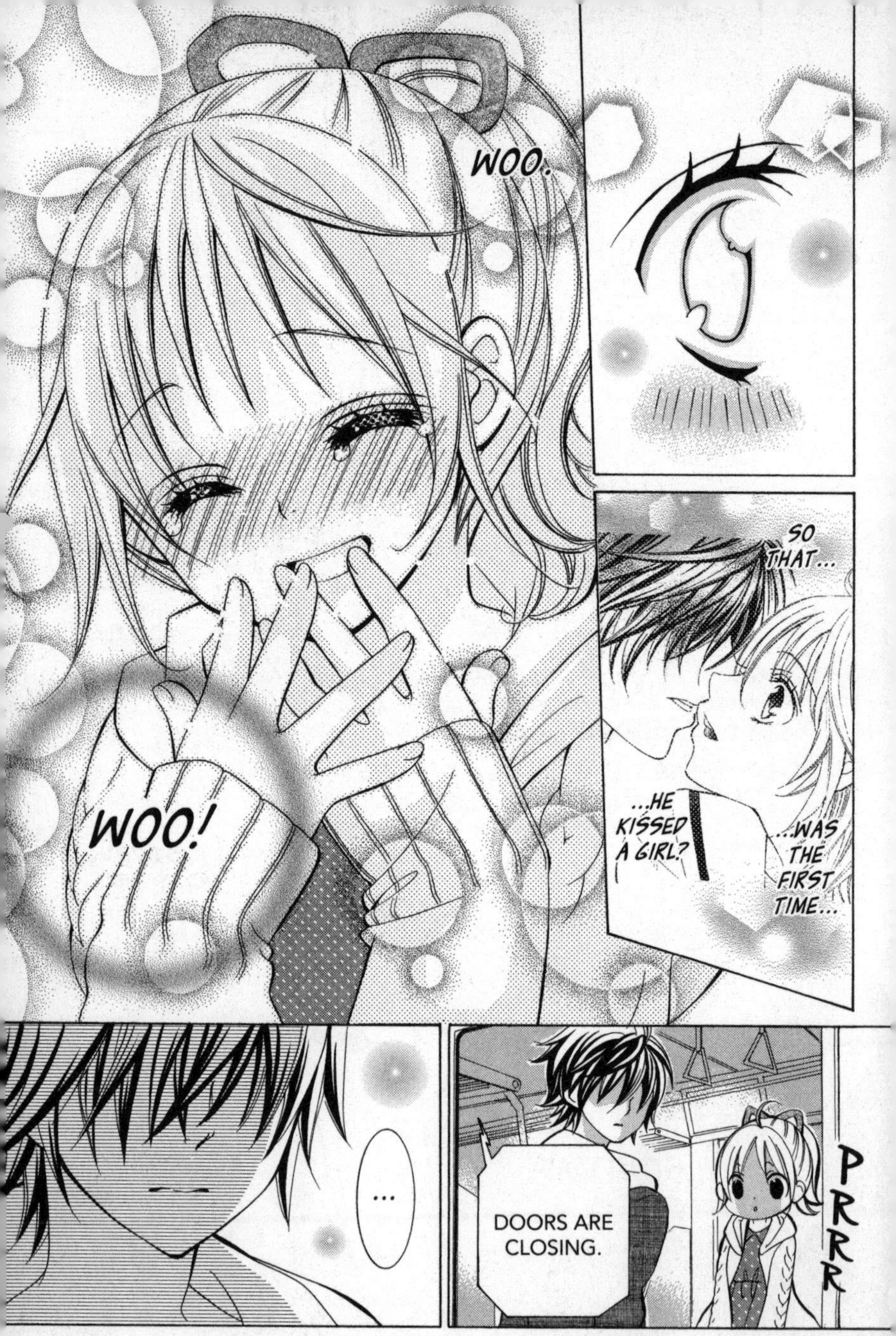
SO THAT...
...WAS THE FIRST TIME...
...HE KISSED A GIRL?
WOO.
WOO!
PRRR
DOORS ARE CLOSING.
...

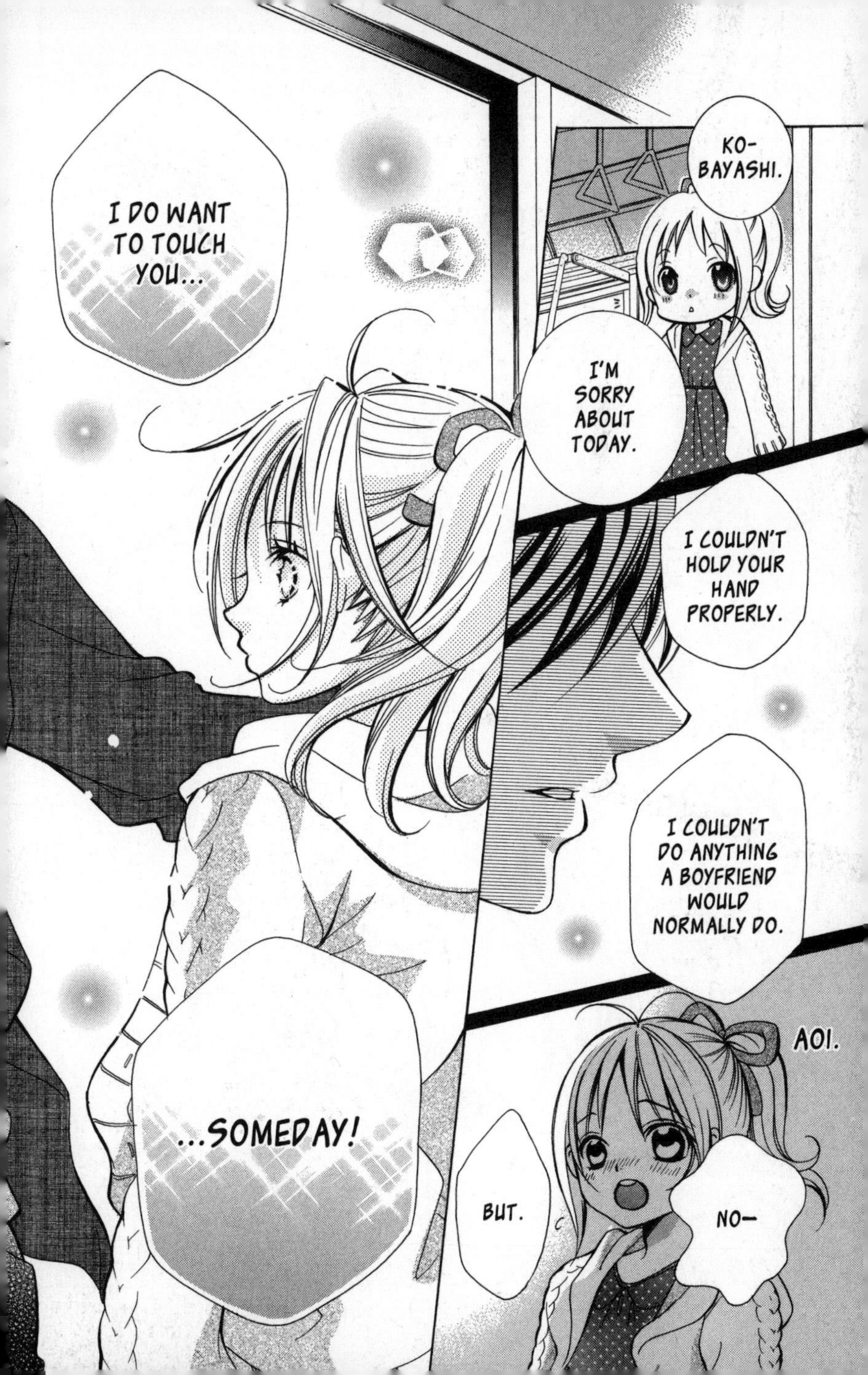
KO-BAYASHI.
I'M SORRY ABOUT TODAY.
I COULDN'T HOLD YOUR HAND PROPERLY.
I COULDN'T DO ANYTHING A BOYFRIEND WOULD NORMALLY DO.
AOI.
NO—
BUT.
I DO WANT TO TOUCH YOU...
...SOMEDAY!

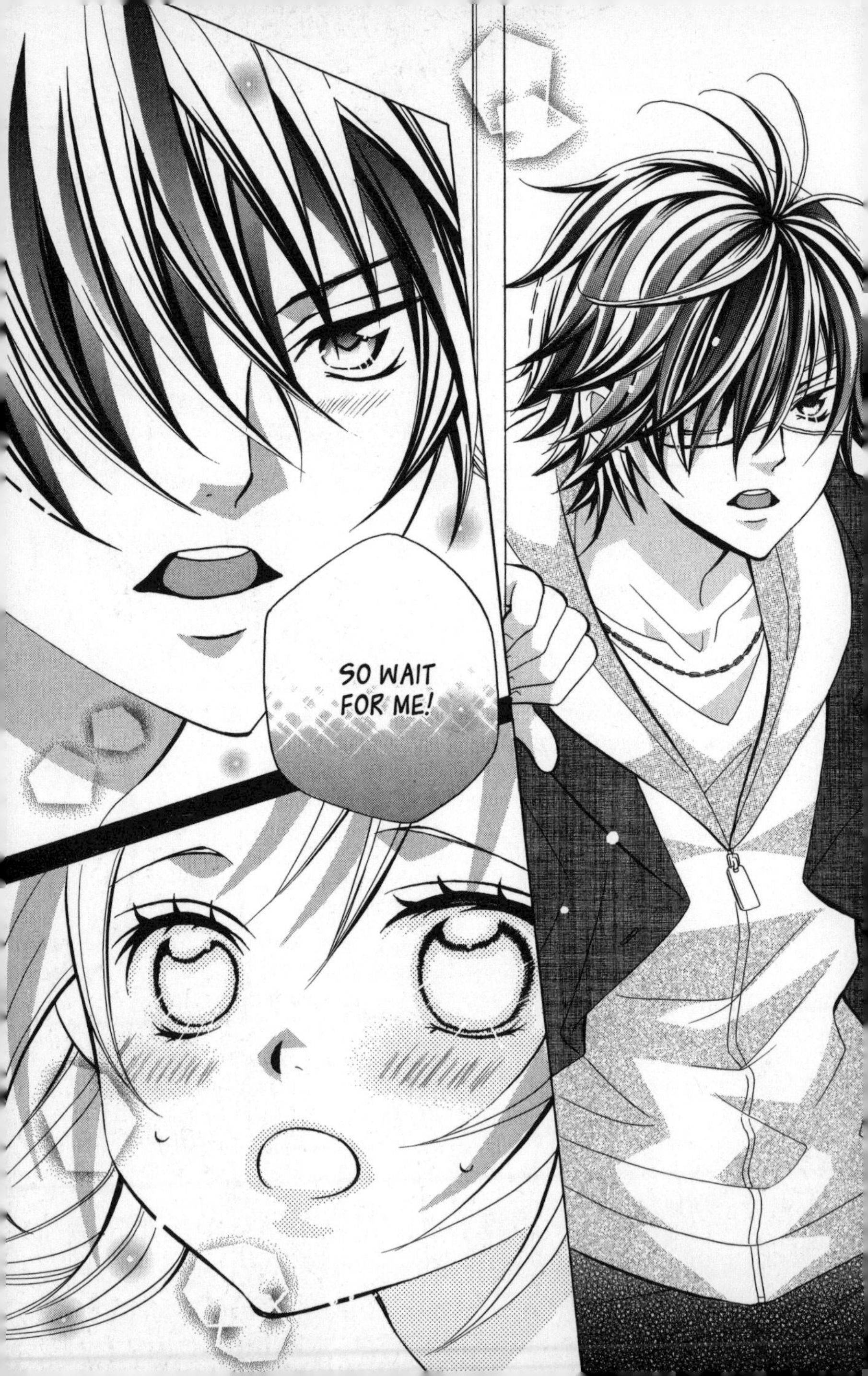
SO WAIT FOR ME!

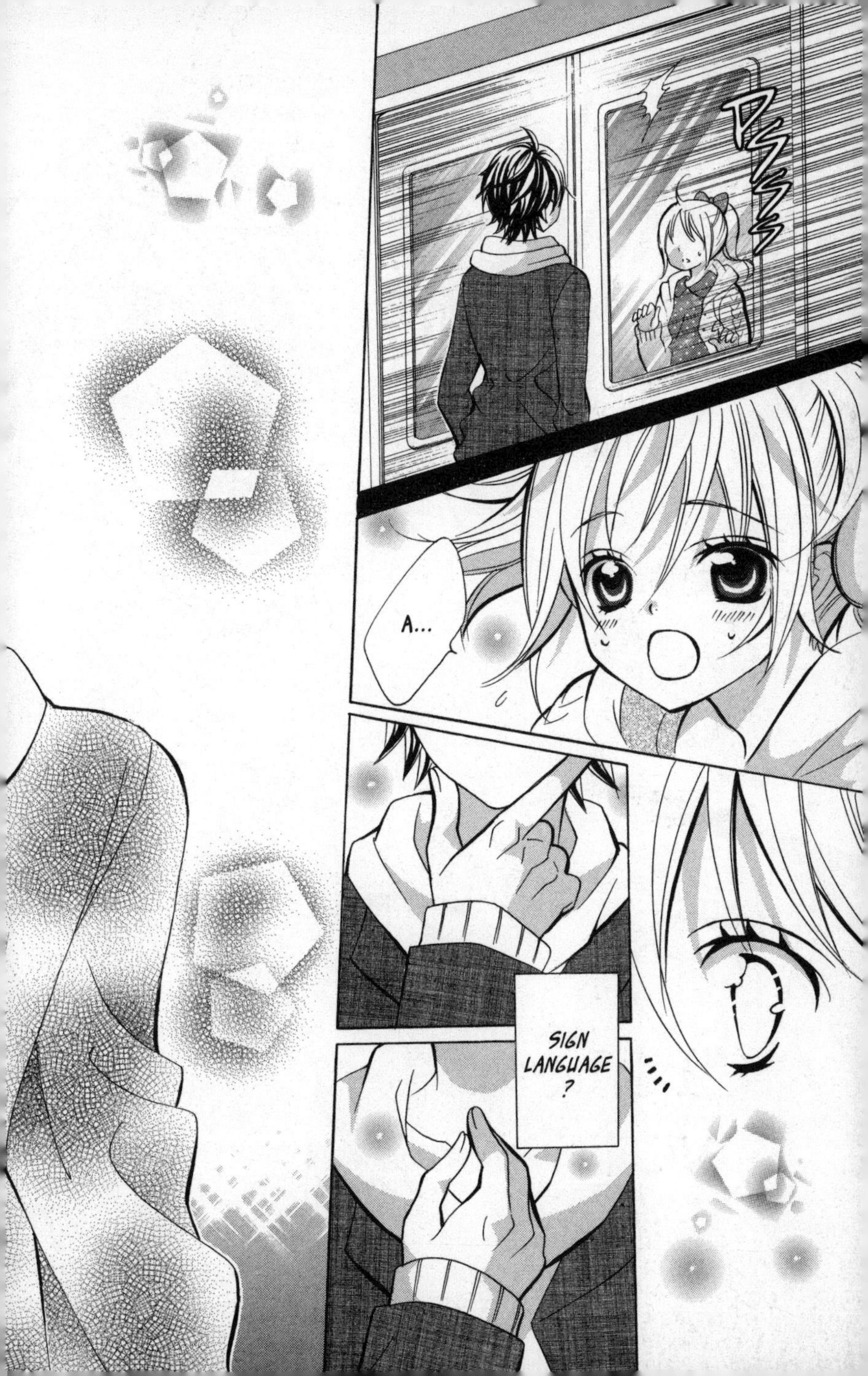
PSSS
A...
SIGN LANGUAGE ?
....

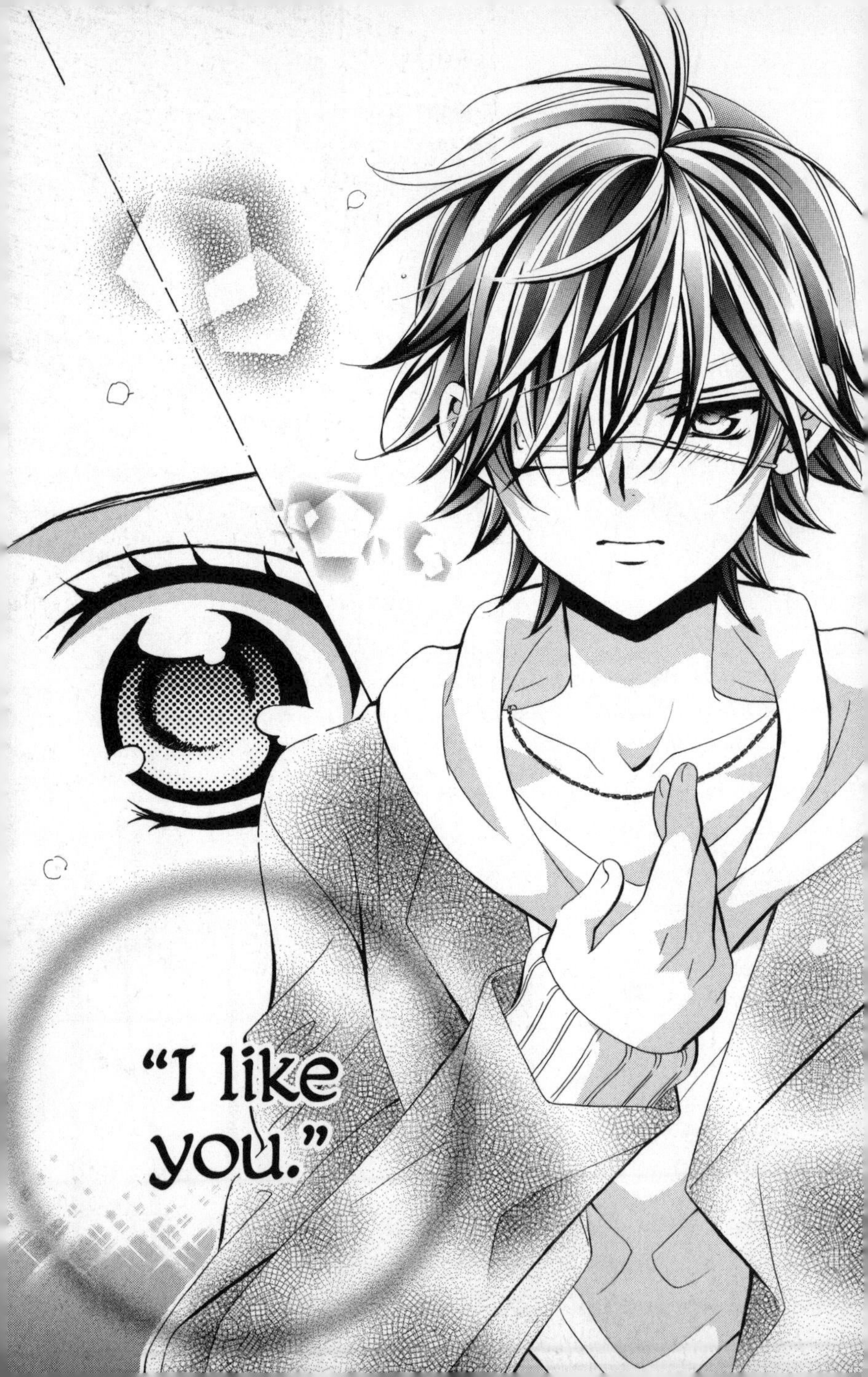
"I like you."

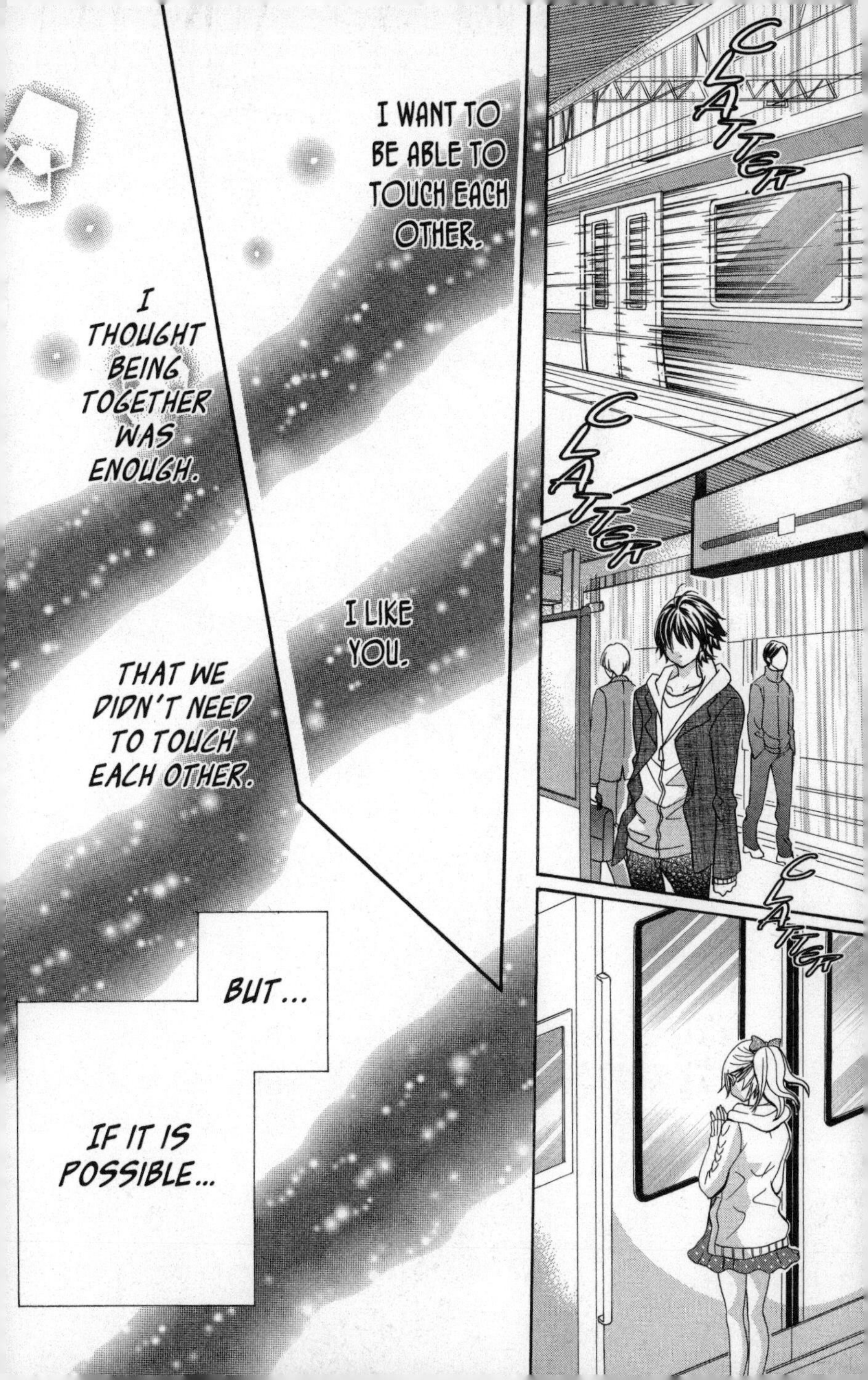
CLATTER
CLATTER
CLATTER
I WANT TO BE ABLE TO TOUCH EACH OTHER.
I LIKE YOU.
I THOUGHT BEING TOGETHER WAS ENOUGH.
THAT WE DIDN'T NEED TO TOUCH EACH OTHER.
BUT...
IF IT IS POSSIBLE...

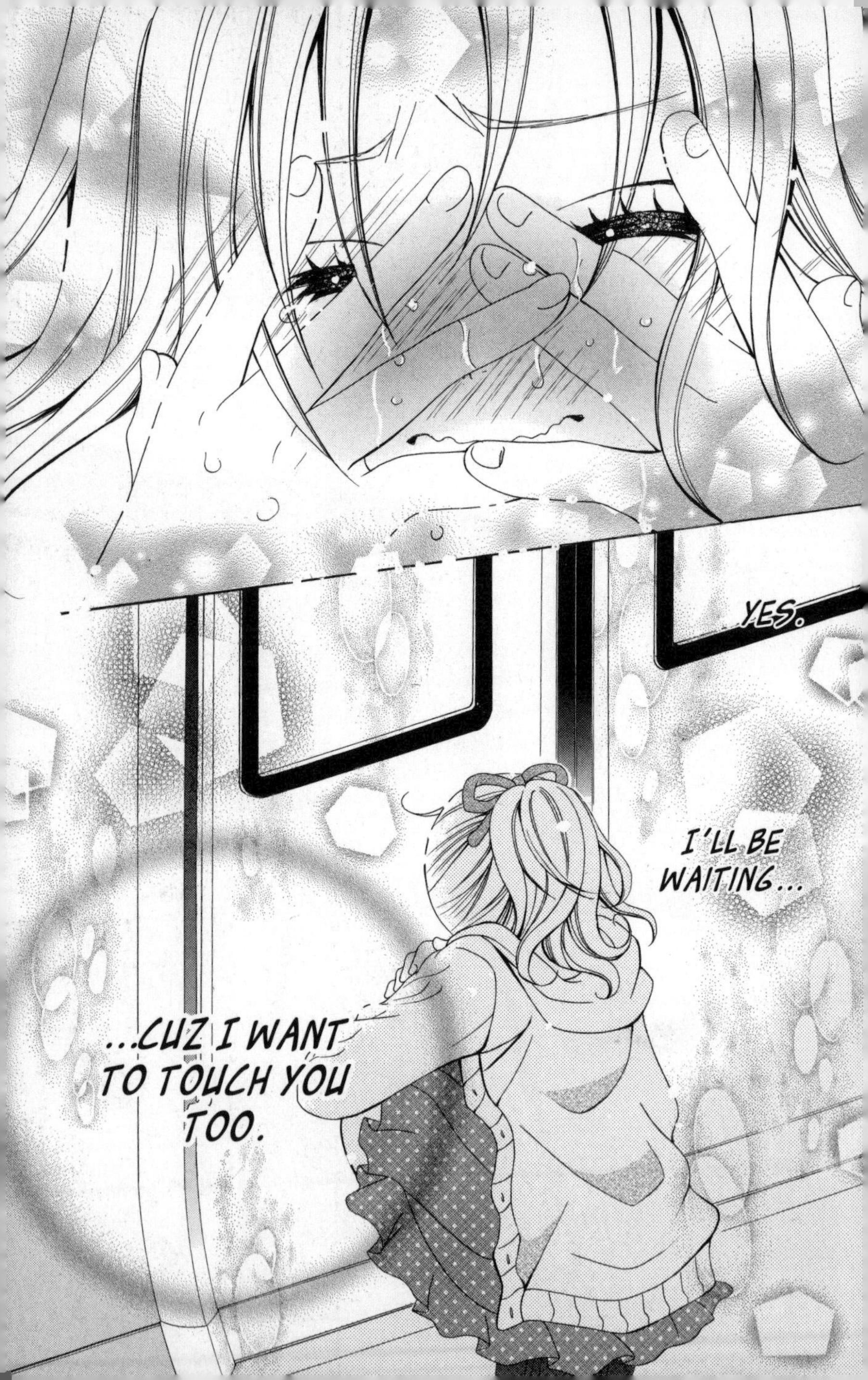
YES.
I'LL BE WAITING...
...CUZ I WANT TO TOUCH YOU TOO.

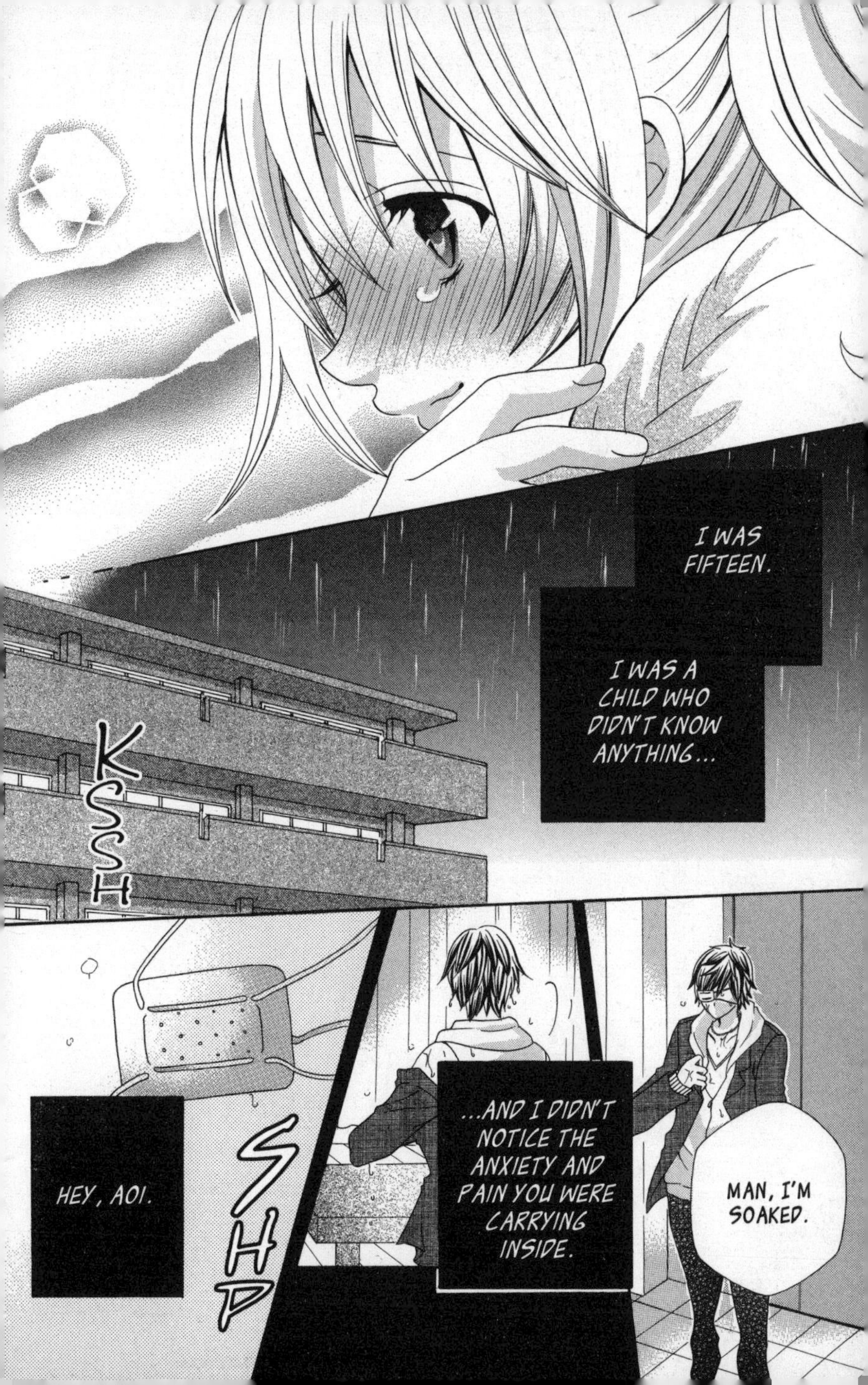
I WAS FIFTEEN.
I WAS A CHILD WHO DIDN'T KNOW ANYTHING...
KSSH
MAN, I'M SOAKED.
...AND I DIDN'T NOTICE THE ANXIETY AND PAIN YOU WERE CARRYING INSIDE.
SHP
HEY, AOI.

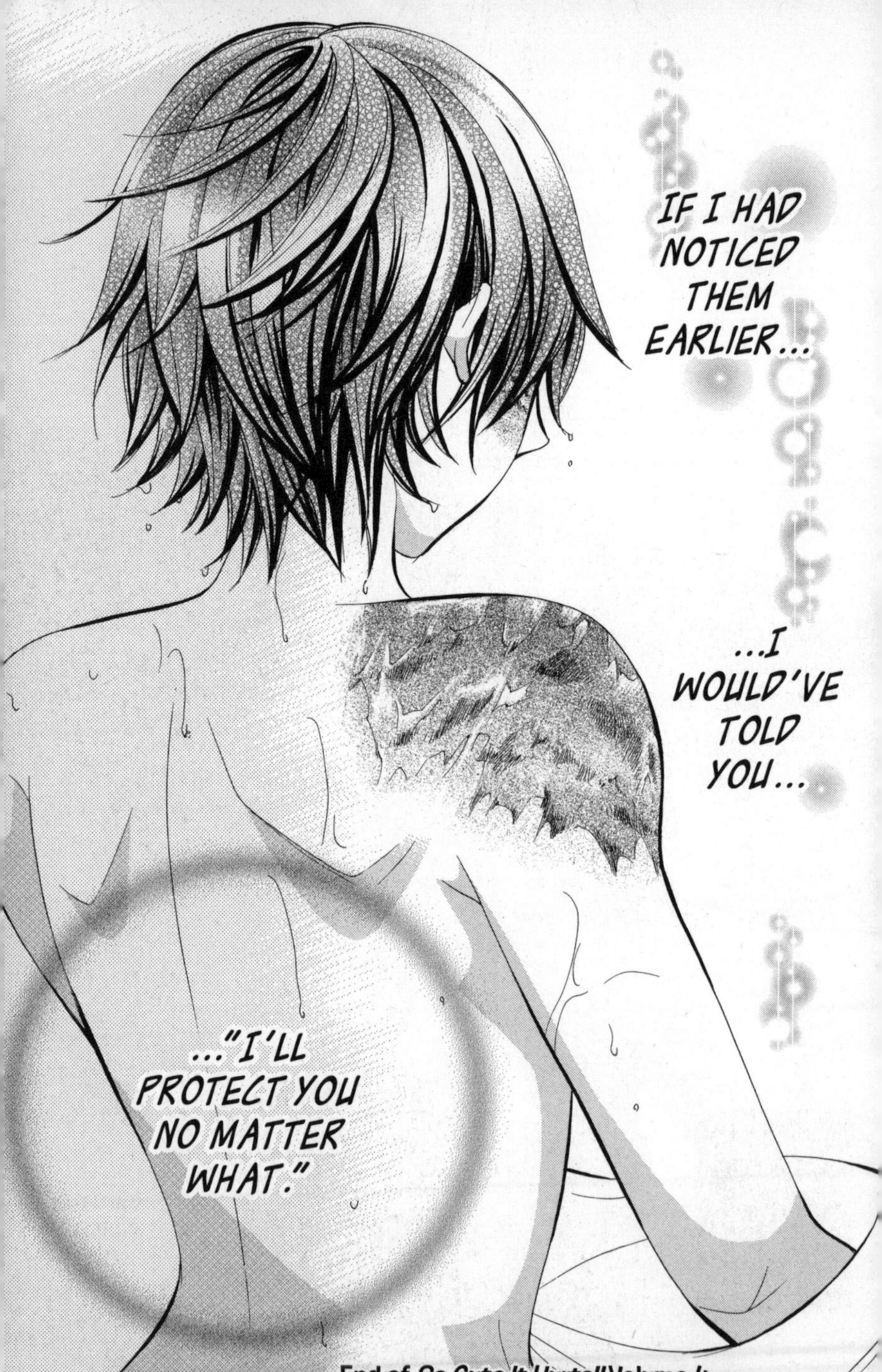
IF I HAD NOTICED THEM EARLIER...
...I WOULD'VE TOLD YOU...
..."I'LL PROTECT YOU NO MATTER WHAT."

End of *So Cute It Hurts!!* Volume 4

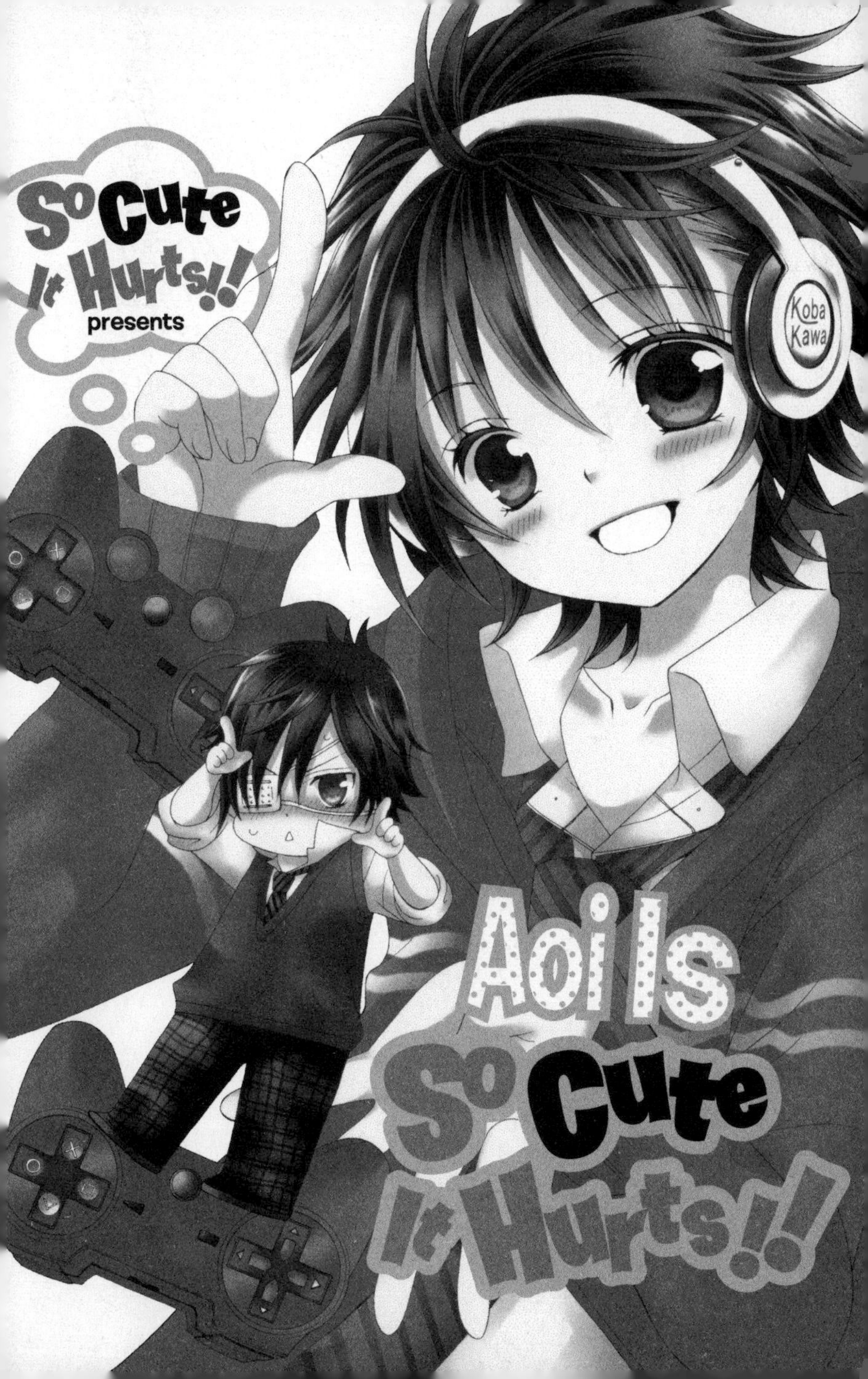
So Cute It Hurts!!
presents
Koba Kawa
Aoi Is So Cute It Hurts!!

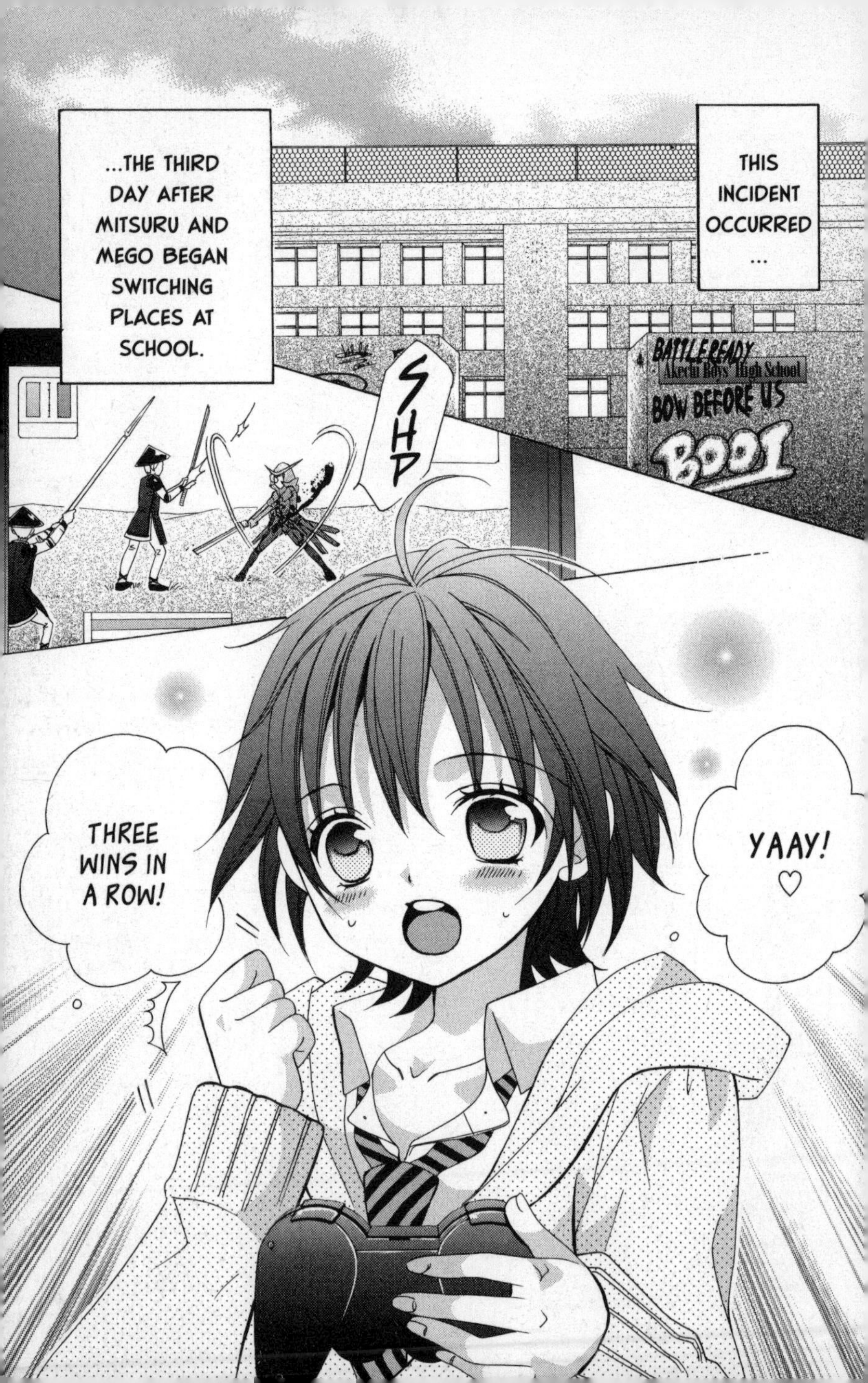
THIS INCIDENT OCCURRED ...
...THE THIRD DAY AFTER MITSURU AND MEGO BEGAN SWITCHING PLACES AT SCHOOL.
BATTLEREADY
Akechi Boys' High School
BOW BEFORE US
SHP
YAAY! ♡
THREE WINS IN A ROW!

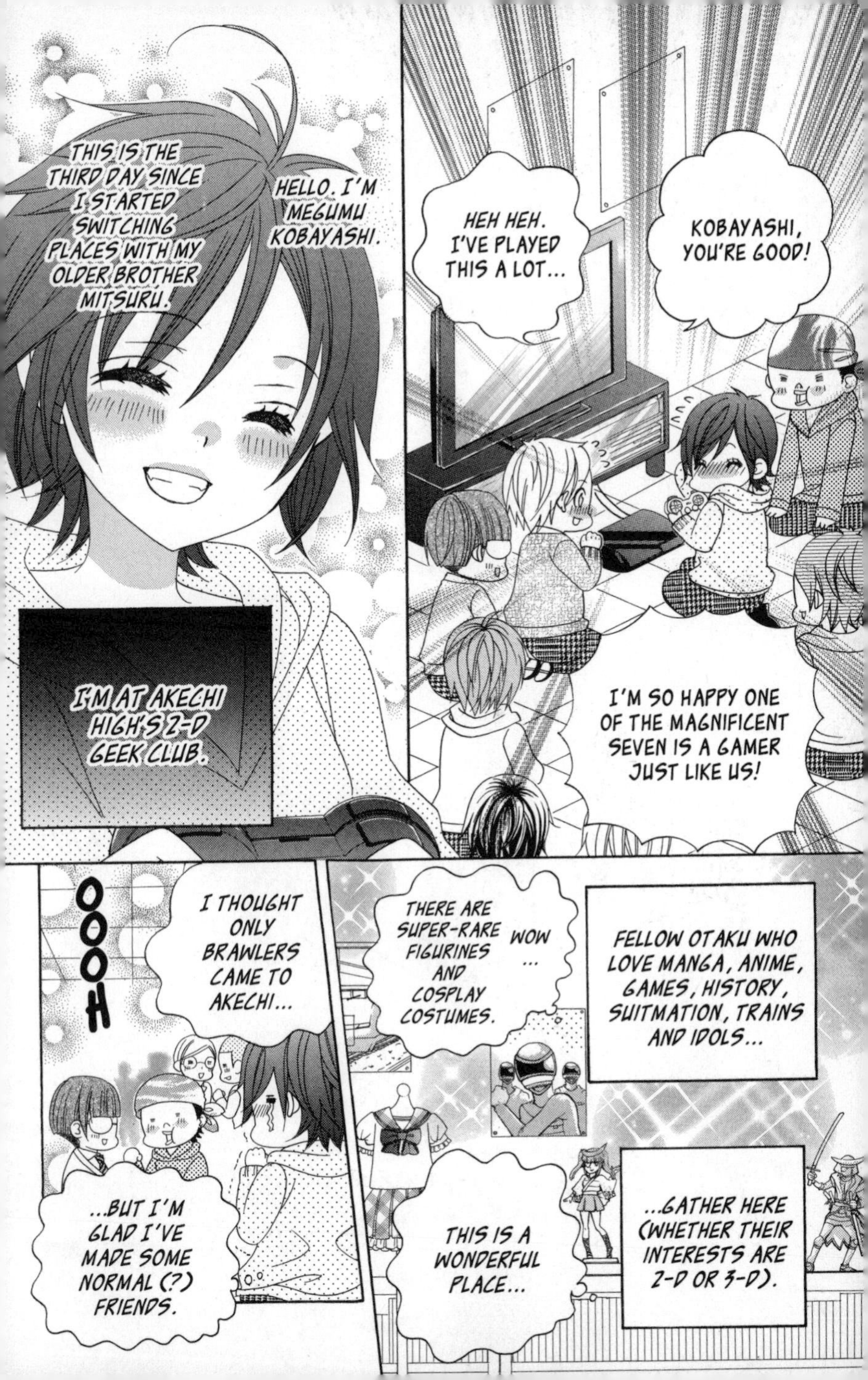
KOBAYASHI, YOU'RE GOOD!
HEH HEH. I'VE PLAYED THIS A LOT...
I'M SO HAPPY ONE OF THE MAGNIFICENT SEVEN IS A GAMER JUST LIKE US!
HELLO. I'M MEGUMU KOBAYASHI.
THIS IS THE THIRD DAY SINCE I STARTED SWITCHING PLACES WITH MY OLDER BROTHER MITSURU.
I'M AT AKECHI HIGH'S 2-D GEEK CLUB.
FELLOW OTAKU WHO LOVE MANGA, ANIME, GAMES, HISTORY, SUITMATION, TRAINS AND IDOLS...
WOW...
THERE ARE SUPER-RARE FIGURINES AND COSPLAY COSTUMES.
...GATHER HERE (WHETHER THEIR INTERESTS ARE 2-D OR 3-D).
THIS IS A WONDERFUL PLACE...
OOOH
I THOUGHT ONLY BRAWLERS CAME TO AKECHI...
...BUT I'M GLAD I'VE MADE SOME NORMAL (?) FRIENDS.

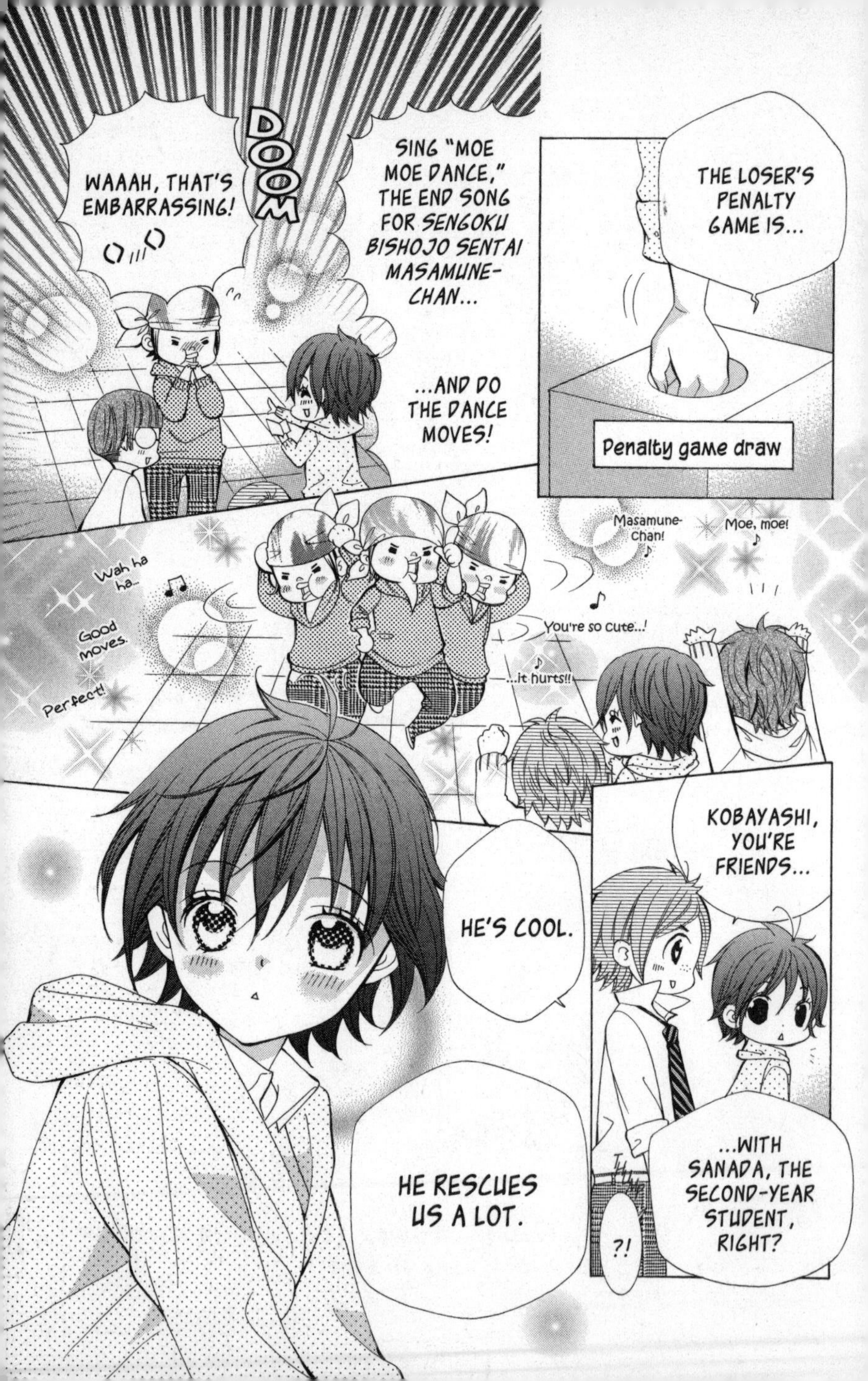
THE LOSER'S PENALTY GAME IS...
Penalty game draw
SING "MOE MOE DANCE," THE END SONG FOR SENGOKU BISHOJO SENTAI MASAMUNE-CHAN...
...AND DO THE DANCE MOVES!
DOOM
WAAAH, THAT'S EMBARRASSING!
Masamune-Chan!
Moe, moe!
You're so cute...!
...it hurts!!
Wah ha ha..
Good moves.
Perfect!
KOBAYASHI, YOU'RE FRIENDS...
...WITH SANADA, THE SECOND-YEAR STUDENT, RIGHT?
?!
HE'S COOL.
HE RESCUES US A LOT.

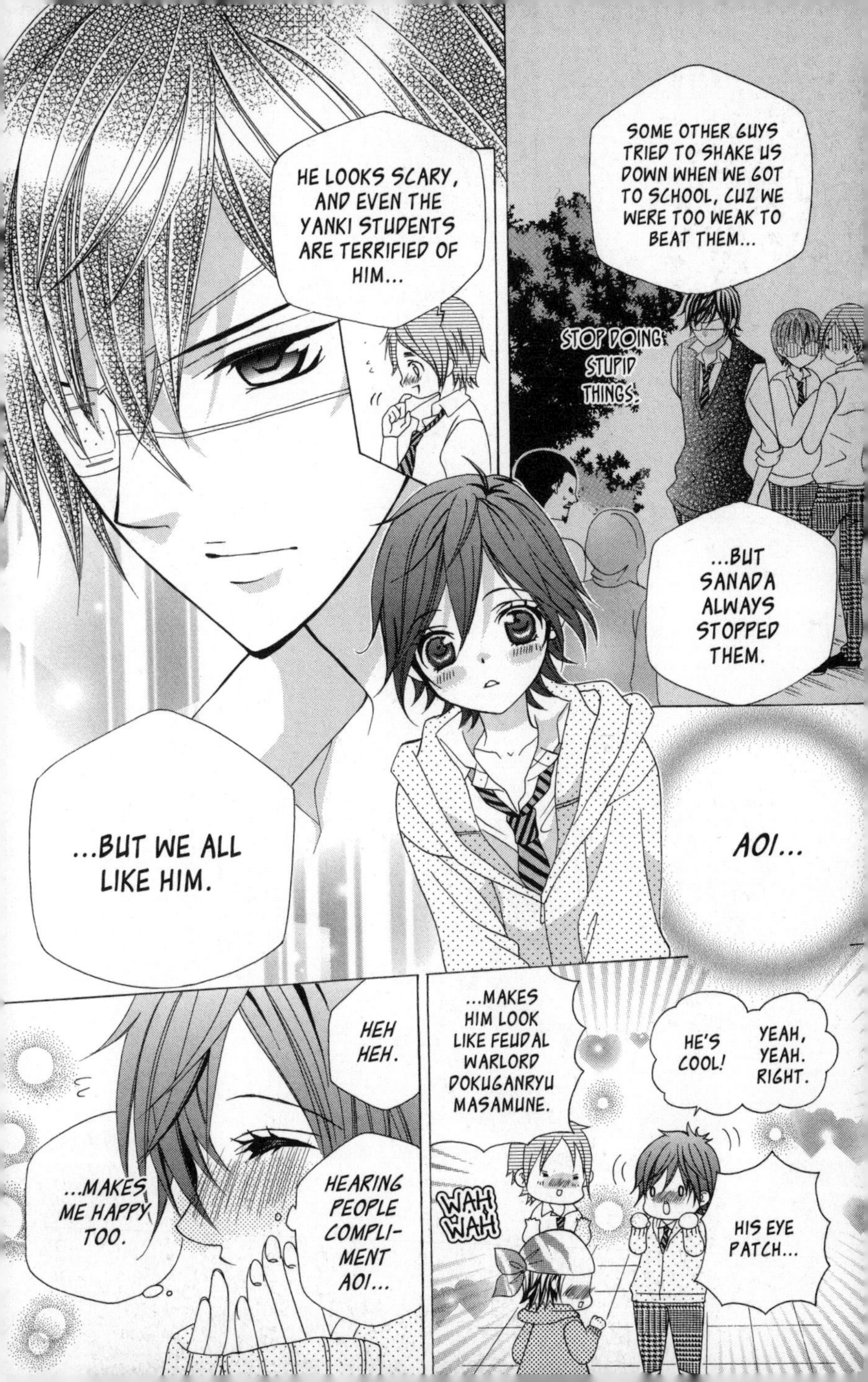
SOME OTHER GUYS TRIED TO SHAKE US DOWN WHEN WE GOT TO SCHOOL, CUZ WE WERE TOO WEAK TO BEAT THEM...
STOP DOING STUPID THINGS.
...BUT SANADA ALWAYS STOPPED THEM.
HE LOOKS SCARY, AND EVEN THE YANKI STUDENTS ARE TERRIFIED OF HIM...
AOI...
...BUT WE ALL LIKE HIM.
YEAH, YEAH. RIGHT.
HE'S COOL!
...MAKES HIM LOOK LIKE FEUDAL WARLORD DOKUGANRYU MASAMUNE.
HIS EYE PATCH...
WAH WAH
HEH HEH.
HEARING PEOPLE COMPLIMENT AOI...
...MAKES ME HAPPY TOO.

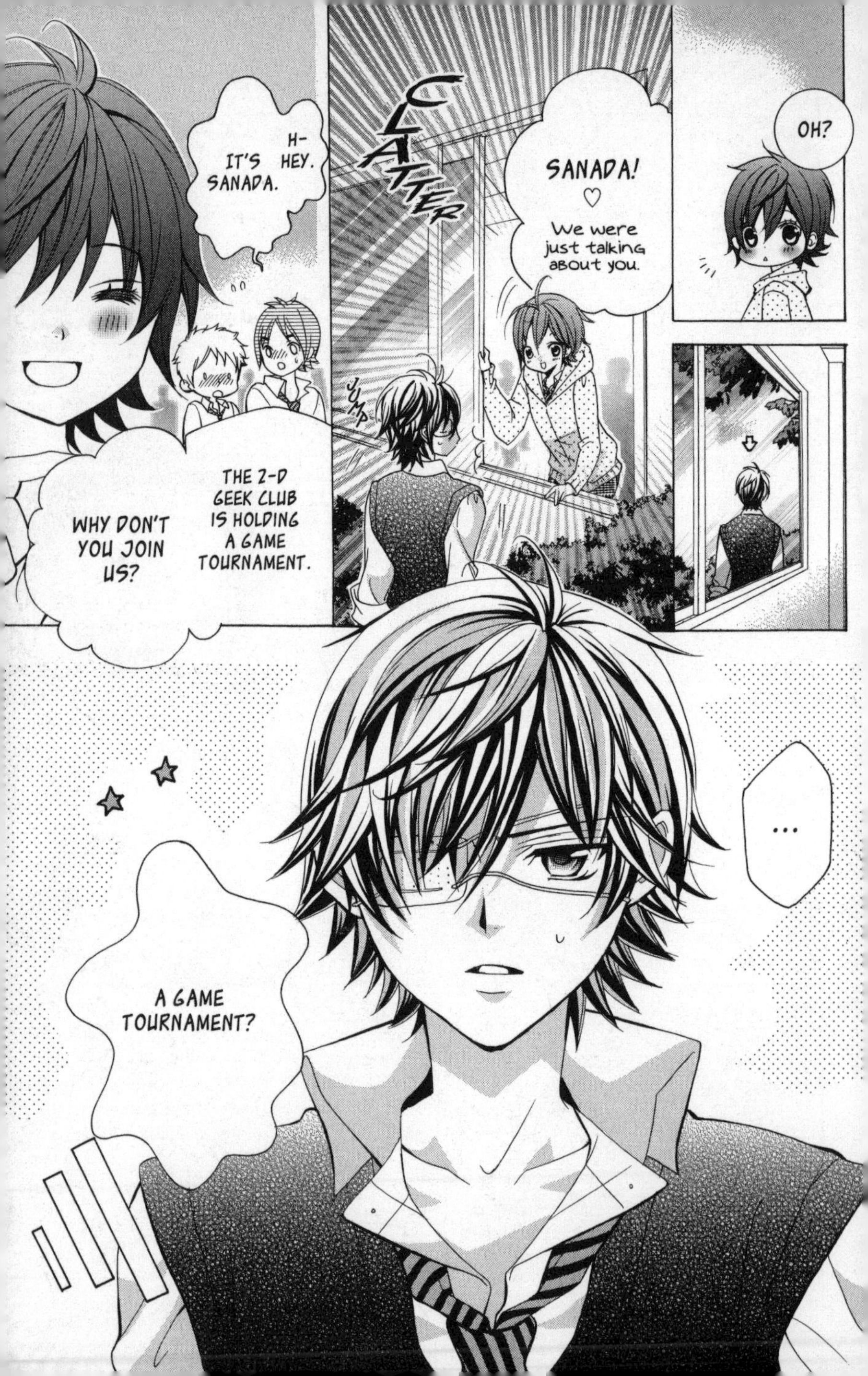
OH?
SANADA! ♡ We were just talking about you.
CLATTER
JUMP
H- HEY. IT'S SANADA.
THE 2-D GEEK CLUB IS HOLDING A GAME TOURNAMENT.
WHY DON'T YOU JOIN US?
...
A GAME TOURNAMENT?

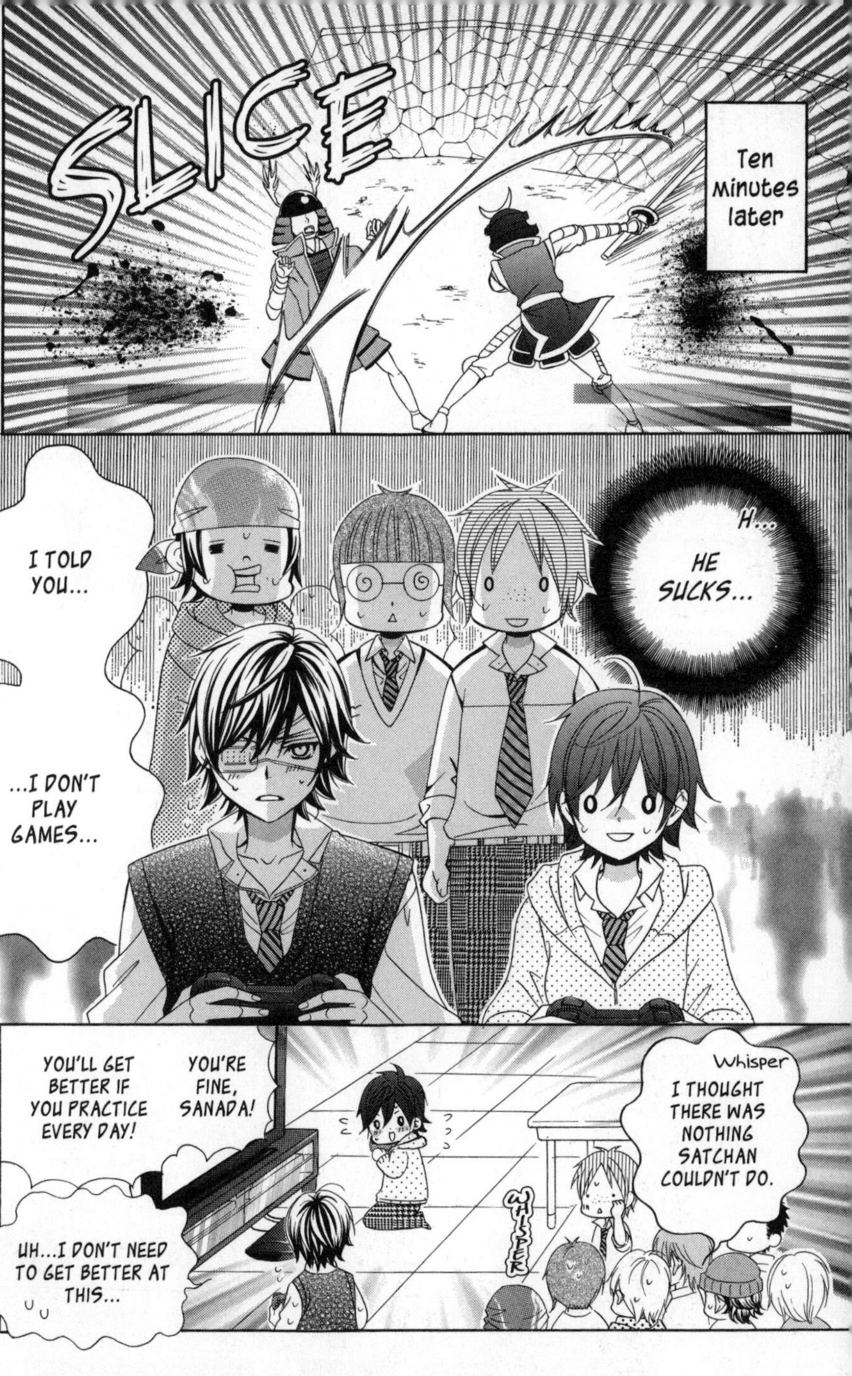
Ten minutes later
SLICE
H...
HE SUCKS...
I TOLD YOU...
...I DON'T PLAY GAMES...
Whisper
I THOUGHT THERE WAS NOTHING SATCHAN COULDN'T DO.
WHISPER
YOU'RE FINE, SANADA!
YOU'LL GET BETTER IF YOU PRACTICE EVERY DAY!
UH...I DON'T NEED TO GET BETTER AT THIS...

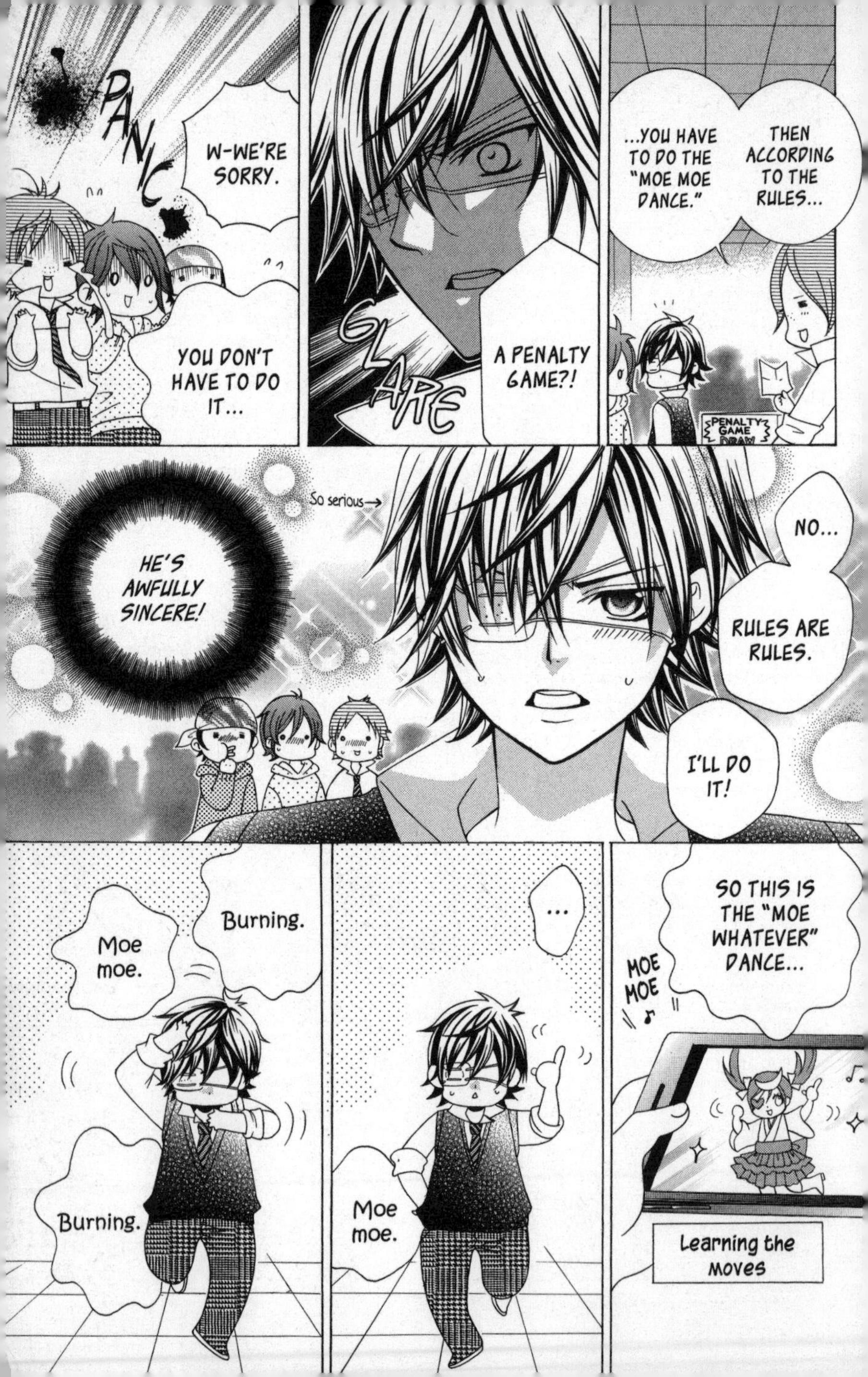
THEN ACCORDING TO THE RULES...
...YOU HAVE TO DO THE "MOE MOE DANCE."
PENALTY GAME DRAW
A PENALTY GAME?!
GLARE
PANIC
W-WE'RE SORRY.
YOU DON'T HAVE TO DO IT...
NO...
RULES ARE RULES.
I'LL DO IT!
So serious→
HE'S AWFULLY SINCERE!
SO THIS IS THE "MOE WHATEVER" DANCE...
MOE MOE
Learning the moves
...
Moe moe.
Moe moe.
Burning.
Burning.

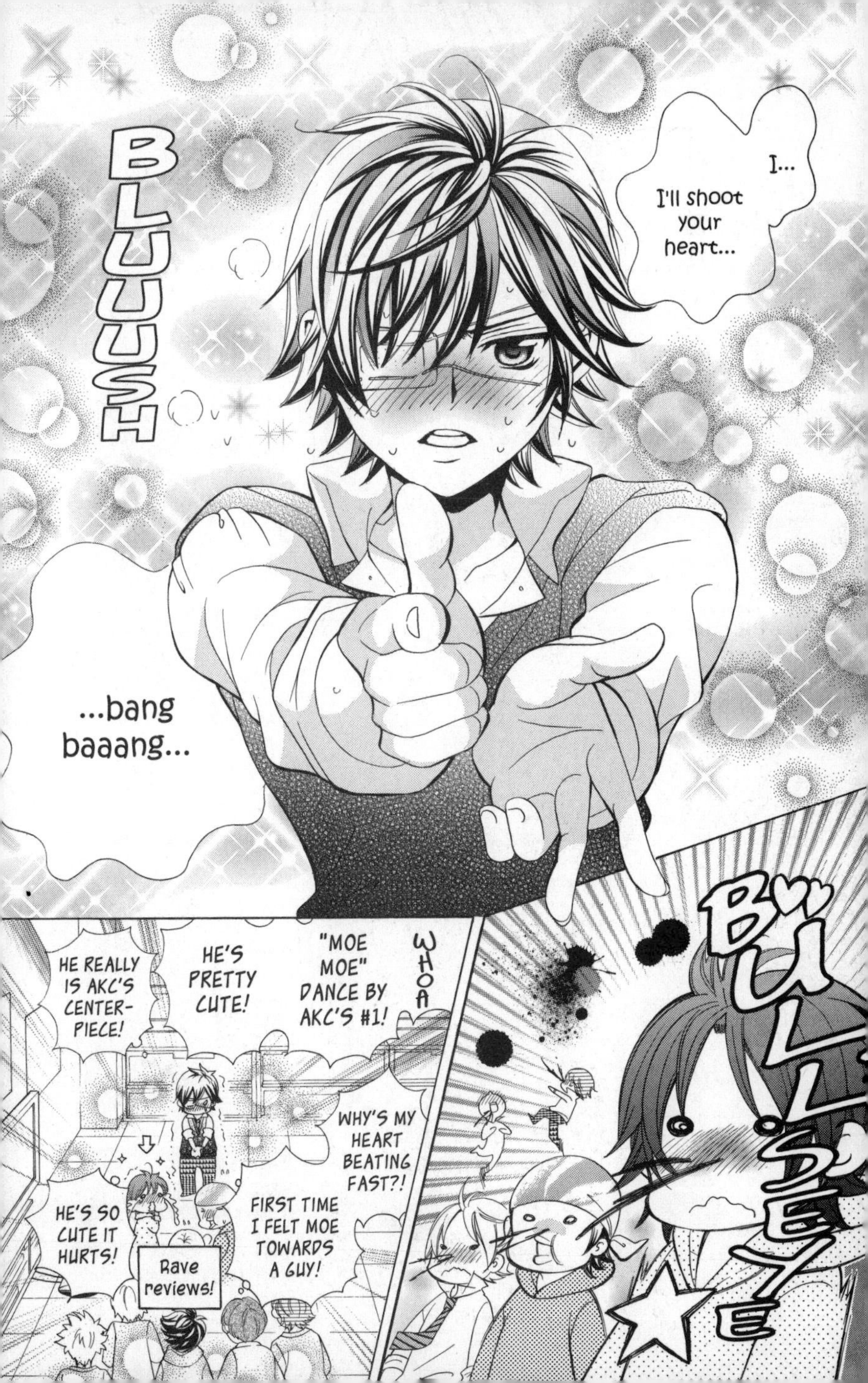
I...
I'll shoot your heart...
BLUUUUSH
...bang baaang...
BULLSEYE
WHOA
"MOE MOE" DANCE BY AKC'S #1!
HE'S PRETTY CUTE!
HE REALLY IS AKC'S CENTER-PIECE!
WHY'S MY HEART BEATING FAST?!
FIRST TIME I FELT MOE TOWARDS A GUY!
Rave reviews!
HE'S SO CUTE IT HURTS!

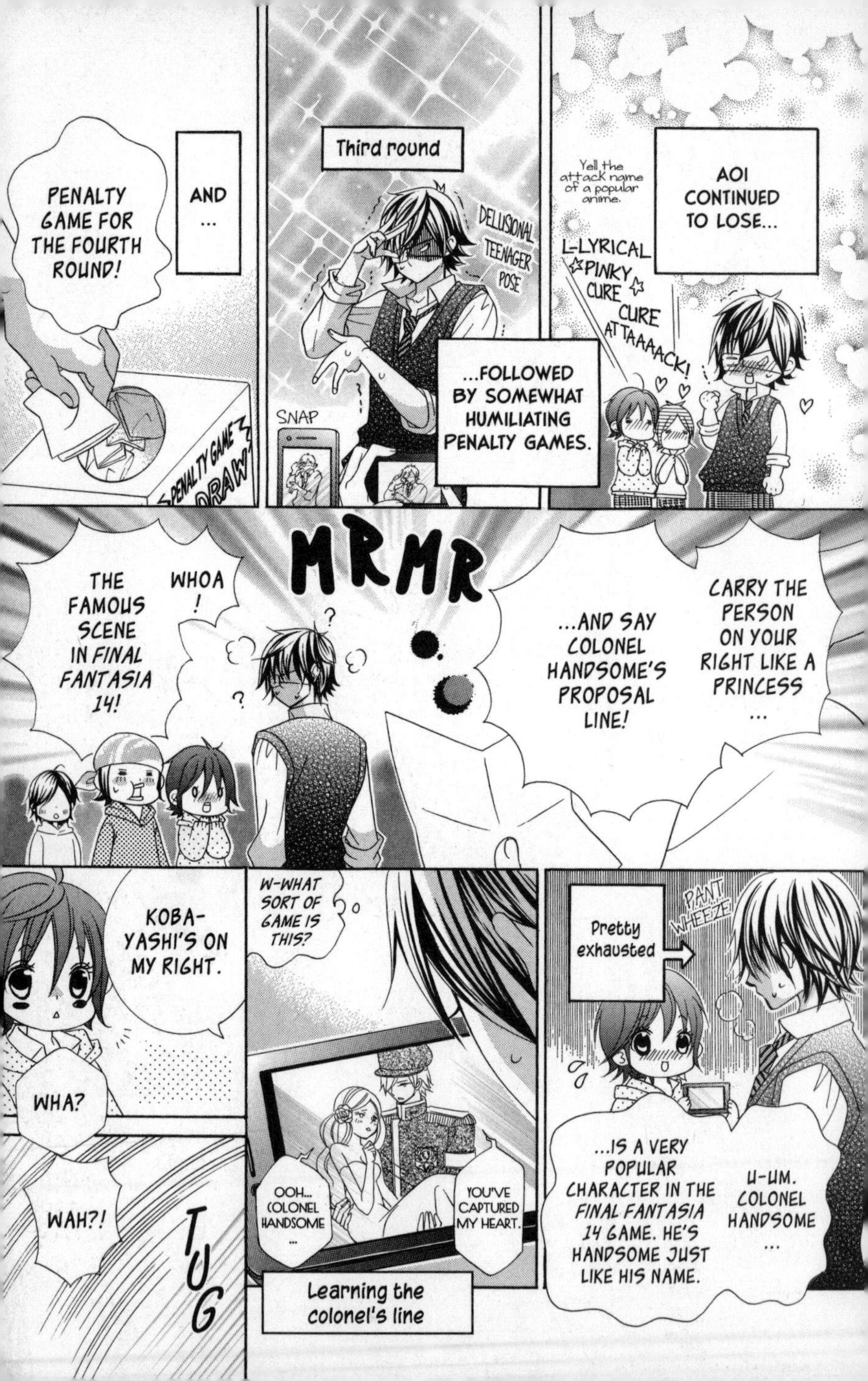
AOI CONTINUED TO LOSE...
Yell the attack name of a popular anime.
L-LYRICAL ☆PINKY CURE ☆ CURE ATTAAAACK!
Third round
DELUSIONAL TEENAGER POSE
...FOLLOWED BY SOMEWHAT HUMILIATING PENALTY GAMES.
SNAP
AND ...
PENALTY GAME FOR THE FOURTH ROUND!
PENALTY GAME DRAW
CARRY THE PERSON ON YOUR RIGHT LIKE A PRINCESS ...
...AND SAY COLONEL HANDSOME'S PROPOSAL LINE!
MRMR
WHOA !
THE FAMOUS SCENE IN FINAL FANTASIA 14!
Pretty exhausted
PANT WHEEZE
U-UM. COLONEL HANDSOME ...
...IS A VERY POPULAR CHARACTER IN THE FINAL FANTASIA 14 GAME. HE'S HANDSOME JUST LIKE HIS NAME.
W-WHAT SORT OF GAME IS THIS?
YOU'VE CAPTURED MY HEART.
OOH... COLONEL HANDSOME ...
Learning the colonel's line
KOBA-YASHI'S ON MY RIGHT.
WHA?
WAH?!
TUG

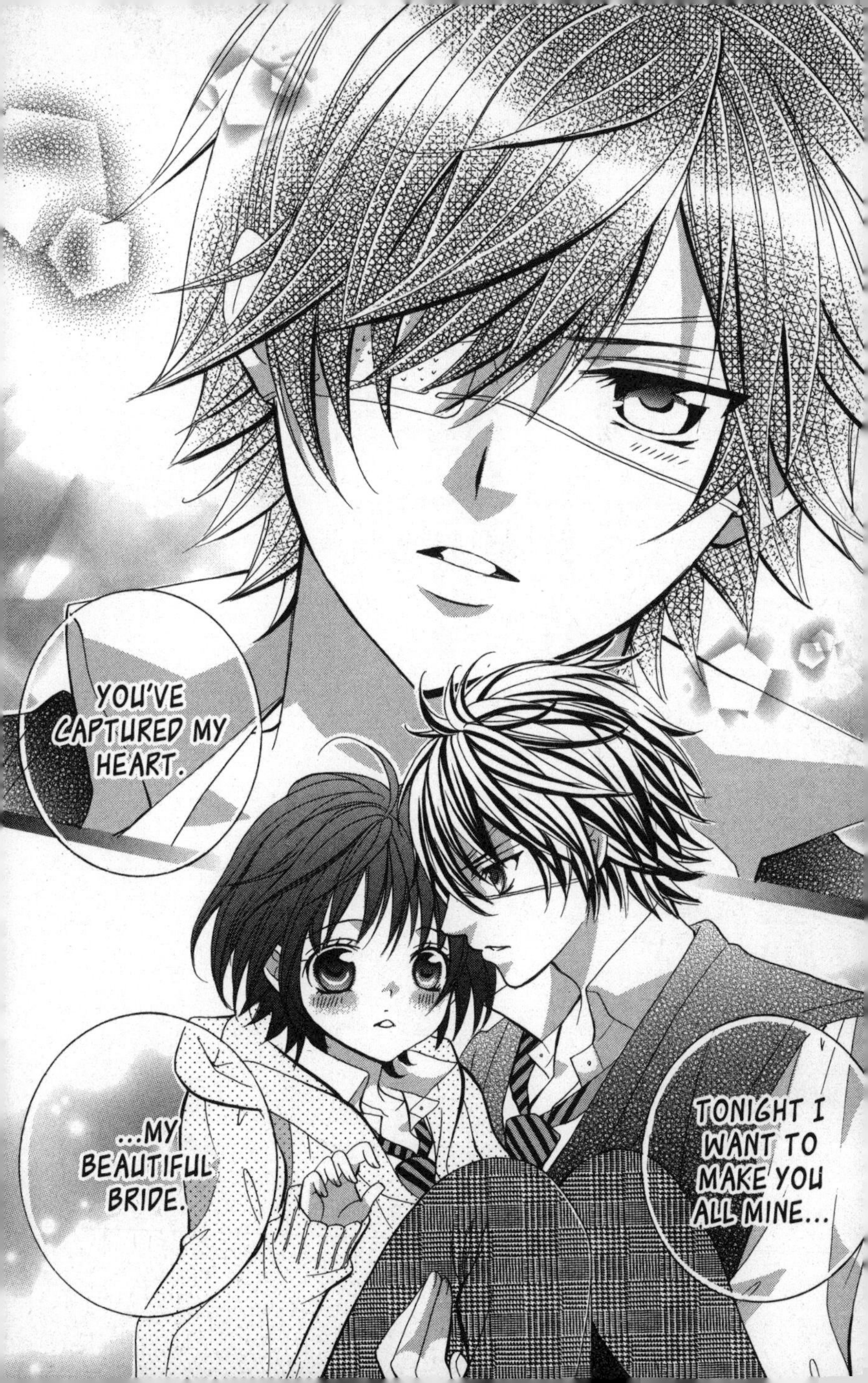
YOU'VE CAPTURED MY HEART.
TONIGHT I WANT TO MAKE YOU ALL MINE...
...MY BEAUTIFUL BRIDE.

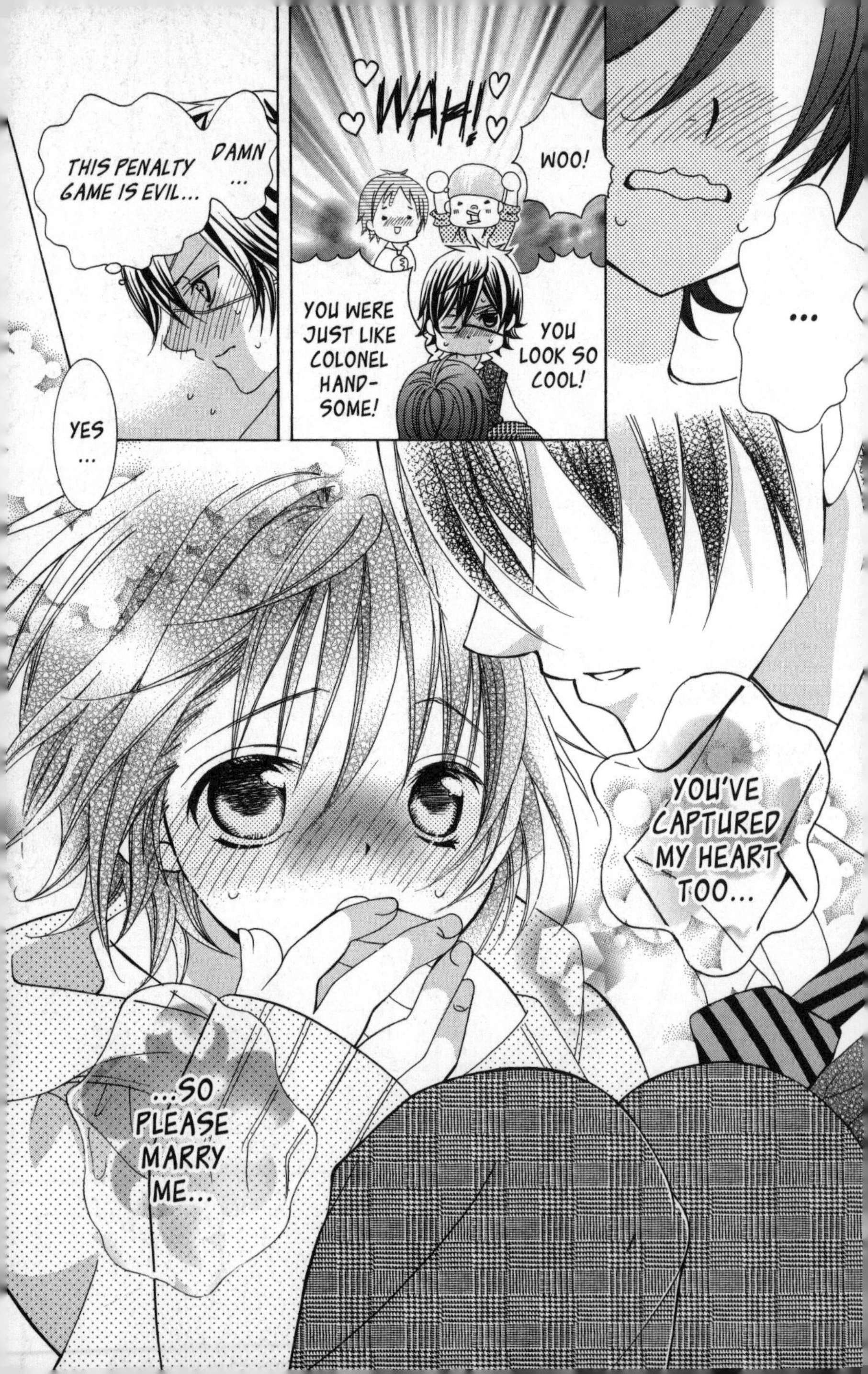
...
WOO!
WAH!
YOU LOOK SO COOL!
YOU WERE JUST LIKE COLONEL HAND-SOME!
DAMN...
THIS PENALTY GAME IS EVIL...
YES...
YOU'VE CAPTURED MY HEART TOO...
...SO PLEASE MARRY ME...

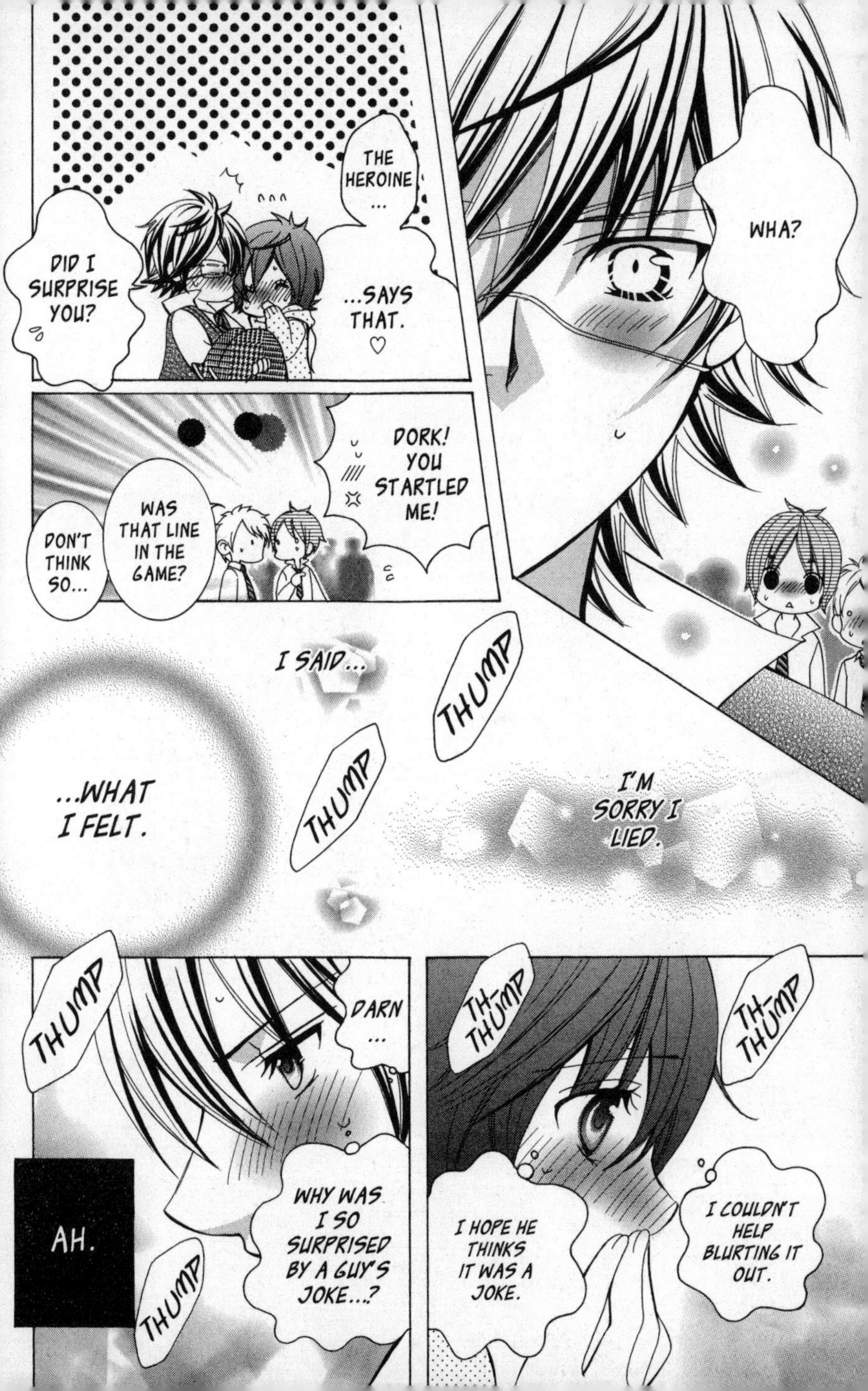
WHA?
THE HEROINE...
...SAYS THAT. ♡
DID I SURPRISE YOU?
DORK! YOU STARTLED ME!
WAS THAT LINE IN THE GAME?
DON'T THINK SO...
I'M SORRY I LIED.
THUMP
I SAID...
THUMP
...WHAT I FELT.
TH-THUMP
TH-THUMP
I COULDN'T HELP BLURTING IT OUT.
I HOPE HE THINKS IT WAS A JOKE.
DARN...
THUMP
WHY WAS I SO SURPRISED BY A GUY'S JOKE...?
THUMP
AH.

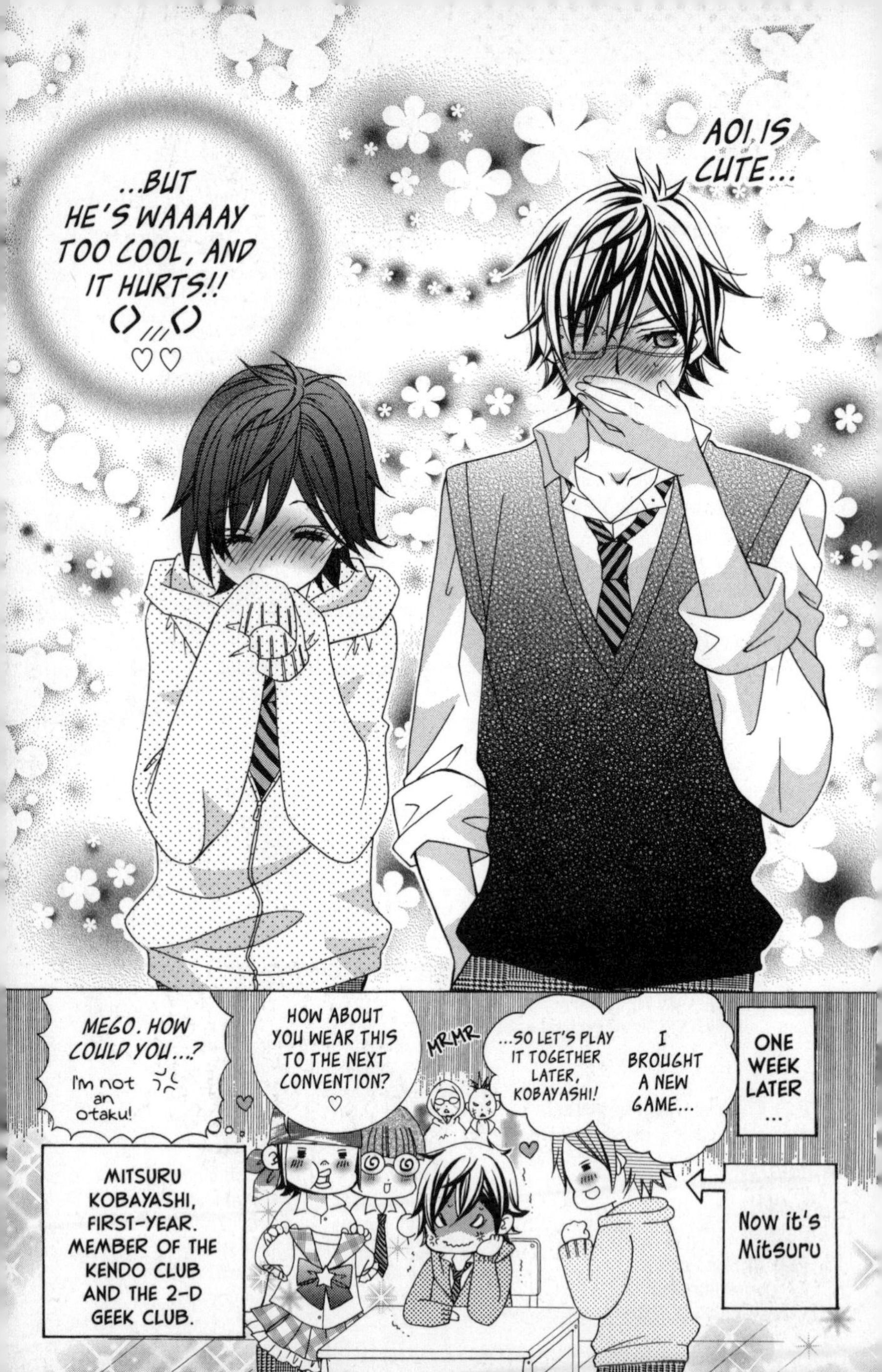
AOI IS CUTE...
...BUT HE'S WAAAAY TOO COOL, AND IT HURTS!!
ONE WEEK LATER ...
I BROUGHT A NEW GAME...
...SO LET'S PLAY IT TOGETHER LATER, KOBAYASHI!
MRMR
HOW ABOUT YOU WEAR THIS TO THE NEXT CONVENTION? ♡
MEGO. HOW COULD YOU...?
I'm not an otaku!
Now it's Mitsuru
MITSURU KOBAYASHI, FIRST-YEAR. MEMBER OF THE KENDO CLUB AND THE 2-D GEEK CLUB.

End of "Aoi Is So Cute It Hurts!!"

GLOSSARY

Page 4, panel 3: Yaoi otaku, idol otaku
Yaoi, also called boys' love, involves stories with male-male romances made for a largely female audience. Idols are media personalities with carefully crafted public personas. An otaku is an extreme hobbyist—basically a nerd.

Page 41, panel 2: Goth Loli
Also called Gothic Lolita, it is a branch of the Lolita fashion culture. Lolita fashion is inspired by Victorian styles, with lots of ruffles, lace and bows. Gothic Lolita incorporates dark colors and typical Gothic style elements.

Page 56, panel 2: Zundamochi, Matsumae pickles
Zundamochi is a type of *mochi* (a sticky dumpling made of rice flour) covered with sweet soybean paste. *Matsumae* pickles are a Hokkaido specialty with dried squid, herring roe and kelp.

Page 57, panel 1: Miso, natto
Miso is a fermented paste (usually from soybeans) used to make broths, sauces and spreads and to pickle vegetables and meat. *Natto* is a type of fermented soybean considered an acquired taste due to its strong smell and slimy texture.

Page 57, panel 2: Kokeshi dolls
Wooden dolls with big round heads and a simple body shape without arms or legs.

Page 58, panel 1: Beef tongue set
A combo meal that consists of grilled beef tongue, oxtail soup, grated yam and barley rice. Sendai is famous for beef tongue.

Page 74: Star Festival, Pageant of Starlight
Sendai's Star Festival is a traditional event that has been held since Lord Masamune Date's days. The city is filled with gorgeous star festival decorations August 6–8.
  The Pageant of Starlight is a winter event held in the second half of December, when a main street is decorated with LED lights.

Page 97, panel 2: Cameo appearance
These are characters from Go Ikeyamada's previous series.

Page 112, panel 2: Purikura
This is a contraction of the Japanese pronunciation of "print club" and refers to the photo booths found in arcades and game centers and the photos they dispense.

Page 178, panel 4: Suitmation
The actors in monster suits stomping on scale model cities, like in *Godzilla* and *Power Rangers*.

Page 179, panel 2: Moe
Moe means to have an affection for or an attraction to something. It is often used in referring to anime, manga and game characters.

Page 180, panel 2: Yanki
A *yanki* is a juvenile delinquent or young gangster. They're young people who smoke, start fights, etc. Some create gangs, and some just wander the streets alone.

Author page message: Tsundere
Tsundere is a term that combines two Japanese words–*tsuntsun* (which means "unfriendly") and *deredere* (which means "lovestruck"). It is used to describe people who can be unfriendly one second but sweet the next.

AUTHOR BIO

オマエって…笑うと花みたいだな
AOI
デレver.

You're like a flower when you smile.
—Aoi, dere version

I hope you enjoyed the anime DVD that came with the special version of the Japanese release of volume 3. (^0^) And this volume is out just one month after volume 3. ♪

In Japan, the first editions of volume 3 (regular version) and volume 4 come with Aoi's tsundere stickers. ♪♪

I drew his bashful "tsun" face for volume 3 and his sweet "dere" face for volume 4. (//∇//) I hope you get both stickers and enjoy Aoi being both tsun and dere. ♥(^0^)

Go Ikeyamada is a Gemini from Miyagi Prefecture whose hobbies include taking naps and watching movies. Her debut manga *Get Love!!* appeared in *Shojo Comic* in 2002, and her current work *So Cute It Hurts!!* (*Kobayashi ga Kawai Suguite Tsurai!!*) is being published by VIZ Media.

SO CUTE IT HURTS!!
Volume 4

Shojo Beat Edition

STORY AND ART BY
GO IKEYAMADA

English Translation & Adaptation/Tomo Kimura
Touch-Up Art & Lettering/Joanna Estep
Design/Izumi Evers
Editor/Pancha Diaz

KOBAYASHI GA KAWAISUGITE TSURAI!! Vol.4
by Go IKEYAMADA
© 2012 Go IKEYAMADA
All rights reserved.
Original Japanese edition published by SHOGAKUKAN.
English translation rights in the United States of America, Canada,
United Kingdom and Ireland arranged with SHOGAKUKAN.

Printed in the U.S.A.

Published by VIZ Media, LLC
P.O. Box 77010
San Francisco, CA 94107

10 9 8 7 6 5 4 3 2 1
First printing, December 2015

www.viz.com   www.shojobeat.com

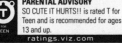